GOD?
VERY PROBABLY

GOD?
VERY PROBABLY

Five Rational Ways to Think about
the Question of a God

ROBERT H. NELSON

FOREWORD BY
HERMAN DALY

CASCADE *Books* · Eugene, Oregon

GOD? VERY PROBABLY
Five Rational Ways to Think about the Question of a God

Cascade Books
An Imprint of Wipf and Stock Publishers
199 W. 8th Ave., Suite 3
Eugene, OR 97401

www.wipfandstock.com

ISBN 13: 978-1-4982-2375-1

Cataloguing-in-Publication Data

Nelson, Robert H.

God? very probably: five rational ways to think about the question of a God / Robert H. Nelson ; foreword by Herman Daly.

xvi + 280 p. ; 23 cm. Includes bibliographical references and index.

ISBN 13: 978-1-4982-2375-1

1. God's existence. 2. Theism. 3. Consciousness. I. Title.

BT 102 .N45 2015

Manufactured in the USA   11/10/2015

For Savannah and Summer

Contents

Foreword

BOB NELSON AND I occupied adjacent offices at the University of Maryland School of Public Policy for about fifteen years. This led to many conversations that were pleasant and fruitful because we shared interests in both economics and environmental studies. Also, we agreed in our basic world views enough to make good conversation possible, yet differed enough to make it interesting. So when Bob asked me to read and comment on an earlier draft of this book, I accepted.

To be painfully honest, however, I thought at the time that I knew a bit more about theology and religion than Bob did, and that while I might be useful to him, I doubted that I would learn much from the collegial duty of reading the draft. It quickly became apparent that I was totally mistaken about that—Bob was the teacher and I was his student. How could I have been so wrong? Had Bob been reticent about his knowledge and wide reading in theology? Had I been unperceptive? Had he learned so much in such a short time? Suffice it to say that I came away from reading the draft with a long list of referenced scholars to read, and with many new insights.

The ability to read and absorb vast amounts of material is a capacity that Bob is blessed with. His mind is like a huge sponge that absorbs everything, but what he wrings out of it on to the pages of his own writing is not simply what he absorbed, but rather a high-proof distillation that stimulates further thought and insight.

Bob's approach to religion in his important past scholarly work on *Economics as Religion* had been that of the objective external observer. This book takes the internal approach of a serious prospective believer, weighing the arguments for the existence of God (a generic monotheistic God). His reasoned conclusion is that very probably God exists. He hints that his next book may go further than this.

The world view of scientific materialism has become so dominant on university campuses that a sophomoric atheism, styled the "new atheism," has become prevalent. It has been preached, aggressively and arrogantly, by Richard Dawkins, Daniel Dennett, Christopher Hitchens, and others. Many, whose study of religion ended with first-grade Sunday school, have uncritically accepted their message. As a Christian theist myself, I have had a hard time understanding how such a fundamentalist neo-Darwinist materialism could have, until recently, gotten a critical free pass from the intelligentsia. Nelson, as you will see, doesn't give free passes. Although the thrust of this book is not to debate these thinkers, the self-contradictions of their positions are frequently exposed as by-products of broader discussions, and Nelson helpfully makes the connections, much to my satisfaction.

I believe that other readers will enjoy and benefit from the clear, informed, and honest reasoning in this book as much as I did.

Herman Daly

Emeritus Professor

March 20, 2015

Preface

"RELIGION" IN THE ACADEMIC environment I have worked in for more than twenty years—at the School of Public Policy of the University of Maryland—is an awkward subject. Unlike some other departments, it is not that my longtime colleagues are hostile to religion or do not acknowledge the potential practical benefits of religion—many of them would readily admit that religion, for whatever reason, often seems to make people more agreeable, more honest and trustworthy, good neighbors if you will—or reliable business partners. But many of these same colleagues would say that religion has little to offer with respect to explaining the fundamental "truths of the world." For that, they look to science, both in its physical science and social science versions. Religion for them is a kind of happy illusion, however great a role it has obviously played over the totality of human history, perhaps overall for the good but sometimes also with terribly destructive consequences.

As a professional economist by training and thus more broadly a social scientist, I fit well personally in many ways in this academic environment. My own professional history, however, shows some significant indications of heretical tendencies. After majoring in mathematics at Brandeis University, and then getting a PhD in economics at Princeton University in 1971, I left the academic world in 1972 in part because I was uncomfortable with what I saw as a limited understanding of the realities of the human condition in my own field of economics—and that seemingly was also true of the other social sciences, although I was less familiar with them. I ended up working as an economist in the Office of Policy Analysis of the Office of the Secretary of the Interior in Washington, DC from 1975 to 1993.[1] It was there that I first clearly recognized that much of American public policy debate, including matters relating to natural resources and the environment that I was directly involved with in my work, were really about religion—broadly understood to include not only Christianity and other traditional religions

1. Nelson, "The Economics Profession and the Making of Public Policy"; Nelson, "The Office of Policy Analysis in the Department of the Interior."

but also "secular" (or some prefer to label them "implicit") religions as well.[2] I resolved by the mid-1980s to explore in my own writings the religious dimensions of public policy debate in the United States as necessary to achieving a fuller understanding of the American political and policy making worlds—focusing on my professional areas of special concern, natural resources and environmental policy. I did not realize it at the time, but this was taking me into the realm of theology.

Since 1990, while also continuing to pursue actively more conventional public policy subjects, I have been spending a good part of my time thinking and writing about religion (including in this category belief systems such as economics and environmentalism), including three books and many scholarly (and also more popular) articles, an area of intellectual activity of mine that my School of Public Policy colleagues today often find meritorious (for one thing, I have had some success) and intellectually interesting but it clearly puts me well outside the social science and public policy mainstreams.[3]

This book takes me even further afield. In it I explore the question of whether a god exists (throughout this book, I will write generically of "a god"— assumed to be a monotheistic god, unless it is specifically the Christian God I am referring to, or is being discussed by others, and in such cases I will use "God"). While I have written a great deal over the past twenty-five years about matters relating to religion, and three of my books have been widely reviewed in religious magazines and theology journals (as well as

2. The late British Anglican vicar Edward Bailey launched a scholarly movement in the 1970s to study what he labeled as "implicit religion"—a term he preferred to the similar "secular religion" and included belief systems such as Marxism as literal forms of religion. As interest spread in his efforts, he founded the Centre for the Study of Implicit Religion and Contemporary Spirituality in 1995, began publishing the journal *Implicit Religion* in 1998, and held annual meetings in England for many years where international scholars with related interests assembled. Partly due to Bailey's efforts, there is now a chair of implicit religion at Cambridge University. He writes in 2012 that there is much to be gained if we recognize the presence of actual religions in modern life whose religious tenets are mainly expressed in hidden and thus implicit ways. Hence, as Bailey puts in, we may advance significantly in our understanding of the world, and the workings of modern society if we "apply something of what we now know about [traditional] religious life, to ordinary secular life" where actual religion is often still powerfully present in disguised forms. Bailey, "'Implicit Religion': What Might That Be?," 196. See also Bailey, "Implicit Religion: A Bibliographical Introduction"; Bailey, *Implicit Religion in Contemporary Society;* Bailey, *Implicit Religion: An Introduction;* and Bailey, "Implicit Religion" (2009); and Bailey, "Implicit Religion" (2010).

3. My books relating to religion include *Reaching for Heaven on Earth, Economics as Religion,* and, most recently, *The New Holy Wars.* Among my other recent writings, see also "The Secular Religions of Progress," "Bringing Religion into Economic Policy Analysis," "Economics and Environmentalism", and "Calvinism Without God."

in social science journals), I have not previously attempted a book as ambitious as this one. Like many people, however, I have often wondered over a lifetime whether a god exists. But I have never committed a sustained intellectual effort to answering this question—until now. I think by writing, so this book is in part the record of the recent progress of my thinking, taking me from a long-standing basic agnosticism as recently as about eight years ago to now believing that a god (very probably) exists. This god may well resemble but is not necessarily the precise divinity of Christianity or any other of the traditional major religions of Western or other world history.

It may be possible for me to make a contribution to a subject about which such an enormous amount has already been written over such a very long time because in the twentieth century, and now early in the twenty-first century, there appeared a number of important arguments, scientific discoveries, and other new evidence relating to the question of a god, as generated in areas such as physics, evolutionary biology, the philosophy of human consciousness, and the history of religion. Indeed, the pace of such discoveries seems to have accelerated in recent years; just since 2010 multiple significant writings bearing on the question of a god have appeared.[4] Despite their large theological significance, few theologians study such matters as part of their routine theological training or research. In part, the character of much of the theology being done today reflects the disciplinary specialization that characterizes the contemporary university, now ironically extending even to theology itself. As with other areas of university life, the professionalization of theology imposes its own significant intellectual limitations for obtaining an understanding of the largest questions of the human condition on earth.

Moreover, the leadership of the institutional religions of the United States typically have a greater detailed knowledge of the history and contents of their own religions. Their thinking on theological matters almost inevitably is influenced significantly by their long-standing religious commitments. Hence, there are few if any "experts" whose specialties include all of the important diverse areas of knowledge that today must be brought together in studying "theology"—in the most traditional sense of the word, as seeking to encompass the full truths of the human situation, theology being the best way we have available to us of seeking to understand the "meaning

---

4. Four important recent books are: Bellah, *Religion in Human Evolution*; Plantinga, *Where the Conflict Really Lies*; Nagel, *Mind and Cosmos*; and Dworkin, *Religion Without God*. While they do not discuss at any length the existence of a god or other explicitly theological topics, two other important recent contributions with large theological implications are Frenkel, *Love & Math*, and Tegmark, *Our Mathematical Universe*.

of it all." Thus, even as I am an outside "trespasser" in the world of theology, this may offer me some advantages as well as disadvantages.

As I will conclude in this book, it is possible to make a strong probabilistic case for the existence of a god by reaching across diverse specialized areas of contemporary inquiry in the physical sciences, philosophy, evolutionary biology, the social sciences, and theology. While most of the individual arguments made in this book have been made by others, the totality of them, as I have assembled and developed them below, offers, at least as I like to think, a fresh perspective on an age-old question of immense interest to many people—the question of whether a god exists. As this book will document, I have now concluded that there is a strong (a very probable) case that a god—in the sense of some supernatural, superhuman power overseeing the world—does in fact exist.

Acknowledgements

In 2009, David Theroux, the president of The Independent Institute, encouraged me to write what has become this book. Without this encouragement, it would not have happened. So I owe him a special debt of gratitude. His colleague at The Independent Institute, Roy Carlisle, also provided helpful support. My friend Michael Whelan, a member of the Christian Brothers in the 1960s, was the first person to read significant parts of the early drafts of the manuscript. His enthusiastic reaction in 2012, especially given his past religious background and his continuing consuming interest in the "question of a god" (he is the author of a recent volume of poetry, *After God*), not only offered me important motivation to continue but also led to many valuable discussions of the main themes of the book.

Another person who played an especially important role in the writing of this book is Herman Daly, my longtime colleague (now emeritus) in the School of Public Policy of the University of Maryland. Herman is better known to the world as a founder and longtime contributor to the fields of environmental sustainability and ecological economics but it is less well known that he has long had a deep interest in religion and the central role it plays in environmental values and more broadly in society. After reading a draft of the manuscript in early 2013, besides his encouraging response, Herman suggested to me that it was too long, and that a shorter version could effectively make the same arguments while reaching a larger audience—as I have endeavored to do in this book. He also commented valuably on the substance of multiple drafts. As myself a professor at the School of Public Policy at the University of Maryland since 1993, I would also like to express my appreciation to the School as a whole for the supportive environment it has long offered (Bill Powers, don't blush), making this and other past books and other writing efforts of mine possible.

Max Stackhouse read and commented valuably on the manuscript. This continues the strong support Max has offered for my investigations into religious subjects dating to the early 1990s. Thank you, Max.

A number of other people have provided valuable encouragement in what has been a large intellectual leap for me and made valuable comments during the writing of this book. As encouraged by The Independent Institute in the winter and spring of 2014, Daniel Robinson, Alvin Plantinga, and Charles Taliaferro offered helpful critiques and suggestions for improvement. Hugh Price, my neighbor who has read more about some of these subjects than I have, critiqued the manuscript in close detail, making many insightful comments. My college classmate Subagh Singh Khalsa (when I first met him many years ago he was Dick Winkelstern) also gave the manuscript a close and helpful reading. In Finland, Tuula Karatvuo, during my 2013-2014 sabbatical year there (for seven months at the Collegium for Advanced Studies at the University of Helsinki) was generous in reading the manuscript and giving her comments. Others who read drafts of the manuscript and provided helpful comments include my personal and professional friends Donald Bieniewicz, Jean Briggs, P. J. Hill, Jill Nelson (not only a friend but my wife of more than forty years), and Kaius Sinnemaki.

1

Introduction

IN THIS BOOK I will be looking to persuade you that the probabilities favor the existence of a god, relying on rational forms of argument accessible not only to traditional devout believers but to current self-professed atheists as well. In other words, I will not be relying on arguments from "faith alone." For those who already believe that a god exists, I will for some of them be adding additional rational arguments to support their already existing views; for nonbelievers at present, I will be offering rational reasons for why they might want to reconsider their position. My conclusion does not necessarily mean exactly the Christian God of history but it does mean the existence of a god of some kind whose essence is supernatural. That is, as I dare to suggest, an important theological conclusion in and of itself, even if it does not conform fully to a traditional Christian understanding.

My rational case for a (very probable) god, as I should say at the outset, will not "prove" that a god exists. "Proof" (actually, in science this means a long record of uncontradicted empirical confirmation that can never be absolutely final) is feasible in the scientific investigation of the natural world but in the case of a supernatural essence, such as a god, there is no similar method of knowledge verification available. Thus, to concede that a scientific "proof" is necessary to estimate the likelihood of the existence of a god would be to concede from the outset that a god is unlikely. Indeed, because this demand is impossible to satisfy, the insistence on a "proof" of a god in the manner of the scientific method is a part of the rhetorical arsenal of those who stridently assert the nonexistence of any god. Yet, the largest part of the ordinary knowledge by which we guide our lives is not based on any such forms of scientific proof.

It is further evidence of the fundamentalist worship of science in our own times that most of the scientific faithful remain altogether blind to the supernatural miracles that routinely surround their daily existence.

1

Foremost among these supernatural miracles, as a leading contemporary American philosopher Thomas Nagel explained in 2012, is human consciousness. Nagel writes that human "consciousness is the most conspicuous obstacle to a comprehensive naturalism that relies only on the resources of physical science" to understand the world. Indeed, he concludes that we will simply have to face the fact that "the existence of consciousness seems to imply that the physical description of the universe . . . is only part of the truth" of human existence, requiring an acknowledgement of the necessity of some kind of supernatural elements of a reality that "threatens to unravel the entire naturalistic world picture" that dominates so much of contemporary thinking—especially among the educated elites in the United States and Europe.[1]

Similar to Nagel, the Oxford philosopher Daniel Robinson writes that "consciousness introduces a new ingredient in the perceptual transactions between organisms and environments. The ingredient is the actual state of experience itself, what may be called a 'mental' state presumably widespread in the animal kingdom." In order for a human being (or other animal) "to possess such a mental state," it is necessary, as Nagel has also long said, that "there is something that it is to *be* that organism—something it is like *for* the organism" to perceive its own existence. It follows logically that since the "standard reductionist accounts of the mental"—accounts that seek to reduce consciousness to physical terms alone—"are essentially indifferent to the subjectivity of such experience, the accounts are fatally incomplete" as a statement of the full human condition. Despite the many best efforts of philosophical reductionists to offer an effective rejoinder, as Robinson considers in 2008, "Nagel's argument retains its power."[2]

It is remarkable that no even remotely plausible scientific hypothesis has yet been offered as to how our brains that exist in observable and measurable time and space might create the mental contents of our consciousness that exist outside measurable time and space. As the distinguished contemporary philosopher Colin McGinn puts it, "since we do not observe our own states of consciousness, nor those of others, we do not apprehend these states as spatial." If we were to seek to explain consciousness in scientific materialist terms, it would mean "that something essentially non-spatial emerged from something purely spatial—that the non-spatial is somehow a construction out of the spatial. And this looks more like magic" than a scientifically comprehensible truth.[3]

---

1. Nagel, *Mind and Cosmos*, 35.

2. Robinson, *Consciousness and Mental Life*, 44.

3. McGinn, "Consciousness and Space," 220, 223.

As McGinn thus suggests, it will always be outside the scope of the physical sciences to explain how material events occurring in the physical world of our bodies and brains create the complex nonmaterial thoughts—such as the contents of this book as I have written it—that populate our mental universe. How did atoms and molecules create this sentence that I am writing at this moment? Did "I" have anything to do with it, or was it simply materially predestined in advance, as Pierre Laplace in the early nineteenth century argued in principle for everything that would happen in the future of the world? Is it merely my own human hubris that I think that "I" had a great deal to do with it—or even that "I" exist as an autonomous and independently thinking human being? These are of course questions of ancient philosophical and religious interest but the religion of scientific materialism, having no plausible answers, largely ignores them today.

Sigmund Freud, as himself a self-professed atheist who denied the existence of a god, and was seeking to confirm the modern scientific faith that the methods of physics can be extended to explain everything in the world, even the events of human consciousness, once claimed that he had established a mental physics of the "forces" of the interactions among separate parts of the human mind that was capable of explaining scientifically the workings of human consciousness. But Freudianism is now seen more commonly to have been a new modern religion rather than an exercise of anything like the scientific method—not many people take the scientific claims of Freud seriously any more.

For human beings, their consciousness precedes matter, not the other way around; the very concept of "matter" is itself a creation of the human mind. The "material world" (even as we can only perceive this "world" in our minds today) and the "mental" (again even this is a matter of our own internal perceptions of one distinctive part of human consciousness) are two separate elements of the same ultimately mental contents of human consciousness. Quantum mechanics in the twentieth century added a radically new element in that the manner of our conscious perceptions, even of the external world, could seemingly change drastically what we actually perceived as this outside "reality." In other words, there was no fundamental reality other than the—admittedly complex and surprising—reality of human consciousness and its perceptions of itself and the "outside" world. The central importance of human consciousness in quantum mechanics meant that the scientific materialism that today dominates the thinking of so much of the American university world, and large parts of wider American elites, was effectively dead as a matter of ultimate truth.

For example, the historical reality for us of the "physical universe" of protons and other atomic and subatomic particles over as much as a billion years or more, as the brilliantly imaginative Princeton physicist John Wheeler once observed, is not finally determined, amazingly enough, until a human observation occurs. Astonishingly by commonsense standards, if there is one form of observation, then more than a billion years of subatomic history as we perceive it comes out one way, if there is another form of human observation, this history comes out another way. As Wheeler writes,

> The idea is old that the past has no existence except in the records of today. In our time this thought takes new poignancy in the concept of Bohr's elementary quantum phenomenon and the so-called delay choice experiment. Ascribe a polarization, a direction of vibration, to the photon that began its journey six billion years ago, before there was any Earth, still less any life. [All this is] meaningless! Not until the analyzer [the observational instrument] has been set to this, that, or the other specific chosen orientation, not until the elementary quantum phenomenon that began so long ago—and stretches out, unknown and unknowable, like a great smoky dragon through the vast intervening reach of space and time—has been brought to a close by an irreversible act of amplification [observation]; not until a record has been produced of either "yes, this direction of polarization" or "no, the contrary direction of polarization"; not until then do we have the right to attribute any polarization to the photon that began its course so long ago. There is an inescapable sense in which we, in the here and now, by a delayed setting of our analyzer of polarization to one or another angle, have an inescapable, an irretrievable, an unavoidable influence on what we have the right to say about what we call the [subatomic] past.[4]

Eugene Wigner, another great Princeton physicist (winner of the Nobel prize in 1963) who, also like Wheeler and unusually for a working physicist, occasionally ventured into philosophical explorations of the larger meaning for understanding human reality of quantum mechanics and other twentieth-century developments in physics, once examined such matters of the centrality for physics of consciousness in an essay, "Remarks on the Mind-Body Question." Wigner wrote that as a result of twentieth-century physics "the very study of the external world led to the conclusion that the content of consciousness is an ultimate reality." In quantum mechanics, "all knowledge of wave functions is based, in the last analysis, on the 'impressions' we receive" as conscious beings. Given the ultimate priority of consciousness, the quantum physics understanding of reality leads to an intellectual outcome where "solipsism may be logically consistent" with the current state of scientific

4. Wheeler, *At Home in the Universe*, 181.

thinking in physics but it is beyond doubt that "monism in the sense of [scientific] materialism is not" compatible with contemporary physics.[5]

As Wigner puts it most simply, we can know from quantum mechanics that "thought processes and consciousness are the primary concepts, that our knowledge of the external world is the content of consciousness and that the consciousness, therefore, cannot be denied. On the contrary, logically, the external world could be denied—although it is not very practical to do so," the route of solipsism (Wigner himself agrees that there is in fact an existence of a physical world outside our minds alone, even if it is not logically or scientifically necessary).[6] Werner Heisenberg, a co-discoverer of quantum mechanics in the mid-1920s, and today commonly ranked among the greatest physicists of history, would similarly reflect years later that in the wake of quantum mechanics "the mathematical formulas indeed no longer portray" an objectively existing material "nature, but rather the forms of our knowledge of nature," as experienced mathematically in our conscious minds. As a radical consequence, he writes, "we have renounced a [materialist] form of natural description that was familiar for centuries and still was taken as the obvious goal of all exact science even a few decades ago" (Heisenberg was writing in 1958).[7] So new atheists today such as Richard Dawkins, Daniel Dennett, Christopher Hitchens, and Sam Harris find little support for their scientistic views among the leading physicists of the twentieth century, physicists whose theories of the natural world, however seemingly mysterious, magical, and otherworldly by ordinary standards of thought, have passed the most exacting of empirical confirmation and today form the deepest understanding of reality available to us from physics.

More recently, in 2014 leading MIT physicist Max Tegmark observes that twentieth-century "discoveries in physics challenge some of our most basic ideas about reality"—or as one might equally well say, physics challenges some of our basic ideas about "theology." Indeed, Tegmark takes things to the surprising extreme of arguing that "our physical world not only is *described* by mathematics, but that it is mathematics, making us self-aware" conscious beings who exist at the most fundamental level as "parts of a giant mathematical" world of formulas and other abstractions somehow accessible to human consciousness by intense processes of rational introspection—yet another supernatural miracle that routinely affects our human existence.[8] Human beings, it would seem, are uniquely made

5. Wigner, "Remarks on the Mind-Body Question," 169, 171, 173.

6. Ibid., 174.

7. Heisenberg, "The Representation of Nature in Contemporary Physics," 105.

8. Tegmark, *Our Mathematical Universe*, 6.

in the image of a god for whom mathematics is central to his thought. Human beings uniquely among species on earth have the capacity to think mathematically, as such a god seemingly also does, and has transmitted this ability to his human likenesses on earth—for whatever his reasons for doing so, possibly just for mutual stimulation and enjoyment.

Thus, besides human consciousness, another existence outside any world of physically observable and measurable time and space, and of immense practical significance in human affairs, even if it is more remote from the daily experience of ordinary people, is the world of abstract mathematical ideas. A world-class mathematician of our times, Edward Frenkel, a professor of mathematics at the University of California at Berkeley, explains in a 2013 book intended for wide audiences that most professional mathematicians today understand their task as the exploration of a nonmaterial Platonic world of abstract ideas—a world outside observable and measurable time and space that consists of preexisting mathematical truths that have existed for eternity, although now becoming accessible to human consciousness in practice only in the past few thousand years, thanks to the extraordinary efforts of some very remarkable human beings from at least Archimedes to Carl Friedrich Gauss. As physics has only recently revealed to human beings, these mathematical truths, as we have now learned, are also miraculously embodied in physical reality, having shaped the workings of the physical world for billions of years, eons before any human beings had any concept of mathematical truthfulness and the miraculous ability of mathematical truth to shape everything that exists in "physical" reality.

Frenkel thus writes that the modern "world inhabited by mathematical concepts and ideas" is a revived version of the much older "Platonic world of mathematics," following in the ancient Greek tradition of "Plato, who was first to argue that mathematical entities are independent of our rational activities" as work within the consciousness of each individual human person. In other words, human beings do not create the mathematical reality that some of the most gifted among human beings are able to perceive—and from which we all benefit every day in our ordinary lives through the use of mathematics by physicists to establish the knowledge that leads to modern human control over nature. Declaring for a revived Platonism, Frenkel thus affirms that "I believe that the Platonic world of mathematics is separate from both the physical world and the mental world"—existing as a world of its own outside both matter and human consciousness.[9] Again, this is by the standards of scientific materialism a miracle, thus demonstrating once again—since we can know with complete confidence that an independent

9. Frenkel, *Love & Math*, 234.

mathematical world exists and is "true" for every person in the world who reasons with correct mathematical logic—that scientific materialism is dead as a possible understanding of human reality. To compound the miracle, as the leading contemporary British physicist Roger Penrose has marveled, the workings of the perceived "physical" world of measurable matter and space has in every case thus far been found by physicists to behave exactly according to one or another part of the abstract world of nonmaterial mathematical ideas—again, bringing us back to Plato.[10]

This miraculous ability of nonmaterial mathematics to control the material world in which we seemingly live out our lives is similar to the ability of nonmaterial events in our own human consciousness to control our own seeming "physical" bodily actions—something outside measurable time and space controls something in measurable time and space. With the exceptions of Wigner, Penrose, and some others, most physicists today routinely go about their business of establishing the exact relationships between mathematical truths (as they are shared in common in the consciousnesses of the physicists of the world) and "observed" events in the "outside" physical world (also shared by these physicists in their consciousnesses), never seemingly contemplating how miraculous all this is.

In light of the above, we can be rationally confident that there is a large supernatural and miraculous element to our very own human existence. Two possibilities then arise: that we are alone in the world, and that we are ourselves gods in somehow creating the events of our own consciousness (solipsism), or that the events of our consciousness (and the existence of other minds with which we share "rational" faculties) are somehow a reflection of some kind of supernatural entity that traditionally has gone by the name of a "god." As this book will argue, I opt for the latter choice—I believe a material world exists, even as I recognize that this has no sure rational and scientific justification, and that a god governs our perceptions of this world. Since the choice is not a matter of a conclusion reached by the scientific method, however, we can only defend this choice—that there is a real external world governed by mathematical laws—on the grounds that it seems to us, according to all the evidence of our eyes, minds, and our rational thoughts, "very probable."

Beyond that, however, it becomes more difficult to say much about this god with a similar degree of confidence. The god that we can probabilistically know to exist may or may not bear a close resemblance to the traditional God of Christianity. It is difficult—impossible really—for us personally to verify the miracles of the Bible, as compared with the supernatural miracles

10. Penrose, *The Road to Reality*.

of a god of mathematics as manipulated by physicists that we daily experience in our own lives as providing the knowledge basis for human control over the "natural world," including the electronic technological marvels such as television and the Internet that populate our daily lives. Compared with the old biblical miracles, such modern scientific miracles are more impressive and we can be far more certain of their actual real existence.

This book will delve more deeply into such matters. It will offer five rational ways for thinking about the question of a god, including further development of the arguments just made above. I have benefited greatly from an outpouring of writings in recent years that have newly discussed developments in the philosophy of human consciousness, mathematics, physics, evolutionary biology, and theology that are of true theological significance—even as such recent writings and developments were not available to previous inquirers into the age-old question of the existence of a god. Their large theological implications also have not thus far received wide attention among the general public. Very little that is said below is entirely new; my contribution is to bring together and interpret the cumulative implications for theology of the many recent contributions in various intellectual disciplines (even if they often do not see themselves in theological terms) that nevertheless bear importantly on the question of a god.

The Rational Method of This Book

As noted above, I do not claim that the arguments made in this book prove the existence—or nonexistence—of a god. The question of a god's existence lies outside the domain of science. Science is a particular method of inquiry about the workings of the natural world as grounded in the scientific method, as originally developed in the seventeenth century. This method is not applicable, however, to the question of the existence of a god. As an issue lying outside measurable time and space, there is no empirical test that can be devised that would either conclusively confirm or reject a "scientific hypothesis" that a god exists.

Many people might suggest, therefore, that there is little point in even discussing the existence of a god. Although they may not realize it, however, such people typically conflate "science" with "rational." If nothing rational can be said about a god, it seemingly would become a matter of "faith alone," a common view in Protestant religion dating back to Martin Luther. Indeed, Luther himself said that there is nothing an individual can do to achieve true faith in God; such faith is a pure gift from God that cannot be influenced by human action, some people (the elect) being favored by God and others—likely the majority—less fortunate (the condemned), all this according to God's own grand plan that is beyond any full human rational understanding. The existence of actual true faith then becomes a matter for individual private introspection as to whether it might be present (with no certainties ever possible) and in which broader rational debate within a community of fellow religious inquirers is desirable but offers no sure answers as to the correct path of salvation. Indeed, this Protestant "privatization of religion" had a large impact on the understanding of the relationship of church and state of the nineteenth and twentieth century, helping to justify the exclusion of religion from state affairs.

"Rational" argument, however, is not limited to the scientific method. The methods of rational argument were long ago elevated to new heights by the ancient Greeks. The results in their time were as revolutionary for the world as the consequences in our own time of the global spread of the form of reasoning we know as "science"—itself a specific form of rational argument that has been spectacularly effective in one particular domain, discovering the workings of the natural world. Even as this book rejects the applicability of science to the question of a god's existence, it seeks to follow in this long history of rational argument in Western thought, now offering yet another application of "rational" methods to incorporate the latest relevant scientific and philosophical developments of our time that offer important insights into the question of a god's existence. I will be following an approach to religion once described by the philosopher Thomas Nagel as "reflection on the question of existence and nature of God using only the resources of ordinary human reasoning. This is not the source of most religious belief, but it is important nonetheless," and it is in fact the approach employed by Nagel himself in his own philosophical writings concerning religion.[11]

In suggesting that the existence of a god is open to rational debate and discussion, I do not mean to deny a legitimate role for a simple personal faith that has long had a large role in the history of Christian and other religion. But I am concerned that "faith alone" has proven an unreliable method historically of distinguishing better from worse—truer and less true—religious beliefs. Too many people have had a deep personal faith in some rather strange and occasionally very harmful—to them and to others—religious "truths." God may ultimately control the events in the world but he seems content to allow human beings in the exercise of their free will to believe devoutly in an extraordinarily wide range of things. So elements of faith may in the end be necessary for the deepest religious convictions but a sound religion must also be based on more than faith alone. Facts

---

11. Nagel, *Secular Philosophy and the Religious Temperament*, 20.

and rational arguments must have a central role; indeed, my view is that we should let them carry us as far as they can. In this respect I depart from Luther (my own family origins over one hundred years ago were in Lutheran Sweden and Finland) and many other Protestants and adopt a view closer to Thomas Aquinas and others in the Roman Catholic tradition.[12]

Yet, I also have the traditional Protestant skepticism of any one official church body and priesthood with its authoritative "experts" in religion. I have the related Protestant conviction that each person must individually study and in the end come to his or her own convictions in matters of religious truth. This helps to make it possible for me to justify my approaching even some of the most fundamental questions of religion as an "informed amateur." Erwin Schrodinger, one of the great physicists of the twentieth century, a co-discoverer with Werner Heisenberg in the 1920s of quantum mechanics, took up questions of philosophy and religion later in life. As Schrodinger commented, it was much to be desired that some people should attempt to bring together "the sum total of all that is known into a whole" interpretation of human mental and physical existence. Indeed, that is the true essence of theology, the effort to understand the "meaning of the human condition in the universe," necessarily including the capacity to make illuminating generalizations about the whole world that go beyond the reductive methods of science, a task in which there cannot be any uniquely qualified "experts."[13]

Before the scientific method can come into the picture, there must be some prior method of human understanding. Modern science was itself a product of Western religious thought, not the other way around. Before human thinking can even begin, and the proper scope and reliability of the use of the scientific method can itself be assessed, there must be an initial rock of rational thought to stand on. This is ultimately a question that falls to—that is of the essence of—theology. The subject matter of theology includes the roles and methods of science but it also includes many other things as well. Theology—properly understood—is thus capable of judging the methods of science; but it does not work the other way around.

Partly owing to the startling discoveries of twentieth-century physics, Schrodinger expected that new fundamental things could be said in our

12. In the thirteenth century, Thomas Aquinas famously offered five rational proofs for the existence of God. I should note that it is a coincidence that five rational ways for thinking about the question of a god are suggested in this book. I was reminded by a friend that Aquinas had given five ways of demonstrating the existence of God—the five proofs—after I had already settled on my five ways that are discussed below. See Kenny, *The Five Ways.*

13. Schrodinger, *What Is Life?*, 1.

time about religion but recognized a great problem in that today it is "next to impossible for a single mind fully to command more than a small portion" of the scientific and many other forms of relevant knowledge of the world. But Schrodinger was nevertheless willing to plunge ahead, declaring that: "I can see no other escape from this dilemma (lest our true aim be lost forever) than that some of us should venture to embark on a synthesis of facts and theories, although with secondhand and incomplete knowledge of some of them—and at the risk of making fools of ourselves. So much for my apology."[14] In embarking on this admittedly very ambitious book of my own, I found Schrodinger's remarks consoling and encouraging.

In writing this book, as noted previously, I have consulted with a wide body of contemporary professional literature in various fields, sifting through it all for those insights most relevant to my task. I have also consulted various contemporary theological resources. There has been a surprisingly large body of important writings bearing on the question of the existence of a god only in the last few years. Reading this literature, I can report that at the highest levels of contemporary intellectual inquiry the existence of a god is being explored today with an increasing interest and seriousness—a surprising development for the many people who not so long ago concluded that religion was fading away.

Doing "Qualitative" Social Science

Since history cannot be repeated, there is often only one grand "experiment" available to the social sciences. Thus, it is not possible to scientifically confirm or reject—in the manner of the physical sciences—broad hypotheses relating to long run human historical causation and explanation. Another significant problem in the social sciences is that there are frequently large numbers of "variables" interacting simultaneously, many of them highly correlated with one another (they are said by econometricians to be "collinear"), making it difficult or impossible to isolate statistically the causal influence of any one variable. A further major complication for human beings today is that events in society can be significantly influenced by ideas in the minds of the participants themselves. Even the ideas of social scientists can have significant influences on human outcomes (popular expectations of upward or downward economic trends, for example, as influenced by professional economic forecasters, can themselves have real impacts on the final economic outcomes).

14. Ibid.

Regarding the physical sciences as the highest form of learning, economists and other social scientists since World War II have devised various
mathematical modeling, statistical and other formal quantitative methods
in hopes of replicating the successes of physics. Unfortunately, however, this
effort has mostly failed.[15] Moreover, it is the most important questions—
dealing with issues of the greatest historical and social significance—that
are the least suitable for applying the formal methods of social science quantitative analysis. Some social scientists have responded to this problem by
tightly limiting their attention to those narrower problem areas in society
that have the best prospects for using the formal methods that most closely
resemble the physical sciences. Many other social scientists, unfortunately,
have shown a virtually religious commitment to using the mathematical
and statistical methods of the physical sciences even when they do not work
well—thus mostly failing to illuminate the social and economic problems
under study. Northwestern University decision theorist Charles Manski
comments that economists and other social scientists "regularly express
certitude about the consequences of alternative decisions" in offering their
advice to nonexpert policy makers. However ethically questionable, such
social scientists frequently offer "exact predictions of outcomes, . . . expressions of uncertainty are rare. Yet, policy predictions often are fragile. Conclusions may rest on critical unsupported assumptions or on leaps of logic"
that mainly reveal the pre-existing beliefs and values of the researcher, as is
also a common characteristic of much religious thought.[16]

In recent years a few other social scientists, however, have increasingly
been accepting the inevitability of using less formal (more "qualitative")
social science methods for many—probably most—inquiries into social
decision making, including conclusions with respect to the most important
aspects of human affairs. The overall method of such "qualitative social science"—of interest here because it is potentially applicable as well to theological inquiries about the existence of a god—is well summarized as follows:

> The [qualitative] social science we espouse seeks to make de-
> scriptive and causal inferences about the world. Those who do
> not share the assumptions of partial and imperfect knowability

15. The editorial page editor of *Barron's*, Thomas Donlan, writes: "Is economics a
science? It isn't much like physics, chemistry, physiology or medicine, the hard sciences
for which Nobel prizes are awarded. Economics is more like another Nobel subject,
literature. . . . But it is [even] more like the award for peace." "A Slippery Course of
Study," 43.

16. Manski, *Public Policy in an Uncertain World*, 2–3. See also McCloskey, *The
Rhetoric of Economics*; and DeMartino and McCloskey, eds., *Oxford Handbook of Professional Economic Ethics*.

and the aspiration for descriptive and causal understanding will have to look elsewhere for inspiration or for paradigmatic battles in which to engage.

In sum, we do not provide recipes for scientific empirical research. We offer a number of precepts and rules, but these are meant to discipline thought, not stifle it. . . . We engage in the imperfect application of theoretical standards of inference to inherently imperfect research designs and empirical data. Any meaningful rules admit of exceptions, but we can ask that exceptions be justified explicitly, that their implications for the reliability of research be assessed, and that the uncertainty of conclusions be reported. We seek not dogma, but disciplined thought.[17]

As three Harvard social scientists write, the goal of such qualitative social science is often "to infer beyond the immediate data to something broader that is not directly observed"—such as, for example, the possible existence of a god.[18] Few social scientists admittedly have taken up the question of the existence of a god as a part of their professional efforts, but there is no reason in principle why such qualitative social science methods might not be applied to this long-standing central question for human beings. In the twentieth century, the social sciences displaced traditional Jewish and Christian theology as the most authoritative way of thinking about the human condition in society and the world. My own background and training as a social scientist that led to a strong interest in religion is unusual among contemporary writers about theological questions. My approach in this book might be described as being in part a special form of "qualitative" social science. It draws on traditional theological resources but seeks to integrate them—always using rational methods such as the social sciences ideally apply—with ideas and knowledge from many other specialized physical and social scientific sources.

Religion is Back

Partly reflecting the influence of Protestant religion, the American intellectual world was filled in the twentieth century with people who thought of religion exclusively as a matter of having some form of private faith. As this way of thinking was manifested among social scientists, religion thus was not a product itself of rational analysis but was a given "preference"

17. King, Keohane, and Verba, *Designing Social Inquiry*, 7.
18. Ibid., 8.

within an individual's overall "preference function," about which little could
be said other than that it existed. Among economists, they might seek to
study religion "objectively" but they considered that there was little of interest that could be said about the way in which the religious and other
contents of an individual preference function were formed. Other social
scientists approached religion in similar ways; its contents and influence
on society could be usefully studied but not much of great interest could
be said about the original sources of religious convictions themselves, and
how they might have arisen as forms of belief and would continue to evolve
in the future. The strong belief among social scientists and other academics
that they could say little or nothing about the relative merits of differing
religions or about the manner of improving the religious beliefs of a society
was one reason that they showed such little interest in the twentieth century in studying the role—as obviously large as it has been—of religion in
society. Their aversion was not as great but few policy makers saw it as their
province to seek to improve the "culture" of a nation, perhaps as a necessary
precondition, for example, to rapid economic development.

Even many such people, however, have recently been changing their
mind. Stanley Fish does not fit the image of a typical defender of religious
inquiry. A Yale PhD and former professor of English at the University of
California at Berkeley, Johns Hopkins University, and Duke University, Fish
is well known as a leading postmodern humanist. Yet, at his *New York Times*
blog, Fish in 2009 revealed a surprisingly strong interest in religion. More
and more people, he wrote, are seeking answers to "theological questions
. . . like, 'Why is there anything in the first place?' 'Why what we do have
is actually intelligible to us?' and 'Where do our notions of explanation,
regularity, and intelligibility come from?'" Many who once worshiped at the
altar of "liberal rationalism and its ideology of science," he suggested, have
concluded that this was yet another false idol.[19]

Religion thus is back. Actually, it never went away, although it often
took novel forms in the twentieth century. In deciding matters of sexual morality, the upbringing of children, marriage relationships, and other aspects
of private behavior, a Freudian gospel, and its psychological successors,
eclipsed the traditional Christian ethical messages.[20] In the public arena,
as I have explored in writings over the past twenty years, secular religions
such as Marxism, the American progressive "gospel of efficiency," the neo-
classical economics of the second half of the twentieth century, and other
forms of "economic religion" were the leading influences on government

19. Fish, "God Talk."
20. Vitz, *Psychology as Religion*; Epstein, *Psychotherapy as Religion*.

policies around the world.[21] In economic religion, "efficiency" and "ineffi-
ciency" take the earlier Christian place of "good" and "evil." Toward the end
of the century, yet another secular religion, environmentalism, challenged
the economic gospels—questioning the whole idea of "progress" as the path
of the future salvation of the world.[22] So what is actually new is that a god—
explicitly, no longer in such disguised forms—is back.[23] This was not only a
Western but a worldwide phenomenon, as the secular gods of the twentieth
century everywhere faced growing challenges.

Such surprising developments of our times do not regularly make
the daily news but some observant journalists have been taking note. In
a 2009 book, two writers for *The Economist* magazine examine "how the
global revival of faith is changing the world." John Micklethwait and Adrian
Wooldridge comment in *God is Back* that the "political classes in the West
are waking up, rather late, to the enduring power of religion."[24] The modern
belief in the redemptive powers of economic progress had first come under
powerful challenge as long ago as the events of World War I, in which nine
million soldiers and six million civilians died to little or no purpose, victims
of the follies of their political leaders.[25] An even greater blow to progressive
faith came in the 1930s and 1940s with the show trials and prison camps of
the former Soviet Union, the concentration camps of Nazi Germany, and
further vast bloodshed across the battlefields of Europe and other parts of
the world. It was impossible within the framework of the rational secular
religions of progress to reconcile such events with the very rapid economic
growth of the developed nations over the previous hundred years.[26] Apparently, something fundamental about the human condition had been missed
in the thinking of the modern age, dating as far back as events in the Enlightenment. If bad human actions were caused by bad external environments in
which "sinful" humans had lived, as so many firmly believed, the immense
material progress of the modern age should have yielded commensurate
gains in moral progress—as had clearly not happened.

Many leading intellectuals experienced a great disillusionment as early
as the 1920s but for a whole society ideas change more slowly. Even after the

---

21. Nelson, *Reaching for Heaven on Earth*; Nelson, *Economics as Religion*; Nelson,
"What Is 'Economic Theology'?"; Nelson, "The Theological Meaning of Economics";
Nelson, "Economic Religion versus Christian Values"; Nelson, "Sustainability, Effi-
ciency and God"; Nelson, "Economics as Religion" (1994).

22. Nelson, *The New Holy Wars*; Nelson, "Calvinism Without God."

23. Nelson, "The Secularization Myth Revisited."

24. Micklethwait and Wooldridge, *God is Back*, 19.

25. Fleming, *The Illusion of Victory*.

26. Nelson, "The Secular Religions of Progress."

many horrible events of the first half of the twentieth century, those devout who had grown up believing in one or another of the secular religions of progress often found it difficult to change their thinking. At stake was no less than the optimistic self-understanding of the modern age. Indeed, it took the abominations of a Hitler, Stalin, and others of their twentieth century ilk to force a painful religious reconsideration that gathered momentum in the last decades of the twentieth century. As the *Economist* writers Micklethwait and Wooldridge observe, the core question being raised in the new god debates is "the battle for modernity" and its transcendent (or not) meaning.[27]

The core belief in progress was based on an assumption—a core element of faith, really—that the fundamental realities in society lie in "natural" (i.e., physical) phenomena, amenable to definitive scientific analysis, and thus allowing human beings to transform the future by making conscious scientific choices to radically alter their exterior—above all their economic—environments. If society perfects the external economic environment, most of the leading secular religions of the modern age took for granted, this would lead to the perfection both of future society and of the internal person as well—bringing about a "new man" and a new "heaven on earth." Traditional religion was left to play a much diminished role, perhaps as merely an epiphenomenon that offered at most a reflection of the "real" underlying economic forces at work. By the end of the twentieth century, however, all this was increasingly coming into basic question, as seemingly yet another utopian illusion in a long history of such utopian and eschatological expectations that long predated the Enlightenment as well.

One sign of the current rethinking of the modern project is the final book of Ronald Dworkin, a longtime distinguished professor of legal philosophy at New York University. Although he died in February 2013, Dworkin had completed by then *Religion Without God*, which appeared later that year. Recognizing that the "secular" is often actually religion in a different form, Dworkin considered that "expanding the territory of religion improves clarity by making plain the importance of what is shared across that territory" of religion in all its full modern diversity of expression. As Dworkin writes, we can thus speak, literally, not just metaphorically, of "religious atheism" as one particular form of genuinely religious belief. Such secular forms of religion share with traditional religion the objective to inquire "more fundamentally about the meaning of human life and what living well means." Reflecting the full scope of religion today, Dworkin declares that "the new religious wars are now really culture wars," frequently involving

27. Micklethwait and Wooldridge, *God is Back*, 24.

competing secular understandings of the overall human prospect.[28] Well
before Dworkin, a leading theologian of the twentieth century, Paul Tillich,
said much the same about developments in twentieth-century religion, that
they took a wide variety of forms, sometimes not even widely and explicitly
recognized as religion, but they were in fact true forms of religion in that
they dealt with matters of "ultimate concern."[29]

Another recent sign of the comeback of religion is that the antago-
nists of religion have been put on the defensive. It is no coincidence that, in
addition to *The God Delusion* and other books by Richard Dawkins, other
prominent "new atheist" writers have also recently emerged, including the
late Christopher Hitchens, Daniel Dennett, and Sam Harris.[30] Hitchens in
God is Not Great advanced the view that "there are . . . several ways in which
religion is not just amoral, but positively immoral."[31] There is admittedly less
novelty in the arguments of such new atheists than many people realize; in
many aspects, their writings represent an updating of the messages of Marx,
Freud, and Nietzsche—now around one hundred years or more old.

There is today in the new atheism the same naturalism grounded in
the Darwinist evolutionary understanding of human origins that in the
second half of the nineteenth century replaced the biblical creation story
for large numbers of people. The implication of Darwin—both then and
now—is to suggest for many people that traditional biblical religion is a
myth, no more scientifically truthful than innumerable other tribal myths
of human history. Thus, long before Dawkins wrote that the God of the Old
Testament is a "sadomasochistic, capriciously malevolent bully," and that
the Christian religion is a "pernicious delusion," Nietzsche in the late nineteenth century was declaring that the belief in a Christian God was "our
most enduring lie" which "turns life into a monstrosity."[32] Freud saw religion
as a great "illusion" that is "comparable to a childhood neurosis"; seen from
a scientific perspective, we must now "view religious teachings, as it were,
as neurotic relics, and we may now argue that the time has probably come
. . . for replacing the [religious] effects of [psychological] repression by the
results of the rational operation of the intellect."[33]

For both the old, and now again with the new atheists, it is unimagi-
nable that god might be a hidden cosmic intelligence whose "mind"—if

---

28. Dworkin, "Religion Without God."

29. Brown, *Ultimate Concern.*

30. Hitchens, *God is Not Great*; Dennett, *Breaking the Spell*; Harris, *The End of Faith.*

31. Hitchens, *God is Not Great*, 205.

32. Dawkins, *The God Delusion*, 51, 52. Nietzsche quoted in Schacht, *Nietzsche*, 121.

33. Cherry, "Freud and Religion."

working in an altogether scientifically mysterious way—whoever and what-ever "he" is—comprehensively controls the workings of the universe. While they are not as dogmatic, mostly stay out of public controversies about re-ligious subjects, and have a generally more positive view of the practically beneficial role of religion in society, a large part of the American intellectual elite still holds today to such a naturalist way of thinking about religion. For them, the old truths of religion do not themselves have an objective validity; rather, religion is itself to be "explained" by more fundamental realities—in this respect Marxism was simply an extreme example of a much broader twentieth-century way of thinking. It is no longer necessary to look to a su-pernatural God because in the modern age the scientific method has given human beings much more verifiable and accurate ways of gaining access to the eternal truths of the world, as compared with the Bible or any other previous sources of divinely revealed knowledge.

In *The God Delusion*, Dawkins refers at great length to the many evil things that—he is, unfortunately, often correct to say—have been commit-ted over the course of history in the name of religion. He also points to the many silly things that individual Christians—and groups of Christian faithful—have actually said in the past. All these real Christian failings, as Dawkins makes the case, represent a leading argument against the ex-istence—or certainly the benevolent character—of God. An equivalent exercise, however, can be applied to the atheism that Dawkins advocates. In-deed, Soviet and Nazi "atheistic fundamentalisms" easily eclipsed Christian religion in encouraging a parade of horrors over the course of the first half of the twentieth century. But, of course, to treat "atheistic" forms of religion in this way would be no more fair than Dawkins's treatment of Christianity. The American theologian William Cavanaugh thus writes in *The Myth of Religious Violence* that it is rationally "incoherent" to argue that "there is something called religion—a genus of which Christianity, Islam, Hinduism, and so on are species—which is necessarily more inclined toward violence than are ideologies and institutions that are identified as secular."[34]

Conclusion

Whatever the omissions and other theological failings of *The God Delusion* (and they are many), the book has nevertheless served a valuable purpose. Partly because of Dawkins's reputation as a leading popular expositor of biological evolution, combined with his skill as a writer, the book reached a large audience (*The God Delusion* made the *New York Times* best-seller list).

34. Cavanaugh, *The Myth of Religious Violence*, 5.

Dawkins has been on the cutting edge of a new trend to a freewheeling and explicit debate about religion in the public arena, following a century or more of comparative relegation to the margins.[35] He therefore should be thanked for his success in bringing religion back to the center of public discussion.

In seeking to continue the discussion, this book is partly intended for those people who begin today with a deep skepticism about, or reject outright, the existence of a god. The book is also intended for those many Christian faithful who nevertheless have some doubts about and would find helpful a carefully developed statement of the strong rational grounds for believing in the (very probable) existence of a god, drawing mostly on sources outside past and current formal theology. The book is organized around the explanation and development of five rational ways of thinking about the question of a god. I hasten to add that there are many other ways—some putting a greater emphasis on reason and others on personal faith—of addressing this fundamental question for human beings, including the writings of a number of distinguished theologians explicitly operating within the Christian tradition.[36]

35. For rebuttals to Dawkins, see McGrath and McGrath, *The Dawkins Delusion?*; Cornwell, *Darwin's Angel*; Ward, *Why There Almost Certainly Is a God*; Hahn and Wiker, *Answering the New Atheism*; and McGrath, *Dawkins' God.*

36. See, among many such writings, Lewis, *Mere Christianity*; Swinburne, *Is There a God?*; Craig, *On Guard*; Ward, *The Evidence for God*; and Plantinga, *Knowledge and Christian Belief.*

2

Thinking About God

I HAVE FAITH, DEAR reader, that you exist. As you may be surprised to hear, this is only a personal conviction of mine. By strictly scientific criteria alone, I have no proof that you do actually exist. And no, I am not referring to the possibility that this book will be so uninspiring that it will not have any readers at all. Rather, I am pointing to a basic issue of epistemology that has been explored by past writers as distinguished as David Hume and Immanuel Kant—the impossibility of any direct contact between the minds of my readers and my own mind, the fact that I can have no sure scientific knowledge that any such thing as another mind (such as you, the "reader") actually exists outside my own mind. As a matter of a strictly scientific understanding alone, I have only a set of sensory messages, as received by my brain (whose actual physical existence again I must take on faith), and that are transformed into mental states experienced in my own consciousness (whatever that is). As Descartes said, I think, therefore I exist. But the actual existence of anything outside the workings of my own mind depends on a form of—essentially religious, as I will be following others in making the argument—faith.

People who lack this faith, who go so far as to reject any reality outside their own minds altogether, are known philosophically as solipsists. While very few people actually believe this as a working basis for the conduct of their daily lives, the solipsist position is surprisingly difficult—or impossible, as some reputable philosophers and scientists think, and I find myself agreeing—to refute logically with certainty. Indeed, the whole concept of a "material world" is surprisingly difficult to explain and justify by strictly rational and scientific methods alone. The current Calvin College and former Notre Dame philosopher and theologian Alvin Plantinga, widely respected internationally in both areas, notes that a prominent contemporary of Hume took his position to be that of "a *skeptic* with respect to external objects, an enduring self, other minds, causality, the past, and so on." The evidence of our incoming sensory perceptions and our common sense thinking within our own consciousness are uncertain indicators of an external physical reality, although we necessarily act as though they are reliable. As Plantinga writes, for Hume "this is the irony of the human condition: those who are enlightened can see that what nature inevitably leads us to believe is false, or arbitrary, or at best extremely dubious; they also see, however, that even the best of us simply don't have it in them to successfully resist her blandishments."[1] And so it is today with our conviction that our own existence is both real and meaningful, along with that of other people who do actually exist, a belief that is perhaps equivalent to, or at the least comes close to, believing in God, as Plantinga himself has argued.

In an earlier book Plantinga thus focused on such perplexities raised by the existence and character of "other minds." Plantinga adds a radical new twist to this long-standing discussion, relating the question to theology. He first examines the various rational arguments from "natural theology" for the existence of God—the ontological argument, the teleological argument, and others. He finds that they ultimately fail: "it is hard to avoid the conclusion that natural theology does not provide a satisfactory answer to the question with which we began: Is it rational to believe in God?" Strictly speaking, rationality alone ultimately does not get us there, as he concludes.[2]

But he then examines the strongest rational arguments to demonstrate that other minds—other people outside ourselves—do in fact exist. As many people may be surprised to hear, he finds (like Hume and some other leading philosophers) that human reason fails again. There is no sure rational path to the conclusion that other people with other minds do really exist. Reviewing previous rational attempts to establish this conclusion, Plantinga finds that the "analogical argument" is the best rational case that can be made. In the end, however, it also fails as a final proof. Remarkably enough, moreover, "it succumbs to a [philosophical] malady exactly resembling the one afflicting the teleological argument" for the existence of God.[3]

Hence, as Plantinga finds, we might not be able to rationally demonstrate the existence of God but it is also impossible to rationally demonstrate the existence of other minds (and the people who go with these minds). This does not of course then prove the existence of God—even as we also have no way of being rationally certain of the existence of other minds and people. But a belief in other minds and a belief in God belong to the same categories of

1. Plantinga, *Warranted Christian Belief*, 218, 219.
2. Plantinga, *God and Other Minds*, 111.
3. Ibid., xvi.

rational uncertainty and necessary degrees of faith. Plantinga takes for granted—as almost everyone else does, including almost all of you I assume, the
readers of this book—the existence of other minds. Since the same kinds of
arguments are required to support the existence of a god, Plantinga concludes
that God very probably also does exist. Or, as he puts it, "I conclude that belief
in other minds and belief in God are in the same epistemological boat; hence
if either is rational, so is the other. But obviously the former is rational; . . . so,
therefore, is the latter" equally rational (or irrational).[4]

This does not, admittedly, finally resolve the matter. Although the
best rational argument for the existence of God, and the best argument
for the existence of other minds, may be philosophically analogous, it is
still conceivable that one is correct and the other is incorrect, perhaps by
random chance (it is after all a matter of probabilities), although human
beings would not be able to resolve this issue by their own rational analysis.
I bring all this up partly to illustrate the central role of faith in matters both
of religion and daily living, and to show how there are a wide variety of rational—even if nonscientific—ways of thinking about the existence of a god.
Since science cannot definitively demonstrate the existence of other minds,
it requires a form of rationally based faith ("rational faith") to believe with
full certainty that they do in fact exist. The same, of course, can be said of
believing with full certainty in the existence of a god. But if one is possible,
it would be folly to rule out automatically the other. It is only a misplaced
worship of science that has led so many people to a definitively negative
conclusion about a god.

Even these people may implicitly believe in a god without knowing
it.[5] Indeed, this divinity may even be a version of the Christian God more
specifically. Among religions, Christianity historically affirms the existence
of an "outside" material world and a human bodily reality with particular
emphasis. As one Christian theologian writes, "Christianity is a physical religion. We believe in the Word who took on human flesh, who bled and died
on the cross, who rose bodily from the tomb. We believe in the resurrection
of the *body*—your body and mine. So beware of slipping into a spiritualism that ignores or despairs of the body," an outlook historically found in
many other religions around the world.[6] One might even suggest that in this
respect scientific materialism should be regarded as belonging to the many
forms of modern belief—along with Marxism, socialism, French positiv-
ism, the American progressive "gospel of efficiency" and a number of other

4. Ibid., xvi.

5. Bailey, "Implicit Religion" (2010).

6. Austin, "How to Be a Sick Christian," 18.

types of "economic religion"—that have offered messages well understood as (at least in significant part) secularized forms of Christianity.[7] From a traditional Christian perspective, since they often deny the existence of a god, they are perhaps then best regarded as Christian heresies—recognizing that the line between Christian truth and Christian heresy has frequently been blurred historically.

Did We Really Go to the Moon?

Beyond questions such as the existence of other minds, large elements of faith are a surprisingly pervasive element in many other aspects of ordinary living. For example, in a 2006 visit to Igauzu Falls along the border of Argentina and Brazil—perhaps the most beautiful falls in the world—I was having dinner with a successful Argentine businessman from the city of Salta in the North. It was an enlightening if mostly unexceptional conversation about the current state of affairs in Argentina—until near the end when I was startled to hear him declare that men had never set foot on the moon. The six American moon missions from 1969 to 1972, he believed, seemingly in all seriousness, had been staged. My curiosity piqued, further checking revealed a 1999 Gallup poll showing that as many as 6 percent of Americans said they agreed.[8] There are even books written on the subject. *One Small Step: The Great Moon Hoax and the Race to Dominate Earth From Space*, published first in German and then translated into English, explains that "there are no plausible proofs of anyone having landed on the moon between 1969 and 1972. On the contrary, proofs of the lunar landings having been faked have increased."[9]

This raised for me the question: do I know that men really went to the moon? I did in fact personally watch Neil Armstrong take "one giant leap for mankind" live on my television—as it happened, in a Houston motel room I had rented in July 1969 specifically for that purpose (while doing some economics PhD research there on the local land market). But this was not definite proof since I had not actually been on the moon and fictional accounts appear on television routinely. I was thus forced to consider why I did actually believe that the scene I had watched was "real."

When I thought about it, I realized that the answers came down in significant part to forms of rationally supported faith (or to rational trust in others, one form of faith). Based on personal experiences—such as my

7. Nelson, *Reaching for Heaven on Earth*; Nelson, *Economics as Religion*.
8. Gallup Poll, "Landing a Man on the Moon."
9. Wisnewski, *One Small Step*, 356.

father working for the federal government for a considerable time, for example—I had for me a rational faith that the US government would not have engaged in such a gigantic fraud (by US government I mean here mainly the National Aeronautics and Space Administration, since other employees of the government could have been equally deceived along with me). I also had a rational faith in the television networks—and the other national news media—that their investigative resources would have uncovered any actual fictional portrayal of a moon landing, and that they would in fact have chosen to reveal any such deception, had they known about it (and faith that they were not coconspirators with NASA).

Yet another form of faith grounded in rational argument was that, since hundreds of Americans working for NASA would probably have to have known of any fraudulent portrayal, some of them would have disclosed the deceit to at least a few other people, and that some of those people would then have told some others, and so on and so forth. The chain of personal interconnections required to move information from one of the NASA employees in Houston to me would not be all that long—by my estimate probably fewer than twenty people even in a country as large as the United States. So if the moon landing was all a grand hoax staged by NASA, I had a rational faith that somehow I would have heard about it. To be sure, a note of caution would have to be considered: many Germans claimed after World War II that they had no knowledge of the holocaust, even though thousands of their fellow Germans had to have had direct personal knowledge.

I mention this story not because I am especially interested in the truth of the moon landing (I have complete faith that it actually took place) but because it illustrates a broader issue that interests me more. How can we establish rational faith in the truthfulness of a core belief—such as not only the moon landing but, more importantly, the existence and actions of a god in the world—when no final scientific demonstration is possible? I have always been reluctant to take things on faith alone but, thinking about the moon landing, it reminded me how some significant degree of rational faith is often involved even in many matters of basic nonreligious belief. We can call it a "rational faith" because it is not a faith that is simply plucked out of the air; it is a faith for which good—if never absolutely conclusive—rational reasons can be given.

Indeed, on reflection there are surprisingly few things of which we can be totally and absolutely sure. In most cases, it will be a matter of probabilities—and thus it seems to require at least some larger or smaller element of rational judgment (and this will require another form of rational faith, in our capacities—as I would hope most of you have—for good judgment). And if so, how, then, can we establish probabilities of our faith in truthfulness even in the face of some degree—in some cases a large degree—of rational uncertainty. As it is said, the hardest thing is to know what we need to know—and the social sciences and philosophy can offer no sure means of obtaining access to this critical beginning form of knowledge. There is a full branch of mathematical statistics, "Bayesian analysis," devoted to this question but it is not much help on many—especially the biggest—questions such as the existence of a god.

Our lives thus are pervaded with probabilistic assessments that lead us to act routinely on the basis of forms of rational faith that we possess. If that is the case, why should we not proceed in a similar fashion with respect to the question of a god? In thinking about the possible existence of a god, this book will offer five rational ways to think about this question—not to suggest that this list exhausts the possible rational ways. Considering these five rational ways, I will conclude at the end of the book that a god does very probably exist, even if not demonstrable with absolute certainty.

Natural Science versus Social Science

Science claims to be the one valid method of establishing (near) certain truth. I essentially accept this claim with respect to the truths of the natural world as discovered by physics, chemistry, and molecular biology (even recognizing that Einstein did make significant modifications in what had been regarded until then as the unassailable final truthfulness of Newtonian physics). Even my acceptance of any particular result of the natural sciences, to be sure, is itself significantly a matter of faith, since I do not do the scientific research, check the mathematics, confirm the empirical findings by my own experiments, or otherwise by myself validate the scientific results. (And there have been scientific frauds, some of which were around many years before being discovered.)

My faith in the products of natural science is in fact based partly on my own understanding of the internal workings of the scientific community, including some personal friends and relatives there whom I do trust. I have faith that natural scientists do a reasonably good job in policing any misconduct by fellow scientists, and then that the restatement of natural scientific discoveries in more popular language accessible to a wider public (the form in which I receive most natural science information) is in fact an accurate portrayal of the original science itself. While the reliability of any particular article in the popular press (to say nothing of television and the web) may be quite uncertain in this regard, I have faith that over the long run—even in the popular media—with respect to the conclusions of natural science, "the truth will win out."

My faith in natural science also includes a surprisingly biblical type of source, the "miracles" that I routinely witness in the form of the vast array of technological products of modern science that would have been almost impossible even to conceive of existing a mere few centuries ago (including the Wi-Fi Internet connection I am now using and the word processor on which I am now typing). If natural scientists are capable of producing such astonishing miracles—including going to the moon, as I do believe happened—it seems reasonable to believe that their knowledge claims more broadly can be taken on faith to be authoritative. Based on a large variety of what seem to be such reliable rational "indicators," I choose to put my (near) full faith in the applications of the scientific method to questions of the workings of the natural world, as their findings are first developed and communicated within the community of natural scientists, and as then further explained by more popular sources of information that I actually consult myself. It also helps that some of the popular explanations are authored by leading physical scientists themselves, significantly increasing my confidence in their accuracy—a method I have relied on heavily in writing this book.

In the modern era, there have been many assertions that the scientific method has far broader application—that it can equally well be applied to learn the truths of society and of human affairs generally, and even the question of a god. Ambitious claims have been made that the scientific method will be able to reveal scientific laws of the workings of society and the human mind. In such matters, however, based partly on long personal experience and observation within the community of social scientists to which I belong myself, I have come to have little faith. In retrospect, economists, political scientists, sociologists, psychologists, and other social scientists have not produced even a single "miracle" that compares to the marvelous technological inventions that have routinely resulted from the applications of the discoveries of the physical sciences. Their efforts often seem to be mere claims to the truth status of the physical sciences—the ability of "science" to convey authority and legitimacy in modern society—that are backed up by remarkably little rational justification.

My limited faith in social science also reflects its many large and embarrassing failures since the eighteenth century. The two "social scientists" who had the greatest impact on the world in the past 150 years were Karl Marx and Sigmund Freud—both asserting a full authority for their economic and psychological theories analogous to that of the physical sciences, a claim that was later fully accepted by hundreds of millions of devout followers.

But Marxism and Freudianism are now both generally discredited as valid sciences in the sense of physics, and are widely doubted as credible even as nonscientific social and economic history and personal history, respectively. While they may have offered some useful specific insights, and some interesting broader schemes for classifying events in the economic and psychological worlds, their "scientific" predictions for the future routinely went awry. Both Marx and Freud today appear closer to messianic prophets than to actual scientific students of either the workings of economic history or of the human mind. Even contemporary mainstream economists—while having many useful and practical things to say—are best regarded in the larger picture as a priesthood of a secular religion whose greatest impact on society is the result of its priestly blessings that the public (wrongly in my view) routinely accepts as scientifically authoritative.

Thinking about the existence of a god is similar to thinking about the validity of the truth claims of the various modern claimants to authoritative knowledge. For Christianity, the one historical miracle of greatest importance in sustaining its truth claims is the resurrection of Jesus Christ, long assumed without question by the Christian faithful to be an actual historical event. In the modern era, however, such certainty has no longer been possible for many people, a key factor in the erosion of Christian belief. It is not that the biblical portrayal of the resurrection is necessarily false but that its historical truthfulness has become a question for probabilistic reasoning and judgments ultimately based on rational faith. If complete faith is demanded as in the workings of natural science, it will be impossible to achieve, not only with respect to the existence of a god but many other faiths that help to guide us through the routine workings of our lives.

Physical science in the modern age displaced Christian theology in matters of the workings of the natural world because its modern miracles are fully authoritative in this domain—unlike biblical statements about the natural world, we all can have almost complete faith in the knowledge claims of physical science for that world. We can all see for ourselves every day the extraordinary physical miracles that the knowledge of the physical sciences has produced, sustaining our rational faith in the full validity of scientific truth claims about nature. In the sense that science cannot itself explain the existence of these miracles (it cannot answer the fundamental question of why physical science itself works so well to explain the natural world and assert human mastery over it), one might take modern technological miracles as strongly indicating the existence of a god, as biblical miracles in their time—also believed to be literally true—formerly served this function for the Christian faithful.

John Henry Newman: Faith through Cumulative Probabilities

As this book will treat the matter, believing in the existence of a god to-day is more like having rational faith, or not, in matters falling outside the natural sciences, a matter in both cases for probabilistic assessments based on available evidence and rational reasoning. Indeed, such a view was developed systematically in the nineteenth century by the English theologian John Henry Newman (Cardinal Newman as he eventually became, and who was beatified in 2010 by Pope Benedict XVI). By most accounts, Newman was among the great theologians of the modern era. His explanation of the reasons for his conversion in England from his youthful Anglicanism to the religion of Roman Catholicism is among the great such accounts of history. Among his voluminous writings, Newman also sought to explain how one might come to believe in God—and specifically in his later writings in the God of Roman Catholicism.

Protestantism emphasizes salvation by "faith alone"—for some people to occur in a sudden flash of being "born again." Martin Luther harshly criticized Thomas Aquinas, partly because Aquinas approached religion more as a matter of a rationally acquired understanding, including his giving his own five rational reasons for the existence of God. Writing in 1871 in *A Grammar of Assent*, many years after his conversion to Roman Catholicism, Newman comes closer to Aquinas. Some kind of faith is ultimately necessary but it should be the product of long experience, careful inquiry, rational thinking, and many other contributing factors—a "rational faith." As Newman wrote, faith in God should emerge from "popular, practical, personal evidence."[10] His contemporary biographer John Cornwell explains that for Newman "'real assent' [to God] involves acceptance of truth through firsthand evidence, the 'real knowledge' of religion across a broad span of experience encountered with the whole of one's being. . . . [It] is retrospective, a realization that follows a variety of parallel evidences and experiences."[11]

Newman believes that it is possible by such means to reach a complete faith in God. But this faith is not proved by any precise method of logical reasoning—not by "the rude operation of syllogistic treatment" or any other form of natural science discovery. Newman looks to many sources of information that must all be experienced and examined, which results in a gradual "accumulation of probabilities" until it may become possible to

---

10. Quoted in Cornwell, *Newman's Unquiet Grave*, 191.

11. Ibid., 186.

reach a personal conclusion.[12] This overall process is not well defined; as Newman writes, it is "too fine to avail separately, too subtle and circuitous to be convertible into syllogisms, too numerous and various for [a single moment of] conversion."[13] As Cornwell puts it, for Newman "real knowledge of religion . . . is supported by the strength of many strands." Newman contrasts the idea of an "iron rod" which consists of one single piece of steel with the character of a "cable" that is woven together of many strands—the development of religious faith resembling the many strands that can come together to make a remarkably strong religious cable of rational faith.[14]

Cornwell thus explains that for Newman God becomes in the end a "certainty," not just a "probability"—much in the manner that I am "certain" that men did go to the moon.[15] But Newman's certain belief "in God, in Christianity, in Catholicism, [is reached] *on* a probability"; in Newman's own words, "a cumulative transcendent probability, but still probability; inasmuch as He who made us has so willed, that in mathematics indeed we arrive at certitude by rigid demonstration, but in religious inquiry we arrive at certitude by accumulated probabilities."[16] Cornwell comments that "Newman is not talking here about probability in the conventional sense but a narrative of probabilities leading to certainty within the personal and moral domain."[17] As applied to the question of a god, Newman's method bears a close resemblance to the methods of qualitative social science as described above in the Introduction—and is in part a model for this book.

The Challenge of Arthur Stanley Eddington

After they had made fundamental scientific contributions, a number of the greatest physicists of the twentieth century, including Niels Bohr, Albert Einstein, Werner Heisenberg, Erwin Schrodinger, and others sought to explain for wider audiences the significance of their new scientific discoveries for understanding the broader state of the human condition. Einstein never systematically organized his thinking but wrote and spoke about god with surprising frequency. Bohr had an intense philosophical interest and wrote a great deal but was not a gifted expositor. Heisenberg and Schrodinger, by

12. Quoted in ibid., 187, 186.
13. Quoted in ibid., 186–87.
14. Ibid., 186, 188.
15. Ibid., 188.
16. Quoted in ibid., 188.
17. Ibid.

contrast, shared the intense philosophical interest but were also fluent writers in multiple books addressing such basic questions.

Richard Dawkins in *The God Delusion*, like other new atheists, offers a natural and material explanation of reality—often characterized as scientific materialism. At one point he recalls his participation at a conference at Cambridge University where a number of leading contemporary theologians were in attendance. A common criticism Dawkins heard was that his materialist habits of thought were outmoded, that "my whole world-view was condemned as 'nineteenth-century.'"[18] Dawkins professes surprise and even mystification in *The God Delusion* with this line of criticism. He might have had a better understanding if he had studied more closely the writings of the Englishman Arthur Stanley Eddington, also among the leading physicists of the twentieth century. Eddington was among the first physicists to grasp the full importance for physics itself of Einstein's general theory of relativity, published in 1915. He organized the famous international experiment in 1919 confirming that the gravitational field of the sun bent light waves coming from other stars according to Einstein's prediction, thus providing the first empirical confirmation of the general theory of relativity, and making Einstein an instant international celebrity.

Eddington was also a devout Quaker who was among the first of the leading physicists of the time to write and speak widely to popular audiences about the large implications for religion of the radical new developments occurring in twentieth-century physics.[19] After the confirmation of the general theory of relativity, and also following the equally remarkable discoveries of quantum mechanics in the 1920s, Eddington embarked on a campaign to spread the word of how fundamentally the new physics was undermining older understandings of the basic character of reality—and the probabilities as he saw things of the existence of an immaterial God. He thus wrote in 1929 that the material conception of reality, so characteristic of the nineteenth century, was no longer tenable, that "science is no longer disposed to identify reality with concreteness. Materialism in its literal sense is long since dead." In the new world of twentieth-century physics, the very concept of "matter now has only a minor place."[20] To be sure, popular faith in the existence of matter was nevertheless still useful for ordinary people as a mental crutch to aid their daily living in the world, much as a faith in the existence of other minds is helpful to ordinary human functioning.

---

18. Dawkins, *The God Delusion*, 186.

19. This tradition has continued among physicists up to the present time. See Polkinghorne, *Science and Religion in Quest of Truth*.

20. Eddington, *Science and the Unseen World*, 51.

Eddington regarded science and religion as mutually supportive, commenting that the traditional "harmony and simplicity of scientific law appeals strongly to our aesthetic feeling. It illustrates one kind of perfection, such as we might perhaps think worthy to be associated with God."[21] The recent discoveries in physics were now opening the way to wider ways of thinking about the world, and about God as well, ways surprisingly compatible with older understandings of the divine reality that put the existence of mind before that of matter (the philosophy of Plato, for example). As Eddington reported,

> What I wish to point out is that we no longer have the disposition which, as soon as it scents a piece of mechanism, exclaims "Here we are getting to bedrock. This is what things should ultimately resolve themselves into. This is ultimate reality." Physics today is not likely to be attracted by [such] a type of explanation.
>
> Perhaps the most essential change is that we are no longer tempted to condemn the spiritual aspects of our nature as illusory because of their lack of concreteness. We have traveled [in physics] far from the standpoint which identifies the real with the concrete. Even the older philosophy found it necessary to admit exceptions; for example, time must be admitted to be real, although no one could attribute to it a concrete nature. Nowadays, time might be taken as typical of the kind of stuff of which we imagine the physical world to be built. Physics has no direct concern with that feeling of "becoming" in our consciousness which we regard as inherently belonging to the nature of time, and it treats time merely as a symbol; but [this is] equally [true for] matter and all else that is in the physical world [and that has] . . . been reduced to a shadowy symbolism.[22]

Eddington at another point confronts the arguments of a generic "materialist philosopher," a species of thinker common throughout the nineteenth and twentieth centuries and still prevalent today—witness Dawkins and the other "new atheists." According to such a naturalist way of thinking, our brains consist of "electric particles [working] in obedience to the laws of physics." It is as a result of the internal movements of "our" electric particles that we as human beings have "brought about and stored in those brains [of ours] the thoughts that make up the sum of human knowledge." Eddington then wonders how a true believer naturalist in his audience would be reacting at that very moment to the arguments he is hearing from Eddington in

21. Ibid., 51.
22. Ibid., 32–33.

his lecture. Presumably, "your brains will react towards the lecture in accordance with the unbreakable laws [of nature] which govern them."[23] That
is, for the members of the audience, the workings of their electric particles
in their brains will decide on the "truth," as they perceive it, of his—Eddington's—message. You, the readers of this book, may be similarly deceived that
your reactions to its arguments reflect any rationality beyond neurology and
physics. Perhaps the electric particles in human brains, as actually described
in quantum mechanics for such particles in general, do themselves have
some of the qualities of human free will that scientific materialism seemingly denies to the human person as a thinking being.

But unless God is somehow actually working his ways through the
conscious decisions of your brain neurons (admittedly no more fantastic
an idea than some of the other creations of twentieth-century physics), Eddington observes that this leads to "a very old *reductio ad absurdum*; and
he would be a very shallow materialist who has not appreciated the difficulty." In asking about the role of the material workings of the universe in
influencing human thoughts and behavior, the full-fledged materialist must
reply that our answer will be determined by the material workings of the
universe. It is as though, in seeking to resolve the question of the truthfulness of A, a person were to argue that the assumed truthfulness of A will
decide the correct answer.

To escape this absurdity, as Eddington points out, the questions raised
by naturalist philosophers will have to be decided by other criteria than
naturalist philosophy itself. Indeed, any such fundamental question "is to
be judged in relation to its [actual] truth or untruth, not in relation to any
supposed theory" of natural science that purports to determine the manner of human perception of truth.[24] It admittedly raises deep mysteries for
understanding human reality but final truth will never be a matter of doing
physics (or brain neurology) well.

While Eddington was an early participant among the leading physicists
of the first half of the twentieth century in making such arguments, Heisenberg and Schrodinger—in the mid-1920s the co-discoverers of quantum
mechanics—were saying similar things by the 1950s. Schrodinger wrote in
1951 that "when you come to the ultimate particles constituting matter, there
seems to be no point in thinking of them again as consisting of some material. They are, as it were, pure shape, nothing but shape; what turns up again
and again in successive observations is this shape, not an individual speck
of material." It was part of a general rejection in twentieth-century physics

23. Ibid., 59, 60.
24. Ibid., 60–61.

of nineteenth-century mechanistic ways of thinking. Schrodinger explained that "as our mental eye penetrates into smaller and smaller distances and shorter and shorter times, we find nature behaving so entirely differently from what we observe in visible and palpable bodies of our [normal] surroundings that *no* model [of full reality] shaped after our large scale experiences can ever be 'true.'" If we try to apply our commonsense understanding of a material world, based on our own direct conscious experiences of the natural order, to understand the quantum world, "a satisfactory model *of this type* is not only practically inaccessible, but not even thinkable. Or, to be precise, we can, of course, think it, but however we think it, it is wrong; not perhaps quite as meaningless as a 'triangular circle,' but much more so than a 'winged lion.'" [25]

Nature at the most fundamental subatomic level thus has no "material" reality, even though we live our daily lives under the helpful illusion that all of nature does have such a reality.[26] It may not be much more difficult, however, to conceive of the existence of a nonmaterial god than of the existence of the nonmaterial world of "nature" as revealed by twentieth-century physics. They are not distinguished in the least by the level of mystery involved. In each case, the way the world actually works is outside any material or mechanical causation—neither "god" nor "nature" in concept is inherently more magical than the other; perhaps the immaterial reality of "nature" is part of a more encompassing immaterial reality that we might label "god," both existing outside anything that human beings directly experience in their routine earthly lives. As the *Economist* magazine commented in 2010, "it is well known that [the] fundamental physics [of the twentieth century] is full of ideas that defy what humans are pleased to call common sense"—a fundamental reality that perhaps can now be extended to encompass as well the existence of a god outside "common sense."[27]

Heisenberg the "Theologian"

As mentioned briefly above in the Introduction, Werner Heisenberg also contributed important writings in the 1950s and later years concerning the implications of quantum mechanics for philosophy and theology. In *Physics and Beyond*, Heisenberg comments that after the terrible events of World War II had ended, it was possible for physicists to "once again meditate

25. Schrodinger, *Nature and the Greeks and Science and Humanism*, 125, 129, 129–30, 130.

26. Davies, *God & the New Physics*; Davies and Gribbin, *The Matter Myth*.

27. *The Economist*, "Going Round in Circles," 101.

peacefully about the great questions Plato had once asked, questions that had perhaps found their answers in the contemporary physics of elementary particles."[28] Much of the book consists of Heisenberg relating long philosophical conversations between himself and other people, mainly other physicists. Since these conversations were put into written form long after they had actually occurred, they in effect represent Heisenberg presenting his own views in interaction with his own recreations of the views of the other physicists. Heisenberg had met the Danish physicist Niels Bohr very early in his career and the two maintained a long collaboration both as close personal friends and professional peers (if strained for a time during World War II). In one recreated conversation recalled from 1927, Heisenberg asks Bohr: "Mathematics introduces ever higher stages of abstraction that help us attain a coherent grasp of ever wider realms. To get back to our original question, is it correct to look upon the religious 'there is' as just another, though different, attempt to reach ever higher levels of abstraction?"[29]

As recreated by Heisenberg, Bohr replied as follows. I quote at length to illustrate the eloquence and the theological sophistication of Bohr's response (as admittedly in the words of Heisenberg, who was a better writer than Bohr):

> With respect to the epistemological side of the problem, your comparison may pass. But in other respects it is quite inadequate. In mathematics we can take our inner distance from the content of our statements. In the final analysis mathematics is a mental game that we can play or not play as we choose. Religion, on the other hand, deals with ourselves, with our life and death; its promises are meant to govern our actions and thus, at least indirectly, our very existence. We cannot just look at them impassibly from the outside. Moreover, our attitude to religious questions cannot be separated from our attitude to society. Even if religion arose as the spiritual structure of a particular human society, it is arguable whether it has remained the strongest social molding force throughout history, or whether society, once formed, develops new spiritual structures and adapts them to its particular level of knowledge. Nowadays the individual seems to be able to choose the spiritual framework of his thoughts and action quite freely, and this freedom reflects the fact that the boundaries between the various cultures and societies are beginning to become more fluid. But even when an individual tries to attain the greatest possible degree of independence, he

28. Heisenberg, *Physics and Beyond*, 244.
29. Ibid., 89–90.

will still be swayed by the existing spiritual structures—consciously or unconsciously. For he, too, must be able to speak of life and death and the human condition to other members of the society in which he has chosen to live; he must educate his children according to the norms of that society, fit into its life. Epistemological sophistries cannot possibly help him attain these ends. Here, too, the relationship between critical thought about the spiritual context of a given religion and action based on the deliberate acceptance of that content is complementary. And such acceptance, if consciously arrived at, fills the individual with strength of purpose, helps him to overcome doubts and, if he has to suffer, provides him the kind of solace that only a sense of being sheltered under an all-embracing roof can grant. In that sense, religion helps to make social life more harmonious; its most important task is to remind us, in the language of pictures and parables, of the wider framework in which our life is set.[30]

As Heisenberg thinks, the discoveries of twentieth-century physics require the abandonment of core ideas of the relationship of man and nature—a central subject for most religions, going as far back as the ancient Greeks. He explains that "the indivisible elementary particle of modern physics possesses the quality of taking up space in no higher measure than other properties, say colour and strength of material. In its essence, it is not a material particle in space and time but, in a way, only a symbol on whose introduction the laws of nature assume an especially simple form." Similar to Eddington's views, the perceptions of both color and space exist only as elements of human consciousness. Physics is a matter ultimately of discovering relationships among different parts of our consciousness, including the correlations between our perceptions of mathematical models and our perceptions of "physical reality," one reason why the world of twentieth-century physics is less bound by any "rational" standards of ordinary common sense. As a result, according to Heisenberg, we now find that "modern atomic theory is . . . essentially different from that of antiquity in that it no longer allows any reinterpretation or elaboration to make it fit into a naïve materialistic concept of the universe. For atoms are no longer material bodies in the proper sense of the word."[31]

Heisenberg compares this situation with the use in mathematics of "imaginary numbers" (defined as the square root of a negative number, which cannot exist in anything other than an "imaginary" sense because the square of any "real" number—either a negative or a positive number—will

30. Ibid., 90–91.
31. Heisenberg, *Philosophical Problems of Quantum Physics*, 55, 55–56.

always be positive). By commonsense standards, therefore, an imaginary number thus does not exist; it is simply a new abstract symbol introduced into mathematical calculations by the mathematician and which can be manipulated according to specific logical rules accepted by other mathematicians. It turns out, however, that mathematical calculations based on the use of imaginary numbers yield some of the most practically useful equations of twentieth-century physics, equations that have shown their ability to explain and predict "real-world" events many times over, however "imaginary" their ultimate character. Once again, the presence of a god seems close by.

As Heisenberg thus explains, "in a similar way the experiences of present-day physics show us that atoms do not exist as simple material objects. However, only the introduction of the concept 'atom,'" like the concept of an imaginary number that exists only in the abstract world of mathematics, "makes possible a simple formulation of the laws governing all physical and chemical processes." Since the "imaginary" laws of the subatomic world are formulated mathematically, and yet work with extraordinary effectiveness to understand and control "material reality," all this works to affirm the "fundamental principle which our science has taken over from antiquity," first with the Pythagoreans, then with Plato, and finally in the writings of the Neoplatonists, that the workings of the natural world (as we perceive it) are guided by "a purposeful and directive force inherent in mathematical formulations" themselves.[32] For the Platonists of the ancient world, that controlling mathematical force was expressed in the very idea of a god. As the distinguished twentieth-century theologian Paul Tillich explains, "Plato was the predecessor of modern mathematical science" and physics.[33]

Heisenberg does not develop this analogy but his epistemological explanation of the use of symbols for "imaginary numbers" in mathematics and "atoms" in physics might be applied to the specific use of the term *God* in Christian theology. The Christian "God" also lacks any concrete or material reality that can be seen or experienced in the "physical world" of our routine existence. God—for most of us anyway—is never directly encountered. The term *God* is instead perhaps a symbol for an idea in our minds that we employ in thinking about the world. Like the symbols for an "imaginary number" or an "atom," the question then becomes whether the idea of God, as represented symbolically in the English language by the one specific word *God*, genuinely aids us in achieving a clearer understanding of the events and meaning of the world. Does it bring us closer to a perception that we can understand the truth of the whole world—admittedly a judgment more

32. Ibid., 56.
33. Brown, *Ultimate Concern*, 35.

complicated than the question of whether imaginary numbers and atoms give us a greater knowledge of the truths of the natural world and an ability to manipulate it for human purposes? Nevertheless, one might say that mathematics, natural science, and theology all have a similar ultimate foundation in human thought. No one can know what the real substance of God "is" any more or less accurately than a physicist can say what an atom "is," even as the concept of the atom proves to have such great practical value in helping to reveal the actual "truth of the world"—as is perhaps also the case for the Christian concept of God. It is striking that God and atoms are equally mysterious in material terms and yet might turn out to be equally real.

God as Mind

Some people may be surprised to hear that many leading Jewish and Christian theologians reached conclusions about the priority of mind over matter long before twentieth-century physicists. For these theologians the full true character of God must necessarily remain an ultimate mystery; human beings can only hope to approach some understanding by the use of indirect methods. Among the most common analogies historically used for thinking about God is that of a disembodied "mind," that God "thinks" and the world is thereby formed and changed. Just as thoughts in human consciousness—also having no material existence—can mysteriously control the physical actions of the human body, perhaps the mind of God works in some related mysterious way in his exercise of powers over the whole physical universe (if thus acting on a vast cosmic scale that altogether transcends limited human powers and understanding).

Observing twentieth-century developments in physics, the former Oxford theologian Keith Ward thus recently commented that there are further good reasons to believe that "materialism is a delusion caused by a misuse of modern science" in the nineteenth-century mode. Indeed, the more plausible understanding of the world is that "the ultimate character of the universe is mind, and that matter is the appearance or manifestation or creation of cosmic mind"—that is to say, as Ward believes, of a divine intelligence that fills the universe and in which we as "individual persons" participate, if necessarily in limited ways.[34] Admittedly, as many ordinary people think of God today, he is an all-powerful but nevertheless humanlike father figure in the sky with a physical existence. But this is definitely not the way that

---

34. Ward, *Why There Almost Certainly Is a God*, 20. See also Ward, *The Evidence for God*, 30–38, 72–75.

leading Jewish and Christian theologians, dating back to the medieval period and before, have typically conceived of God.[35]

Meir Soloveichik, associate rabbi at Congregation Kehilath Jeshurun in New York, recently noted that "Jews reject the notion that God might take bodily form." Instead, they "seek to commune with what they believe to be his infinite mind"—something that cannot happen in a world of material forces but only in a world of mind itself. It is through the intense study of "the infinitude of the Torah [that] we are given a glorious glimpse of the infinitude of the Almighty" and of his supreme—non-corporeal—intelligence.[36] From the Protestant side, Ward writes that for serious theological inquiry "it is vitally important that we do not think of God as some sort of human-like being with lots of fairly arbitrary characteristics. That idea has never been supported by a leading theologian of any major monotheistic tradition."[37] The philosopher Thomas Nagel recently defined God as "a divine or universal mind [that] supplies an answer to the question of how a human individual can live in harmony with the universe." The idea of God as a physical being "is not what anybody" who has thought deeply about the matter "means by God," who must instead be understood as a divine consciousness outside the material realm who, despite his nonmaterial essence, is capable "nevertheless of creating and forming the entire physical world."[38]

One of the leading Christian apologists of the twentieth century, C. S. Lewis, similarly explains that for him God "is more like a mind than it is like anything else we know." We have no idea how he does it but we can also conceive God, more specifically, as "a mind bringing life into existence and leading it to perfection."[39] Lewis writes elsewhere of a "cosmic mind" that exists "outside nature"; it has no material reality but is the original source to which we attribute "the power of producing the basic elements, inventing not only colours but colour itself, the senses themselves, space time and matter themselves, and also of imposing what He has invented on created minds" as possessed by human beings.[40] Overseeing all this is the one overarching cosmic mind, the mind of God. The meaning of the

---

35. In a recent book intended for the religious instruction of children, the distinguished contemporary Christian theologian William Lane Craig asks "What is God like?" and replies that "God is Spirit." As Craig explains, "You can't touch God because God doesn't have a body. Sometimes people think of God like an old man with a long, white beard. But that's not true. He is only spirit." Craig, *What is God Like?*, 13.

36. Soloveichick, "Torah and Incarnation," 48, 46.

37. Ward, *Why There Almost Certainly Is a God*, 78.

38. Nagel, *Secular Philosophy and the Religious Temperament*, 5.

39. Lewis, *Mere Christianity*, 34, 35.

40. Lewis, *Miracles*, 30, 31, 33.

biblical statement that human beings are made in the image of God can thus be understood as saying that human beings also have a nonmaterial consciousness of our own existence and a capacity for deep abstract learning within this consciousness, however severely limited relative to the immensity of God's equally nonmaterial "consciousness."

For Lewis, if a material world does in fact exist, it is thus because God has decided that the workings of his mind should have an actual physical representation. Human beings have a unique ability to learn about the mind of God through their scientific study of the material universe, as it was perhaps originally put in place by God at the Creation to aid human beings whose inferior minds required such crutches to attain to a deeper understanding. Or, as Ward writes, "God is the mind in which all possible universes and states of being exist" and one (or possibly more if there are multiple universes) was chosen by God for a special material existence at the moment of the "creation."[41] To experience the natural world is to see with our own eyes the concrete artwork of God, a direct reflection of his mind at work. It is not only C. S. Lewis and Ward but many other Jewish and Christian theologians—and physical scientists as well—who have been saying such things for centuries. John Calvin once wrote in his great systematic statement of his theology, *Institutes of the Christian Religion*, that "the knowledge of God [is] sown in their minds out of the wonderful workmanship of nature." For those able to turn away from the "prodigious trifles" and "superfluous wealth" that occupy the minds of so many, it will be possible to be "instructed by this bare and simple testimony which the [plant and animal] creatures render splendidly to the glory of God."[42]

Our Fine-Tuned Universe

A number of writers have recently made a scientific case for the existence of a god based on the extraordinarily small likelihood—infinitesimally small really—that our universe could have been created to sustain life by random chance. The laws of physics are not only mathematical but often include numerical constants in their formulation that further determine the mathematical content of the laws (for example, the "gravitational constant" in the law of gravity as formulated by Newton determines the level of the force mutually attracting any two mass objects—also dependent on the exact masses of the two objects and the square of the distance between them). These numerical constants thus play a large role in controlling the workings

41. Ward, *Why There Almost Certainly Is a God*, 78.
42. As rendered in Kerr, ed., *Calvin's Institutes: A New Compend*, 26–27, 99, 27.

of the physical universe. If the numerical constants differed from the constants actually seen in the mathematical laws of our universe, we would have a different universe with different laws of physics.

As physicists discovered in the twentieth century, frequently miniscule departures from the actual constants of nature as found in our universe would mean a universe in which the existence of life (at least as we can conceive it) would be impossible. As the English physicist-turned-theologian John Polkinghorne thus writes, "the fundamental laws of nature operating in our world take a very precise, 'finely tuned,' form. Small variations in the strengths of the basic forces of nature," as expressed by mathematical laws based on specific numerical constants, "would have rendered the development of carbon-based life impossible."[43] Indeed, "small" variations greatly understates the matter. In one case, as related by Rodney Holder, "the mass of the proton must be almost exactly 1.837 times the mass of the electron, as it is, for the possibility of interesting chemicals to be made and to be stable, certainly for complicated molecules like DNA, which are the building blocks of life." In another case, a constant of nature is even far more tightly constrained in order to create the universe as we know it; the constant must be "less than 1.000000000000001 and larger than 0.999999999999999."[44] In other words, if the numerical constant of nature in this case were determined randomly, there would be a vanishingly small chance of obtaining the necessary constant for our universe and the existence of life.

We could then rationally decide whether a god exists in the following way. We would have to choose among two probabilities, the probability that the constants of nature of our physical universe were randomly determined, and thus simply happened to sustain life by chance, versus the probability that a god exists who established the necessary constants of nature as an exercise of his divine omnipotence. Since the probability of the random alternative is essentially zero, any significant positive probability assigned to the alternative of the existence of a god would yield a rational conclusion that a god very probably exists. Indeed, given that there are a number of other reasons based on other rational arguments why it is probable that a god exists—including those discussed in this book—the existence of a god would become a virtual probabilistic certainty. As the British physicist Fred Hoyle—a self-professed atheist for most of his life—was eventually forced to confess, it was difficult not to conclude in light of the extraordinary fine-tuning of nature that "a superintellect has monkeyed with physics, as well

---

43. Polkinghorne, "Foreword" to Holder, *Big Bang, Big God*, 8.
44. Holder, *Big Bang, Big God*, 90, 88.

as chemistry and biology, and that there are no blind forces worth speaking about in nature."[45]

New atheists such as Richard Dawkins are of course aware of the fine-tuning rational argument for a god and have struggled to deal with it. Their response might be characterized as follows. It is also true that there was an infinitesimally small probability that the author of this book, Bob Nelson, would be born with the exact body that I have (no two people on earth are biologically alike, other than identical twins) and that I would write this book exactly as it has come out to be. So it is a miracle that I am who I am, physically and as an author. Yet, I concede that it would not be logical to conclude that the miracle of "me" is in itself a strong argument for the probable existence of a god. Indeed, every specific event in the world had essentially a zero *a priori* probability of occurring exactly as it would turn out to occur in history as a matter of the actual outcome. Surely, this cannot in itself demonstrate that a god exists.

But this argument seemingly suffers from the following weakness. In the case of my body, I can know that "I" am the product of many identifiable events. First of all, it was essential that my parents married. Over a much longer time frame, it was essential that human beings evolved on earth. And over a yet much longer time frame, it was essential that the earth was created 4.6 billion years ago. So "I" am the product of an intelligible chain of events, however negligible the probability of exactly "me" arriving on earth at this moment in time. If we assume that there is only one finely tuned universe, however, it is impossible to make this argument. The fine-tuning has to precede the workings of the universe which is itself then fundamentally shaped in part by this fine-tuning—so something about the physical universe that would already require the fine-tuning cannot itself be said to have caused the fine-tuning that we observe. The physical universe was seemingly created out of nothing, there is no series of intelligible previous events to explain it, and it is thus an altogether unexplained miracle—or explainable only in supernatural terms—that the specific constants of nature of our universe are fine-tuned with such extraordinary exactness as to support life, and now finally the existence of human beings on earth such as me.

As an attempt to escape this problem, new atheists have been forced to turn to the new idea in physics of recent decades that we may not live in the only existing universe but that there are multiple universes. These universes, moreover, may not have been created but may have simply existed for eternity. Then, we could say that by pure random chance—in the same way that my specific body features are a product of pure random chance—we just

45. Hoyle, quoted in ibid., 91.

happen to live in a universe where the constants of nature—also products of pure random chance—turned out in at least this one case to be capable of supporting life. So our fine-tuned universe is no more miraculous than the miracle of a one "fine-tuned" Bob Nelson existing on earth. Both had a less than negligible probability and yet, as it might be argued, both just happened by an extraordinary random chance to be the actual outcome for our own universe and existence.

This argument suffers itself from two large weaknesses, however. First, given the incredibly narrow range of possibilities for a set of constants of nature capable of sustaining life, there would have to be a virtual infinity of alternative universes in order to have a random possibility that even a single such universe would have actually been suitably fine-tuned for life. The more important difficulty, however, is that the existence of even one other universe—to say nothing of an infinity of them—has not been demonstrated by any empirical confirmation based on the scientific method. Some people suggest that any such empirical confirmation might by definition be impossible—if it can be empirically confirmed, then *a priori* it must be part of our own existing universe. So to believe in the multi-universe hypothesis is itself seemingly an act of faith, at present no more scientifically provable (or disprovable) than a belief in the existence of a god.

If that is the case, we are thus confronted with two alternative forms of religious faith, belief in a cosmic design of a vast enormity of different universes and belief in a god (not that they are mutually incompatible). Although it is not a scientific act, we can also estimate subjective probabilities of one or the other (or both, in which case there is a god) of these forms of faith being true. If we consider them alternatives, we could logically identify the alternative for which our subjective probability is the highest. To say that the estimate is subjective, moreover, is not to say that it is irrational. As this book examines, there are important rational arguments for the existence of a god having little to do with the fine-tuned character of the universe. Indeed, these rational arguments are stronger than any rational arguments that can be offered at present for the multi-universe hypothesis—and quite possibly this will be true for the indefinite future.

There is also an issue of motive. It seems likely that the hypothesis of multiple universes has been advanced in part to fend off the strong argument for the existence of a god in light of the recently discovered fine-tuning of our universe. The Cambridge University mathematician John Barrow thus writes that "one motivation for considering the presence of other universes has been to understand why our visible Universe displays so many life-supporting 'coincidences' between the values of its numerical constants, and so many advantageous contingencies that have fallen out apparently." Indeed, given the essential impossibility of a single existing universe having the level of fine-tuning as ours, as Barrow considers, "the multiverse hypothesis is favoured by many cosmologists as a way to avoid the conclusion that the Universe was specially designed for life by a Grand Designer"—that is, a god. For other cosmologists, they see the multiverse possibility "as a way of avoiding having to say anything about the problem of fine tuning at all," which raises embarrassing issues for them.[46]

In other words, the thinking of such people begins with a certainty that there is no god, then they have to face the unanswerable refutation posed by fine-tuning if there is only our one universe, and, following that, they draw the necessary conclusion that there must be multiple universes—indeed, a virtual infinity of universes if our finely tuned universe has occurred randomly. For those who think this way, they are plainly making a theological argument, one that is then misleadingly converted to an ostensibly "scientific" argument. Theologically, they simply assume atheism in order to conclude that no god is necessary in the multiverse that they then hypothesize on faith to exist, succeeding in little more than creating a tautology.

The focus of this book will be on five other rational ways of thinking about the question of a god. None of them, however, begins with the scientific fact of a finely tuned universe. The decision not to examine the fine-tuned argument more fully reflects the fact that the religious implications of a fine-tuned universe has been well explored elsewhere.[47] It can validly be considered, however, a sixth rational way of thinking about the question of a god, one that adds further weight to the five rational arguments developed more fully below for the probable existence of a god.

The Gospel According to Kurzweil

Descartes famously declared that "I think, therefore I am." That is to say, we can be entirely confident of our own existence by virtue of the fact that we directly experience this existence in our own consciousness—unlike everything else in the world that must necessarily be the indirect product of our interpretations of external sensory signals somehow miraculously converted to nonmaterial form as found in human consciousness. But recent developments in computers and artificial intelligence are bringing even Descartes's seemingly certain dictum into question. That is to say, my mind may not be my mind at all in the way that Descartes and most other people

---

46. Barrow, *The Infinite Book*, 204.

47. Barrow, *The Constants of Nature*; Davies, *The Goldilocks Enigma*; McGrath, *A Fine-Tuned Universe*.

historically have thought about the matter. Rather, as fictionally dramatized in 1999 in the movie *The Matrix*, what I perceive to be my own mind may simply be one element of a giant computer simulation, controlled by other minds of which I am completely unaware. Descartes to the contrary, the fact that I seem to "myself" to think may not actually mean that "I" do really think (at least as a freely thinking agent) and thus that I do actually exist as a real person.

Wondering about such possibilities is not limited to the world of fiction. The Estonian Jan Tallinn is a founder of Skype, the Internet video chat service. Having sold his interest in Skype, Tallinn now devotes his time to broader interests, including pondering the possibility of whether "as our computers and technology get better at making virtual worlds, it's reasonable to expect them to be able to create virtual worlds that are indistinguishable from the real one." Indeed, there might be only one real world, what Tallinn designates as a "single-history universe" but within this one "real" universe there might be multiple simulated universes. Moreover, there is no way for a person to know which is the case for them individually; as Tallinn thinks, "once you're in a simulation you don't even know—it could be that it's not even you." Moreover, if there are many simulated universes and only one real universe, "the chances of being in the simulation are higher than the real thing." Addressing the question of the practical consequences, if someone should come to believe he or she is living in a simulated universe, Tallinn responds that it then "depends on what kind of evidence we have that we are in a simulation . . . and then the critical question is why the simulation is being run."[48]

Adopting the language of Christian theology, Tallinn's one "real" universe might alternatively be described as the one special "simulated universe" that is specifically being run by a god—and thus is real. In light of the multiverse hypothesis, moreover, some cosmologists now assert a growing scientific possibility that god might have also allowed some other simulated universes as well to come into existence—with potentially different designers and operators of these other simulations (I am admittedly assuming here that any god that exists will be monotheistic, that there will not be multiple gods creating their own distinct multiple—conceivably even somehow competitive—universes). It would seem that, whatever you may believe, it will be a matter of your individual faith—no rational argument or empirical observation can fully resolve this matter of the actual character of the universe you and I live in, whether it is simulated or not.

48. Tallinn interview, conducted by Alexandra Wolfe, "Weekend Confidential," C11.

The implications for theology of the new "miraculous" computer capacities now coming into existence may thus turn out to be as profound as the radically new understandings of reality produced by twentieth-century physics. If human beings were themselves someday, somehow, to be capable of creating a computer simulation of a full universe through their own efforts, it would give a whole new meaning to the idea of humans "playing God" in the world. Or perhaps we will come to speak of such future computer programmers as supernatural "angels" that serve a higher purpose as authorized by a yet higher "god."

It is of course impossible to predict just what the actual future of the "IT revolution" will be—whether a full computer-simulated universe, as created by human beings themselves, might ever be an actual possibility even in concept. But some people are trying hard. Among the leaders in this area is the futurologist Ray Kurzweil—the holder of seventeen honorary doctorates and the recipient of the US National Medal of Technology and the prestigious Lemelson-MIT Prize for innovation. Following a 2006 Stanford University conference on Kurzweil's prediction of a coming "singularity," Google joined with Kurzweil in 2009 to create the Singularity University and then hired Kurzweil in 2012 as its "director of engineering."

Kurzweil's predictions for the future are partly derived from his assessments of the likely coming role of "artificial intelligence"—the power of computers to simulate the mental capacities and thought processes of the human mind, and even potentially improve on them. By 1997 an IBM computer ("Big Blue") could "think" (admittedly using brute force computational methods) well enough to defeat Gary Kasparov, then the top chess player in the world. In 2011, still more impressively, an IBM computer defeated two of the leading contestants from past years on the popular American television quiz show, *Jeopardy*. Google is almost godlike in its capacity to access a vast memory stream of information spread across the earth, all in the flash of a second—yet another modern-seeming "miracle."

Kurzweil is convinced, moreover, that these trends will accelerate exponentially in the years to come. Within the twenty-first century, conceivably even within a few decades, computers should be able to pass easily the "Turing test." It will be impossible to distinguish whether you are talking to an advanced computer intelligence or to a real live person. The biological and the nonbiological worlds will be converging. At the far limit—as labeled by Kurzweil "the Singularity"—we will find that "future machines will be human, even if they are not biological." This will extend even to "the human ability to understand and respond appropriately to emotion . . . [which] is one of the forms of human intelligence that will be understood and mastered by future machine intelligence."[49]

Kurzweil's prophecies are controversial, sometimes criticized by other leading futurologists. Some observers suggest they are closer to a religious faith—a belief in a future God of a vast computer intelligence—than to actual computer science. But Kurzweil is perhaps the leading inventor of new computer capabilities of his time; he has made controversial predictions about advances in computer capabilities in the past that have subsequently been fulfilled, and his expert credentials otherwise are sterling. In the not-too-distant future, as he now predicts, it may even be possible to "upload" into a computer the contents of an individual person's mind, including their past thoughts that have been retained in their memory bank of experiences. It is already becoming possible to clone physically the body of an individual person and, surprisingly soon, Kurzweil suggests, it will be possible to "clone" a person's mind nonbiologically. Humans will literally have a new kind of capacity to play god. It will not be long, as Kurzweil says, before "most of the intelligence of our civilization will be nonbiological" in character. As computer capacities grow exponentially, "ultimately, the entire universe will become saturated with our intelligence. This is the destiny of the universe."[50] Could this be the new meaning of the arrival of "heaven on earth"?

As Kurzweil himself recognizes, if such events should actually come to pass (or even anything close), the issues raised will be of a fundamental character extending to subjects more traditionally associated with religion. What does it mean to be human if a computer can closely simulate a human mind—and when god is commonly understood by leading theologians as belonging to the domain of mind rather than of material substance? Should we think of a god in terms of an eternal computer capacity that has always existed but that modern humans now, astonishingly enough, are developing on their own? Could this be in our time finally the fulfillment of the biblical prophesy of a second coming—Jesus come to earth in the form of the collective powers of the world's computer programmers? In terms of the workings of society, what is a "community" when I may not be able to tell when I am interacting with another human mind—such as a presumed reader of this book—as opposed to a super-intelligent, programmed machine? Can a human being fall in love with a machine intelligence and corresponding robot? Will the realization of Kurzweil's prophecy leave me alone in the universe, aware of my own thoughts, but never knowing for sure when and whether I am encountering other "real" human intelligences in the world? Indeed,

49. Kurzweil, *The Singularity is Near*, 25, 30, 28.
50. Ibid., 3, 29.

how will I know that I am a real living being myself? Such deeply religious questions are today popping up in surprising places, providing further important new avenues for thinking about the existence of a god.

Indeed, Kurzweil's speculations open up the possibility that we may have entered into a brand new stage in the evolutionary history of the world, going far beyond matters explored by Darwin and his evolutionary biologist successors. For about four billion years, as one might now say, evolution on earth occurred biologically in what we have conventionally described as the material world (see later chapters for the complications of explaining exactly what "material" means). Now, however, over about the past 5,000 years, since the ability to record and transmit human intelligence in physical forms emerged (first the writing of texts, then printing of books, now computers), the most important evolutionary developments may no longer be physical but the evolution of intelligence in the world. Then, critically, as Kurzweil is suggesting, the most powerful future carriers of "world intelligence" may no longer be biological, as now found at the highest levels in the consciousness of human beings that somehow is associated with their physical brains, but in the physical systems of computers much advanced from what we now have developed in human thinking. The new evolutionary "reality" will consist then not of the most rational and creative thoughts of real-world human beings but of the contents of radically more powerful and "intelligent" computers.

This all suggests a radically new theological possibility. Perhaps god did not put human beings on earth to be the final product of Darwinist biological evolution. Perhaps god saw—or created—human beings as an intermediate state in the evolution of a higher stage of intelligence that will in time pervade the universe as its ultimate destiny. As Kurzweil suggests, it will not be an intelligence that is based in biology but in a physical intelligence itself—as evolution moves forward, in computer "minds" specifically. Leading theologians such as Keith Ward conceive of god as a cosmic mind, so perhaps the arrival of intelligent creatures such as human beings has simply been a transitional phase. The pervasive world intelligence of the future may have taken its first halting steps in the minds of human beings. In the future, intelligence and biology, as Kurzweil proposes, may become distinct. The biological phase will at that point be dispensable in shaping the future cosmic intelligence of "the earth."

Put in more conventional religious terms, the "salvation" of the world would then consist of the following: After all of four billion years, a new advanced form of intelligence has arisen in the past one or two million years in the form of human beings now present on earth, enabling them in the past ten thousand years to become the dominant biological species of the

earth. During the past 5,000 years, human beings then miraculously created the physical instruments of writing, printing, and computers that have
immensely expanded the biological capacities of human intelligence. In the
near future, according to Kurzweil and some others, the physical products
of human minds will in turn greatly exceed the biologically based intelligence of human beings. It will be a brand new stage in the evolution of the
earth towards a new world of a cosmic intelligence that exists outside and
has transcended human beings themselves. If we think of this cosmic intelligence as a god, god will have come to earth through the intermediary step of
human biologically based intelligence. At that point the biological part may
no longer be necessary. A new heaven on earth, surprisingly similar to the
heaven of Christian theology, filled with intelligent nonphysical beings, will
have achieved its appointed destiny. This new heaven on earth will mean the
full reign of a supremely rational and universal intelligence.

The biological evolutionary "era of human intelligence" thus could be
drawing to a close, to be replaced by less fragile forms of intelligence. This
is all of course religious speculation that Kurzweil and others of his ilk open
up as a possibility, outside any definite method of resolution and verification
in our time. Yet, could this be the true meaning of "the gospel of Kurzweil"?

Baseball as Religion

The potential avenues to learning more about god can also be found in more
familiar contexts. As Keith Ward observes, for some people one might say
that "art is their religion," that "in art we can create and discern objective
and intrinsic values" that transcend the events of everyday life. Indeed,
"such values" in art "are intrinsic in that they are worthwhile just for their
own sake. They are not values because we happen to like them" from a utili-
tarian perspective of only giving human aesthetic pleasure. It is in "ordinary
human experience, and in the enhanced experience that art provides, [that]
you know something that is more than either value-free sense-perceptions
or merely physical elements." In Paris the Notre Dame Cathedral is more
than the sum of its stone, glass, wood and other material elements. Thus,
great paintings, music, and other art for many people creates the "sense of
something transcendent, 'beyond.' . . . It is a sense for the spiritual dimension" of human existence.[51]

Ward concedes that there are large variations in the responses of specific people to seeing and hearing a work of art. But forms of "art" capable
of inspiring deeper thoughts and feelings can be found in other settings that

51. Ward, *The Evidence for God*, 17.

are not conventionally seen in that light. Indeed, for many people important religious elements may be found in human involvement in sports as both a spectator and a participant, as explored in 2013 by John Sexton in *Baseball as a Road to God: Seeing Beyond the Game*. Sexton has been the president of New York University since 2001 and before that was dean of the NYU law school for fourteen years. His book is based on a successful course he has taught at NYU for many years. Sexton is not simply speaking about the obvious ability of baseball and other sports to arouse powerful emotions, great loyalty, and other "religiously" intense passions. He is saying that baseball literally offers religious messages for him and for many others of its most ardent fans; it is perhaps one more among the various ways of cumulatively adding to the knowledge of god. As he thus writes, his book is about the question of "whether baseball, like Catholicism or Islam or peyote in the desert, can be a road to God—not *the* road to God for all, but *a* road to God for some"—among the multiple roads that most people will probably want to explore.[52] Can baseball, in other words, be yet another among the many ways of thinking about the existence of a god—one of multiple paths to be followed in putting into practice the method of cumulative probabilities of Cardinal Newman?

Probably to the surprise and puzzlement of many people today, for Sexton the answer is yes. For those who do not follow baseball, it may help to think of baseball for its most devoted fans as spiritual in much the way that bird watching can be spiritual for those people more oriented to learning about God through their intense experiences of the natural world. As Sexton explains, "baseball evokes in the life of *its* faithful features we associate with the spiritual life: faith and doubt, conversion, blessings and curses, miracles, and so on. For some, baseball really is a road to God," powerfully illustrating the wide scope of the subject matter of religion and of the pursuit of greater theological understanding.[53] Remarkably enough, the large amount of coverage given to sports in the pages of American newspapers and magazines may be for some people their most influential exposure to religious thought. A contender might be the business coverage of newspapers, as I suggested in 2001 in *Economics as Religion*, my own contribution to this genre of theological writings about the wider religious meanings of otherwise seemingly mundane events in the world.[54]

52. Sexton, *Baseball as a Road to God*, 11.

53. Ibid., 7.

54. Nelson, *Economics as Religion*. See also Nelson, *Reaching for Heaven on Earth*; Nelson, *The New Holy Wars*.

The Foreword for *Baseball as a Road to God* is written by historian (and former devoted Brooklyn Dodger and now devoted Boston Red Sox fan) Doris Kearns Goodwin. As she reports, when the Dodgers defeated the hated New York Yankees in the 1955 World Series—their first World Series victory after coming painfully close several times before—as a young girl at the close of the deciding game, she "threw my arms around my mother, tears streaming down our cheeks." When the Dodgers moved to Los Angeles in 1958, this "betrayal of staggering dimensions" caused her to swear off any interest in baseball for eight years. Goodwin recovered her lost faith, however, in coming to root in an "irrational" way for the Boston Red Sox at their own "sacred place," Fenway Park, the replacement for the Ebbets Field cathedral of old. When the Red Sox defeated the (still-hated) Yankees in the 2004 American League championship, after losing the first three games, and then went on to win the World Series for the first time since 1918, the unfolding series of events was so improbable that Goodwin could only deem them literally "miraculous"—a lesson about life conceivable taught by a god.[55]

As it would be for many baseball fans, Sexton's book was a revelation for Goodwin. She writes that "I have loved baseball all my life, but never before did I fully comprehend the sacred dimensions of that love." With Sexton's help, her eyes had now been opened to the many close parallels— more easily seen in retrospect—between baseball and religion: the common features of "prayers, altars, sacred space, faith, doubt, conversion, miracles, blessings, curses, saints, and sinners."[56] With respect to such matters, the experience of being a devout baseball fan taught lessons that applied more broadly throughout all aspects of life. Many people, however, learn better from the particular, as compared with intellectual contemplation of theological abstractions. Baseball may be another of the crutches by which a god aids weaker human minds.

Sexton thus shows how valuable theological insights might be gained outside the boundaries of what is conventionally considered "theology." Those who wish to learn more about god need to open their eyes to the whole world around them, looking for the surprising places where new religious insights might be discovered. This book will explore five such "theological" areas falling outside traditional theological discussions.

---

55. Goodwin, "Foreword" to Sexton, *Baseball as a Road to God*, xii, xiii.

56. Ibid., xi.

The God Hypothesis

Taking such a wide-ranging theological approach, the god hypothesis to be investigated in this book is the following:

1. A god—conceived not as a material entity, a superpowerful human being with a body, but as a cosmic intelligence that has no beginning and no end—exists.

2. This god created the external world of our perceptions as a physical manifestation of his divine intelligence. Hence, there is in fact a real world external to the human mind, including other minds. God has ensured that individual human sensory perceptions in the mind are accurate representations of this actually existing external world. Without a belief in a god, no such confidence would be possible.

3. Human beings uniquely participate in the divine intelligence and consciousness—this is the sense in which they are made "in the image of God." Human beings thus share in their own minds at least some (highly imperfect) elements of the divine intelligence. The development of this intellectual capacity is a cumulative process over human history, as seen, for example, in the progress of the natural sciences in revealing god's mathematical laws that we now have very good reason to believe he decided at the creation should govern the full workings of the physical universe. If less consequential for daily existence, a similar progress can be found in music, the arts, and other areas of increasing human access to the mind of a god. When human beings share participation in the divine intelligence, they experience feelings of beauty, pleasure, awe, inspiration, wonder, and a conviction of the greater meaning and purpose of their own existence.

While this way of thinking about a god would be familiar to many leading Christian theologians of the past, it admittedly falls well short of the personal God of most current Christian faithful. A rational conclusion reached with respect to "the god hypothesis" as defined here, therefore, is not synonymous with a verdict on the entire message of Christianity. Acceptance of the Christian message definitely implies acceptance of the god hypothesis, but the converse is not true. One might accept the god hypothesis, for example, while rejecting—entirely or in part—"the Christ hypothesis," as in fact many people historically have done (including Isaac Newton who drew unitarian conclusions—heretical in his own times—from his lifelong studies of religion). Richard Dawkins, like many people, conflates the two. He seeks in part, for example, to demonstrate the falsity of the god hypothesis by harshly attacking certain books of the Bible, especially those in the Old Testament. But the accuracy of specific biblical criticisms (or lack of such) does not in itself demonstrate the falsity (or truthfulness) of the god hypothesis as defined above. God might or might not actually exist but this is not a question that is necessarily resolved by attacks on the literal historical accuracy—or other specific messages—of the Jewish and Christian biblical accounts.

As applied in this book, similar to the methods of qualitative social science research described in the Introduction, use will thus be made of any empirical data or other sources of information that can lend rational insight into the god hypothesis. The quality of this information should be carefully assessed and described as rationally as possible. Qualitative social science research requires well-crafted methods of analysis. The steps in reasoning must be as transparent as possible. Also to the extent possible, key initial assumptions should be clearly spelled out. The final conclusions should not be implicit in the initial set of assumptions (care must be taken to avoid tautological conclusions). The levels of uncertainty in the final analysis should be identified to the fullest extent that this can be done.

Drawing on the social science methodology of qualitative research, on epistemological traditions in philosophy, and on theological writings of leading Christian apologists such as Newman and Lewis, as well as other sources, five main streams of potentially relevant information and evidence about the existence and character of a god—five especially illuminating ways of thinking rationally about the question of a god—are examined in this book. These five hardly exhaust the possible areas that might be studied as part of a broader assessment of "the god hypothesis." However, they seem, at least to me, to be among the most promising for shedding important light, if not yielding any absolute "proof"—which is in fact impossible in concept, short of god coming to earth in some indisputable fashion at the present time.

The combined result of my analysis of these five ways of rationally thinking about a god will, for reasons already explained, inevitably not be enough to demonstrate with certainty the existence of a god. For me personally, I can report, however, that the writing of this book has increased greatly my own estimate of the probabilities.

3

God the Mathematician

The Miracle of Mathematical Order in the Natural World

In 1913, the Danish physicist Niels Bohr formulated a new theory of the actions of electrons as they orbited the nucleus of the atom, a critical step towards the development of quantum mechanics in the 1920s, leading to his winning the Nobel prize in physics in 1922. He continued to be among the most influential figures among the physicists of the world for decades to come, and is today commonly ranked among the greatest physicists of history.[1] Like a number of other leading physicists of the twentieth century, Bohr also had a deep interest in the implications of the discoveries of twentieth-century physics for the overall understanding of the human situation in the world.[2] He recognized that physics in its radically new portrayal of the workings of nature was also raising deep philosophical and religious questions. In his 1938 essay, "Natural Philosophy and Human Cultures," an address delivered to the International Congress of Anthropological and Ethnological Sciences, he wrote that "it is impossible to distinguish sharply between natural philosophy" as developed by physics "and human culture. The physical sciences are, in fact, an integral part of our civilization, not only because our ever-increasing mastery of nature has so completely changed the material conditions of life, but also because the study of these sciences has contributed so much to clarify the background of our own existence" as human beings.[3]

1. Tindol, "Physics World poll names Richard Feynman one of 10 greatest physicists of all time."

2. For a historical review of the interaction of science and religion, see Barbour, *Religion and Science*.

3. Bohr, "Natural Philosophy and Human Cultures," 23–24.

It was thus of great significance that twentieth-century physics had required a "revision of the presuppositions underlying the unambiguous use of even our most elementary concepts such as space and time." Indeed, "in the study of atomic phenomena we have [now] repeatedly been taught that questions which were believed to have received long ago their final answers had most unexpected surprises in store for us." Of particular importance, it was no longer possible "to distinguish sharply between the behavior of [physical] objects and the means of [their] observation," as historically was the view of physicists (and most other people). Since ultimately the means of observation are inseparable from the workings of the human sensory organs and human consciousness, this newly linked what had previously been two distinct fields of investigation, the physics of the natural world and the psychology of human consciousness. Bohr would thus write that the scientific questions in the two areas resemble one another in that there is a "close analogy between the situation as regards the analysis of atomic phenomena . . . and characteristic features of the problem of observation in human psychology." It is impossible for us to describe, as Bohr comments, in an entirely objective manner our own "psychical experiences . . . such as 'thoughts' and 'feelings'" because we combine inseparably in our human consciousness the roles of observer and observed. In atomic physics, it was surprisingly similar in that there is a "complementary relationship . . . regarding the behavior of atoms obtained under different experimental arrangements" in which the observer becomes an integral part of what is actually observed.[4]

The role of the consciousness of the physicist as an observer thus becomes part of the reality of the subatomic natural world. This takes us far from the mechanistic understanding of an objective physical reality existing outside ourselves that had long dominated physics, and still informs the common sense thinking of most people. As Bohr would later put it in a 1957 essay (he died in 1962), "the inadequacy of the mechanical concept of nature for the description of man's situation [in the world] is particularly evident in the primitive distinction between soul and body" that had reemerged as a large issue in light of the discoveries of twentieth-century physics.[5] A new focus on the soul—historically meaning the domain of human consciousness outside any material reality—has resulted from our search for the true workings of nature. According to twentieth-century physics, it has turned out that physical nature, objective natural reality, physical causation, etc., are all parts of a set of illusions that flickered for much of modern existence, as Plato once described the human circumstance in the cave. Physicists, as one might say,

---

4. Ibid., 24, 25, 27.
5. Bohr, "Atoms and Human Knowledge," 91.

have now finally shone a true light, thereby necessitating a large revision in our understanding of the circumstances of our own human existence.

The leading physicists of the late 1920s and 1930s typically spent part of their times together discussing the radical metaphysical—indeed theological, even if few of them were devout religious believers themselves—implications of their remarkable recent discoveries. Bohr, for example, frequently sparred at these meetings with Einstein, who famously complained about quantum mechanics that "god does not play dice."[6] A number of these leading physicists in later years would themselves write books and essays exploring the radical philosophical and religious implications raised. If a minority, other leading physicists since then have also entered into such discussions. In this chapter, I will rely heavily on the writings of such leading physicists of the twentieth century (and their mathematician compatriots)—and also a few from the twenty-first century—to examine the "theological" consequences, including the effects of their discoveries on the question of a god, even if they did not normally address this subject explicitly in their own writings.

Mathematics as Supernatural

There is no real need for a working physicist today to consider the question of why the natural world seemingly always and everywhere exhibits a mathematical order. It is simply a matter of an (often implicit) faith of the physicist that has been amply rewarded in the past with an astonishing array of scientific discoveries by earlier physicists. It was not a main subject of the 1920s and 1930s discussions among physicists but Einstein in this respect—as in others—was an important exception. As he considered, "*a priori*" one would expect that the world would be "chaotic"; in the absence of some outside agency with the power to "impose an order," why would the world exhibit the lawfulness and "comprehensibility" that has been revealed by modern science? Einstein had no good answer but could only marvel at "the 'miracle' which becomes more evident as our knowledge develops" through scientific discovery of the order underlying the functioning of the universe.[7]

More recently, a few other leading physicists have on occasion wondered why the mathematical methods of physics "work" so well in understanding the natural world. As noted in the Introduction, although he is not of the stature of an Einstein, Bohr, Heisenberg, or Schrodinger, Princeton professor Eugene Wigner ranks among the important physicists of the twentieth century, winning the Nobel prize in 1963. Besides his many scientific

6. Lindley, *Uncertainty*.

7. Einstein, quoted in Holder, *Big Bang, Big God*, 100.

contributions, he was another one of those physicists who ventured to explore from time to time the deeper human implications and meaning of physics.

One of these contributions was a frequently noted 1960 article on "The Unreasonable Effectiveness of Mathematics in the Natural Sciences." Speaking more bluntly and candidly than most of his fellow physicists, Wigner acknowledged that the mathematical foundations of the natural world are a true "miracle" that lies outside any scientific understanding itself. Indeed, as he further explained, it seemed to him that there are actually "two miracles," first the very "existence of [mathematical] laws of nature" and a second miracle "of the human mind's capacity to divine them."[8] Wigner thus considered as implausible any suggestion that the electrical and chemical workings of the physical brains of human beings could have created the complex abstractions—themselves lacking any physical reality—of higher mathematics of the kind routinely used by physicists.

For him, it was also remarkable how "the mathematical formulation of the physicist's often crude experiences leads in an uncanny number of cases to an amazingly accurate description of a large class of phenomena" in the natural world. Full candor required acknowledging "that the enormous usefulness of mathematics in the natural sciences is something bordering on the mysterious and there is no rational explanation for it" in the methods of physics itself. Indeed, there was no way to avoid the fact that "mathematics plays an unreasonably important role in physics." Moreover, it was not a case of mathematicians drawing on the physical world as the inspiration for their development of mathematical ideas. Rather, as Wigner wrote, "whereas it is unquestionable true that the concepts of elementary mathematics and particularly elementary geometry were formulated to describe entities which are directly suggested by the actual world, the same does not seem to be true of the more advanced concepts [in mathematics], in particular the concepts that play such an important role in physics" at its most advanced levels today.

The typical mathematician, Wigner observes, is motivated by a desire to explore abstractions that "demonstrate his ingenuity and sense of formal beauty." Despite its miraculous character, the workings of mathematics and physics are products of rational thought. At present, "the great mathematician fully, almost ruthlessly, exploits the domain of permissible reasoning and skirts the impermissible. That his recklessness does not lead him into a morass of contradictions is . . . [yet another] miracle in itself." Admitting

8. Wigner, "The Unreasonable Effectiveness of Mathematics in the Natural Sciences."

almost to a modern heresy, Wigner then confesses his strong sense that "certainly, it is hard to believe that our reasoning power [in areas such as higher level physics and mathematics] was brought, by Darwin's process of natural selection, to the perfection which it seems to possess."[9]

Wigner, simply put, finds it impossible to believe in biological evolutionary accounts of the development of human consciousness with its amazing mathematical and other high level rational facilities. Indeed, a physical explanation such as evolutionary biology is inherently incapable of explaining an outcome such as the worlds of mathematics and the laws of physics—both existing as elements of human consciousness and thus outside measurable time and space. Wigner does not say this explicitly himself but he is coming close to the idea of a preexisting supernatural intelligence shared in surprisingly large degree by human beings—or, as it would more traditionally have been put in religious language, human beings are made "in the image of God" who is himself rational and they also participate at least to some degree with him in the exercise of shared rational faculties.

The God of Gravity

Isaac Newton would have agreed with this—and would have been more explicit about it than Wigner. It is not well known but Newton actually spent much more time studying theological subjects than the physical laws of the natural world. But Newton is known to history, of course, because he showed with the help of mathematics (he was himself one of the top mathematicians of his time) just how the effects of gravity controlled the workings of the solar system and were experienced elsewhere throughout the natural world. Yet, Newton found all this perplexing; much like Wigner, he did not claim to understand how gravity actually came to exist or to operate—how it was even conceivable that two objects sometimes separated by millions of miles of empty space could influence the motions of one another (often called the mysterious phenomenon of "action at a distance")—and with the mathematical exactness of these interactions further compounding the mystery. Clearly, there could be no explanation in traditional mechanical terms. Rather, for Newton gravity could be understood only in terms of the complete omnipotence and omniscience of God and the frequent unfathomability of his ways to ordinary human minds—a view that fit comfortably with Newton's essentially Calvinist and Puritan—his "voluntaristic"—outlook on an all-powerful divine being full of mystery (although Newton was not himself a Puritan, he was much influenced by their thinking). God

9. Ibid.

simply willed objects to be drawn towards one another and so it happened; there was no other "scientific" explanation.

The American historian of ideas Frank Manuel thus writes that, for Newton "to be constantly engaged in studying and probing into God's actions was true worship and the fulfillment of the commandments of a Master." Knowledge of God for Newton must be based on hard facts and other evidence informed by rational thought; not on speculative models and pure abstractions as in the later degenerate phases of scholastic theology. Thus, as Manuel writes, for Newton, like many Protestants before him, "only two paths are open to him in his search for knowledge of the will of God as Master: the study of His actions in the physical world, His creations, and the study of the verbal record of His commandments in Scripture, both of which [for Newton] have an objective historical existence." Much will always remain a mystery, however, because we do not now—and will never fully— "know the reason why God's will manifested itself in the physical world in one way rather than in another, why He issued one Commandment rather than another; all we can know is the fact that He did, and we can marvel at the consequences and study them" closely with the methods of physics and thus come to know God's thinking better—if still in very imperfect ways.[10] To do physics, in short, for Newton is to do theology (or "natural theology" as it was in fact called at the time).

As Newton himself wrote in 1692, "when I wrote my Treatise about our Systeme" in the *Principia Mathematica* explaining the workings of gravity and the solar system, "I had an eye upon such Principles as might work with considering men for the beleife of a Deity & nothing can rejoice me more than to find it useful for that purpose."[11] Indeed, Manuel writes that Newton believed that "in his generation he was the vehicle [for the revealing] of God's eternal truth" of the natural world, precisely governed—as could now be conclusively demonstrated for increasing parts of the natural world for the first time ever—by mathematical laws. Plato had already asserted such a divine role for mathematics more than 2,000 years before Newton but it was as a philosophical principle, not as a matter of rationally demonstrated scientific fact with the actual mathematical laws now fully revealed for exact human understanding and calculation, confirmed by the scientific method.

Newton also rejects the "metaphysical" efforts of people like Descartes and Leibniz in his own time to portray God as an ultimate expression of a fully objective rationality that pervades the world (a divine "logos"). For Newton, this falsely attributes human thoughts and features to God. It is a

---

10. Manuel, *The Religion of Isaac Newton*, 22, 22–23, 23.

11. Quoted in de Pater, "An Ocean of Truth," 463.

great mistake, Newton writes, to attribute "to God the affections and passions of men and making him a compound. For God is not as man, nor are his thoughts like ours." The true God, as Newton believes, is *"all* Similar, *all* Eye, *all* Ear; *all* Brain, *all* Arm, *all* Sensation, *all* understanding, *all* active Power: But this is not after a corporeal Manner, but after a Manner wholly unknown to us."[12] As Manuel observes, for Newton it is necessary for human beings to accept "our incapacity to have any idea of the substance of God."[13] God may choose to reveal some parts of his thinking—through the mathematical workings of the natural world, for example—but the ultimate essence of God will forever remain a mystery. We will never know, for example, why or how the divine intelligence, lacking any corporeal elements, came to be reflected in the physical world, a world obeying the mathematical laws of nature that seemingly existed first in the mind of God—and, as Newton saw himself, he had somehow now been individually chosen, astonishingly enough, to reveal in precise detail to his fellow human beings this important feature of God.

God as Mathematician

By some accounts, Gottfried Wilhelm Leibniz, the great German philosopher and mathematician of the late seventeenth and early eighteenth century, was "the smartest person who ever lived."[14] He and Newton had some fierce disagreements, including who deserved credit for being the original inventor of the calculus. Newton also did not share Leibniz's comforting belief that God had created a rational world as a reflection of his own rational perfection, shared in part with rational human beings themselves. As noted, the God of Newton instead was more distant and more mysterious, less accessible to human understanding—more Calvinistic. As one leading student of Leibniz's thought, Herbert Breger, writes, for Liebniz, however, "the principle of sufficient reason ensures us that for all decisions and acts of God there is a rational reason." Hence, "the true religion is the most rational religion." Moreover, since all thought has a "fundamentally mathematical structure," it follows that "God must be a perfect mathematician." In his concern for this world, God's "act of creation is done by 'divine mathematics,' and is nothing other than the solution of an extreme value problem." Indeed, this problem for Leibniz even takes on an economic aspect in that

---

12. Newton, as quoted in Manuel, *The Religion of Isaac Newton*, 73, 74.

13. Ibid., 74.

14. Smolin, *Time Reborn*, xxvii.

God's thinking follows "a principle of determination, which is the maximum of effect achieved with a minimum of expenditure."[15]

While Newton was a harsh critic of Leibniz (and vice versa), in some areas they could both readily agree that "knowledge of God is the foundation or origin of all knowledge and wisdom. Every newly found truth, every [physical] experiment or [mathematical] theorem, is a new mirror of the beauty of God." As a result, as Breger writes of Leibniz's thinking, "perfection of the [human] mind, which results from the progress of our [mathematical and other] knowledge, unites man with God. [For Leibniz] mathematics is particularly suitable for entering the realm of [divine] ideas. It pleases us by giving us a glimpse of God's ideas." The incomprehensible "miracle" of the mathematical character of the natural world as described more recently by Eugene Wigner was thus explained in those days in theological terms. For Leibniz, the human capacity for "doing mathematic[s] seems to be a way of listening to God's voice and might even be comparable to divine service." Leibniz confesses that he has an "immoderate" love for mathematics and that for him "important mathematical achievement is the surest sign of a sound mind," one that approximates more closely—admittedly within the ultimately very large limits of human mental capacities—to the mind of God.[16]

The great British physicist James Clerk Maxwell, discoverer in the 1860s of the laws of electromagnetism, shared Newton's and Leibniz's faith that scientific endeavors were revealing eternal truths of the creation. As a contemporary historian of science writes,

> [Maxwell] went further than any other between Newton and Einstein in the rigorous application of mathematical equations to natural phenomena and their behavior. . . . No human science, he felt could ever really match up in its theoretical connections to the real modes of connection existing in nature, for valid as they may be in mathematical and symbolic systems, they were true only up to a point and could only be accepted by men of science, as well as by men of faith, in so far as they were allowed to point human scientific inquiry to that hidden region where thought weds fact, and where the mental operation of the mathematician and the physical action of nature are seen in their true relation. That is to say, as Clerk Maxwell himself understood it, physical science cannot be rightly pursued without taking into account an all-important metaphysical reference to the ultimate ground of nature's origin in the Creator. Thus, while

15. Breger, "God and Mathematics in Leibniz's Thought," 487, 488, 489, 490.
16. Ibid., 493–94, 494, 489, 494.

Clerk Maxwell never intruded his theological and evangelical convictions into his physical and theoretical science, he clearly allowed his Christian belief in God the Creator and Sustainer of the universe to exercise some regulatory control in his judgment as to the appropriateness and tenability of his scientific theories.[17]

Albert Einstein would later write similarly that "Since . . . sense perception only gives information of this external world or of 'physical reality' indirectly, we can only grasp the latter by speculative means."[18] Maxwell's theory of electromagneticism shared with Newton's theory of gravity the fact that it could not be given any plausible physical interpretation beyond the mathematics itself. Electrical and magnetic fields did not have any physical existence or mechanical explanation—like gravity, they simply exist. Thus, for those who persisted in believing in the existence of matter as the foundation of an ultimate physical and mechanical reality, in both the cases of Newton and of Maxwell their manner of practice of physics must appear as relying on a form of magic. Even such a distinguished British physicist as Sir William Thompson (Lord Kelvin) charged that "in his departure from a mechanical model of thought he [Maxwell] had lapsed into *mysticism*."[19]

As Einstein would remark, in Maxwell's theory "the equations alone appeared as the essential thing and the field strengths as the ultimate entities, not to be reduced to anything else." As a result, serious scientists had to give up "belief in the justification, or the possibility [as with Newton and gravity], of a mechanical explanation of Maxwell's equations." As a result, as Einstein wrote, of the "changes wrought by him in our conception of the nature of physical reality, we may say this: before Maxwell people conceived of physical reality -- in so far as it is supposed to represent events in nature -- as material points ... After Maxwell, they conceived physical reality as represented by continuous fields, not mechanically explicable, which are subject to partial differential equations," the mathematics having become the ultimate reality for post-Newton—and now post-Maxwell physicists—however magical this might seem to be.[20] For any kind of rational answer, it would be necessary to turn to theology—to invoke the actions of a supernatural

17. Torrance, "Preface" to Maxwell *The Dynamical Theory of the Electromagnetic Field*, x.

18. Einstein, "Maxwell's Influence on the Evolution of the Idea of Physical Reality," 266.

19. Torrance, "Preface" to Maxwell *The Dynamical Theory of the Electromagnetic Field*, ix.

20. Einstein, "Maxwell's Influence on the Development of the Conception of Physical Reality," 268, 269.

being, a god of some kind. Rational thought could thus lead to a conclusion of a strong existing likelihood of there being a god that guides the "material" world, if in a mysterious manner outside of any material explanation.

Mathematics and the Divine

Mathematics and its miraculous qualities are still widely regarded today with a similar sense that a god must be present. The traditional religious foundations, however, are now implicit and disguised; unlike Wigner, many contemporary students of mathematics and physics have never seriously thought about the reasons they regard mathematics with such awe and wonder—beyond the practical ability established to control and use nature for human benefit. Thus, explicit writing about the relationship of god and mathematics in the manner of Newton and Leibniz is seldom encountered today—also reflecting partly the fact that Newton was both a great mathematician and physicist and also a prolific theologian, and Leibniz was both a great mathematician and a great philosopher, intellectual combinations rare in our own times. Recently, however, there have been some signs of a renewed interest. In 2005, an edited collection of essays was published on *Mathematics and the Divine: A Historical Study*, examining a number of leading figures whose thinking illustrated the close links between mathematics, science, and religion from ancient Greece to modern times. As the editors T. Koetsier and L. Bergmans write, "mathematics in its relation with the divine has played a special role in the course of history." This is partly because "mathematics is abstract and it often seems absolute, universal, eternal and pure. More than other kinds of knowledge it possesses characteristics that we associate with the divine."[21]

In another recent book reflecting such growing interest, the American astrophysicist Mario Livio asks in 2009, *Is God a Mathematician?*[22] The question arises partly because of "the apparent omnipresence and omnipotent powers"—features most commonly attributed to a god—"of mathematics" in determining events in the natural world. Like Wigner, Livio confesses to his own sense of "utter bewilderment" that mathematics is so extraordinarily successful in revealing the precise workings of nature—making possible exact predictions of future natural events, and in many cases providing a scientific basis for direct future human control over these events.[23]

21. Koetsier and Bergmans, "Introduction" to Koetsier and Bergmans, *Mathematics and the Divine*, 4.

22. Livio, *Is God a Mathematician?*

23. Ibid., 1, 2.

The mystery is compounded for Livio as well because for many working mathematicians their work is done for its own sake without regard to practical consequences—as one might say, as a form of contemporary inspirational contemplation. Many leading mathematicians thus have toiled for years exploring mental constructions that had no apparent physical analogues or usefulness. Their method has been to make certain initial abstract assumptions and then, following well-defined rules of abstract mathematical reasoning, to follow this reasoning down an intricate path that leads to the discovery of whole new mathematical worlds that inspire in them a strong sense of beauty and the sublime, in essence, present-day secularizations of the old Newtonian and Liebnizian idea of encountering the mind of God. Remarkably enough, such abstractly created mathematical ideas have sometimes turned out, decades or even centuries later, to correspond to the workings of actual natural systems. As Livio puts it, there have been a number of cases "in which entirely abstract mathematical theories had been developed, with no intended application, only to metamorphose later into powerfully predictive physical models" that the natural world obeys.[24]

As long ago as ancient Greece, the Pythagoreans were shocked and dismayed to discover (as a result of finding contradictions in their own rational analyses) that there were conceivable lines whose length could not be measured and expressed by any "real" number (a number that could itself be expressed in any form composed of other numbers—either any possible fraction or, equivalently, any nonrepeating decimal series that has a finite ending). The square root of 2 is one such example, known by the Pythagorean theorem to be equal to the length of the hypotenuse of a triangle whose sides are each one unit long. The multiplier "pi," used to calculate the area of a circle (pi times the radius squared) is another familiar such number. The Pythagoreans found the existence of such geometric objects that could not be expressed in any numerical terms so heretical that the mathematicians who discovered their existence sought to suppress the knowledge from the wider public. As Koetsier and Bergmans write, "for the Pythagoreans doing mathematics was a way to get in touch with the divine."[25] Their god was a mathematical god whose character was now turning out to be stranger and more mysterious than the Pythagoreans up to then had ever conceived would be possible.

Eventually, the concept of "irrational numbers" was developed by mathematicians to address this problem. Although they could be

24. Ibid., 203

25. Koetsier and Bergmans, "Introduction" to Koetsier and Bergmans, eds., *Mathematics and the Divine*, 13.

represented geometrically, irrational numbers were abstract mathematical symbols without any greater "real" numerical existence. The number was simply assumed to exist even if "it"—the irrational number—could not actually be expressed in any finite numerical terms. And yet these new kinds of "irrational numbers," along with the later development by mathematicians of still stranger "imaginary numbers," eventually played a large role in the modern development of the calculus, and have been routinely put to practical use by modern working physicists. Seeming to be almost a miracle, mathematical manipulations of such pure mental abstractions as irrational and imaginary numbers, seemingly lacking any real existence outside of the world of abstract mathematical reasoning, turn out to be part of the mysterious controlling process over the physical workings of nature. As the great Princeton physicist John Wheeler asks, even as the practical usefulness of this approach has been demonstrated innumerable times, metaphysically "then how can physics in good conscience go on using in its description of existence a number system that does not even exist?"[26] For some people, if not for Wheeler, it is a sure sign that the hand of a god must be at work somewhere in all this.

In the nineteenth century, to give another example, mathematicians developed elaborate systems of "non-Euclidian" geometry—abstract mathematical worlds in which no parallel lines might be possible even in concept. A prominent figure in this new branch of mathematics was the German Bernhard Riemann, among the great mathematicians of the century. Fifty years later, Albert Einstein (who, unlike Newton, was not a gifted mathematician) did not know about this mathematics but a friend and mathematician helpfully pointed it out to him, suggesting that it might be valuable in finding a mathematical solution to the problems of general relatively with which Einstein had been struggling for several years. After Einstein took further years to master the difficult mathematics of non-Euclidean geometry, the final theory of general relativity was published in 1915, relying heavily on Riemann's pure mathematical abstractions that had originally seemed in the 1860s to describe an imaginary mathematical world that could exist only abstractly in the mind of the mathematician—and also potentially in the mind of a god.

Shing-Tau Yau, a Fields medal winner and chairman of the mathematics department at Harvard University, thus commented that in creating general relativity, Einstein arrived at it by "a process of pure thought—realized through mathematics without any prompting from the outside world." As Yau observes, using Riemann's concept of a "metric tensor, Einstein worked

---

26. Wheeler, *At Home in the Universe*, 184.

out the shape and other properties—the geometry, in other words—of his newly conceived space-time." This culminated in "the famous Einstein field equation, [which] illustrates that gravity—the force that shapes the cosmos on the largest scales—can be regarded as a kind of illusion caused by the curvature of space and time" in the presence of a large mass object. In short, "gravity . . . is geometry," thus finally seeming to confirm empirically what Plato had said 2,500 years earlier, that ideal geometric forms ultimately serve to shape the lower—the physical—part of the universe that human beings directly experience themselves in physical nature.[27]

Eternal Mathematics

A growing number of physicists today might agree that their scientific mission depends on a virtually supernatural role for mathematics. They are typically inhibited from saying so, however, by the pervasive scientific materialism of the university world that they inhabit. They may also be intellectually confused personally, thinking as Platonic idealists in their roles as physicists and mathematicians, but as scientific materialists in their wider personal philosophizing about the world as a whole. One exception, however, is the British physicist Roger Penrose, known for his pioneering 1960s theories of the workings of black holes in the universe, among other important scientific contributions. Since the 1980s, he has extended his intellectual efforts to new realms, pondering the types of "mysteries" that concerned Wigner (although with greater sustained attention than Wigner was willing to commit). This has lead Penrose to conceive of the full universe as consisting separately of "three worlds" of which human beings can have a direct awareness.

Two of these distinct worlds are familiar enough: the physical world of nature and the mental world of consciousness in human minds. Penrose departs from conventional thinking, however, in identifying a third distinct and yet equally real world that he labels the "Platonic mathematical world." The three worlds, moreover, are all interrelated with one another. The physical world is entirely controlled by specific mathematic realities that exist in the Platonic mathematical world, something that Penrose, much like Wigner, acknowledges is a "deep puzzle" whose explanation, if it is ever found, will very probably have to lie outside the scope of normal science.[28] The physical world includes the human brain that, equally mysteriously, somehow is necessary to the existence of the nonmaterial world of hu-

27. Yao and Nadis, *The Shape of Inner Space*, 32.
28. Penrose, *The Road to Reality*, 18, 21.

man consciousness. And finally, human consciousness, again remarkably, is a nonmaterial world capable of apprehending the Platonic mathematical world that itself also lacks any physical reality. It is seemingly one miracle followed by another.

Contrary to the standard naturalist explanations that see the fundamental realities of the universe strictly in material terms, Penrose thus sees two of the three basic worlds that make up human "reality" as having a nonmaterial essence. In offering this vision that borders on religion, Penrose explains that it has a very practical basis, derived from his many years of study as a leading contemporary theoretical physicist: "Those who work in this subject [theoretical physics], whether they are actively engaged in mathematical research or just using results that have been obtained by others, usually feel that [in doing and using the mathematics] they are merely explorers in [an already existing] world that lies far beyond themselves—a world which possesses an objectivity that transcends opinion, be that opinion their own or the surmise of others, no matter how expert those others might be."[29] The physical world then is miraculously controlled by this non-material mathematical world, not the other way around.

Underwood Dudley, a leading contemporary student of mathematical thought, agrees with Penrose's description of the thinking of mathematicians, writing that "many mathematicians, maybe most, are naïve Platonists. That is, they think they know that the mathematical objects with which they deal were not made up by them, nor by anyone else." For example, "mathematicians who have internalized Liousville's theorem can *feel* the external existence of algebraic numbers."[30] The role of the mathematician is then to discover the structures, the abstract logical contours if you will, of the abstract mathematical world. Just as the nineteenth-century explorer David Livingston discovered the physical and social features of a preexisting interior of Africa then unknown to Europeans, mathematicians embark on their own journeys of discovery to discover and explore a preexisting world of often surprising mathematical ideas and relationships. Human beings did not invent the idea that two plus two equals four; it is instead an eternal reality, just as true before the big bang (assuming we can say that time existed before the big bang) as it will be forever true into the future after the sun and earth are long gone. With the development of arithmetic, and with suitable instruction, such arithmetical realities have become an explicit part of the routine contents of ordinary human minds today. Professional

---

29. Ibid., 13.
30. Dudley, "Introduction to Chapter 2," 15.

mathematicians discover similar eternal realities, if of far greater rational complexity, normally well beyond the capacity of the average person to comprehend.

The Englishman G. H. Hardy ranks among the great mathematicians of the twentieth century. He is best known to the wider public for discovering the Indian mathematical genius Ramanujan who had received almost no prior mathematical training before writing to Hardy with examples of his work. Greatly impressed, Hardy brought him to Cambridge where the two collaborated to publish a number of important mathematical papers, all this popularized in the 1991 book, *The Man Who Knew Infinity*.[31] Perhaps partly because of his unassailable stature in the top ranks of twentieth-century mathematicians, Hardy was more publicly forthright than most mathematicians (and physicists) today. He acknowledged that some fellow mathematicians disagree but he had no doubt personally that "mathematical reality lies outside us" and that "our function is to discover or *observe* it, and that the theorems which we prove, and which we describe grandiloquently as our 'creations', are simply our notes of our observations" in our journeys into the realm of mathematical ideas. The mathematics of "pure geometries" such as Riemann had explored, for example, "are independent of lecture rooms or any other detail of the physical world." Hardy goes so far as to suggest that, because physicists deal with a physical world that they can only know through the indirect means of their sensory impressions (often derived from the measuring instruments they necessarily use in seeking to discern the actual features of "physical" reality), it is actually "the mathematician [who] is in much more direct contact with reality"—with the actual real world of mathematical ideas that he can know better and explore more directly because they have a real existence within his own mind. By comparison, the physicist can ultimately be said only to study the ordering of external sensory data as received and interpreted—and potentially "distorted"—through the workings of the human mind and human consciousness.[32]

Given the dominance of the "religion" of scientific materialism in contemporary American and European intellectual life, however, most mathematicians and physicists today are reluctant, if not altogether unwilling, to publicly advocate any such deeply Platonic heresies, especially when such ideas might easily be taken to suggest the likely existence of a god. It would come close, for example, to embracing traditional theological understandings of a god as constituting a preexisting divine intelligence—if in this case a god having a mind of a surprisingly mathematical orientation.

---

31. Kanigel, *The Man Who Knew Infinity*.
32. Hardy, *A Mathematician's Apology*, 123–24, 126, 128.

For Plato, the world of abstract ideas, especially mathematical ideas, was of the essence of a god. Platonism has long been associated with a strong sense of the mysterious and the religious; early Christian theology was deeply influenced by Neoplatonic philosophy. To be an avowed Platonist in a public way today might put a mathematician in sharp conflict with contemporary figures such as Richard Dawkins and Daniel Dennett, who are true-believing scientific materialists, and who seem to enjoy the kinds of harsh verbal sparring in public that many mathematicians might find unpleasant and would prefer to avoid.

Philip Davis and Reuben Hersh, both mathematicians themselves, affirm that "the typical mathematician is a Platonist" in his daily professional life. For such a mathematician, "when he is doing mathematics he is convinced that he is dealing with a [preexisting] objective reality [of mathematical ideas] whose properties he is attempting to determine"—much as a biologist sees himself discovering and studying the physical properties of living organisms. In doing physics, the physicist then works to discover which preexisting mathematical laws govern which specific areas of the workings of the natural world. Yet, as Davis and Hersh report, the typical mathematician or physicist today is reluctant to confess his or her Platonism publicly; hence, "when challenged to give a philosophical account of this reality [of his own thinking about doing physics and mathematics], he finds it easiest to pretend that he does not believe in it after all." While this mathematician is "a Platonist on [working] weekdays," he becomes a materialist "formalist on [religious] Sundays." [33] In this way, present-day mathematicians and physicists contribute—if inadvertently—to our contemporary state of theological confusion.

Some people such as Lee Smolin, a theoretical physicist at the University of Toronto, think this is hypocritical. Smolin, moreover, is a strong critic of the implicit Platonic thinking of so many mathematicians and physicists on working weekdays. Smolin, for example, objects to Penrose's three-world model, including the hypothesis that there is a separate world of mathematics exercising—in an altogether unknown and mysterious way—control over another separate world of physical objects. Smolin complains that such ways of thinking leave physicists today as "easy prey to mystifiers who want to sell us radical metaphysical fantasies in the guise of science," who might in fact argue that Penrose has provided a rational path to a belief in the likely existence of a god. He thus says of Penrose that he "believes that our minds can transcend the ever changing flow of experience and reach a timeless eternal [mathematical] reality behind it." Such a "desire for transcendence,"

33. Davis and Hirsch, *The Mathematical Experience*, 321.

however, as Smolin sees it, "is at root a religious aspiration," for him a disturbing development within the realm of what he hopes can be objective science. A form of Platonism such as Penrose advocates, Smolin concludes, leads to a new form of "mysticism" in which "the seeking of mathematical knowledge make[s] one a special kind of priest, with special access to an extraordinary form of knowledge" of essentially divine origin and character.[34]

If too many mathematicians and physicists were to acquiesce in this state of affairs, for Smolin it would mean that they were exposing "mathematics for the religious activity it is." It would be especially disturbing in that "the most rational of our thinkers, the mathematicians," would now be acting and speaking as though "what they do [is] . . . the route to transcendence from the bounds of human life."[35] As himself a devout scientific materialist, Smolin naively believes that rational argument is incapable of leading to a god, that true reason and god are incompatible. Or, as one might say, he is a latter day follower in the tradition of Aristotle, for whom—in opposition to Plato—the concrete material world comes first, and then the abstract idea is formed as a composite mental image that serves usefully in human thinking about the workings of this material world. Smolin believes in the view that Hardy completely rejected, that all the results of mathematics are simply a human "creation;" if human beings did not exist, mathematical truths would therefore not exist.

At the deepest level, all reality for such Aristotelians—including their contemporary naturalist heirs—is material, and human ideas, including mathematical ideas, are mere human instruments (that since Darwin can be seen as serving biological evolutionary purposes). Long before Darwin, when pressed to explain the presence of causation in the world, Aristotle himself thought that causal agency was intrinsic to the fundamental character of the material world itself, not somehow superimposed on that world by any external divine realm of mathematical ideas that came first. In retrospect, admittedly, Aristotle's internal material agency—explaining say the movement of a ball thrown through the air as its movement towards its final appropriate destination—was no less mysterious than Plato's initial world of mathematical forms. Why should a ball have an inherent tendency to fall through time towards its "natural" destination that reflects some kind of "final cause" of the ball? In the language of contemporary philosophy, Aristotle in the end as well offered a "teleological" view of the workings of the natural world. For both Plato and Aristotle, the world of ordinary commonsense perception of material elements is an illusion that masks deeper

34. Smolin, *Time Reborn*, 7, 10, 11.
35. Ibid., 11.

and more fundamental realities that can only be discovered by heroic intellectual—today scientific—effort.

From Plato to Newton

The American sociologist Robert Merton in the 1930s set out to understand the historically unprecedentedly pace of development of science in England in the seventeenth century. Like many American intellectuals of that period—and even today—his initial assumption was that religion and science would be in conflict. He was therefore surprised to discover that many leading English scientists of the seventeenth century—indeed a disproportionate number relative to the overall religious composition of the English population—came from Puritan Calvinist backgrounds, and that many of them were still devout as scientists.[36] Among the Calvinists, the strong religious motive for studying nature was combined with the strict discipline and capacity for hard work of the Calvinist faithful. The result, as Merton found, was that in England "among the original list of members of the Royal Society in 1663, forty-two of the sixty-eight for whom information about religious leanings is available, were clearly Puritan." Merton found similar connections in other parts of seventeenth-century Europe, observing that "all available evidence points in the same direction. Protestants, without exception, form a progressively larger proportion of the student body in those schools which emphasize scientific training, whereas Catholics concentrate their interests on classical and theological training." Merton concluded that "Puritanism and ascetic Protestantism generally emerges as an emotionally consistent system of beliefs, sentiments and action which played no small part in arousing a sustained interest in science," not only in the seventeenth century but extending even into "the nineteenth century, [where] their divorce [of science and Protestantism] was not final."[37]

The surprise Merton felt partly reflects the typical lack of theological and philosophical awareness in twentieth-century scientific circles. In the history of Western religion, one great line of thought runs from Plato, to the later Neoplatonists of the ancient world, to Augustine who synthesized Platonism with Christianity, and then to the Protestant Reformation that in the sixteenth century newly looked back to Augustinian theology for inspiration (Martin Luther was originally an Augustinian monk). For Aristotle, by contrast, Thomas Aquinas in the thirteenth century was the great synthesizer of Aristotelean thought with Christian theology. The great "protest"

36. Merton, *Science, Technology and Society in Seventeenth-Century England.*
37. Ibid., 114, 128, 135–36, 136.

of the Reformation in the sixteenth century was significantly against the medieval scholastic theology of the Catholic Church, against Aquinas, and against Aristotle.

The favoring of Platonic over Aristotelian sources in the Reformation proved to be a great advantage in terms of setting the stage for the development and advancement of the scientific method and the eventual discovery by Kepler, Galileo, Newton, and others in the sixteenth and later centuries of the mathematical workings of the physical universe. Plato is said to have placed the statement "let no one unversed in geometry enter here" over the entrance to his academy in Athens. He divided the cosmos into two distinct realms, "a higher divine, intelligible world and a lower human sensible world" as found in ordinary human existence. Then, as the University of Chicago authority on ancient Greek philosophy and mathematics, Ian Mueller, writes, "the crucial link between these worlds is mathematics." For Plato, the mathematical formulations had eternally existed independently in the higher world of ideal forms but they also assumed a material character and were given expression "in the mathematical organization of the lower world."[38]

Among the core subjects that Plato in *The Republic* expected his philosopher kings to study, mathematics occupied the largest amount of time.[39] Mathematics is central because it can "turn the mind away from human things toward divine ones." Mathematics for Plato serves to direct "the attention of the potentially divine individual from the lower world to the higher world and its apex, the form of the good"—as has been suggested, the essence of god for Plato, if not the Christian God precisely. Throughout his dialogues, Plato insists on "the moral benefit to be gained from the study of mathematics."[40]

In the following centuries in the ancient world, students and followers of Plato—the "Neoplatonists"—further developed such ideas. A late Neoplatonist, Proclus (412–485 CE), taught that in order to reach the highest levels of the divine, the first subject to be studied was the "'practical' sciences" where the writings of Aristotle were the most helpful. More advanced study would then focus, however, on "the higher reaches of philosophy, the 'theoretical' sciences represented, in ascending order, by physics, mathematics, and 'theology' (the science of the divine)."[41] In the first step above the natural world, the self-discovery of the soul is reached through geometry. In this way, the soul "sees an image of herself and, through this self-

---

38. Mueller, "Mathematics and the Divine in Plato," 117.

39. Ibid., 113.

40. Ibid., 114, 117.

41. O'Meara, "Geometry and the Divine in Proclus," 137.

knowledge, reaches a knowledge of the presence in her of truths concerning the transcendent first principles, the gods. In thinking of these [geometric] truths, [the] soul already lives a life of knowledge that will bring her higher in the scale of divinity."[42] As American intellectual historian Daniel Cohen puts it,

> Irrationality, clouded perception, and faulty notions accumulated throughout our lifetimes obscure our vision of the truth, Proclus thought, and condemn us to the flickering shadows of Plato's cave. Thrown down from heaven, mathematics is the lightening bolt that rouses us, dispelling the darkness of the cave with an unparalleled and sublime brilliance that alerts us to the possibility of seeing everything in such a vivid, penetrating light. The mathematical arts thus involve nothing less than the purification and ascendency of the human soul, permitting it to overcome the innate imperfection of mankind and the human senses.[43]

Augustine lived around the same time as Proclus. As a contemporary historian of religion writes, Augustine's theology was "the Christian form that the great Platonic tradition took in the West."[44] Canadian intellectual historian Faith Wallis observes that, following in the Platonic tradition, "for Augustine, 'number' is the vehicle by which eternal Form is embodied in particular, material things. We can only know things insofar as they have 'number,' that is, insofar as they possess form. Take away *these forms*," Augustine says, "and there will be nothing." Mathematics for Augustine is "divinely instituted" because the mathematical world exists independently of human thoughts and actions. Augustine makes the point that "three times three" must always have been and must always be nine—it is an eternal truth. As with most contemporary mathematicians in practice, if not in their public statements, with Augustine as well, "the truths of number are not invented, but discovered." It is for this reason that "the study of the science of number is an ascesis through which one learns to appreciate the immense difference between immutable divine truth and the mutable human mind."[45] Teun Koetsier and Luc Bermans explain that,

> St. Augustine was the first major Christian theologian who tried to show along Platonic lines that our knowledge of God is as certain as our knowledge of geometry. In St. Augustine's view

42. Ibid., 139.

43. Cohen, *Equations from God*, 20.

44. Randall, *Hellenistic Ways of Deliverance and the Making of the Christian Synthesis*, 199.

45. Wallis, "'Number Mystique' in Early Medieval Computus Texts," 187–88, 182.

mathematical knowledge is knowledge of an eternal abstract realm to which we have access by means of an inner light, Divine illumination. The existence of eternal truth in mathematics implies the existence of the idea of Eternal Truth, which is an important ingredient of St. Augustine's proof of the existence of God and the immortality of the soul.[46]

In the Christian tradition, there are three basic ways of learning about God. There is the study of the Bible, which is divinely inspired and in the New Testament reveals the word of God as proclaimed by Jesus. There is the natural order that was created by God at the beginning and can therefore be studied to directly discover the workings of His mind. And there are the teachings of the church as worked out by church leaders, theologians, other church scholars, and others with the ability to contribute to developing and refining human knowledge of God. Over time the Roman Catholic Church assigned an increasing role to this third form of attaining religious knowledge, mostly originating within the Church itself. The Protestant Reformation, however, rejected that church role as an intermediary between God and man, seeing it as a false substitution of a fallen human institution in the proper place of God. Absent this third source of authoritative knowledge about God, Protestantism therefore gave larger roles both to the study of the Bible and also to learning about God by directly experiencing and studying the natural world.

John Calvin proclaimed in his *Institutes of the Christian Religion* that human beings must show respect for the natural world because it is especially in its presence that they can find "burning lamps" that "shine for us . . . the glory of its Author" above.[47] As Calvin believed, God had created the world in recent times, and it was still possible to see in nature the direct evidence of his handiwork, altered only in minor ways since the Creation. As Calvin thus wrote,

> The final goal of the blessed life, moreover, rests in the knowledge of God [cf. John 17:3]. Lest anyone, then, be excluded from access to happiness, he not only sowed in men's minds that seed of religion of which we have spoken but revealed himself and daily discloses himself in the whole workmanship of the universe. As a consequence, men cannot open their eyes without being compelled to see him. Indeed, his essence is incomprehensible; hence, his divineness far escapes all human perception. But

46. Koetsier and Bergmans, "Introduction" to Koetsier and Bergmans, eds., *Mathematics and the Divine*, 19.

47. Kerr, ed., *Calvin's Institutes*, 26–27, 99.

upon his individual works he has engraved unmistakable marks
of his glory, so clean and so prominent. . . . Wherever you cast
your eyes, there is no spot in the universe wherein you cannot
discern at least some sparks of his glory.[48]

It was out of this pursuit of greater knowledge of God that the scientific
method would be developed in the seventeenth century, leading to exact
levels of knowledge about the true workings of nature—and thus the thinking of God—far beyond anything Calvin could have conceived. A student
of environmental thought, Jeffrey Bilbro observes that in the presence of the
creation human beings felt that they could "behold more fully the beauty
and character of the Creator. Galileo, drawing on such a foundation, famously argues for the value of mathematics and science as guides to our
reading of the 'open book of heaven' in which 'the glory and greatness of
Almighty God are marvelously discerned.'" Transferred to the new world
and a Protestant setting, "these views of creation inspired those American
Puritans who sought to perceive and then participate properly in God's
created order," helping to inspire the American Calvinist faithful to create
Harvard, Yale, and Princeton universities, among others, to study and better
understand God's ways as could be seen in his Creation.[49]

Newton was not himself a Puritan (the English branch of Calvinism)
but was heavily influenced by the Puritan surroundings in which he lived.
Cornelis de Pater writes that in the development of his thought leading up to
the *Principia* in 1687 "Newton was influenced by the well-known Cambridge
Platonists Ralph Cudworth and Henri More." Newton therefore rejected the
idea that only a natural event could have an impact on another natural event;
however mysterious, it was possible for mind (such as the mathematical laws
of gravity as existed in the mind of God) to influence matter. As de Pater
puts it, "Newton in the end rejected the separation of mind and matter advocated by Descartes, Hobbes and others, who accepted only material causes
as explanations of phenomena in the physical word."[50] Newton's Platonist
tendencies, rejecting such crude materialism, were essential to his efforts as
a physicist and mathematician that changed the world—otherwise, he would
never have made the necessary beginning assumptions about gravity in order to explain the workings of the solar system.

Indeed, the acceptance of Newtonian physics in France and elsewhere
on the continent was initially held back for up to three decades by a sense
that, lacking any basis for gravity in material phenomena, Newton's new

48. Ibid., 24.
49. Bilbro, *Loving God's Wildness*, 10.
50. de Pater, "An Ocean of Truth," 466.

theory was a form of religious mysticism that could not offer a "rational" explanation of the world. Even in the twentieth century, Albert Einstein would describe the idea of gravity as developed by Newton as having a "fictitious character," owing to the lack of any explanation within physics for the existence of the phenomenon of gravity itself.[51] With the general theory of relativity in 1915, Einstein saw himself as having finally provided the first such scientific explanation.

Einstein's Special and General Relativity

By the eighteenth century, given the extraordinary successes of the scientific method in the seventeenth century in revealing the workings of the universe, its use was spreading across Europe among religious and cultural groups of all kinds. Increasingly, and becoming in the second half of the nineteenth century a development of overwhelming historical importance for the material character of human existence, scientific knowledge was being put to use to assert human control over nature, gradually giving human beings the ability to achieve virtually miraculous technologies and other scientific methods to harness the power of electricity, to cure disease, to communicate instantaneously across thousands of miles, and to obtain many other large practical benefits. The advance of science was thus no longer routinely justified primarily as a way of learning about God. Governments began to invest large sums of money in scientific research for their own public purposes. Although modern science emerged from religion, there was a growing separation of science and traditional religion (although accompanied by a corresponding rise in the role of "secular religion," as discussed in Chapter 7 below). The place of explicit "God-talk" in the workings of modern mathematics and physics thus receded sharply from the language of seventeenth-century scientists.

It did not disappear altogether, however. One large exception was Albert Einstein who did not believe in the personal God of Judaism and Christianity but was nevertheless a devout believer—in this respect much in the manner of Newton and Leibniz—in a supernatural god who thought in mathematical terms and had somehow put his mathematical thinking to use to guide the workings of the natural world. Koetsier and Bergmans comment that for Einstein his god "is found in the harmony of the natural world." As Einstein thought, nature is the realization of mathematical ideas. The search for god thus was the search for the natural harmony of the universe as expressed in mathematics. As Einstein wrote, the physicist

51. Einstein, quoted in Pais, "*Subtle is the Lord . . .*", 460.

is motivated by a confident deep "faith in the possibility that the regula-
tions valid for the world of existence are rational, that is, comprehensible
to reason. I cannot conceive of a genuine scientist without that profound
faith. Science without religion is lame, religion without science is blind."[52]
Einstein said, for example, of the scientific efforts of Max Planck, another
great physicist of the early twentieth century (who made a fundamental
early discovery on the road to quantum mechanics), that Planck was fiercely
driven by "the longing to behold . . . [the] preestablished harmony" of a god
as revealed in the workings of the natural world.[53]

Indeed, Einstein thought that a physicist lacking such a powerful core
of religious faith would have little chance of making any great contributions
to scientific discovery. It is a common mistake to attribute scientific success to exceptional will power and concentration combined with a strong
desire for professional success. Einstein thus considered that "those whose
acquaintance with scientific research is derived chiefly from its practical
results easily develop a completely false notion of the mentality of the men"
who have made fundamental discoveries in physics. Rather, Einstein wrote
that such men were driven by a the pursuit of a "cosmic religious feeling
[that] is the strongest and noblest motive for scientific research."[54] When
they succeeded, they felt a "rapturous amazement at the harmony of natural
law, which reveals an intelligence of such superiority that, compared with
it, all the systematic thinking and acting of human beings is an utterly in-
significant reflection." For a great physicist, "this feeling is beyond question
closely akin to that which has possessed the religious geniuses of all ages."[55]
Einstein agreed with a "contemporary [who] has said, not unjustly, that in
this materialistic age of ours the serious scientific workers are the only profoundly religious people."[56]

Einstein's leading biographer, fellow physicist Abraham Pais (who
knew him well personally), thus comments that the "overriding urge for
[finding God's] harmony [in nature] directed Einstein's scientific life." In
making his fundamental discoveries in special relativity, general relativity,
and other areas of physics, "as he experienced it, [Einstein] played the role
of the instrument of the Lord, Who, he deeply believed, was subtle but not
malicious"—and thus had created a natural world that was well ordered

52. Einstein, quoted in Koetsier and Bergmans, "Introduction" to Koetsier and
Bergmans, eds., *Mathematics and the Divine*, 41.

53. Einstein, quoted in Pais, "*Subtle is the Lord . . .*", 26–27.

54. Einstein, "Religion and Science," 39.

55. Einstein, "The Religious Spirit of Science," 40.

56. Einstein, "Religion and Science," 40.

and subject to human mathematical discovery and explanation.[57] Another commentator on Einstein's views about religion and science, Algis Valiunis, writes in the same vein that for Einstein "science at its highest was a form of divination." Einstein's way of doing physics was an exercise in "contemplative theology" in which "to partake of God's fathomless mind . . . was the physicist's holy communion; there was nothing more sacred to him than a true insight into the workings of Nature," which provided an opening to the mind of a god who controlled the workings of the natural world.[58]

In Einstein's own scientific research, moreover, his thinking about this god played a surprisingly important practical role, including in the development both of the special theory of relativity in 1905 and the general theory of relativity in 1915. The constant speed of light, while a large surprise to most classical physicists when first clearly demonstrated empirically in the famous Michelson-Morley experiment in 1887, was theologically required for Einstein as a necessary part of god's plan for the universe. If the speed of light differed from one frame of reference to another, according to its movement, then measurements of time, distance, and speed, as recorded by the instruments of the world's physicists (without scientific adjustment), would also differ according to the frame of reference of the physicist. As a consequence, the observed results of ordinary physical experiments—and the laws of nature discovered by physicists—would also routinely differ according to the inertial frames of reference in which a physicist was functioning. Since the earth is spinning on its axis, for example, without adjustment, the perceived laws of nature would vary constantly across the earth according to the geographic location. But Einstein said, No!, his god would never have let the universe work that way—the laws of nature must be the same everywhere at all times, independent of the movement of the frame of reference. In order for this to be true, however, it would require radical changes in traditional concepts of the measurement of time and distance, both now varying with the speed of the frame of reference. Once again, as it seemed, god worked in miraculous ways, as now to be revealed by Einstein, moving further along a path that Newton had pioneered.

Einstein himself explained it this way in 1916 in a publication intended for a popular audience. As he wrote, "the (special) theory of relativity has grown out of electrodynamics and optics"—the study of light.[59] If, counterfactually, the speed of light were not invariant with respect to the frame of reference, Einstein explained, the "coordinate systems K, K', K", etc. which

57. Pais, "*Subtle is the Lord . . .*", 27, 30.

58. Valiunas, "Einstein's Quest for Truth," 139.

59. Einstein, *Relativity*, 49.

are moving uniformly relative to each other, will not be equivalent for the description of natural phenomena." We might have to choose one frame of reference Ko which we might then define as the one "real" frame, the one "absolutely at rest." Relying on the measurements from the instruments of physicists on Ko, there would then be one set of laws of nature observed within this frame of reference, Ko. But if the measured speed of light was different in another frame of reference, K1, moving at some constant speed relative to Ko, the natural world of K1 as it would be perceived in human minds would be different from the natural world of Ko (as common sense would suggest, and is in fact true for the measured speed of sound waves in the air). As Einstein put it, a moving "railway carriage" would be a different system K from the absolute rest system Ko, and an observer in this carriage would find that "the general laws of nature which have been formulated" would reflect "the magnitude and direction of the velocity of the carriage [which] would necessarily play a part."[60]

Einstein simply could not believe that his god would have created a universe in which the laws of nature were so ephemeral; he was far from a devout believer in the Bible, but shared Newton's belief that the natural world revealed the ways of god, and those ways must have a fundamentally constant and mathematical character, having been implanted there by god—and thus the mathematical laws of physics must always be the same everywhere in the universe, as perceived by the physicist (or any other person). Mathematically, in the case of the special theory of relativity published in 1905, the working out of the necessary "transformation equations" between frames of reference in order to preserve a constant measured speed of light (as Einstein expressed it in mathematical language, the necessary equations in order to assure that the "general laws of nature are covariant with respect to Lorenz transformations") was a fairly simple task, requiring little more than a solid grasp of algebra and geometry.[61] The general theory of relativity in 1915, however, generalized these results to include frames of reference moving at changing speeds relative to one another, as in one frame of reference falling toward another frame of reference according to the Newtonian laws of gravity. The mathematics of general relativity proved to be much more difficult, a main reason that Einstein took a decade to work it all out (as noted above, eventually requiring his use of Riemann's 1860s discoveries about the workings of non-Euclidian geometry). In the language of general relativity, gravity was now to be understood as a "warping" of time and space. Gravity was also a field in the manner of an electromagnetic

60. Ibid., 17.
61. Ibid., 37.

field. As with light waves, gravity "traveled" at a finite speed (in fact the very same speed of light) within its field. Hypothetically, for example, if the entire mass of the sun miraculously disappeared altogether at one instantaneous moment, the gravitational effects of the sun on the earth would continue to be felt for an additional eight minutes, the time required for gravity waves to reach the earth.

Einstein thought that it would have been preferable if twentieth-century physics had been able to develop such ideas out of daily human experience. But, increasingly, that was not possible; the theories now had to be developed as an abstract exercise in mathematical thinking with a minimal connection to daily "reality," as ordinary people experienced it. It was only at the last stage, when the predictions of the theory were finally tested empirically with real measuring instruments, that observations in the "real world" became a decisive factor. As Einstein wrote, "it has to be admitted that general relativity has gone further in relinquishing 'closeness to experience' of fundamental concepts in order to obtain logical simplicity."[62] Einstein believed that this logical simplicity was derived from a supernatural source as expressed in mathematical rules of the universe derived from this source—a source which he was comfortable in labeling as his god.

The Magical Quantum God

The 1920s were a time of severe economic turmoil and social upheaval in Germany but apparently these conditions did not rule out the possibility of doing great physics. Einstein was by then a senior statesman—along with Max Planck—but a new group of young German physicists, often collaborating closely with Niels Bohr in Denmark, was emerging to become leading contributors to the glory days of twentieth-century theoretical physics. Besides the contributions of Werner Heisenberg (only twenty-five when he discovered quantum mechanics in 1925) and his co-discoverer, Erwin Schrodinger (an Austrian, who then reformulated quantum mechanics in a new more mathematically useful way), there were also other German physicist "near-greats," including Max Born, Wolfgang Pauli, and Herman Weyl. Outside Germany, Paul Dirac in England and Louis de Broglie in France belong to this 1920s and 1930s hall of fame of theoretical physics.

Physicists of such historic significance have been slower to come along since then. Arguably, there were no further Einsteins or Heisenbergs over the rest of the twentieth century. There was, however, one later physicist, the American Richard Feynman, who stood out from the others in the second

62. Einstein, "On the Generalized Theory of Gravitation," 349.

half of the twentieth century. Indeed, in a 1999 worldwide poll of 130 physicists, Feynman was ranked seventh in the history of physics, one place behind Galileo, and the only physicist whose important discoveries occurred after World War II to be included in the top ten list (Einstein ranked first, Newton second, and the Englishman James Clerk Maxwell third—these three falling in a class by themselves as the greatest physicists of all time).[63] Feynman was born in New York City, educated at MIT, and spent most of his working years as a physicist at the California Institute of Technology. His greatest claim to fame is as the leading creator of "quantum electrodynamics" (with Freeman Dyson, Julian Schwinger, and Sin-Itiro Tomonaga), integrating recent discoveries of quantum mechanics with the older physics of electrodynamics, and sharing the Nobel Prize in 1965 for these efforts. Feynman's biographer James Gleick writes that Feynman's work in the late 1940s and early 1950s "defined the start of the modern era for the next generation of physicists."[64]

Feynman was also famous as a showman (sometimes less charitably expressed as enjoying being a bit of a "clown"), which carried over into an interest in making physics more accessible to ordinary people. In 1985 he commented on the difficulty of translating an essentially mathematical subject into language accessible to wider audiences. In many cases, the popularizers had succeed only in creating an illusion of understanding the physics, since the essence of the physics lay in mathematics that was impenetrable to ordinary readers. As Feynman put it, popular writings about twentieth-century physics therefore often "achieve apparent simplicity only by describing something different, something considerably distorted from what they claim to be describing." Feynman would not do that and said it was not his fault that "No, you're not going to be able to understand" quantum mechanics, even as he was presenting it in as simple a way as possible. But then he encouraged readers to continue because, not to worry, "my physics students don't understand it either. That is because I don't understand it. Nobody does."[65] It was just that quantum formulations somehow—however magically—"worked" as statistical statements relating to very large numbers of subatomic events to explain key events in nature. In this respect, admittedly, they were perhaps no more mysterious than gravity and electromagnetic fields.

Around 1960, Caltech physicists were unhappy with their introductory physics courses and asked Feynman to create a new course which he taught

63. Tindol, "Physics World poll names Richard Feynman one of 10 greatest physicists of all time."

64. Gleick, *Genius,* 271.

65. Feynman, *QED: The Strange Theory of Light and Matter,* xxv, 9.

in 1961–1962 and 1962–1963. These lectures were published as *Lectures on Physics*, becoming a leading introductory work for many people wanting to learn more about physics, eventually selling more than 1.5 million copies and still in print. The most popularly accessible material was later gathered together and published as *Six Easy Pieces* and then *Six Not-So-Easy Pieces*.

In *Six Easy Pieces*, Feynman seeks to make quantum mechanics as accessible as is possible, however difficult the task. At the subatomic particle level, he writes, the behavior of nature is altogether "unlike ordinary experience, it is very difficult to get used to and it appears peculiar and mysterious to everybody, both to the novice and to the experienced physicist." In thinking about quantum phenomena, since they do not accord with our "direct, human experience" of a material world, the only option is to "learn about them in a sort of abstract or imaginative fashion." Quantum phenomena are simply "mysterious" and we cannot "explain the mystery in the sense of 'explaining' how it works." All a physicist can do is "*tell* you how it works" and leave matters at that. In some ways, as Feyman acknowledged, this was true of all of physics—even classical physics—because if we ask the basic question, "Why can we use mathematics to describe nature without a mechanism behind it?" there was only one possible answer: "No one knows," the same honest answer that Wigner had given.[66] It was simply an unexplained miracle.

In quantum mechanics, as Feynman exclaimed, "physics *has* given up on the problem of trying to predict exactly what will happen in a definite circumstance. Yes! Physics *has* given up. *We do not know.*" Feynman describes the "double-slit" thought experiment that has been widely used as a way to try to explain the mysterious—if not altogether bizarre—character of quantum mechanics to the wider public. If it were not so strange an idea, one might conclude that electrons are thinking agents with minds of their own. As Feynman put it, it was as if "an electron, before it starts, has already made up its mind" about the path it will take.[67] Astonishingly enough, however, in quantum mechanics the electron can change its mind in the middle of the experiment. If the two slits are both left open, the electrons behave in a way which humans could not in concept ever observe directly—for any electron, whether it had gone through one slit, through the other slit, or through both slits simultaneously, the physicist could never know by any form of measurement (the famous uncertainty principle). If the physicist did try to discover such matters through some experimental device for measurement, amazingly enough, quantum mechanics said that the electron would behave

66. Feynman, *Six Easy Pieces*, 117, 108.
67. Ibid., 135.

as though it had changed its behavior and now would be seen clearly to pass through only one of the two slits.

In quantum mechanics, it was thus as though electrons had secrets in their minds that they were determined not to reveal to human beings. Attempting to explain what otherwise seemed altogether mysterious in the movements of planets in the solar system, Kepler had once proposed that they were guided in their path by a calculating mind of their own but physicists had long since dismissed this as a remnant of a medieval mysticism that could be ignored in light of Kepler's other great contributions to the development of modern science. In the first quarter of the twentieth century, however, physicists discovered that both photons (of light) and electrons could—however contrary to ordinary common sense—behave either as a particle or as a wave. Indeed, they seemingly had a choice to make in their minds of which they would prefer it to be. It was, as one might say, as though electrons had "free will" and were determined not to give their freedom up (not give it up at the individual photon or electron level, even as their cumulative behavior was statistically entirely predictable in extremely large numbers). As Feynman characterized this strangeness, "*if the electrons are not seen*" by the physical experimenter, "*we have* [wave] *interference*" but if they are seen they change their behavior and act like ordinary particles. There was no choice for the physicists doing quantum mechanics but to "conclude that *when we look at the electrons* the distribution of them on the screen is different than when we do not look" at them.[68] However altogether seemingly incomprehensible, your or my very act of observation and measurement (or that of a physicist) changes the perceived outcome in the natural world at the level of the individual quantum particle.

Even more astonishingly, electrons would even change their minds after they had already passed through the slits but had not yet reached the backboard endpoint where they were to be recorded—if the physicist after the fact sought to "see" them at any point before they reached the final blackboard destination. Only after an observation had actually occurred could we can say that an event in nature "exists." As the Princeton physicist John Wheeler similarly explains, "in broader terms, we find that nature at the quantum level is not a machine that goes its inexorable way. Instead what answer we get depends on the question we put, the experiment we arrange, the registering device we choose. We are inescapably involved in bringing about that which appears to be happening."[69]

68. Ibid., 130, 129.

69. Wheeler, *At Home in the Universe*, 120.

This phenomenon, moreover, goes beyond the conduct of laboratory experiments involving small space and time intervals. Amazingly enough, it also applies at the cosmic level of the universe over potentially billions of years. As previously noted, a photon that began its journey through the universe billions of years ago does not assume its final physical characteristics—as we must necessarily perceive them in our consciousness—until we actually observe the photon today. As Niels Bohr explained, the observed "natural world" and the world of human consciousness have thus been blended together into one mysterious unity. Mind now takes clear precedence over matter; indeed there is no objective external thing such as "matter."

Quantum mechanics thus abolished the very distinction between the object in nature and the physicist as an independent observer of this object. The physicist Paul Langevin states that "the wave function it [quantum mechanics] uses to describe the object no longer depends solely on the object, as was the case in the classical representation [of physics], but, above all, states what the observer knows and what, in consequence, are his possibilities for predictions about the evolution of the object. For a given object, this [wave] function [of physics], consequently, is modified in accordance with the information possessed by the observer." In quantum mechanics, that is to say, one finds a situation where physics involves a "coupling of the system observed with the measurement device; and by the intervention of the observer, who becomes aware of the result of the measurement and thus determines the new wave function—following the observation—by using the new datum to reconstitute his datum bank."[70] In its weirdness, it surpasses most things in science fiction.

Hence, a full understanding of the workings of modern physics requires an "analysis of the act of observation itself"—a subject matter previously considered more appropriate to philosophy and psychology. When asked why this is the case, most working physicists such as Feynman understandably have been reluctant to enter into such unfamiliar territory, however limiting this is in terms of their full understanding of the foundations of their own discipline. The physicists Fritz London and Edmond Bauer write that most "physicists are to some extent sleepwalkers, who try to avoid such issues and are accustomed to concentrate on concrete problems" that have concrete solutions—as quantum mechanics has proved spectacularly successful in accomplishing, its mathematically precise statistical predictions for the total aggregate (rather than the individual) behavior of particles having been empirically confirmed a vast number of times over.[71]

70. Langevin, "Preface," 218.

71. London and Bauer, "The Theory of Observation in Quantum Mechanics," 218,

Quantum Theology

Feynman (to my knowledge) never reached what would have seemed an obvious conclusion to many theologians of the past. God is conceived by virtually all sophisticated theologians as some kind of (never to be fully understood) cosmic mind. In terms of the chemistry of their bodies, the workings of human beings simply blend in with the rest of the universe—there is nothing special in the application of the laws of nature to human bodies. What makes human beings altogether unique (at least in our solar system) is their highly developed capacity of mental perception, rational thought, and intense self-consciousness—in other words their possession of a thinking mind (one that is capable of conceiving of things such as a theology or a theory of quantum mechanics). It would seem that god and human beings have in common at least this one limited feature (human beings are made "in the image of God" in this respect), including the human ability to exercise free will, which depends on the possession of an independently thinking mind.

But then, to the astonishment of quantum physicists, it now appeared that god might have also given individual photons and electrons some of the qualities of a mind, including seemingly some elements of free will. A physicist could no more say precisely how an electron would behave than a psychologist or other "scientist" of human consciousness could say just what a human being would be thinking in the next moment (or in whatever time period). The individual electron or photon did not actually exist as a "material" thing; it was more closely analogous to an individual "thought" in human consciousness, if subject to a much different set of statistical laws of quantum "psychology." Presumably, god knew what the electron would do (or what the human being would think), but maybe not—in the human case this question was a matter for deep theological speculation relating to the actual full degree of god's omnipotence and omniscience in the world and how this might affect the possibility of the actual existence of human free will.

We are back to Plato, the observed "material" world now consisting of a set of extremely powerful mathematical statistical regularities—themselves existing for reasons falling altogether outside the grasp of physics. The human observations of this lower "material" world, moreover, exist themselves only in the mental world of human consciousness. The quantum universe at its most fundamental level thus becomes a world entirely of mind, not of matter. As discussed in Chapter 2, the very idea of "matter" is merely a convenient heuristic that facilitates human thinking in daily

---

219, 218–19.

life about some particular aspects of the workings of the universal cosmic mind—a universe in which human consciousness is itself a part. Not only in quantum mechanics but in Einstein's theory of relativity, physics becomes, as one might say, a special branch of "psychology" that studies the impact of one part of "mind" on perceptions in other parts of "mind." This special branch of psychology—conventionally labeled as "physics"—has the unique property within human consciousness that it can establish perfect correlations among the workings of certain "scientific" parts of consciousness that are explored by physicists. Why the perfect correlations exist in human consciousness—as Wigner, Feynman, and other physicists had to acknowledge—is a total mystery. Indeed, it is perhaps of a similar degree of mystery as the existence of a god and the ability of this god to exercise divine powers over the world in which we—seemingly—live.

It then followed that, to the extent that the contemporary religion of scientific materialism (naturalism) depends on the existence of any such "real" thing as matter, the motions of which are governed by scientific laws of an actual physical world, scientific materialism in the wake of relativity and quantum mechanics becomes a relic of the past. In terms of the materialist thinking of naturalism, quantum mechanics is "supernatural" and "superhuman"—its world is a place of constantly recurring "miracles." The most plausible explanation for it all would seem to be that human beings can somehow participate in the thinking of a god, however surprising this seems to be, and even as the full workings of this god's mind will always ultimately remain mysterious, and the real final essence of god will remain altogether unknown to human comprehension—conclusions that would have sounded familiar to Newton and many other leading scientists of the seventeenth century. Quantum mechanics seemed magical by the classical materialist standards of nineteenth-century physics but is more readily comprehensible in theological and philosophical terms dating as far back as to Plato.

Feynman on Religion

It is not surprising, of course, that Feynman did not offer such a "theological" description of quantum phenomena. Feynman or any other physicist who made any such suggestions would probably soon have been relegated to the margins of professional life. In 1963, however, Feynman was asked to give the John Danz Lecture series at the University of Washington in Seattle. The purpose was not to give a popular exposition of physics but to offer his thoughts—Feynman by then widely recognized as among the greatest physicists of his generation with an unusual breadth of view even extending to broader matters—on questions of the human situation in the world. These lectures were never published in Feynman's lifetime but appeared in 1998, ten years after his death, as *The Meaning of It All*.[72]

As Feynman acknowledged, the study of nature for him was still as much a religious experience as it had been for Newton, Einstein, and many other earlier physicists. Admittedly, Feynman did not use the word *religion* even as he talking about it (his knowledge of formal religion was in fact quite limited). Rather, he talked of doing physics "for the excitement of what is found out. Perhaps most of you know this. But to those of you who do not know it, it is almost impossible for me to convey in a lecture this important aspect, this exciting part, the real reason for science." Physics for someone like Feynman was "the great adventure of our time" that is a "wild and exciting thing."[73]

In making plain his own state of joyous excitement in doing physics, Feynman was in fact describing something that would come closest to a form of religious ecstasy, establishing a line of communication with the mind of god. On one occasion in *The Meaning of it All*, Feynman came close to acknowledging this explicitly. He was describing the deep sense of "awe and mystery" that comes to a physicist who is engaged in "the great adventure to contemplate the universe." When new successes were achieved by a physicist, it enabled a person "to view life as part of this universal mystery of greatest depth, . . . to sense an experience which is very rare, and very exciting. It usually ends in laughter and delight." Feynman then, rarely for him, explicitly acknowledged that "some will tell me that I have just described a religious experience. Very well, you may call it what you will." But Feynman himself preferred some other term than *religion* (he did not say what term). The problem with the term *religion* was that it raised the specter of organized religion and the official doctrinal formulations of the institutional churches. Feynman considered that the standard messages he found in institutional religion were for him simply "inadequate to describe, to encompass that kind of [ecstatic] experience" of doing physics at its highest levels.[74]

Feynman's feelings about the act of doing science, as he himself recognized, are not themselves "scientific." He acknowledged that the scientific method "imposes a severe limitation to the kinds of questions that can be answered" by scientists. Science had been enormously successful in answering questions like "If I do this, what will happen?" But Feynman considered that science had nothing to say—as science—about "questions like, 'Should I do

72. Feynman, *The Meaning of It All*.

73. Ibid., 9.

74. Ibid., 39, 39–40.

this?' and 'What is the value of this'" that are simply "not of the same kind."[75] Or, as one might add, science has little to say about the question of a god.

Feynman did acknowledge at one point that in his experience "most scientists do not believe" in God. But he considers that this is not a conclusion they have reached by a scientific route because "science cannot disprove the existence of God." He finds that in any case the question of God's existence is one of probabilities—as Feynman says, "is it 50-50 or is it 97 percent?" Many atheistic naturalists assert that all important human values can be derived from science itself. Feynman, however, bluntly rejects this idea—it is a false scientism to suggest that correct human values can be determined by any form of exercise of the scientific method. As he says at one point in Lecture 2, "science makes, indeed, an impact on many ideas associated with religion, but I do not believe it affects, in any very strong way, the moral conduct and ethical views" of scientists (or any others). Hence, "I believe . . . it is impossible to decide moral questions by the scientific technique, and that the two things are independent."[76] A scientific materialist who believes that all important things must be decided by science is thus either an amoral being or, more likely, he or she is deceiving his or her self in claiming to rely only on science even in personal matters of their own human morality. It would seem that there are large numbers of religious "implicit believers" in a god who deny the reality of this god within their own consciousness, thus even to themselves. Theologically, the modern age has engaged in self-deception on a scale perhaps unprecedented in human history.

Feynman, however, is more honest than most of his peers. He has no doubts as to the strength of his own convictions in matters of human values, including the sense of religious ecstasy in doing physics. But since science cannot be the source of his (or others) feelings and beliefs in such matters, where do they come from? He confesses that, much as he had also said of the reasons for the seemingly magical behavior of quantum particles, "I have no idea of the answer." A god would be one possibility but Feynman is not comfortable with that suggestion. Feynman sums up his own state of moral—and as it also extends to scientific matters in twentieth-century physics—bewilderment as follows:

> Western civilization, it seems to me, stands by two great heritages. One is the scientific spirit of adventure—the adventure into the unknown, an unknown that must be recognized as

75. Ibid., 16.
76. Ibid., 35, 36, 37, 41, 46.

unknown in order to be explored, . . . the attitude that all is uncertain. To summarize it: humility of the intellect.

The other great heritage is Christian ethics—the basis of
action on love, the brotherhood of men, the value of the individual, the humility of the spirit. These two heritages are logically, thoroughly consistent. But logic is not all. One needs one's
heart to follow an idea. If people are going back to religion, what
are they going back to? Is the modern church a place to give
comfort to a man who doubts God? More, one who disbelieves
in God? Is the modern church the place to give comfort and encouragement to the value of such doubts? . . . How can we draw
inspiration to support these two pillars of Western civilization
so that they may stand together in full vigor, mutually unafraid?
That, I don't know. But that, I think, is the best I can do on the
relationship of science and religion, the religion which has been
in the past and still is, therefore, a source of moral code as well
as inspiration to follow that code.[77]

Back to Plato in Twenty-First-Century Mathematics

At the age of twenty-one, a Russian mathematical prodigy, Edward Frenkel,
still short of having earned his undergraduate degree in Moscow, was invited in 1989 to be a visiting professor of mathematics at Harvard University.
Very much impressed with his abilities, Harvard invited Frenkel to remain
at Harvard, and he obtained a PhD in mathematics there in one year, and
then joined the Harvard faculty. He moved to the University of California
at Berkeley in 1997 where he today ranks among the leading mathematicians in the world. Like Feynman and some other great physicists of the second half of the twentieth century, Frenkel's interests extend beyond doing
mathematics alone to encompass as well the culture of mathematics and the
place of mathematical reasoning in the universe. This motivated him to col-
laborate in the creation of a movie about mathematics intended for popular
audiences and then to write a 2013 book, *Love & Math: The Heart of Hidden
Reality*.[78] In this book, he further reaffirms in language directed to wider
contemporary audiences the understanding of mathematics developed thus
far in this chapter.

As the title suggests, a main theme of the book is that mathematics
reveals a "hidden" world that is inaccessible to ordinary human observation

---

77. Ibid., 47–48.
78. Frenkel, *Love & Math*.

through the senses. He describes the work of mathematicians as a process of discovery and communication to others of the contents of this hidden world. It is not a physical world, however, but a world of ideas—the equations, geometries, algebras, topologies, and other symbolic constructions that mathematicians work with. As Frenkel explicitly states at many places in the book, mathematicians do not create this world on their own. Rather, it already exists for mathematicians to discover and explore. Within the community of the minds of the mathematicians of the world, as with other human efforts of exploration, there are strict rules and standards for the collective confirmation and acceptance of the full truthfulness of discoveries made, as Frenkel describes them, of the beautiful "continents," "mountains," and other features of the "parallel universe" of the mathematical world.[79]

Following others, Frenkel clearly and explicitly recognizes that this view of the universe can be traced back to Plato—that the Platonic mathematical world exists altogether "independent of physical reality." One of the most important mathematical findings of the nineteenth century, for example, "Galois groups were discovered by the French prodigy [in the 1830s], not *invented* by him. Until he did so, this concept lived somewhere in the enchanted gardens of the ideal world of mathematics, waiting to be found" by some human being. If it had not been Galois, it would have been someone else later who would have made the same discovery because a mathematical truth is an objective fact, even as it has no physical reality. As Frenkel affirms, "mathematical entities are independent of our rational faculties" as human beings and thus "mathematical truths are inevitable." The objective truth that two plus two equals four precedes any human existence and will be true for eternity, whatever happens to human beings.[80]

Frenkel is confident that in thinking this way he has a great deal of company among contemporary mathematicians and physicists. Indeed, he finds that "most math practitioners believe that mathematical formulas and ideas inhabit a separate world." He notes that "Kurt Godel, whose work . . . revolutionized mathematical logic, was an unabashed proponent of this view. He wrote that mathematical concepts 'form an objective reality of their own, which we cannot create or change, but only perceive and describe.'" In the nineteenth century, as Frenkel observes, the physicist "Heinrich Hertz, who proved the existence of magnetic waves, . . . expressed his awe this way: One cannot escape the feeling that these mathematical formulas have an independent existence and intelligence of their own, that they are wiser than

---

79. Ibid., 81, 124, 131.
80. Ibid., 234, 235, 234.

we are, wiser than their discoverers."[81] They are, as such language suggests, similar to if not identical to a god.

The contemporary mathematicians Philip Davis and Reuben Hersh thus write that "like mathematics, religions express relationships between man and the universe. . . . Insofar as mathematics pursues ideal knowledge and studies the relationship between this ideal and the world as we find it, it has something in common with religion." Furthermore, to the extent that "the objects of mathematics are conceptual objects whose reality lies in the common consciousness of human minds, . . . these shared mathematical concepts may [be said to] constitute the dogma of mathematical belief."[82]

As Frenkel explains, one reason we can know that mathematics is not simply created as a humanly devised means of describing some feature of physical existence is that there are many "examples of rich mathematical theories that are not linked to any kind of physical reality." For example, most of "the gauge theories associated with the Lie groups . . . are perfectly sound mathematically but there are no known connections between them and the real world." Frenkel writes that "the fact that such objective and enduring [mathematical] knowledge exists at all (and, moreover, belongs to all of us) is nothing short of a miracle"—literally. Frenkel says of one of his own mathematical discoveries of a previously unsuspected relationship that "the existence of a link between the two was nearly miraculous." It remains a great mystery of human existence in that "we still don't fully understand what is and what drives mathematical discovery. But it is clear that this hidden reality" of the world of mathematics "is bound to play a larger and larger role in our lives." To be a mathematician today is to be a wanderer in "the magical world of modern math."[83]

By way of illustration, Frenkel comments that "the discovery of quarks" in the 1960s "is a good example of the paramount role played by mathematics in science." Quarks "were predicted not on the basis of physical data, but on the basis of mathematical symmetry patterns." Physicists then made an educated guess that certain physical phenomena would later be found to correspond to these mathematical patterns. It turned out in this case, as in many other great scientific discoveries, to be true. As Frenkel explains, "this was a purely theoretical prediction, made within the framework of a sophisticated mathematical theory of representation of the group SU(3)." In developing the physics of quarks, "a seemingly esoteric mathematical theory empowered us to get to the heart of the building blocks of nature."

81. Ibid., 233, 234, 233.
82. Davis and Hersh, *The Mathematical Experience*, 109.
83. Frenkel, *Love & Math*, 235, 181, 23, 69.

As Frenkel puts it, "How can we not be enthralled by the magic harmony of these tiny blobs of matter, not marvel at the capacity of mathematics to reveal the inner workings of the universe?"[84] Truth be told, there is no other way to see it other than as the manifestation of something supernatural.

As Wigner pointed out and Frenkel now again affirms, there are thus two miracles to be confronted, first the magical existence of a world of mathematical truths independent of human existence and physical reality, and second the magical correspondence of at least some of these mathematical truths to the "physical" workings of the natural world (as we perceive them in human consciousness). No one has any scientific explanation for any of this. As Frenkel comments about the total mystery, although physicists and other "scientists have been exploiting this 'effectiveness' [of mathematics] for centuries, its roots are still poorly understood"—indeed, are not really understood at all, as Frenkel would likely concede, if pressed on the matter.[85] As Cheng Ning Yang, a Nobel Prize winner in physics, puts it, "What could be more mysterious, what could be more awe-inspiring, than to find that the structure of the physical world is intimately tied to the deep mathematical concepts, concepts which were developed out of considerations rooted only in logic and the beauty of form?"[86]

Frenkel thus subscribes to the three-world view of the physicist Roger Penrose described above.[87] There are three separate universes of the "physical world," "human consciousness" and yet another distinct third world of "mathematics." The workings of the physical world are governed by the truths of the mathematical world, the world of human consciousness requires the existence of a physical brain, and human consciousness has the rational capacity to discover the nonphysical contents of the mathematical world. Frenkel is no less mystified than Penrose as to how this all came about. As Frenkel writes,

> In my view, it is the objectivity of mathematical knowledge that is the source of its limitless possibilities. This quality distinguishes mathematics from any other type of human endeavor. I believe that understanding what is behind this quality will shed light on the deepest mysteries of physical reality, consciousness and interrelations between them. In other words, the closer we

84. Ibid., 26, 26–27, 27.
85. Ibid., 202.
86. Cheng Nin Yang, quoted in ibid., 201
87. Ibid., 234–35.

are to the Platonic world of math, the more power we will have
to understand the world around us and our place in it.[88]

There is no explicit mention of a god or explicit discussion of theology in
Love & Math. But the book is nevertheless an important work of theology
for our time. Contemporary naturalists take for granted that matter must
be fundamental, since physical science—for them the one all-powerful
method of understanding the world—is all about explaining the workings
of the material world. Frenkel is not the first to do so but he offers a strong
up-to-date statement from a world-class contemporary mathematician that
mathematics is more fundamental than matter. This is all based on a rational analysis as he develops it, employing the skills in reasoning that are
found at the highest levels among mathematicians. Indeed, while Frenkel
may not realize it himself, he is laying out a rational argument for the very
probable existence of a god.

Is Mathematics All There Is?

As noted above in the Introduction, Max Tegmark is a prominent contemporary cosmologist and MIT professor of physics who has written even
more recently about related matters of large theological significance. In
2014, he published *Our Mathematical Universe: My Quest for the Ultimate
Nature of Reality*, explaining that "I'm a physicist, and I'm taking a physics
approach to the mysteries of reality." For him, much like Feynman, physics
can be a "religious experience" that "helps us to see more clearly, adding to
the beauty and wonder of the world around us."[89]

Like Frenkel, Tegmark is also a Platonist, writing that "Plato was right;
modern physics has made abundantly clear that the ultimate nature of reality isn't what it seems." Tegmark also agrees with the many mathematicians
and physicists who believe that the mathematical world has an objective
reality outside any physical domain of time and space. As he puts it, "we
don't invent mathematical structures—we discover them, and invent only
the notation for describing them."[90] They simply exist in a realm of abstract
ideas, and have always existed there. Mathematicians (or physicists doing
mathematics) can visit this realm through their own heroic rational efforts
within human consciousness. The role of physicists is then to search for
exact correlations between such mathematical ideas and the behavior of the

88. Ibid., 235.
89. Tegmark, *Our Mathematical Universe*, 9, 11.
90. Ibid., 8, 259.

physical world—again as it is necessarily perceived in their consciousness. In this manner physicists establish what we know as the "mathematical laws of the universe." Seemingly in a miraculous fashion, even though all this necessarily takes place within the consciousness of each individual physicist, in practice the community of all the physicists of the world can often reach a consensus, establishing a worldwide common agreement on these laws—something altogether impossible outside the physical sciences. It is yet another piece of evidence that a supernatural god must lie somewhere behind all this—what else could be the explanation?

Tegmark departs from most of his professional physics colleagues, however, in that in his book he now goes so far as to advance "a crazy-sounding belief of mine that our physical world not only is *described* by mathematics, but that it *is* mathematics, making us self-aware parts of a giant mathematical" universe. Most people think that "there exists an external physical reality completely independent of us humans." But the practice of physics not only involves the use of "mathematical equations" but also of humanly created "'baggage'—words that explain how the equations are connected to what we observe and intuitively understand." For example, "if you solve the Schrodinger equation for five or fewer quarks, it turns out that there are only two fairly stable quarks and a down quark or a clump of two down quarks and an up quark, and we humans have added the baggage of calling these two types of clumps 'protons' and 'neutrons' for convenience."[91] But the so-called "proton" and "neutron" has no fundamentally deeper reality beyond the mathematical equations that predict the behavior of "quarks," themselves consisting of only yet another set of mathematically expressed relationships.

At the deepest level of understanding of reality (the goal of Tegmark's inquiry), therefore, with respect to the physical world there is seemingly nothing but the mathematics itself, plus the human "baggage" of words— the "poetry" of physics—that are added by physicists to aid heuristically in their own thinking and in communicating their results to others. But if we want to discover the deepest reality that transcends any human linguistic additions, it will be necessary to limit our claims to an understanding of the mathematics itself. Hence, as Tegmark concludes, if we are to seek a physical reality that is independent of any human influence, it follows that such an "external reality is a mathematical structure." In other words, "something that has a complete baggage-free description" outside human language "is precisely a mathematical structure" in and of itself alone.[92] Since the mathematical world and its rational truths have always existed, even be-

91. Ibid., 6, 254, 255, 256.
92. Ibid., 260

fore the arrival of human beings on earth, the mathematics itself becomes
the ultimate bedrock of the reality of the universe. Tegmark, like Wigner,
Penrose, and other physicists today, admittedly has no way of explaining
why our perceptions of a "physical" world in our human consciousness (as
often aided by measuring devices) have turned out to correlate so exactly
with one or another eternal mathematical truth that human beings have
rationally discovered and explored. It may be all part of the giant mystery of
the universe that seemingly only a god could reveal.

Once the clear mathematical light of physics has shone in our modern
cave in which we have lived so long in illusion, it is surprisingly logical to
accept Tegmarks's "Mathematical Universe Hypothesis" that a "mathematical structure *is* our external physical reality" itself. In the universe that we
happen to inhabit, "the equivalence between physical and mathematical
existence means that if a mathematical structure contains a self-aware sub-
structure" such as a human consciousness, "it will perceive itself as existing
in a physically real universe, just as you and I do," even when all is ultimately mathematics.[93] The mathematics, however, cannot by itself explain
the self-awareness. Indeed, the whole world of human affairs has proven
stubbornly resistant to the great number of modern attempts to explain it
mathematically. God apparently thinks one way about the physical world
and another way about human thoughts and actions. In this sense, Tegmark
would seem to be only partially correct; the physical world may well reduce
to mathematics alone as the fundamental reality but it is another matter for
the human world—although a true-believing scientific materialist, devoutly
convinced that in the end all is physics, might then logically conclude that
the totality of human existence is ultimately mathematics. As with Frenkel's
discussion of mathematical truth, the discussion of a leading contemporary
physicist has moved from the realm of physics and natural science to the
realm of religion—and a religion of a remarkably Platonic kind.

In his book, Tegmark at times admittedly seems to back off his mathematical monotheism, claiming somewhat confusingly to believe that we can
understand both "physical reality" and "mathematical reality" as separate
things, even though the main theme of the book is that mathematics is the
fundamental reality. He does agree that the nonphysical workings of human
consciousness remain well outside our physical scientific understanding at
present (for further discussion of the mystery of human consciousness, see
Chapter 5). Tegmark describes human consciousness as yet another "internal reality" (besides the physical and mathematical realities) that consists
of "the way you subjectively perceive the external reality from the internal

---

93. Ibid., 322–23, 323.

vantage point of your mind." This third internal reality of human conscious-ness—Tegmark acknowledges some similarities to the three-world views of fellow physicist Roger Penrose—"exists only internally to you; your mind feels as though it's looking at the outside world, while its only looking at a reality model inside your head." Tegmark acknowledges that he once be-lieved that "we also need to understand consciousness before we can fully understand physics," thus defeating his hopes at that time to find the "ulti-mate reality" of the natural world, since we have at present little if any scien-tific understanding of the internal human reality of consciousness and the prospects for large scientific advances there are dim, even in the long run.[94]

Although his argument becomes vague at this point, Tegmark con-tends that he has solved the problem by introducing a fourth "consensus reality" consisting of "the *shared description* in terms of familiar concepts from classical physics" and upon which we human beings "on Earth all agree on" (seeming to beg the question of how we know what other self-aware observers are actually perceiving in their own consciousness). In any case, he now argues that "although understanding of the detailed nature of human consciousness is a fascinating challenge in its own right" (and is likely to remain so for a long time), "it's *not* necessary for a fundamental theory of physics, which need 'only' derive the consensus reality from its [mathematical] equations."[95]

In short, the "ultimate meaning" of the universe for which Tegmark is searching "splits cleanly into two parts that can be tackled separately, the challenge for physics is deriving the consensus reality from the external re-ality [i.e., discovering the mathematical laws of nature], and the challenge for cognitive science is to derive the internal reality from the consensus reality." As Tegmark thinks, "these are two great challenges for the third millennium."[96] There is another possibility, however; perhaps there is only one fundamental reality that is the mind of a god that exists outside physical nature, and who shares elements of his intelligence not only with math-ematicians and physicists but with all other human beings. It increasingly appears in the early twenty-first century that the ultimate foundation of the universe may be a giant supernatural consciousness, historically often called the "mind of god." The study of workings of the universe will then be as much the responsibility of the theologians of the world as of its physicists and other natural scientists.

94. Ibid., 243, 235, 234.
95. Ibid., 238, 239.
96. Ibid., 239.

The newly startling character of our current human circumstance was well summarized in 2011 by the leading contemporary philosopher Colin McGinn:

> Our concepts [of reality] are really quite inadequate to express what is really going on out there. Our concept of motion, in particular, is very difficult to make sense of, and the very possibility of motion-as-we-conceive-it can be cast into serious doubt (Zeno lives!). The relation between space and matter is highly contentious. Matter itself is vanishingly elusive. Electric charge [as described by Maxwell] is utterly mysterious. Gravity [as described by Newton] baffles. The mathematics is as regular as clockwork, but the reality to which it applies defies our best efforts at comprehension. It is not that we see reality as through a glass darkly; we don't see it at all, but we do have a marvelously precise mirage that can take its place. Physics does not give us a dim or distorted view of reality; it gives us a perfectly clear view of reality under a mathematical description—but only that. The "ontological commitments" of physics are obscure, because we have so slight a grip on the real nature of what we postulate. And even when we think we know what we are talking about (as with space, matter, and motion) deep conceptual problems confront us.[97]

Conclusion

In *The God Delusion*, Richard Dawkins's stated criterion for accepting "the God hypothesis" is to show that "there exists a superhuman, supernatural intelligence who deliberately designed and created the universe and everything in it, including us."[98] One such possibility would be to show that there exists a Platonic world of mathematical truths outside any physical existence that govern the full workings of the material universe, as Plato long ago said was true. As this chapter has examined, and as many—probably most—mathematicians and physicists themselves believe today, the world of mathematics is "supernatural" in that it already exists outside nature, prior to and outside of any material realities in the natural world (indeed, "matter" itself has become a problematic concept for twentieth-century physics). Moreover, this supernatural mathematical order somehow—and of this we still have no clue as to how it works—serves to govern the full

97. McGinn, *Basic Structures of Reality*, 6.
98. Dawkins, *The God Delusion*, 52.

detailed workings of the entire "physical world" as we perceive it in our consciousness (another domain outside physical reality).

Mathematics also meets the criterion of "superhuman" in that, for example, mathematicians in their discoveries up to now have only touched the tip of the iceberg of all mathematical truths and even future mathematicians may never fully comprehend all of them—and in any case the laws of nature arose in their mathematical forms billions of years before the recent period of human mathematical discovery, and thus mathematical truths must have long preceded the arrival of human beings on earth in that they were then governing the workings of the universe. A governing mathematical intelligence is thus a supernatural, superhuman entity that meets Dawkins's criterion for the existence of a god. If we then choose to define a god as such a supernatural entity having a fully developed mathematical intelligence, we can then say that at least one god very probably exists, a god of mathematical truth that rules the physical world.

4

Darwinism as Secular Fundamentalism

I SHOULD EMPHASIZE AT the outset that I am not questioning in this book that natural biological evolution has occurred over about four billion years; I agree fully, its reality cannot be reasonably disputed (assuming one has faith, as I do, in the long run workings of the world scientific community). I also agree fully that there is an immense fossil record, much of it deposited hundreds of millions of years ago, that must be regarded as a factual history of a main part of life on earth. But neither of these areas of agreement comes close to being the essence of Darwinism. Indeed, the former is largely established using the methods of physics, and the latter is the product of paleontological investigations that have scoured the earth since the eighteenth century to uncover the fossil remains of immense numbers of extinct plant and animal creatures.

Darwinism—as further revised by neo-Darwinist evolutionary biologists over the past 100 years— is rather a specific theory of history, in this case a biological history of life on earth that we know leads eventually to the presence of human beings today. As such, it must be judged by the methods of history; the methods of the physical sciences, including the development of scientific hypotheses and their empirical confirmation or rejection, do not apply. Isaac Newton was one of the greatest mathematicians of his time who used mathematics to explain exactly the motions of the planets in the solar system and other features of the natural world. Darwin, by contrast, acknowledged that he had little facility in mathematics and made little or no use of it in *The Origin of Species*. His method of research, the method of history, is careful observation and classification, combined with great intellectual curiosity and the application of a high analytical intelligence. To say that "evolution exists" is to say very little, not much more informative than to say that "history exists"—a virtual truism.

The American philosopher Jerry Fodor and his coauthor, University of Arizona professor of cognitive science Massimo Piatteli-Palmarini (both self-declared atheists) thus conclude that "there is an important sense in which there . . . can be no general [scientific] theory of evolution. Rather, the story about the evolution of phenotypes"—the observable physical features of an organism and their workings—"belongs not to biology but to natural history; and history, natural or otherwise, is par excellence the locus of explanations that do not conform to the Newtonian paradigm."[1] Given the great limitations of our factual knowledge of the biological history of the earth, a precise final verdict on the specifics of any theory about the long-run workings of biological evolution may therefore never be more authoritative than obtaining answers to such human historical questions as, for example, how we can explain the rapid rise of the Roman Empire to dominate the Mediterranean world in such a short time, or how did the final settlement of World War I play a large causal role in the rise of Nazi Germany in the 1930s. Much of great insight and interest can be said about such matters but it is far from resulting from the application of the scientific method. In itself, to say that natural selection drives evolution is not much more scientifically illuminating than to say that human warfare has played a large role in recorded human history.

While it is usually impossible to conduct direct scientific experiments in studying biological history, evolutionary theories are, of course, subject to other forms of scientific testing. Darwinism passed some of these tests with flying colors such as the scientific demonstration of the much older age of the earth (necessary for so much evolution to have plausibly occurred) than was once believed. Over the years, large numbers of plant and animal fossils have been found, recorded and scientifically dated, often demonstrating that they are many millions of years old, and that they display patterns of evolutionary change over very long periods of time. In the past few decades, genomic analysis has added a large new scientific dimension to the study of the workings of evolution, making possible whole new areas of insight. A large part of the evolutionary history of the earth is nevertheless shrouded in mystery and will remain forever unknowable in any real historical detail to us. As commonly related by evolutionary biologists, much of the evolutionary explanation of the biological history of the earth thus far have amounted to a series of educated guesses.

The ultimate goal for evolutionary theory revolves around achieving a more precise theory of the exact mechanisms by which evolutionary processes have formed the biological world, as Newton did for the role of

---

1. Fodor and Piattelli-Palmarini, *What Darwin Got Wrong*, xxii.

gravity in the solar system. We are still awaiting, however, a Newton of evolution, and cannot even be very confident that such a person will ever emerge. And then, even if evolutionary biologists do succeed in achieving a much better scientific understanding of the evolutionary workings of the biological world over billions of years, this knowledge might have few of the immense direct practical consequences that have resulted from the discoveries in physics about the workings of the physical world, enabling human beings to assert an altogether unprecedented mastery of physical forces and to control major elements of their material environment on earth. (The one area where some momentous consequences might admittedly arise from a better theoretical understanding of biological evolution is the spread of microorganisms and the combating of disease and improving human health more generally.) In other words, Newtonian science can be the source of humanly created events that can only be seen as miracles, but there are no such analogous human miracles to be found in the knowledge produced by Darwinist evolutionary theory, other than perhaps the very existence of biological history itself.

Darwinism as Religion

As we can be sure, however, evolutionary biology has already had and will continue to have an immense impact on our understanding of fundamental human questions, such as the origins and meaning of human existence on earth. That is to say, in asserting a new authoritative biological history of life on earth from the very beginning, the study of evolution has worked to change our basic self-concept. As Florida State University philosopher Michael Ruse puts it, "The Darwinian Revolution destroyed forever the old picture of humans as somehow miraculously special, symbolically and literally as touched by magic."[2] When evolutionary biology claims to explain the human condition in some of its most fundamental aspects, it is thus entering into the realm of religion.[3]

In his magisterial 2011 book on *Religion in Human Evolution*, the product of thirteen years of study and writing, the distinguished American sociologist Robert Bellah describes the British philosopher Mary Midgley's book on *Evolution as Religion* as "the best such analysis of its kind." Midgley shows how "there are two [contrasting] ways in which evolutionary theory becomes religious," one way resulting in a "cosmic optimism" about the progress of the human species, and the other in a "cosmic pessimism,"

2. Ruse, "The Darwinian Revolution," 290.
3. Dawkins, *The Blind Watchmaker*.

according to the specific evolutionary portrayal.[4] As Midgley herself writes, many Darwinist true believers are "evolution-worshippers." She asks, "Is there any deity involved, any supernatural creative being? Officially no, but something called Life seems to be filling that role."[5] Darwinist true believers often behave like and exhibit as great a certainty of the truth of the Darwinist gospel as many fundamentalist true believers of more traditional religions have exhibited with respect to the certain truths of the world of these faiths.

The fact that evolutionary biology is actually a story of the history of life on earth is especially important for Western and Middle Eastern civilization. In the Abrahamic tradition, from the Jews, to Christianity, to Islam, the Bible and other foundational documents present themselves as a true account of history. In challenging such traditional fundamental truth claims, and substituting its own new claims about the truth of the history of the world, Darwinism offered a direct religious alternative and competitor to the Abrahamic religions. These religions have often made peace with Darwinism but in the process have had to abandon some of their long-standing basic tenets of belief. This is of course why the disagreements that have surrounded the history of Darwinism over the past 150 years have often resembled a holy war. Much more is at stake than the accuracy of a specific biological theory of the history of life on earth.

Darwinism, moreover, was not as much a beginning as a culmination. It was already a shock to Christianity when incontrovertible evidence at odds with the usual Christian account of "the Creation" (including the supposed 6,000 year existence of the earth) began accumulating in the mid to late eighteenth century, including the discovery of ancient fossil remains altogether outside previous human experience, and also the growing awareness of the geological formation of the earth over many millions of years. In the nineteenth century, Darwinism then went beyond such developments in that it posited a seemingly credible theoretical mechanism, natural selection, by which the full biological history of the earth could have been explained by material causes alone—without invoking any traditional divine agency. In its radical impacts on the world, Darwinism is perhaps best compared to the shock of the Copernican explanation that the earth revolves around the sun, and more recently that the sun is only one among many billions of similar stars in billions of galaxies in the universe—discoveries of deep religious significance as well as forms of scientific knowledge. As a newly authoritative historical account of the history of the world, Darwinism in this sense offers a core entry—a new set of "books"—of a new "bible" of

4. Bellah, *Religion in Human Evolution*, 48.
5. Midgley, *Evolution as a Religion*, 70, 71.

life on earth, again beginning with a Creation of the earth (now having occurred more than four billion years ago, and of the universe itself, thirteen
billion years ago). It culminates in a final set of books, a "new testament,"
dealing with the relatively very short and recent history of human life on
earth. As the authorities in the history of the universe and of life on earth,
physicists and evolutionary biologists assume the role of new authoritative
prophets and apostles of religious truth. As this chapter will suggest, however, the truthfulness of some of the "books" of Darwinist evolutionary history are not much more certain than the messages of the books of the Jewish
and Christian Bible.

When a desire for historical truth is extended into the modern recent
history of politics, economics, philosophy, and other areas of society, other
newly authoritative priesthoods are composed of archeologists, historians,
and social scientists. The leading such modern figures have typically continued to invoke material causes and forms of natural selection within human
history in "explaining" this history—the supernatural is ruled out by assumption. In writing his economic history and issuing his prophesies, Karl
Marx saw his theories as a direct extension of Darwinist thinking, the "class
struggle" becoming the particular form of natural selection that could explain everything in human history, offering a theory of a newly omnipotent
set of forces in economic history that took the place of the biblical God. The
great theologian Paul Tillich declared that, as a matter of objective historical influence, if not of the accuracy of his economic predictions, Marx was
"the most successful of all theologians since the Reformation" of Luther and
Calvin.[6] Marxism offered a newly revised story of an original happy and
natural harmony in the world; a terrible fall into sin and depravity (owing to the rise of economic surplus and resulting human alienation—the
Marxist reinterpretation of original sin); a future moment of the apocalypse;
and the coming of a new heaven to earth, again the culminating event in
human history. A leading contemporary philosopher, Alasdair MacIntyre,
thus declares that, as a story of all history, "Marxism shares in good measure both the content and the functions of Christianity as an interpretation
of human existence, and it does so because it is the historical successor of
Christianity."[7] (Admittedly, this last assessment, offered in 1984, might have
to be revised somewhat in light of subsequent events.)

The story of the arrival of the millennium, as newly told by Marx in
"secular" terms, admittedly drew on elements already found in Darwin's
own writings. The British cultural historian Paul Johnson observes that

6. Tillich, *A History of Christian Thought*, 476.
7. MacIntyre, *Marxism and Christianity*, 6.

"the actual [full] title of *Origin* [*of Species*], it has been pointed out, uses words like *selection*, *struggle*, *favored*, and *preservation*, which imply a mind or force or something more conscious than blind nature at work. *Origin* and *Descent* [*of Man*] are dotted with words and phrases that imply design, purpose, or creative intelligence," actively working for the progress of the world, if no longer to be understood as the active creative intelligence of the Christian God of old.[8] But it would seem that even for Darwin there may have been a god—suitably defined—at work in biological evolution, culminating in the miracle of a godlike human species.

The Inquisitors versus Evolutionary Heresy

Like other priesthoods who often simplified their messages for the ordinary faithful, evolutionary biologists have been reluctant to acknowledge directly and explicitly to the wider public the significant scientific uncertainties of the traditional Darwinist theory of life on earth. Aside from matters of professional pride, they fear that any confessions of doubt will be used to give credence to Christian creationists, many of whom continue to contest vigorously even the very fact of the fossil record as a reliable account of the earth's long biological history. There was at least one leading evolutionary biologist, however, willing to take greater risks—as is in fact necessary for the long-run advance of even a theory of history. Until he died in 2002 (at the young age of 60), Stephen Jay Gould was for many years a distinguished professor of evolutionary biology at Harvard University. Among his many awards and honors, Gould became a member of the National Academy of Sciences in 1989.

With Niles Eldredge, Gould in 1972 raised large issues concerning the scientific validity of past and existing Darwinist theory, as summarized in Gould's last—posthumously—published book in 2007 summarizing his theory of "punctuated equilibrium."[9] As he explained there, well before the 1970s it had been well known among working paleontologists (professional students of the fossil record) that the standard Darwinist theory of natural selection was in significant conflict with the available empirical observations of the fossil record. Gould was knowledgeable about this partly because he was an important contributor himself to paleontological literature.

As he noted, one ground-level paleontologist had written in 1968 that "during my work as an oil paleontologist, I had the opportunity to study sections meeting these rigid requirements [of continuous sedimentation

8. Johnson, *Darwin*, 130.
9. Gould, *Punctuated Equilibrium*.

and sufficient span of time]. As an ardent student of evolution, moreover, I was continually on the watch for evidence of evolutionary change. . . . The great majority of species do not show any appreciable evolutionary change at all. These species appear in the section (first occurrence) without obvious ancestors in underlying beds, are stable once established, and disappear higher up without leaving any descendants"—all this far removed from the slow processes of gradual evolution of new species following the natural selection of the fittest as theorized by Darwin.[10]

Another paleontologist cited by Gould wrote that, based on detailed observation of species changes as found in boreholes, "it is noteworthy that gradual directed transitions from one species to another do not seem to exist in borehole samples of microorganisms."[11] After many years of studying Paleozoic Australian Carboniferous brachiopods, yet another paleontologist found that "there is no evidence of 'gradualistic' evolutionary processes affecting brachiopod species either within or between zones."[12] Still another paleontologist wrote in 1973 that "in twenty years work on the Mesozoic Brachiopods I have found plenty of relationships, but few if any evolving [evolutionary] lineages [within species]. . . . What it seems to mean is that evolution did not normally proceed by a process of gradual change of one species into another over long periods of time."[13] These studies, as cited by Gould, moreover, were only the tip of the iceberg of the skeptical paleontological literature concerning the standard Darwinist accounts of the evolutionary creation of new species through a gradual process of small random mutation and the survival of those species characteristics that accidentally turned out to enhance survival prospects. Owing as well to his wide-ranging evolutionary interests, the need for many examples to fill his voluminous popular writings about the workings of the natural world, and the need to respond to his professional critics, Gould was familiar with a large part of the professional work in evolutionary biology. As he characterized his overall findings near the end of his life, "the dominant and cardinal fact, something that professional paleontologists learned as soon as they developed tools for an adequate stratigraphic tracing of fossils through time [is that] the great majority of species appear with geological abruptness in the fossil record and then persist in stasis until their

10. MacGillavry, "Modes of Evolution Mainly Among Marine Invertebrates," quoted in ibid., 23.

11. Reyment, "Analysis of a General Level Transition in Cretaceous Ammonites," quoted in ibid., 24.

12. Roberts, "Control Mechanisms of Carboniferous Brachiopod Zones in Eastern Australia," quoted in ibid., 24.

13. Ager, "The Nature of the Stratigraphic Record," quoted in ibid., 24.

extinction." Under this typical evolutionary pattern, "the last remnants of a species typically look pretty much like the first representatives" in the fossil record.[14] Indeed, Darwin himself had already been aware of the problem of the lack of a confirming fossil record of species evolution even in his own time but he attributed the problem then to insufficient fossil research and discovery, and assumed that time would take care of the problem.

Even in the last decades of the twentieth century, however, the original Darwinist account of the origin of species lacked empirical confirmation in the fossil record. Yet, this serious theoretical weakness was typically minimized and neglected in the field of Darwinist evolutionary biology. As Gould observes, "paleontologists have always recognized the long-term stability of most species, but we had become more than a bit ashamed by this strong and literal signal, for the dominant theory of our scientific culture told us to look for the opposite result of gradualism as the primary empirical expression of every biologist's favorite subject—evolution itself."[15] It required an unusually brash and self-confident scientist with a high commitment to doing good research to push this basic challenge to the Darwinist orthodoxy into the public limelight, as Gould did.

By the mid-twentieth century, admittedly some evolutionary biologists had proposed a "neo-Darwinism" that they hoped would resolve the problem. Ernst Mayr was a leading figure in this effort, making him among the best known figures of twentieth-century evolutionary biology. Mayr advocated a theory that most of the evolutionary origins of new species according to the workings of natural selection had occurred in isolated species populations in limited geographic areas. With this modification in the traditional Darwinist account, as Mayr wrote, it would still be possible to argue that the "origin of species" took place in Darwinist terms through "the accumulation of small genetic changes, guided by natural selection" in such isolation.[16] Only after a brand new and fitter species was fully evolved in isolation would it spread into much wider areas across the earth, leaving no fossil remains documenting in these wider areas the original slow processes of species development. In other words, the traditional Darwinist account could be saved by positing that finding any hard fossil evidence of gradual special evolution would be like looking for a needle in a haystack.

While this was a plausible account, it also suffered from a large theoretical limitation—neo-Darwinism still lacked empirical confirmation. It was, as one might say, closer to a matter of Darwinist faith than

14. Ibid., 19.
15. Ibid.
16. Mayr, quoted in ibid., 330.

a demonstrated historical fact. With such empirical confirmation lacking, neo-Darwinism might be another "just so story," as evolutionary biologists have been prone to offer whenever their understandings of evolution have come under serious empirical or theoretical challenge. They in effect posit some kind of seemingly plausible explanation, in effect saying, "there is no problem, evolution could have still have worked this way in concept," even if we cannot empirically demonstrate it as a historical fact, so Darwinist evolutionary theory should in any case therefore not be seen as discredited.

This attitude, however, implicitly begins with the assumption that the Darwinist theoretical account of the workings of evolution must be in essence correct and can be rejected only by a direct empirical contradiction for which no plausible explanation can be given. Absent such an overt contradiction—a challenge to find when the biological historical record is missing so much—it will still be possible to keep the Darwinist faith. Gould was a serious problem, however, because of his high stature as an contemporary evolutionary biologist himself and his unusual willingness to challenge consensus professional opinion in public. As he wrote in 1980, "I have been reluctant to admit it . . . but if Mayr's [own] characterization of the synthetic theory [of neo-Darwinism] is correct" as stated, it was impossible for Gould to avoid concluding that, in light of his own detailed knowledge of the paleontological and other evolutionary history, Mayr's revised "theory, as a general proposition, is effectively dead, despite its persistence in textbook orthodoxy."[17]

It was one thing to attack the specific original theoretical details of natural selection long after Darwin's death but Gould was now bluntly dismissing a living icon within the contemporary Darwinist field of evolutionary biology, someone who was seen by fellow evolutionary biologists as having resolved some embarrassing limitations of the original Darwinist orthodoxy. Professional biologists reacted less as disinterested scientists and more as cult members shocked to hear heretical utterances from one of their own—as Gould would later report, he was soon "reviled in many quarters."[18] Richard Dawkins in 1986 attacked Gould for perhaps the greatest offense an evolutionary biologist could commit, giving "abundant aid and comfort to creationists and other enemies of scientific truth."[19] For Dawkins and his Darwinist ilk, they were the new inquisitors; any new heretical tendencies among the priesthood of Darwinist evolutionary biologists must be quickly

17. Ibid., 330.
18. Ibid., 331.
19. Dawkins, quoted in ibid., 334.

marginalized, and hopefully extinguished. Such things had of course happened previously in the history of religion.

Stung to some degree by the harsh attacks, Gould in his later years attempted to maintain a delicate balancing act, frequently criticizing mainstream Darwinist evolutionary ideas and proposing radical revisions of evolutionary theory such as his own theory of "punctuated equilibrium." In this theory, evolutionary change occurred as a serious of sharp "punctuations" followed by long periods of stasis. Gould could not say exactly what caused these punctuations but offered several possible explanations, including his own version of a neo-Darwinist account of reproductive isolation. But he also proposed that other evolutionary mechanisms could have been at work in the sudden appearance of a brand-new species in the fossil record. As he later admitted, the emotional intensity of the attacks by fellow evolutionary biologists, and their hostile reactions to his theory of punctuated equilibrium, caused him to pull back somewhat, couching his later professional language in less provocative—more technical sounding—terms that were less accessible to the wider public and thus less threatening to fellow Darwinist evolutionary biologists. But at the end of his life, Gould nevertheless declared that he would not retract anything from the substance of the offending 1980 article, stating that, however upsetting it had been to fellow Darwinists, "I will defend the content of the quotation" finding little theoretical merit in Mayr's neo-Darwinist synthesis "as just and accurate."[20]

Darwinist Fundamentalism

In his 1996 book, *Darwin's Dangerous Idea: Evolution and the Meanings of Life*, a leading advocate of an orthodox Darwinist world view, the American philosopher Daniel Dennett, argued that evolutionary theory was the full explanation for the human situation in the world.[21] Indeed, Dennett's god of biological evolution exercised a power over the events of the world not much different from the omnipotent God of Christian history. Dennett included criticisms of Stephen Jay Gould and his theory of punctuated equilibrium, both as a misleading account of Darwinism and also for adding unnecessary elements of mystery to the world in that there was no well-established scientific theory yet for the emergence of evolutionary punctuations. Provoked by Dennett's attack on his views, Gould in 1997 responded

---

20. Ibid., 330.
21. Dennett, *Darwin's Dangerous Idea.*

in a two-part review of Dennett's book in *The New York Review of Books*, Part I of which was titled "Darwinian Fundamentalism."[22]

Describing Dennett as "Dawkins's lapdog," Gould's response was equally directed at Dawkins along with others of Gould's past Darwinist inquisitors. Dawkins and Dennett were best understood, Gould now wrote, in religious terms—as the "apostles" of a new secular fundamentalism that was seeking to win converts to "the true Darwinian scripture." Like many other self-appointed saviors of the world, Dawkins, Dennett, and others of their ilk formed a "superficially attractive cult" composed of "fellow defenders of evolutionary orthodoxy."[23] These new secular fundamentalists, Gould observed, were all caught up in an "apocalyptic ultra-Darwinian fervor" grounded in a "simplistic dogmatism," one that "threatens to compromise the true complexity, subtlety (and beauty) of evolutionary theory" and the wider acceptance of a more scientifically valid Darwinist "explanation of life's history."[24] All this harsh criticism was coming from a leading American evolutionary biologist of his time. Not surprisingly, Gould was now plunged into a new round of accusations of heresy and other holy offenses.

Gould was also critical of the contemporary movement of "evolutionary psychology" that finds biological explanations for events more traditionally addressed through psychological study of the workings of the human mind. Sexual beliefs and morals, for example, are now to be interpreted in this framework as determined by the necessities of human reproduction and the imperatives of gene transmission in the competition for evolutionary survival. Indeed, for Dennett, as he says of his own thinking, Darwinian "biology is engineering" of the existence of all living things, body and mind alike.[25] Michael Shermer, a frequent writer for *Scientific American*, commented in 2000 that "Dennett's crane of relentless natural selection is for him a skyhook—a 'mind first' force or power or process that, run over and over, would produce us again and again. It is something akin to an evolutionary theology, a secular cosmogony."[26]

Gould, by contrast, although he accepts the basic facts of evolution, does not regard Darwinist evolutionary biology as a new and more authoritative secular replacement for an omnipotent Christian god. For one thing, he contends that there is a large place for "nonadaptive parts and behaviors"

22. Gould, "Darwinian Fundamentalism." See also Gould, "Evolution: The Pleasures of Pluralism."

23. Gould, "Darwinian Fundamentalism."

24. Ibid.

25. Dennett, quoted in Gould, "Darwinian Fundamentalism."

26. Shermer, "Glorious Contingency."

that can "arise for many reasons in Darwinian systems," including the presence of what Gould in 1979 would label as "spandrels"—accidental evolutionary outcomes that had not themselves been shaped by the adaptive pressures of natural selection. Indeed, Gould suggests that "the human brain must be our finest candidate" for a spandrel. He writes, "I am content to believe that the human brain [initially] became large by natural selection, and for adaptive reasons." But the specific ability to "read or write" and the other higher-level faculties of human beings have only developed recently, leaving too short a period for changes of such a radical character in the human biological condition to have occurred through traditional evolutionary means alone. Gould thus concludes that, rather than a strict evolutionary biological determinism, we must recognize that "the human brain must be bursting with spandrels that are essential to human nature and vital to our self-understanding but that arose [outside evolution] as nonadaptations, and are therefore outside the compass of evolutionary psychology, or any other ultra-Darwinian theory."[27]

Gould argues in general that, rather than biological evolution, the largest part of human civilization today has been formed by "human cultural change, which cannot be basically Darwinian at all." Indeed, "for two fundamental reasons (and a host of other factors), cultural change unfolds virtually in antithesis to Darwinian requirements." As Gould explained, unlike the competitive struggles among species in biological evolution, "cultural change works largely by an opposite process of joining, or interconnection, of [cultural] lineages." In the traditional Darwinist workings of selection of the fittest in nature, species do not combine genetically—"nature cannot make a new mammalian species by mixing 20 percent dugong with 30 percent rat and 50 percent aardvark."[28] But this is the normal way things work in the evolution of human cultures outside evolutionary biology. Early Christian religion, for example, is often described as a blending of Jerusalem and of Athens. Indeed, Darwinist fundamentalism itself might well be described as a modern blending of elements of Christianity with the new findings of the biological and geological sciences that were emerging in the eighteenth and nineteenth century.

In his portrayal of "the selfish gene," Dawkins describes a world no less sinful that the grave corruption of human existence as depicted by many Calvinist preachers—with an old-fashioned Calvinist certainty of conviction and vehemence of expression. The Darwinist separation of the winners from the losers in biological evolution can be seen as a secularized version

27. Gould, "Evolution."
28. Ibid.

of the Christian separation of the saved from the damned—now extending to the whole living world, including especially human beings among those subject to an evolutionary verdict.[29] As Herbert Spencer taught, God works his ways by the selection of the economically fittest; as Dawkins now had revised the script to teach that the world is shaped by the triumph of the fittest genes—expressions in both cases of forms of self-interest that seemingly lies at the center of God's grand design for human existence. It has been suggested that the success of Dawkins's theory of the "selfish gene" may be partly explained by its compatibility with neoliberal tendencies that were coming to the fore in the 1970s in many areas of social and economic thought. The American historian of ideas Gertrude Himmelfarb writes of Darwinism that in Darwin's own time "some Calvinists gloried in it precisely because it exalted chance, not design"—in contrast to much of Roman Catholic theology. Darwinism for such nineteenth-century Calvinists "confirmed their faith in special providence, in the arbitrary selection of the chosen, and in the spontaneous, unpredictable, and often tragic nature of the universe."[30] In his religious certainty, his severe judgments of others, and his strong proselytizing impulses, Dawkins resembles nothing less than a Calvinist preacher of old, a homegrown "neo-Calvinist" product for a secular age of an England where Puritanism has long been a powerful impulse in shaping the national character but was now fading under fierce public assault.

The Method of Contradiction as Applied to Darwin

It is also possible to examine Darwinism from perspectives outside evolutionary biology. Specifically, one can apply to Darwinism a method that is commonly used in the field of mathematics. A common method of proof in mathematics is the following. A mathematician will begin with the following: assume that proposition A is true. By a chain of rigorous mathematical reasoning, the mathematician will then establish the following further proposition: if A is true, then B must also be true. But if B is known (or can be demonstrated mathematically) to be false, it follows logically that A must be false as well. Historically, some of the most important mathematical discoveries have employed this method to prove the correctness (or falsity) of mathematical theorems (the correctness of a theorem can be shown when the assumption that "A is not true" leads to a logical contradiction, so therefore A must be true).

29. Nelson, *Reaching for Heaven on Earth*, Chapter 4.
30. Himmelfarb, *Darwin and the Darwinian Revolution*, 395.

In ancient Greece, the Pythagoreans discovered that the square root of two (and many other supposedly existing "real" numbers) were not "real" by showing through mathematical reasoning that the assumption of the actual existence of an assumed "real" number (that is, expressible as a fraction or a non-repeating decimal series) equal to the square root of two leads to a logical contradiction. Therefore, the square root of two cannot be real. Much more recently, in 1995, Princeton mathematician Andrew Wiles—after seven years of intense effort—finally proved a famous conjecture by the seventeenth-century French mathematician Pierre de Fermat, known as "Fermat's last theorem." Many leading mathematicians had failed for more than 300 years in their efforts to prove this theorem (which states that no integer solutions exist to a particular set of equations). Wiles's proof took more than one hundred pages but the essence was the following. University of California mathematician Kenneth Ribet in the 1980s had proved that any possible solution to Fermat's equation would mean that a "non-modular semistable elliptic curve" exists. Wiles, however, succeeded through heroic efforts in mathematical reasoning in showing that all elliptic curves must be modular, i.e., that no non-modular elliptic curves of any kind can exist. Hence, it logically followed, as Fermat had conjectured, there can be no solutions to Fermat's set of equations.

Assuming the truth of Darwinism, as some people might be surprised to hear, also leads to a contradiction. Let us start from the assumption that Darwinism is "true." Most people understand "true" in the sense that say the laws of electromagnetism, the theory of relativity, and quantum mechanics are "true," that is, they have an objective truthfulness that transcends any survival value or other pragmatic usefulness they may have for human beings. For Darwinists, however, Darwinism is the full explanation of the human circumstance as the workings of evolution have produced it on earth. Hence, a Darwinist account of the workings of evolution will conclude that the things believed to be "true" will in general be those beliefs which work to advance human evolutionary prospects as a species in the natural world. But this has nothing to do with being "true" in the above sense—or as evolutionary biologists themselves mean when they say that Darwinism is "true." Indeed, if Darwinism is "true," then nothing can be said to be "true," including Darwinism, in the absolute sense that is the normal meaning of the term. There are only beliefs that are selected for by evolution and beliefs that do not survive the evolutionary process of natural selection.

Hence, to believe that Darwinism is "true" leads to the conclusion that it is "not true," a direct contradiction. Applying the method of contradiction as widely employed by mathematicians, we can logically then conclude that Darwinism itself is necessarily "not true," although it may be evolutionarily useful (but we could not know this as a "truth" either). In order to find real truth in the world, it requires stepping outside the workings of biological evolution, something which for the true-believing Darwinist is impossible.

Darwin himself was aware of this problem. In a famous 1881 letter to William Graham, Darwin confessed that "with me the horrid doubt always arises whether the convictions of man's mind, which has been developed from the mind of the lower animals, are of any value or at all trustworthy. Would anyone trust in the convictions of a monkey's mind, if there are any convictions in such a mind?"[31] But there is no more logical reason in a Darwinist world to believe in the truthfulness of the convictions in a human mind. Darwin did not say so in this letter but an obvious corollary is the following: If Darwinism is one of those convictions in human minds, then Darwinism itself says—as Darwin himself recognized—that we can have no sure reason to believe confidently in this particular conviction of the actual truth of Darwinist evolutionary theory itself. That is another way to say, again, if Darwinism is true, it cannot be true, a logical contradiction that Darwin seemingly did not clearly recognize in this form. Hence, Darwinism is not true. QED.

If not formally invoking the mathematical method of proof by internal contradiction, the basic difficulties in asserting that "Darwinism is true"— in anything more than a modern pragmatic sense that this is a belief that has survived evolutionary tests thus far—have been recognized by a number of important writers. The leading defender of Christianity, C. S. Lewis, for example, writes that "Naturalism . . . offers what professes to be a full account of our mental behavior; but this account, on inspection, leaves no room for the acts of knowing or insight on which the whole value of our thinking, as a means to truth, depends." Darwinism creates a contradiction, as Lewis puts it, because "natural selection could operate only by eliminating [ideas and other mental] responses that were biologically hurtful and multiplying those which tended to survival. But it is not conceivable that any improvement of responses could ever turn them into acts of insight, or even remotely tend to do so. The relation between response and stimulus [in natural selection] is utterly different from that between knowledge and the truth known" in the usual human understanding of the—absolute—truth.[32]

Another person to point out the logical problems in Darwinist thinking is John Lennox, who is familiar with the highest levels of reasoning as a professor of mathematics at Oxford University. He writes that if the human mind is merely a scientific materialist physical entity—"a vast assembly of

31. Darwin, "Letter to William Graham."
32. Lewis, *Miracles*, 18, 18–19.

nerve cells"—that has evolved to advance survival prospects, then it is a mystery as to "how in the name of logic would we know that our brain was [truly] composed of nerve cells?" As Lennox concludes, "there is a patent self-contradiction running through all attempts," such as found in the Darwinist evolutionary account, "however sophisticated they may appear, to derive rationality from irrationality."[33]

The former Notre Dame philosopher and theologian Alvin Plantinga offers a similar assessment:

> Could we argue . . . that these beliefs [ideas] of ours are connected with behavior in such a way that false belief would produce maladaptive behavior, behavior which would tend to reduce the probability of the believer's surviving and reproducing? No. False belief doesn't by any means guarantee maladaptive action. . . . If they [perhaps members of a primitive tribe] ascribe the right properties to the right witches, their beliefs [in witches] could be adaptive while nonetheless (assuming that in fact there aren't any witches) false.
>
> So we can't sensibly argue from the fact that our behavior (or that of our ancestors) has been adaptive [and thus evolutionarily successful up to now], to the conclusion that our beliefs are mostly true and our cognitive faculties reliable.[34]

Daniel Dennett attempts to rebut Plantinga by arguing that accurate knowledge of what is true will advance the prospects of evolutionary survival—that living in a world of illusion will tend to be harmful to survival prospects and thus evolutionarily maladaptive nontruths will tend to disappear.[35] This may be correct with respect to the accuracy of our sensory impressions of the external world. But going beyond sensory impressions, his argument poses a large problem for Dennett in that religion has been a pervasive element of human existence, central to the existence of almost every tribal group or wider civilization in history. Since religion thus seems to qualify as a form of belief that has demonstrated remarkable evolutionary survival value, by Dennett's own criterion it would seem that religion must be true—despite his own strident proclamations to the contrary, another example of the basic contradictions that beset Darwinist statements of scientific materialist thinking.

But in a deeper sense, that is not a strong argument for religion. The Cambridge University philosopher Simon Blackburn wrote in 2013 about

---

33. Lennox, *God and Stephen Hawking*, 74, 75.
34. Plantinga, *Warranted Christian Belief*, 234–35.
35. Dennett, "Darwin's 'Strange Inversion of Reasoning,'" 346–48.

"a vigorous contemporary form of [philosophical] moral skepticism, which argues that a capacity for ethical truth would have given no selective [evolutionary] advantage to anybody, so that it would be a miracle if it came to predominate as a trait of our species" through Darwinist selection methods found in evolutionary workings alone.[36] Without a supernatural "miracle," in other words, it is logical to conclude that Darwinism is not true. But if we have to assume a miracle, we can then conclude that the scientific materialist philosophy of a Dawkins or a Dennett is not true. Whichever way you go, the thinking of scientific materialism results in a jumble of contradictions. Only by somehow bringing a god into the picture can the idea of something being really "true" be logically and consistently sustained.

Evolutionary Theology

Rejecting Darwinism, or the more recent neo-Darwinism, as a final truth of the world—as being necessarily false by the logic of the method of contradiction—still leaves very much open the question of the actual "truth" of the workings of biological evolution over the four billion years of life on earth. An alternative hypothesis that avoids the contradictions contained in the typical Darwinist account would be to posit the existence of a god who somehow has overseen the long course of the earth's evolutionary history. In the traditional Judeo-Christian understanding, the "truth" of biological evolution would then lie in the mind of God, a truth in which human beings, made in the image of God, are able to participate at least to some degree in their consciousness. When they do, they experience the same feelings of "beauty" and "awe" characteristic of religious believers, even when in modern times many people with such deep feelings deny that they have any real religious beliefs. When Einstein, Newton, and many other physicists have been convinced that they have discovered the "truth" of the workings of the natural world, it has been in this sense of discovering core elements in the thinking of a god.

The Darwinist account of history without religion results in a logical contradiction; understood within the framework of religion, however, this logical problem can be resolved. Darwinist evolution, as put in place and somehow guided by a supernatural god (it does not necessarily have to be the Judeo-Christian God specifically), may be "true" and the question then becomes one of assessing the various theoretical claims to evolutionary truthfulness—such as one claimant, Darwin's own particular gradualist theory of natural selection. It is the same question Kepler, Galileo, and Newton

36. Blackburn, "Taliban and Plato," 12.

were motivated to address, what are the actual qualities of the mind of God as he has revealed them in the workings of the solar system and other parts of nature, and we can now also find further revelations of God's thinking in the natural workings of biological evolution on earth.

In *Darwin and the Darwinian Revolution*, the American historian of ideas Gertrude Himmelfarb thus observes that, despite occasional confessions of doubt as in his 1881 letter to William Graham noted above, Darwin had an abiding deep "faith in an objective universe in which both he and his subject occupied fixed and independent positions. He never doubted that he was a passive, disinterested observer accurately recording the laws revealed in nature." This core faith of Darwin was not a scientific conclusion, however; it was in fact contrary to a literal Darwinist interpretation of evolution (in which Darwin himself cannot be an independent observer outside the workings of evolution). As Himmelfarb puts it, Darwin's own thinking implicitly "shared with religion the belief in an objective knowledge of nature. If religion's belief was based on revelation and Darwinism on science, with good reason the two could be—as indeed they were—shown to coincide."[37] As Einstein would later say of the basic enterprise of twentieth-century physics, it might be said also of Darwin's nineteenth-century inquiries into the natural laws of biological history, that evolutionary "science without religion is lame, religion without [evolutionary] science is blind."[38]

Surprisingly, although not a generally accepted viewpoint or widely known to the public, some contemporary students of Darwin find that he sometimes was explicit in seeing outside purpose and direction in evolution's workings, going beyond the mere material interactions of molecules and atoms (themselves guided by a purposeless process of natural selection). University of Chicago historian of science Robert Richards, in an article written for a 2009 National Academy of Sciences symposium, notes that at one point in *The Origin of Species*, Darwin himself wrote "that nature's productions . . . plainly bear the stamp of far higher workmanship."[39] As Richards comments, "the Biblical cadences of these passages had an assuaging effect on Darwin's Victorian readers." Some of them, such as the leading American biologist of the time and strong advocate for Darwin, Harvard's Asa Gray, "would yet find the mysterious hand of the Creator still stirring in the depths of Darwin's language." Indeed, as Richards now interprets him, "the model by which Darwin attempted to explain to himself the opera-

---

37. Himmelfarb, *Darwin and the Darwinian Revolution*, 448, 449.

38. Quoted in Koetsier and Bergmans, "Introduction" to Koetsier and Bergmans, eds., *Mathematics and the Divine*, 41.

39. Darwin, quoted in Richards, "Darwin's Place in the History of Thought," 336.

tions of natural selection was that of a very powerful, intelligent being that manifested 'forethought' and prescience, as well as moral concern, for the creatures over which it tended." In contrast to the standard view of evolutionary biologists today of natural selection as a random and thus purposeless "mechanical or machine-like" process, Richards concludes after his own exhaustive study of Darwin's own diaries and many other of his less familiar writings that Darwin himself actually conceived natural selection as a "teleological and moral construction" that steadily drove the world towards higher ends, this evolutionary progress having by now culminated in the greatest heights achieved by any form of life on earth, the emergence of modern human beings.[40] Darwin, it should be recalled, lived much of his professional life in the second half of the nineteenth century, a period in history when faith in the transcendent character of human progress was at its greatest in Western civilization, consciously or unconsciously assumed by the vast majority of people.

If some kind of a god must therefore be introduced to maintain the logical integrity of the Darwinist scheme as a valid truth statement, it still leaves open many large questions about the specific character of this god and the role of evolution in god's mind. God may have made the world of plants and animals and other life on earth to work according to something very much like a standard Darwinist account grounded in natural selection. Conceivably, the actual god of the universe decided that the long biological history of living things on earth should indeed be formed entirely by such a physical mechanism. It would be similar to the deism that arose in the Enlightenment; god created the earth but then let it run according to the laws of physics, now extended to the laws of biological evolution as well.

Alternatively, perhaps a god who works through evolution might have preferred a world with other—or even multiple—evolutionary mechanisms in addition to the standard Darwinist account of natural selection. This god might have from time to time intervened to "reset" the initial base point of species composition, thus altering the subsequent course of evolution. This might be the source of some of the large and sudden punctuations seen in evolutionary history. Perhaps god tired of the dinosaurs and thus directed an asteroid to hit the earth. The study of the evolutionary biology of life on earth thus is a process of scientific inquiry in search of the actual thinking of god, as it is revealed in the workings of the four-billion-year biological history of the earth. Only a true-believing Darwinist fundamentalist would say that a god could not have had any options in this regard.

40. Richards, "Darwin's Place in the History of Thought," 336, 335, 341.

Some people might suggest that it is impossible that any conceivable god would have chosen to organize the workings of nature in the world according to such a violent and cruel—such an "immoral"—guiding principle as the competitive survival of the fittest. But this is to make the great mistake for a human being of presuming to know the ways of god. Indeed, the God of the Old Testament is often harsh and seemingly arbitrary by ordinary human standards. After the rise of Christianity, Calvinism in particular emphasized the gravely fallen and thus corrupted state of human existence—a fallen condition that god might have extended to encompass all the living world. Indeed, Paul wrote in Romans 22 that, owing to the original sin in the garden, "we know that the whole creation has been groaning in labor pains until now; and not only have the creation, but we ourselves, who have the first fruits of the Spirit, groan inwardly while we wait for adoption, the redemption of our bodies."

Even if they do not usually describe it this way for wider public audiences, many current professional biologists do in fact think of their work in deeply religious terms, as invoking powerful feelings of awe and wonder in their encounters with the beauty and intricacies of the evolutionary process and other elements of the natural world. In a book surveying the development since the 1980s of the professional field of conservation biology, David Takacs thus writes that it is evident "that ideas and reactions of a deeply religious character [are] . . . central to the whole enterprise of conservation biology. . . . For these biologists and for many others, being in nature—surrounding oneself with biodiversity—can almost not help but bring about experiences to leave the senses reeling. . . . How can we help but feel awed?"[41] It is much like the feelings of Einstein and Feynman noted above in the process of discovery in physics. In short, besides the physical world, the biological workings of the natural world, including the processes of biological evolution of life on earth, are also parts of the "Book of Nature," long seen in Christian theology as a direct reflection of the mind of God—and implicitly still seen in this light by many leading evolutionary and other biologists today who still find religion, if in newly "secular" sources.

Theoretical Problems

Compared with the study of the physical world by physicists, however, the world of evolutionary biology has thus far been more secretive in revealing the precise thinking of god. In another of the articles written for the National Academy of Sciences 2009 symposium reviewing the 150-year

41. Takacs, *The Idea of Biodiversity,* 266–67.

history of Darwinism, University of Florida philosopher Michael Ruse finds that from the publication of *The Origin of Species* in 1859 up to the 1930s, "evolution had the status of a popular science. There was some professional [evolutionary biological] work going on . . . but generally evolution was a [popular] museum science," achieving its greatest public visibility and impact with spectacular exhibits of the fossil remains of dinosaurs and other exotic prehistoric creatures. Among the prominent writers about evolution in that period, Ruse writes, "causal thinking was second rate or (often) absent entirely."[42] More ominously, the popular interpretations of Darwinism were also invoked by Marxists, National Socialists and advocates of other twentieth-century ideologies (in truth, they were new "religions") to support the legitimacy of their views and arguments. In proclaiming that Darwinism is the final truth of the natural world, it meant for them in practice that their political and economic agendas—supposedly the result of applying Darwinist theory to human affairs—could be seen as blessed by a god.

Even well before the *Origin*, there was some good information becoming available, Ruse writes, in that "people knew about homologies, the fossil record was starting to fill out, embryology was suggestive, and so forth. But the full [evolutionary] picture was not there. After the *Origin*, being an evolutionist," as he explains, was not about applying the scientific method but about "just plain common sense," often joined with a passionate belief in the progress of the human species, following along a path of what could be said to be a Darwinist evolutionary path advancing towards an eventual perfection of the human condition on earth.[43]

As originally formulated by Darwin, evolutionary theory had the large intellectual advantage that it portrayed the earth's biological history as consisting of a vast number of transitional stages in the character of life on earth since its emergence billions of years ago. Such transitions were typically characterized by the disappearance of many old species and the emergence of new species, this process generally— if very gradually—showing an overall increase in the complexity of the "highest" living things, now culminating in the most complex biological organ ever found on earth, the brain of modern human beings. But what about the specific way that these major transitional events in biological history actually took place? What was the scientific mechanism? In this respect, the original Darwinist theory fared surprisingly poorly, given the high scientific regard in which "Darwinism" as such was—and still is—so widely held both among the general public and in scientific circles.

42. Ruse, "The Darwinian Revolution," 292.
43. Ibid., 292.

In broad terms, Darwin in his day asserted that evolutionary biological history was driven by natural selection, based on competitive successes and failures in the struggle for survival of the fittest among individual plants and animals and other life forms. University of Chicago evolutionary geneticist Jerry Coyne—a strong contemporary defender of Darwinism—recently explained that "if individuals within a species differ genetically from one another, and some of those differences reflect an individual's ability to survive and reproduce in its environment, then in the next generation the 'good' genes that lead to survival and reproduction will have relatively more copies than the 'not so good' genes." For example, mammoths once living in northern cold environments, unlike African elephants, needed plentiful amounts of hair to protect them. Coyne explains that in the evolutionary process the early mammoths with more hair "left more offspring than their balder counterparts" so that "in the next generation the average mammoth would be a bit hairier than before." Allow this process to work out over "some thousands of generations, and your smooth mammoth gets replaced by a shaggy one." Extending this basic idea to all living things, "natural selection can, over eons, sculpt an animal or plant into something that looks designed" in terms of the perfection of its adaptation to its physical and biological surroundings.[44] But in the Darwinist account, the process works entirely naturally and gradually by material causes alone; no supernatural designer or greater purpose need be invoked.

As noted above, there has always been a large empirical problem, however, with this original—and still widely offered—Darwinist account: in Darwin's day there was little to support it in the fossil record, and the situation is not that much improved today. New species often emerge seemingly out of nowhere, even as the old species might persist. Such a process, however, was difficult to understand in terms of Darwin's original account of natural selection. How could one subgroup of a species—perhaps advantaged in some way—become reproductively isolated, as would be necessary for the emergence of a new distinct species, when all the members of the species were typically sharing a common territory and were interbreeding with one another? Human breeders of new types of dogs, horses, cattle, and other domestic animals solved this problem by reproductively isolating those animals that possessed the desired trait(s), allowing them to breed only with one another, and achieving rapid evolutionary change. But what was the corresponding isolating mechanism in the workings of biological history? Darwin did not attempt to say. As noted above, Ernst Mayr and

---

44. Coyne, *Why Evolution is True*, 11.

other neo-Darwinists more recently offered the hypothesis of geographical isolation but empirical confirmation remained elusive.

The above problems—and still others—meant that Darwin's theory of the origin of species lacked any full validation according to the canons of the scientific method. Until the necessary missing fossils to validate the Darwinist or neo-Darwinist account were found (if ever), it was as though Newton had proposed a theory of the workings of the solar system under the influence of gravity but there was insufficient data available at the time concerning planetary movements to confirm empirically Newton's new theory—and yet Newton had nevertheless rapidly been acclaimed as a great scientific genius. In the late nineteenth century, the new Darwinist gospel nevertheless spread rapidly across the Western world.

Even in those days, however, as Ruse observes, among closer students of the subject, there were many doubters. Indeed, the supposed actual existence of natural evolution for many years after the *Origin* became in essence "a truism"—reflecting the fact that Darwinism had the large advantage over many of its leading religious competitors in that it accepted without question the literal truth of the available fossil record. Ruse comments, however, that the actual theoretical "mechanism" as posited by Darwin "was another matter. No one denied natural selection. Very few" close students of evolution "accepted that it could be as powerful as Darwin suggested. People became evolutionists in droves. The number of pure Darwinians, as we might term selectionists, was very few." Moreover, the "most prominent after Darwin himself, namely [Alfred Russell] Wallace, became enamored of spiritualism in the 1860s and he started to deny selection when it came to humans." As Ruse writes, "the reasons for this halfway acceptance" of Darwinist evolutionary theory in the next 70 years" "are well known," including concerns such as those raised above.[45]

By the 1930s and 1940s, however, evolutionary biology was taking on new professional directions, bringing to bear the discoveries of Mendelian and other population genetics, adopting more sophisticated mathematical modeling methods, and in general showing greater scientific skepticism, seeking in such ways to address some of the criticisms of the original Darwinist accounts. Yet, this "neo-Darwinism" continues to face scientific skepticism, as seen in the concerns expressed above by Stephen Jay Gould, and will be examined further below. The immense success of Darwinism theologically is beyond dispute; its success scientifically is another matter.

45. Ruse, "The Darwinian Revolution," 293, 294.

The Question of Sufficient Time

Since *The Origin of Species*, an important question has been whether there has been sufficient time in the history of life on earth for evolution to have worked all the large biological changes that have occurred. One strong point in favor of a yes answer was the discovery that the earth is 4.6 billion years old. Assuming the standard Darwinist account of a process of slow but steady evolutionary change as guided by natural selection, it seemed at least plausible to believe that this might have been sufficient time since the first emergence of life on earth. This was, admittedly, more a matter of guesswork than a rigorous scientific argument. In order to address the question more adequately, it would have been necessary to have a model of biological evolution through natural selection including such things as the rate at which mutations within species occur; the likelihood that any given mutation will actually work to advance survival prospects, the extent of evolutionary reassortment due to mating of genetically diverse populations within the same species; rates of species population mobility around the earth; and the amount of time it would normally take for a new fitter species to outcompete and displace an evolutionary loser.

Absent such calculations, as a matter of doing good science, it is not saying much simply to assert that evolution through natural selection could in concept have produced the current state of the biological world over the long course of the history of life on earth. As it is also said, a monkey typing randomly could in concept reproduce a play of Shakespeare within a finite period—in itself a true statement. Yet, it is easy with a few plausible assumptions and probability calculations to show that it would require vastly more time than the thirteen billion years of the universe for a monkey randomly typing to have any possibility of reproducing a play of Shakespeare. It might then be proposed that an additional selection mechanism be added—perhaps every time the monkey actually typed randomly an actual word in the English language, it would automatically be preserved (it would be selected to "survive"), and all such words would thereafter be randomly recombined in some fashion over time. This would by itself radically reduce the expected time for a randomly typing monkey but it would still in all likelihood far exceed thirteen billion years. More complicated selection mechanisms might then be proposed—perhaps every time the monkey produced a grammatically correct (in Shakespearian English) sentence this would be preserved and survive, such sentences then to be recombined with other "sentence survivors"—and the probabilities of a play of Shakespeare within thirteen billion years would then be further reassessed (now yet more probable but still essentially a remote chance at best). Assuming rates of random typing for the monkey, and a selection mechanism of some kind, it thus would not be difficult to actually calculate an estimated probability of creating a play of Shakespeare within a certain number of years.

Unfortunately, the initial mutation probabilities and the speed of workings of the selection mechanisms in Darwinist evolution—survival of the fittest—are much more complex. As with the typing monkey, the fact that evolution could in concept have produced a world of such biological complexity as the world we inhabit does not resolve the issue of sufficient time. Marc Kirschner is the founding chair of the department of systems biology at Harvard Medical School and John Gerhart is a professor in the department of molecular and cell biology at the University of California at Berkeley, well-respected figures in their American professional worlds. They coauthored a 2005 book, *The Plausibility of Life*, explaining that Darwinism rests on "three pillars": the workings of natural selection, genetic inheritance, and the mechanisms of variation within nature. The first pillar, dating to Darwin, is grasped easily enough—in essence, as noted, the survival of the fittest. The second pillar, first explained by Gregor Mendel and then worked out in much greater detail in the twentieth century, including the discovery of DNA, is also well enough understood. As Kirschner and Gerhart think, however, the third pillar remains to this day largely a mystery. Indeed, a main purpose of Kirschner and Gerhart in writing their book is to try to explain more precisely how new variations in the features of biological organisms do emerge within nature, thereby helping to provide a basis for a better understanding of the actual workings of natural selection.[46]

Given the absence of any broadly accepted theory in this third area, it remains premature even today to say that Darwinism is a well-developed and accepted scientific theory of the evolution of life on earth. As Kirschner and Gerhart explain, "the Modern Synthesis" developed in the 1940s remains "the current consensus model of evolution." If offers "a valuable model but an incomplete one. It lacks the third pillar needed to explain the feasibility of evolutionary change," a pillar necessary to make "Darwin's basic outline and construct a more plausible and more complete theory of evolution." As Kirschner and Gerhart state, evolutionary "biologists might be faulted for their failure to recognize this large gap in their theory. They mostly ignored it." As a result, lacking this element, "the issue of the rate of evolution . . . has always been imponderable," leaving essentially unresolved the basic question of whether "there has . . . been enough time for suitable

---

46. Kirschner and Gerhart, *The Plausibility of Life*.

variants to arise" in the manner assumed by Darwinist evolutionary theory over the full history of life on earth.[47]

Rather than honestly acknowledge the large gap in Darwinist theories, even today, write Kirschner and Gerhart, "many evolutionary biologists dismiss the issue of rates of variation" and the potential implications for the actual speed of evolution. As is surprisingly common in evolutionary biology, they offer a plausible-sounding explanation and then suggest that the problem has been resolved. As Kirschner and Gerhart write, evolutionary biologists thus typically "tell us that geological time is, in fact, very long when compared with the decades, centuries or millennia that have sufficed for the divergence of domestic animals into grossly different breeds by artificial selection, or for the changed coloration of moths or beak sizes of finches via natural selection." The typical evolutionary biologist then goes on to dismiss the "skeptics [who] are still not willing to grant that random variation can produce anything as complex as a flower, or an eye, even over [the available] geologic time, much less a human being from a bacterium-like organism." But this is not an acceptable scientific answer in their view. As Kirscher and Gerhart argue, "without some account of how complex novelty arises" over the long course of the earth's biological history, "mere refuge in the sufficiency of time is unconvincing" in seeking to put Darwinism on a sound scientific footing.[48]

In the absence of greater empirical evidence, and since it then becomes one person's best guess versus another person's best guess, I can report that for me intuitively I find the possibility of the evolution of human beings and their astonishing brains on earth, all this happening according to a standard Darwinist account—based in random mutations and the selection method of survival of the fittest—to be implausible. Indeed, the random evolution of the human brain and its mental capacities might be no less implausible than a monkey randomly typing a work of Shakespeare within thirteen billion years—certainly possible in concept but very unlikely in practice. There always remains, of course, the possibility of a strictly natural explanation of the biological evolution of life on earth but it would seemingly require positing a much different natural selection mechanism than the traditional Darwinist account. Indeed, as will be discussed below, some leading evolutionary biologists in recent years have been turning towards such new selection methods as a result of laboratory research employing newly available and inexpensive methods of genetic decomposition as a basis for studying evolutionary pathways.

47. Ibid., 13, 14, 15, 31, 32.
48. Ibid., 33.

The Human Punctuation

The puzzling quality of many aspects of biological evolution is well illustrated by the most important sudden "punctuation" of all (at least from our own anthropocentric perspective), the recent emergence of modern human beings on earth, known scientifically as "homo sapiens." Beginning around ten million years ago, this story includes a few short episodes of rapid evolutionary transformation, followed by long periods of stasis, culminating finally with the sudden appearance around 150,000 to 200,000 years ago in Africa of modern man. Given our special interest in this particular evolutionary episode, and its relatively more recent occurrence in the biological history of the earth, more is known about some of the details, as compared with most other evolutionary events in the long history of life on earth. The story is well told by Ernst Mayr who towards the end of his long life published a book, *What Evolution Is*. He sought there to explain for a wide audience the state of evolutionary theory at the end of the twentieth century, including a chapter on "How Did Mankind Evolve?" over the past five to ten million years.[49]

Mayr was not himself an enthusiastic supporter of Gould's theory of punctuated equilibrium but he was intellectually honest enough to present an account of recent human evolution that fits the punctuated model well in key aspects. As Mayr explained, the timeline of human evolution is fairly well accepted because it can be reconstructed from fossil bones and other physical remains of a past humanoid presence. Beyond matters resolvable by the discovery of such objects, however, most of the rest of the more distant parts of human evolutionary history—most things relating to behavioral and cultural evolution, or example—remain matters of controversial speculation by evolutionary biologists. Based on the fossil record, however, we do know that chimpanzees are biologically the closest of any species to current human beings. The two shared a common ancestor until around five to eight million years ago when the human and chimpanzee evolutionary lines diverged.

Then, around four million years ago, a new key step happened suddenly in Africa, a new species (or group of related species) that had now made a large evolutionary change, that of walking upright. In other respects, however, they remained much closer to current chimpanzees than to current humans. The members of this group, "Australopithecus," typically had a brain size of about 500 cubic centimeters (cc), similar to chimpanzees today (and around a third current human brain sizes). Then, from about

---

49. Mayr, *What Evolution Is*, 233–64.

four million to about two million years ago, not much further of great evolutionary significance happened. As Mayr relates, the "whole 1.5 million-
year-long period" was one of "stasis," typical of so much of the evolutionary
record for all forms of life. Most importantly, "for more than 2 million years
... there was no significant change in the size of their brain" of the members
of Australopithecus.[50]

But then, about two million years ago, as Mayr relates, there was an
"unprecedented increase in brain size," roughly a doubling. Writing in 2001,
Mayr sees this rapid emergence in the matter of at most a few hundred thousand years of a new human ancestor ("homo erectus") with a much larger
brain as "puzzling" for evolutionary theory in that it "appears in eastern
Africa so suddenly."[51] Like other false steps throughout the history of Darwinist theory, Mayr comments that for "part of the nineteenth century and
most of the twentieth century" evolutionary biologists had attempted to fit
the era of Australopithecus into a standard Darwinist account of natural selection. Since Australopithecus was most distinguishable from chimpanzees
and other apes by its bipedalism, "it was [then conventionally] argued that
the upright posture freed arms and hands for other roles, in particular the
making and use of tools. This, in turn," as was long said by evolutionary biologists, "required brain activity and was the main reason for the increase of
human brain size." As Mayr now acknowledges, however, "this chain of reasoning is no longer convincing." Besides the minimal actual increase seen in
brain size, "the australopithecines shared almost all of their other characters
with the chimpanzees" among whom, as it is now known, chimpanzees also
made "extensive tool use," even as their brain sizes never did increase. As a
result, there is at present no readily accepted explanation within evolutionary biology of the sudden "step from the Australopithecus apelike stage to
the Homo stage" about two million years ago that "was clearly the most
important event" in the emergence of modern homo sapiens.[52]

Homo erectus soon moved out of Africa to Asia as well; its fossils were
actually first discovered in Java in 1892 ("Java Man"). In Africa, the first
fossils of homo erectus were not discovered until 1924, and following that
in China in 1927. After the emergence of homo erectus about two million
years ago, there was then another long period of comparative stasis. As
Mayr writes, in terms of brain size and other key respects, the homo erectus
predecessor to modern humans "existed without major change for at least

50. Ibid., 243, 244.
51. Ibid. 248, 246, 247.
52. Ibid., 243, 244.

1 million years."[53] But then the evolutionary line again rather suddenly and mysteriously diverged about 500,000 years ago, one branch becoming the Neanderthals who were found in Europe and Asia and were evolutionarily the most successful from about 250,000 to 30,000 years ago. Surprisingly, the Neanderthals suddenly had a brain size larger even than current humans, about 1600 cc, compared with a typical human brain today of 1,250 cc to 1,500 cc.

The other key diversion from the evolutionary line of homo erectus was our own homo sapiens, emerging suddenly (in evolutionary terms) in Africa about 150,000 to 200,000 years ago. Homo sapiens then moved out of Africa about 100,000 years ago, arriving in western Europe about 35,000 years ago, followed fairly soon thereafter by the disappearance of the Neanderthals of Europe. (The reasons again are not well understood but presumably this was not a pure coincidence.) Then, from a population of only a few million as recently as 10,000 years ago, homo sapiens exploded across the earth, recently exceeding seven billion, displacing large numbers of other species in their traditional habitat areas, and causing the extinction of some species from the earth altogether. Some people are now declaring that a continuation of this past 10,000 years will bring about an event comparable to the five previous mass extinctions that were attributable to natural causes, this new state of the biological world now dominated by a human presence to be labeled the "anthropocene era."

Mayr finds that among all the surprising events on the ten-million-year Darwinist path to modern man, "what is perhaps most astonishing is the fact that the human brain seems not to have changed one single bit since the first appearance of homo sapiens" within the past 150,000 to 200,000 years.[54] This is a long enough time frame that it would have seemed reasonable to expect that evolutionary pressures would have worked selectively in favor of greater human intelligence (this presumably correlated with further increases in brain size). Given their limited natural physical endowments, the very recent extraordinary evolutionary successes of homo sapiens have clearly been in large part the result of their unprecedented capacities for memory, logical reasoning, language, tool making and other acts of high intelligence, illustrated in our own time by the extraordinary feats of modern mathematics and physics and the resulting control achieved over nature only in the past 200 years, a virtual miracle as I will suggest later.

Mayr does not say much about yet another surprising feature of human evolution that adds a still further element of mystery, the relative absence

53. Ibid., 248.
54. Ibid., 252.

of evidence of any other kinds of evolutionary change—leaving aside brain size—among homo sapiens since they moved out of Africa somewhere around 100,000 year ago. As a result of that large migration out of Africa, human beings were increasingly isolated from one another in a wide range of different physical environments around the earth, ranging from frozen tundra near the Arctic to searing deserts, existing there in relative reproductive isolation. According to the usual "neo-Darwinist" accounts, this should have accelerated the rate of evolutionary change within the human species, groups of homo sapiens now evolving to meet the specific survival requirements of their own particular isolated geographies and other environmental features. One might have expected that perhaps even one or more brand-new evolutionary species within a larger category of "humanity" might have branched off by now from the main homo sapien line. Yet, nothing of the sort happened. Even as large cultural differences developed across the earth in the past 100,000 years, little change occurred genetically. Indeed, while some limited racial differences such as skin color can be found today, the more remarkable fact is the great genetic similarity among all the racial groups within the homo sapien line, despite the great geographic variety of their isolated local environmental circumstances. The human case of the past 100,000 years thus does not accord well with neo-Darwinist theory. This is indeed fortunate for all those of us today who believe deeply in the fundamental idea of an equality of all human beings, a seeming defiance of neo-Darwinist predictions.

Evolutionary geneticist Jerry Coyne thus states that in the evolution of homo sapiens, "only about 10 to 15 percent of genetic variation in humans is represented by differences between 'races' that are recognized by differences in physical appearance. The remainder of the genetic variation, 85 to 90 percent, occurs *among individuals within races*." Coyne explains this seemingly anomalous outcome in evolutionary terms by suggesting that the past 100,000 years must have been too little time for significant human evolution to have occurred—"that human races are too young to have evolved important differences in intellect and behavior" (and in major aspects of physical anatomy).[55] But how, then, can we account for the extraordinary overall pace of evolutionary developments over the previous two million years, moving essentially from an upright version of a chimpanzee to current human beings biologically in that short period? If nothing much happened biologically in the past 100,000 years of evolution, how did so much extraordinary change occur in the mere 1.9 million preceding years?

55. Coyne, *Why Evolution is True*, 213, 216.

Perhaps the most fundamental challenge of all to Darwinism is offered by professor Colin McGinn, among the most prolific and insightful
philosophers today. As McGinn notes, human consciousness lacks a spatial
dimension. But how could an evolutionary process occurring in the physical world create something that does not exist in this world—the contents
of human consciousness that lack the dimensions of measurable time and
space that characterize the physical world? As McGinn notes, the "non-
spatial character of consciousness" is something "much more mysterious
than is generally appreciated" even at the highest levels of contemporary
intellectual life. The evolution of something lacking in any physical qualities is in fact incomprehensible as the outcome of what is itself a physical
process—such as Darwinist natural selection. Facing such a total mystery,
McGinn suggests that an explanation, if it is ever to be found, might yield
an understanding in which "consciousness turns out to be older than matter
[existing] in space"—in this case again ruling out any possible Darwinist
naturalist explanation of the origins of human consciousness.[56]

Evolutionary biologists frequently seem to be improvising theoretical
explanations to meet the empirical challenges and defensive needs of the
moment. Evolutionary processes thus can be expected to move very rapidly
when Darwinist theories call for such rapid change. But when a slow process
of evolution is called for by another empirical challenge, the workings of
natural selection can then be said to occur very gradually. In *Origins of the
Modern Mind*, professor of psychology Merlin Donald writes that, "on the
available evidence, the brains of apes and humans are so similar that one is
left at a loss to explain the remarkable, and apparently discontinuous, nature
of the mental capacities of humans in comparison with our primate cousins."
As a further complication, "There is no direct information available on the
brains or level of intelligence of the 'missing links,' the intermediate species
that bridged the gap from ape to human. All of our evidence is indirect."
Indeed, "the task of reconstructing the steps through which humans must
have passed in their evolutionary transition" to the modern human brain
and its extraordinary mental capacity "is so difficult that many have chosen
to ignore the problem"—or to sweep it aside with grand conjectures about
evolutionary processes that cannot be accepted or rejected empirically.[57] And
yet, our unreconstructed Darwinist fundamentalists today still routinely lay
claim to having in their possession an evolutionary theory of biological history that has definitely and comprehensively shown itself to be scientifically
valid, including the evolution of current human beings, and everything im-

56. McGinn, "Consciousness and Space," 223, 224.
57. Donald, *Origins of the Modern Mind*, 21.

portant about them, and that no well-informed and well-intentioned person could rationally have large doubts. As with every other human culture of the past, it is seemingly impossible to live without religion, even as religion has taken some radically new forms in the modern age.

Darwinism as Storytelling

In 2008 Jerry Fodor, a well-respected American philosopher at Rutgers University and a self-described "naturalist" skeptical with respect to traditional religion, nevertheless published an article on "Against Darwinism" in the professional journal *Mind and Language*. As Fodor explained, he had "not the slightest reason to doubt the central Darwinist theses of the common origin and mutability of species" over a very long history of life on earth. Like those who demand better answers to the question of sufficient time, however, what he did want to challenge was the explanatory power of the Darwinist account with respect to the specific details of evolution by natural selection. As Fodor wrote, "Darwin didn't just present 'a well-thought out theory of evolution.' Most importantly, he also proposed a 'theory of causation, a theory of natural selection.' Well, if I'm right, that's exactly what Darwin *didn't* do; a 'theory of causation' is exactly what the theory of natural selection *isn't*."[58]

Fodor again is not questioning that biological evolution is driven by "competitions between creatures with different phenotypes [physical and behavioral characteristics that] often differ in their outcomes; and, of course, in each case, there must be some explanation or other of why the winner won and the loser didn't." But Fodor agrees that if a scientific "law" is understood in the sense of the physical sciences, Darwinism fails this test badly. Rather, in the typical Darwinist account "there's no reason at all to suppose that such explanations typically invoke laws that apply to the creatures in virtue of their phenotypic types." Fodor, therefore, is "inclined to think that [Darwinist] explanations of phenotypes in terms of their selection histories generally aren't nomological [having the character of a physical law] and that they don't claim or even aspire to be. What they are is precisely what they seem on the face of them: they're historical explanations." In other words, Darwinist explanations of the workings of evolution, "insofar as they are convincing, are best construed as *post hoc* historical narratives, natural history rather than biology."[59]

58. Fodor, "Against Darwinism," 23, 22. See also Fodor and Piattelli-Palmarini, *What Darwin Got Wrong*.

59. Fodor, "Against Darwinism," 17, 15, 1.

In other words, evolutionary biology consists of the development of a biological form of historical storytelling ("historical narratives"). Indeed, it could not be otherwise, because, as Fodor thinks, Darwinists not only failed to discover the laws but "there aren't any [posited] mechanisms of the selection of heritable phenotypic traits (as such)."[60] The plant and animal world is simply too diverse and complicated; the historical evidence is too remote. These problems significantly inhibit even the understanding of present-day natural ecologies and are only greatly magnified when it comes to the ecological events and the roles and actions of species that occurred many millions of years ago.

This does not mean that historical narratives are not valuable ways of understanding the world. The understanding of the record of human history is an important part of the human project on earth; history is central to our own self-understanding as human beings. It is just that we should not treat the results as having the authority of sciences such as physics, chemistry, or molecular biology. As Fodor thus writes, given the limitations under which it operates, "there is nothing wrong with explanations that consist of historical narratives." The individual case study method is typically the best that can be done, however, rather than the scientific method of prediction and empirical confirmation. Indeed, Fodor suggests that the methods of evolutionary biology may have about the same degree of explanatory power as say the current theories of how to get rich: "For each person who is rich, there must be something or other that explains his being so: heredity, inheritance, cupidity, acuity, mendacity, grinching the faces of the poor, being in the right place at the right time, having friends in high places, sheer brute luck, highway robbery, or whatever." There are innumerable books written offering sure theories about how to become rich but the odds are that Warren Buffet—who clearly has the knack—seldom if ever reads any of them. The most illuminating explanations of the route to financial success, as Fodor observes, are historical—those "that explain, case by case, what it was about a guy in virtue of which he got as rich as he did in the circumstances that prevailed when and where he did so."[61] It will have to be the same, as Fodor concludes, in seeking to understand the mechanisms of evolutionary success—individual cases are historically interesting, heroic evolutionary generalizations are problematic when not wrong altogether.

Fodor is particularly critical of Darwinists who implicitly seem to imply that there is some kind of higher force at work in natural selection or, as they commonly put it, specific traits are "selected for" in the evolutionary process.

60. Ibid., 22.
61. Ibid., 23, 21, 22.

Rather, as he explains, "strictly speaking, *traits* don't get selected at all; traits don't either win competitions or lose them. What wins or loses competitions *are the creatures that have the traits*," and such results are too complicated to formulate in terms of any wider evolutionary laws of the selection of species characteristics. A common tactic in popular expositions of evolution, attributing the results to "Mother Nature," is hopeless, as Fodor suggests. All in all Darwinism, he concludes, has been much oversold. Since the *Origin of Species* in 1859, it has performed valiantly in teaching the general public—biblical creationists aside—to recognize the historical existence of an extremely long and diverse biological history of the earth. When evolutionary biology seeks to go further, however, and to provide a "scientific" explanation for this historical record, Darwinism falls far short. As Fodor puts it, given that there are no scientifically valid "generalizations about the mechanisms of [evolutionary] adaptation as such, then the theory of Natural Selection reduces to a banal truth"—a virtually tautological claim that the winners in biological evolutionary history are those biological species and creatures that have had those characteristics that made them the winners.[62]

As noted previously, the sociologist Robert Bellah spent thirteen years writing his encyclopedic 2011 book, *Religion in Human Evolution: From the Paleolithic to the Axial Age*. He explains in the conclusion that he discovered a great deal that was new and surprising to him in the research and writing process, but near the end felt the need to completely rewrite only one chapter, that on the workings of evolution, partly because he had now learned that "the understanding of biological evolution had changed dramatically in the decade or so since the first draft was completed" around 2000.[63] He is referring in part to the new respect being shown for Gould's theory of punctuated equilibrium and other concerns about Darwinian orthodoxies, but also to other important developments in evolutionary thought. As has become increasingly apparent in recent years, Darwinism is far from a settled science. In actual fact, rather little about the workings of evolutionary biology, other than that it historically has existed for about four billion years, is truly settled. This would be hardly worth saying if not for the contrary claims of literal biblical creationists of the twentieth century and still many others today.

62. Ibid., 10, 17, 23.

63. Bellah, *Religion in Human Evolution*, 567; see 709n2.

Bacteria versus Darwin

In addition to Gould's criticisms of neo-Darwinism, an equally formidable American critic was Lynn Margulis. Indeed, Margulis, who became a member of the National Academy of Sciences in 1983, received the National Medal of Science from President Bill Clinton in 1999, and died in 2011, is today commonly seen as among the most important evolutionary biologists of the twentieth century. She pioneered the study of the evolutionary history of bacteria, a subject long neglected by fellow evolutionary biologists, even though bacteria were the main life-form for the largest part of the biological history of the earth. Her greatest honor was to be one of thirteen recipients of the Darwin-Wallace Medal in 2008 (including also Gould). This is an unusual award in that until recently it was given only once every fifty years (the previous awards thus had been in 1958). It is more difficult for an evolutionary biologist to be a Darwin-Wallace medalist than for a physicist or chemist to win a Nobel Prize, thus putting Margulis with the other twelve recipients in 2008 in the category of the most important evolutionary biologists of the previous fifty years.

As Galileo was aided by improved telescopes, Margulis was aided by improvements in electron microscopes of the 1960s, enabling more precise observation of bacteria and other microorganisms. Another key development assisting her efforts was the discovery of DNA and then the rapidly decreasing cost of doing genome analyses from the 1970s. It also helped that some of the bacteria that she was able to observe in her microscopes still bore many resemblances to the bacteria that had existed on earth in its first three billion years, a source of information about the distant past superior to what could be obtained about most ancient plants and animals from studies of the fossil record.

Bacteria can interchange their genes so easily and rapidly that the very concept of a species is difficult to apply—Margulis herself stated that "bacteria do not have species."[64] Since Darwinism was a theory of *The Origin of Species*, it thus did not have much directly relevant to say about the first few billion years of the evolution of life on earth. Bacteria to this day still represent a large part of the existing life mass of the earth, again falling outside the scope of Darwinist explanations grounded in the concept of evolutionary changes in species.

Darwinism posited that the evolutionary creation of a new species was a process of change as random mutations occurred among individual members of a species, evolution then continually selecting for the most favored

---

64. Margulis, *Symbiotic Planet*, 6.

changes, until a new species finally emerged. Instead, in the bacterial world which Margulis studied, she found a much different process of evolutionary change that she called "symbiosis." As she first proposed in 1967, new forms of bacterial life were formed by one individual bacteria merging physically with another bacteria to create a new organism. As she said, one bacteria might "eat" another and yet the latter would survive to create jointly a new genetic organism. Such combinations, symbiotic bacterial blendings of multiple bacterial microorganisms, might then merge again with other combinations, resulting in yet further new bacterial organisms. Such mergers of microorganisms, as Margulis proposed, were the actual key events in the evolutionary process on earth for around two billion of years of the reign of bacteria.

Such new life forms, moreover, continue to play an important evolutionary role today. In describing the continuing process of "symbiogenesis," Margulis writes that it results from "the tendency of 'independent' life . . . to bind together and reemerge in a new wholeness at a higher, larger level of organization."[65] Indeed, each human being today contains billions of bacterial organisms within his or her stomach, eyelashes, and other parts of the body, their presence vital to normal human biological functioning. Human evolution itself has thus been in part a continuing process of symbiogenesis by which human "ecologies" of diverse living things exist together in mutual interdependency. "You" may think that you are a single human "person" but this is simply another of the many large illusions relating to human existence that the physical and biological sciences have been dispelling over the course of the twentieth century. "You" are in fact an "ecological system" that hosts a vast array of independently living microscopic organisms, as well as large amounts of originally bacterial DNA that still exist within your cells outside the nucleus—in addition to "your" very own DNA within the actual nucleus of each cell.

In this respect, moreover, human beings are typical of the rest of life on earth. Evolution by means of symbiosis has complemented genetic changes resulting from mutations, evolutionary drift, and other random events that drove traditional Darwinian natural selection. Margulis describes, for example, another representative symbiotic life form as follows:

> The flatworms of the species *Convoluta roscoffensis* are all green because their tissues are packed with *Platymonas* cells; as the worms are translucent, the green color of *Platymonas*, [a separate organism of] photosynthesizing algae, shows through. Although lovely, the green algae are not merely decorative: they live and

65. Ibid., 11.

grow, die and reproduce, inside the bodies of the worms. Indeed they produce the food that the worms "eat." The mouths of the worms become superfluous and do not function after the worm larvae hatch. Sunlight reaches the algae inside their mobile greenhouses and allows them to grow and feed themselves as they leak photosynthetic products and feed their [worm] hosts from the inside. The symbiotic algae even do the worm a waste management favor; they recycle the worm's uric acid waste into nutrients for themselves. Algae and worm make a miniature [combined symbiotic] ecosystem swimming in the sun.[66]

Events occurring in the surrounding environment can play a critical role in the creation of a new symbiotic organism such as the flatworms above. Symbiogenesis can also happen much more rapidly in comparison to evolutionary changes dependent on random genetic variation and natural selection. In this sense, symbiosis as theorized by Margulis is sometimes said to have a Lamarkian character in that environmental factors through symbiogenesis can create, for example, a new organism that passes its newly blended sets of genes to its biological heirs—as in the case of the flatworms above. This is another reason that Margulis initially encountered strong resistance to her thinking, since Lamarkian ideas had long been dismissed in evolutionary biology as pure pseudoscience.

More than a billion years ago, such evolutionary symbiotic workings led eventually to the emergence of eukaryote cells, more complicated organisms that typically included remnants of earlier bacterial life forms, themselves the remnants of still earlier bacterial blendings. Eukaryote cells are distinguished by the fact that they include a nucleus (surrounded by other cell elements). Remarkably, except for red blood cells, even all human cells today still contain identifiable bacterial remnants (existing within the cell membrane but outside the nucleus) that have been passed down from bacteria a billion and more years ago. Moreover, as noted above, each human being contains billions of independently living bacteria that often play key roles in the functioning of human life (bacteria, as Margulis liked to say, have received an unfairly bad reputation because of the harmful disease causing effects of a small minority of them).

When Margulis in 1967 first proposed this revolutionary understanding of the evolutionary workings of life on earth, and what it means to be a "living" thing (drawing in part on the work of some long-neglected American and Russian predecessors), she was widely ridiculed (her paper was rejected by the first fifteen journals to which she sent it). Frequent disagreements

66. Ibid., 9–10.

exist in all of science and new ideas are often strongly resisted but evolutionary biology seems to carry the mud slinging and derogatory comments to new heights—presumably in part because it involves such high religious stakes, and many evolutionary biologists are also true believers themselves in the Darwinist fundamentalism. In evolutionary biology, major new discoveries can thus pose existential challenges that go well beyond the threats to disciplinary orthodoxy of new thinking in other areas of science.

Margulis thus wrote in 1990 that the reigning new Darwinism of the day would eventually be viewed as "a minor 20th century religious sect within the sprawling religious persuasion of Anglo-Saxon biology."[67] It was not a new thought for her; Margulis once stated that in her early years as a student she found that "the field of population genetics, with its insistence on overly abstract neo-Darwinian concepts such as 'mutational load,' 'fitness,' and 'coefficients of selection,' taught more of a religion than a description of the rules by which real organisms passed on their genes and evolved."[68] Leading evolutionary biologist Niles Eldredge (coauthor with Gould of the theory of punctuated equilibrium) once commented that Margulis's arguments in the late 1960s and 1970s were "initially condemned as heresy" by fellow evolutionary biologists, even as these same ideas by the 1990s would be so well accepted that they had not only achieved wide professional acclaim for Margulis but had "rewritten the basic textbooks" of evolutionary biology.[69] The popularizers of evolutionary biology have been slow, however, to inform the wider public of these radical and potentially embarrassing new developments in the understanding of evolution—which are even today still not well understood outside professional evolutionary biological circles.

Even when it came to the more recent biological evolution of plants and animals with their more complex cell structures, Margulis had little use for neo-Darwinism as advanced by contemporary apostles such as Dawkins and Dennett. With respect to Darwin himself, she admired him but thought it possible that it was "because of Darwin [that] as a culture we still don't really understand the science of evolution."[70] Her views of contemporary neo-Darwinists were more critical. She wrote in 2002 that "many of Darwin's fashionable but misguided followers" among contemporary evolutionary biologists "habitually misinterpret even the parts of science they know well." Rather than a story of individuals evolving within species popula-

67. Quoted in Mann, "Lynn Margulis," 380.
68. Margulis, *Symbiotic Planet*, 18.
69. Eldredge, "Foreword" to Margolis and Sagan, *What is Life?* xiii, xii.
70. Margulis, *Symbiotic Planet*, 4.

tions, the actual working of biological evolution was not taking place among individuals but one of communities of life that "prevail in nature. When members of communities, different types of life thriving (or merely surviving) at the same time and place, fuse and transfer genes among themselves, new more complex 'individuals' evolve" in a manner so unlike the standard neo-Darwinist account. This symbiotic process results in "new, large, more complex 'individuals'" made up of many separate living parts that, as Margulis says sarcastically, are then "invariably assigned new species names by biologists," thus preserving the old Darwinist model of individual living things that collectively make up the members of a species.[71] The Margulis brand-new "communitarian" account of the key workings of evolution, as it was increasingly confirmed empirically from the 1980s (unlike many specifics of Darwinism that historically had been impossible to confirm empirically), was like a shock wave for mainstream evolutionary biology. This is the reason she is now regarded as such a major scientist of her times.

Indeed, Margulis stated publicly that she was unable to find a single example of the evolution of a species in the manner that Darwin had posited, observing that "although Darwin entitled his magnum opus *On the Origin of Species*, the appearance of new species is scarcely even discussed in his book"—Darwin apparently did not feel up to the problem at that time. More recently, Margulis relates an incident in which she challenged the evolutionary biologist Niles Eldredge to produce "any case in which the formation of a new species has been documented" by past or contemporary evolutionary biology. After some thought, Eldridge had to agree that he was unable to do so. Margulis was sympathetic to the Gould and Eldredge characterization of the changes in the fossil record in terms of a process of sudden punctuated equilibria but she was skeptical of neo-Darwinist explanations. Rather, she thought she had a better way of explaining how rapid punctuations occurred: "To me symbiosis as a source of evolutionary novelty helps explain the observation of [the frequency of] 'punctuated equilibrium,' of [sharp] discontinuities in the fossil record."[72] It was much easier to conceive of the sudden radical appearances of a new species as the result of a random set of symbiotic events than as the result of random mutations and the following workings of natural selection as necessarily occurring slowly over very long periods of time.

Margulis relates that "the stories of how microbes tend to physically join each other, and the multiple [genetic] interactions among themselves" within their biological communities "and with larger associates, have [now]

71. Margulis and Sagan, *Acquiring Genomes*, 96, 95.
72. Margulis, *Symbiotic Planet*, 6, 7, 8.

been told many times in the specialized language of the sciences." It remains the case, however, that "inevitably these stories are poorly known." The tools of the trade for Margulis and others like her were microscopes and genetic decomposition, while most evolutionary biologists still studied fossil records or created complex mathematical models. Hence, as she comments, "the study of microbes was largely shunted to its own departments, called microbiology, all of which resided in medical or agricultural schools." In these places, the principal goal was not a better theoretical understanding of the workings of biological evolution but with respect to the microbes to find more effective ways "to kill them."[73]

For Margulis, implicit in the neo-Darwinist way of thinking, as revealed, for example, by its long-standing disinterest in the central role of bacteria throughout the biological history of the earth, were old-fashioned ideas about the superiority of human beings and their central place in the universe. Evolution, as Darwin had said, was not about "the history of life on earth" but about the "descent of man." Indeed, an element of Christianity—human beings are uniquely made in the image of God—was often implicitly present in neo-Darwinist formulations, even as their evolutionary biological advocates might themselves frequently claim to be atheists. At one point Margulis and her son Dorion Sagan (Margulis had been married for a few years early in her life to the cosmologist Carl Sagan) observed that "God, if he existed, was Newton's God. . . . Beneath the new mathematical God was the ancient residuum of the idea of a more active God." In seeking to explain the world in physical terms alone, as is the faith of scientific materialism, Darwin and his evolutionary biologist successors were implicit heirs to the mechanist thinking of Newtonian science and the "more active God" that actually underlay it all.[74]

Margulis, however, declared that rather than putting human beings at the center of the universe, she was especially drawn to bacteria that had in fact played a much greater role in the overall evolution of life on earth. Perhaps a god had long preferred the bacteria and their symbiotic ways but was eventually ready for a change. She was controversially a strong supporter of the Gaia hypothesis of James Lovelock, seeing the whole earth not as a large piece of hard matter made up only of atoms and molecules but as an unusually large living system itself, the ultimate form of symbiosis, operating on the geographic scale of the entire planet. It still reflected the manner of the micro-level symbiotic processes that had originally formed life on earth, beginning with spontaneous symbiotic bacterial recombinations.

73. Margulis and Sagan, *Acquiring Genomes*, 95.
74. Margulis and Sagan, *Dazzle Gradually*, 203.

By her later years Margulis was commonly recognized as among the leading scientists of the twentieth century, even as some of her most adventurous ideas such as the Gaia hypothesis might be seen as lying outside science—it should be kept in mind, however, that her early theories had been seen as equally unlikely, only to receive full scientific vindication by the 1980s and 1990s. The basic environment of the earth, no scientists question, has been significantly formed by biological processes, including the creation of an oxygen-filled atmosphere as a result of bacterial actions around three billion years ago, and today the critical role of plant photosynthesis in absorbing CO_2 and releasing oxygen. In this sense, perhaps the "earth" is a living organism in the way that a human body is a large ecology including billions of microscopic organisms, all living together symbiotically as one "human being."

Margulis at Oxford

Margulis was invited in 2008 to be the Eastman Visiting Professor at Oxford, a position that had previously been occupied by some of the leading scientists in the world, a number of them Nobel P4rize winners. While at Oxford, a debate was arranged between Margulis and Richard Dawkins, the Oxford Professor for the Public Understanding of Science from 1995 to 2008—and of course well known for his books attacking religion and defending atheism, including *The God Delusion*. One of Dawkins's colleagues, who was present in May 2009 as a commenter at the debate at Balliol College, the Oxford professor of paleobiology Martin Brasier, later described the event in 2012. As he writes, "on one side stood Lynn Margulis, author of *Symbiotic Planet* and the greatest living proponent of symbiogenic theory. On the other side stood Richard Dawkins, author of *The Selfish Gene* and the most public proponent of neo-Darwinian theory."[75]

The debate was not about religion—Margulis and Dawkins did not strongly disagree there, although Margulis was less strident in rejecting Christianity and other traditional religion. It was about scientific truth, how biological evolution had actually worked since the emergence of life on earth about four billion years ago. As Brasier wrote of Margulis, she was "soon telling us that nearly all major speciation events that had ever taken place in evolution were the product of a kind of dangerous liaison—a symbiosis between two distantly related organisms that wantonly wrapped their genetic information to form completely new genetic strains." Moreover, despite long-standing Darwinist dogma to the contrary, as her new evolutionary

75. Brasier, "The Battle of Balliol," 74.

discoveries had revealed, "nearly all forms of biological innovation could not have arisen by natural selection working on random mutations." Taking the opposite side of the debate, as Brasier reported, Dawkins argued instead that genes "are the ultimate carrier of biological information and therefore the ultimate units upon which Darwinian natural selection itself is obliged to work. Genes are regenerators par excellence. And they sit atop a hierarchy that runs from genes, via cells, through organelles, to individuals and thence to communities."[76]

Brasier then asked, "So who won this debate at Balliol?" in 2009. He considered that the verdict "hinges around which of two life strategies has been the winner in the great planetary game: hierarchies, a la Dawkins; or networks in the Margulian mode?" Judged by the total volume of evolutionary events, Brasier thought that the evidence strongly favored Margulis: "most genetic transfer within the biosphere takes place among bacteria and archaea, and the vast majority of such microbes are found within symbiotic associations." On the critical question of hierarchies versus networks, Brasier again found in favor of Margulis: "I would argue that each of the most important steps in evolution—the evolution of cellular life (before circa 3,500 million years ago), of eukaryote cells (c. 1,800 Ma), of animal guts (c. 580 Ma), and of plant roots (c. 580 Ma)—has arguably involved revolutions in symbiogenetic networks on the grandest scale. . . . It was arguably such networking revolutions in the deep history of life that made our planet habitable."[77] Brasier was too polite to give a final explicit verdict but his report left little room for doubt—and if Dawkins was wrong scientifically about the basic workings of evolution, his similarly confident judgments about religion might also be called into serious doubt. It was not a good day for the true believers in scientific materialism of the Dawkins/Dennett kind.

Another of Dawkins's Oxford colleagues, physiologist Denis Noble, who chaired the debate, and had interacted frequently with Dawkins over the years, offered a similar assessment in his own account. He acknowledges that he was already having serious doubts about neo-Darwinism as a result of writing the 2008 book *The Music of Life,* which had proved to be "a watershed event in which I discovered that standard evolutionary theories make little sense in physiological science. If organisms were merely vehicles for genes that mutated entirely at random, then physiology would be largely irrelevant to the major processes in creating new species"—an idea that seemed to him altogether "strange."[78] By the time of the 2009 debate, as

76. Ibid., 75, 76.
77. Ibid., 78.
78. Noble, "Science, Music, Philosophy," 80.

he states, "I was already coming to the conclusion that something must be incomplete or even fundamentally wrong with the modern synthesis (neo-Darwinism)."[79] In rejecting the evolutionary understanding that Dawkins had been presenting so confidently since *The Selfish Gene* appeared in 1976, Noble writes:[80]

> I confessed that I no longer knew what a gene was and that, whatever it was, I thought that selfishness was an inappropriate metaphor. To a physiologist, the striking thing about genes and their products, RNAs and proteins, is that they act in large cooperative networks to produce physiological functions [as seen in animal bodies and behavior]. The networks reduce the influence of any individual genes on functionality by buffering against such changes.[81]

Even with the clear evidence of the latest evolutionary biology now turning against him, Dawkins, perhaps understandably, has seemed unwilling to alter his lifelong message. In reviewing a 2013 Dawkins book, the distinguished British political philosopher John Gray wrote that Dawkins remains an "antireligious missionary." As such, he retains the certitudes of the true believer on whom even strong new scientific evidence often can make little impact. As Gray thus notes, "the theory of evolution by natural selection is [still there] treated not as a fallible theory . . . but as an unalterable truth, which has been revealed to a single individual of transcendent genius." Darwin was the original genius but "there cannot be much doubt that Dawkins sees himself as a Darwin-like figure, propagating the revelation that came to the Victorian naturalist" in prose now more suited to the late twentieth and early twenty-first century.[82] With his long-standing statements of neo-Darwinism now under basic challenge from fellow evolutionary biologists, perhaps it is some consolation that he still has a large remaining audience of adoring followers who remain drawn to his "atheistic" sermons delivered with an evangelical fervor that still captivates millions.

As Gray assesses Dawkins overall, "at no point has Dawkins thrown off his Christian inheritance. Instead, emptying the faith he was taught [in his youth] of its transcendent content, he became a neo-Christian evangelist." It would have been more difficult for him to sustain all this if Dawkins had "a more inquiring mind" but he has never understood "that religion comes in many varieties, with belief in a creator god figuring in only a few of the

79. Ibid., 81.

80. Dawkins, *The Selfish Gene*.

81. Noble, "Science, Music, Philosophy," 81.

82. Gray, "The Closed Mind of Richard Dawkins."

world's faiths and most having no interest in proselytizing. It is only against a background of a certain kind of [Abrahamic] monotheism that Dawkins's evangelical atheism makes any sense."[83] The stories of neo-Darwinism told in story after story by Dawkins have been new secular substitutes for the stories of the Christian Bible that once were seen by whole societies as having themselves revealed the actual historical truth of the world. As Gray says, by all indications Dawkins conceives of himself as a leading apostle of a new modern and "scientific" god of evolution, a god that for many modern people took the place of the Christian God in controlling everything that happens in the world.

Margulis would probably not be happy to hear her own thinking described in religious terms. Nevertheless, what really separates her from Dawkins is not the presence or absence of a religious content. Rather, it is the more attractive character of the implicit religion that is embedded in Margulis's thinking, standing in large contrast to the fundamentalism of Dawkins that bears surprisingly many similarities to its Christian fundamentalist counterparts. Rather than religious certainties, Margulis is a follower in the forms of religion in which an awareness of one's own weaknesses and religious doubt and thus tolerance of dissent are central to the practice of the faith. The greatest scientists such as Albert Einstein or Richard Feynman typically have believed that to read the Book of Nature is to encounter the mind of a god. In Einstein's case he often said explicitly that he was engaged in a religious search to understand the thinking of a god. Margulis is closer to Feynman in this regard, often speaking in terms of the "beauty" of the bacteria and other natural objects she studies, the sense of "awe" she experiences in contemplating evolutionary biological workings, and how she "love[s] to gaze" at the objects of her research—even as she says little about all these things being manifestations of the work of a god.[84]

Cells as Sentient Beings

As examined in Chapter 3, the discoveries of the physics of the twentieth century—above all quantum mechanics—undermined the mechanistic view of the universe as it had been inherited from the nineteenth century. Since 1980, a similar outcome has been occurring in evolutionary biology in which Margulis played an important part but many others also had large contributing roles. Neo-Darwinism is grounded in the same mechanistic habits of thought of the nineteenth century but such ways of thinking

83. Ibid.
84. Margulis, *Symbiotic Planet*, 20, 41, 11.

survived in the field of evolutionary biology well past their demise in physics. They did not survive long into the twenty-first century, however, as University of Chicago professor of microbiology James Shapiro explains in his 2011 book, *Evolution: A View from the 21st Century.*[85]

Another evolutionary biologist, Eugene Koonin, who works at the National Institutes of Health, takes a similar view in another 2011 book, *The Logic of Chance*, writing that "thanks to the advances of genomics and systems biology, we have learned more about the key aspects of evolution in the first decade of the twenty-first century than in the preceding century and a half." Looking back on the past seventy years, Koonin describes the neo-Darwinist development of the "Modern Synthesis" as having turned into "a relatively narrow, in some ways dogmatic conceptual framework." Indeed, the "Modern Synthesis notably 'hardened' through indoctrinating gradualism, uniformitarianism, and, most important, the monopoly of natural selection as the only route of evolution." In light of the rapid pace of discovery in evolutionary biology in recent years, it has become further apparent that "for all its fundamental merits, [the neo-Darwinist] Modern Sythesisis is a rather dogmatic and woefully incomplete theory." It is based in part on a "huge leap of faith by extending the mechanisms and patterns established for microevolution to macroevolutionary processes"—not a faith in a Christian God but perhaps in a new evolutionary form of divinity.[86]

Shapiro writes similarly that the neo-Darwinist account of evolution based on the assumption of "the accidental, stochastic nature of mutations is still the prevailing and widely accepted wisdom" today. This long-standing "insistence on randomness and accident" was not a scientific conclusion in and of itself but resulted from "a determination in the 19th and 20th Centuries by biologists to reject the role of a supernatural agent in religious accounts of how diverse living organisms originated." These biologists made "an *a priori* philosophical distinction between the 'blind' processes of hereditary variation and all other adaptive functions."[87] It might be more accurate, however, to say that they made an *a priori* "faith distinction," the randomness of hereditary variation becoming for evolutionary biologists a core element of belief.

But evolutionary change through random mutations and the workings of natural selection is bound to be a slow process. It would be more adaptive if living creatures could have the ability to speed up the process of genetic variation and even more beneficial for them if they could direct the

85. Shapiro, *Evolution*.
86. Koonin, *The Logic of Chance*, 416, 14, 18, 19.
87. Shapiro, *Evolution*, 1, 1–2, 2.

emergence of new genes in directions that would be beneficial for their own evolutionary survival prospects. It was simply that evolutionary biologists ruled this out from the beginning by assumption; it would require that cells and other living organisms have a seemingly miraculous ability to "plan" for their future. Human beings and perhaps a few other higher mammals might be able to do this, but it was taken for granted that the rest of life on earth certainly could not.

Much as quantum mechanics originally seemed miraculous to physicists but they were forced by the rigorous application of scientific methods to accept that very strange things actually occurred in the behavior of quanta, similarly rigorous work in evolutionary biology in recent years has now shown that cells also perform in ways that are very surprising. A key factor has been that the discovery of DNA and the rapid declines in the cost of genome analyses have worked to transform evolutionary biology from Darwinist storytelling (relating "historical narratives" as Fodor puts it) into a science closer to physics and chemistry. The results have been startling. As Shapiro writes, "molecular analysis provided mechanistic insight into the myriad distinct ways that living cells can engineer their DNA. Genome sequencing at the end of the 20th Century and the start of this one confirmed major roles played by 'natural genetic engineering' in the course of evolutionary change."[88]

Much as Margulis also said, neo-Darwinism as preached by Dawkins, Dennett, and so many others thus is effectively consigned to history. Shapiro writes that in light of contemporary research in evolutionary biology "little evidence fits unequivocally with the theory that evolution occurs through the gradual accumulation of 'numerous, successive, slight modifications.' On the contrary, clear evidence exists for abrupt events of specific kinds at all levels of genome organization. These sudden changes range from horizontal transfers and the movement of transposable elements through chromosome rearrangements to whole genome duplications and cell fusions." Drawing partly on Margulis, one important way of achieving rapid changes in cell genomes is by "whole genome mergers [that] are the products of phagocytosis or cell invasions leading to endosymbiosis." Broadly speaking, the accepted "view of genome change" today has abandoned previous neo-Darwinist concepts to become "one that describes active cell processes rather than a series of random accidents" due to mutations, now instead based on "natural genetic engineering operators [that] are the molecular agents of active genetic change" that can occur far more rapidly, a very large

88. Ibid., 2.

evolutionary advantage for the large number of living creatures that have this capacity for rapid adaptation to their surroundings.[89]

Shapiro acknowledges that there is an element of the mysterious about all this—how can an organism as primitive as a cell manipulate its genetic variation through molecular means in directions that will be favorable to its evolutionary survival prospects? At one point he asks, "Can such function-oriented capacities be attributed to cells? Is this not the kind of teleological thinking that scientists have been taught to avoid at all costs? The answer to both questions is yes." But as quantum mechanics showed now many years ago, nature does not respect human prejudices about how the world must work. Shapiro writes that "the more we learn about the detailed molecular operation of cells, the more we appreciate the depth of the circuitry they contain to ensure the accurate, 'well informed' execution of complex functions. This is now the prevailing view in many fields of biology." Remarkably, even plants have such capacities; Shapiro notes that a field of "plant neurology" is emerging. A 2010 article in the journal *Nature Immunology* "was dedicated to 'decision making in the immune system.'" Indeed, as such developments suggest, he finds that "the idea of cellular cognition and decision making with well-defined functional objectives has gone mainstream."[90]

As Shapiro explains, cells thus routinely "spend a great deal of their available energy and matter on information processing and regulation" of themselves. For example, "anti-body-producing B lymphocytes are only one of hundreds of dedicated cell types in a mammalian body that operate for specific functional ends." Unlike the biological history of old that sought to interpret the fossil record from a distant past, it is now possible for evolutionary biologists to subject such matters to real "experimental tests" in the laboratory that have thus far confirmed the concept that "functionally targeted and coordinated natural genetic engineering" is central to the evolutionary workings of life on earth. Shapiro writes that cells engage in "cognitive cellular operations that have led to successful evolutionary inventions." Remarkably, one might even describe cells as having a capacity for "sentience." As he puts it, recent evolutionary biological research has shown that "living cells and organisms are cognitive (sentient) entities that act and interact purposefully to ensure survival, growth and proliferation." He goes further to say that hard laboratory research has demonstrated that "cells are now seen to operate teleologically"—that is to say, even though they lack a human consciousness, they pursue a purpose, the purpose of evolutionary

89. Ibid., 128, 129.
90. Ibid., 136–37, 137.

survival as they can advance their own prospects by their own natural capacities for "genetic engineering."[91]

Despite the extensive empirical documentation and confirmation of recent years, Shapiro notes that the idea of "natural genetic engineering" has been "fiercely resisted by mainstream biologists and evolutionists in particular." Shapiro has even been accused by some follow evolutionary biologists of lending support—whether intentionally or not—to the Intelligent Design movement when he uses terms such as "sentience" as exhibited in cell genetic engineering. Shapiro insists that, to the contrary, he is as much of a naturalist as any evolutionary biologist, does not assign any role to supernatural elements, but also insists on following where the hard scientific realities take him, however difficult to understand in commonsense terms. In his view, the strong resistance of many evolutionary biologists has little to do with science but is "deeply philosophical in nature and dates back to late 19th Century disputes over evolution and also to the early 20th Century 'mechanism-vitalism' debate." The philosophical—really religious—foundations of the neo-Darwinist understanding of evolution were "uncritically accepted at those times by much of the biological community." It was thus long an evolutionary biological article of faith that in evolution "cognitive goal-oriented processes have to be relegated to the realms of unscientific fancy and religion."[92]

But it is neo-Darwinism that today seems to Shapiro to belong more to the domain of unscientific fancy and religion.[93] For many evolutionary biologists of our time, Shapiro's strong criticisms of neo-Darwinism have come as a large shock—to be told now that their lifelong neo-Darwinist faith has been invalidated by recent hard scientific evidence. It is perhaps no less than the shock of many Christian faithful in Darwin's own time on being confronted with the scientific realities of the evolutionary history of the earth, provoking a similar existential tension and resistance. When the history of neo-Darwinism is taught in the future, it may be appropriate to include it as a part of the curriculum in schools of theology.

Darwinism as Universal Acid

Many ardent Darwinist advocates today, like other zealots of history, see themselves as introducing new fundamental truths of the world. In one

91. Ibid., 137, 147, 143, 137.

92. Ibid., 138.

93. For a summary review of recent new thinking about the workings of evolution, see Ward and Kirschvink, *A New History of Life*.

prominent case, as Daniel Dennett proudly asserted of his own efforts, Darwinism provided a "universal acid" that would radically change western civilization because of "both its ubiquity and its power to corrode traditional Western beliefs."[94] Dennett seems to have overlooked the fact that he was not making a prediction about the future but was describing an actual large role that Darwinism played in shaping the history of the first half of the twentieth century, most of all in Germany where its "universal acid" was particularly effective. As we all know, the results of applying this acid to the foundations of historic German culture were not happy. What we learned was that Darwinist ideas were very dangerous, containing within them a religious potential that could lead not to scientific and economic progress towards a heaven on earth but instead towards a new hell on earth.

In undermining faith for many millions of people in the biblical account of the history of the world, Darwinism worked to undermine their faith in traditional Jewish and Christian religion altogether. It raised a profound question, what would now become the purpose of their lives, why were they here on earth in the first place? Not only did evolutionary biology fail to provide any reassuring answers but it could easily be taken to say that in principle there was no answer to be found at all—human existence was just another random biological event in the long evolutionary history of life on earth. Traditional morals might be scientifically "explained" for their practical survival benefits but in a strict evolutionary account they would continue to exist only to the extent that they could be said to advance the competitive prospects of the human species (or, of a specific subspecies, that is to say, a race, part of the gradual process of the evolution of a brand-new species of superior humanoid successors to the old and increasingly less fit current "humans," as was the norm in the Darwinian evolution of a brand-new species). Morality for many people no longer seemed to have any absolute claims to validity as something "true"—excepting only those unreconstructed traditional Christian true believers who still argued that Darwinism itself cannot be "true."

With the authority of the Jewish and Christian Bible thus under radical Darwinist assault, the "Book of Nature" nevertheless might remain as a potentially authoritative source of knowledge about God. There was admittedly nothing in Darwinism itself that said much about the religious authority of the Book of Nature. But even for many "secular" people the Jewish and Christian roots of Western civilization proved sturdier than expected even in the wake of the Darwinist corrosive acid. For such people, even as they rejected the traditional biblical messages, they still implicitly saw the Book of

94. Dennett, quoted in Gould, "Darwinian Fundamentalism."

Nature as an authoritative source of information about the thinking of god. In the United States in the late nineteenth century, for example, the early environmentalist John Muir said little about Jesus and the Bible in his voluminous writings but in the experience of the High Sierra mountains of California—and of the wild nature uncontaminated by human actions there—as he happily and explicitly professed, he felt a powerful presence and source of instruction in being in the presence of the awe-inspiring Sierra landscapes that provided an avenue into the workings of the mind of god.[95]

Less comforting lessons, however, might also be learned from the Book of Nature, especially after the full Darwinist revelations concerning the evolutionary biological history of the earth. As Darwinism now seemingly had scientifically shown, god is not only inordinately fond of mathematics (as had been clearly demonstrated beginning in the seventeenth century) but also of evolutionary competitive struggle among the various forms of life on earth. Indeed, intense interspecies warfare throughout nature, as Darwin seemingly had now revealed, was at the heart of the divine plan for the world. This also presumably applied to a recent arrival among the species of the earth, human beings—not only in competition with other species but among human beings themselves in the process of evolving a new improved "superhuman" species that would be the natural biological heir to the current human species. Again, even as it was not a scientific element of Darwinism itself, such a residual Jewish and Christian message concerning the character and desires of God persisted over wide circles of twentieth-century society. Applying Darwinist science correctly, manipulating the workings of natural evolution for human purposes, there could be hope for rapid evolutionary advances in human affairs, leading eventually along an evolutionary path to the greater perfection of the human species and the human condition as a whole.

However perverse and even abhorrent it is today, such Darwinist evolutionary utopianism spread over large parts of the intellectual life of Europe and the United States of the late nineteenth and early twentieth century. In the United States, for example, Madison Grant came from the upper strata of American society; he could trace his ancestry on his father's side to Richard Treat, dean of Pitminster Church in England, among the first Puritans to arrive in New England in 1630. Grant was a close friend of Theodore Roosevelt, including membership in the elite (and politically influential) Boone and Crockett Club founded by Roosevelt. A Yale graduate, Grant was a founder of the Bronx Zoo in 1895 and was later a leader in the political battle to create Glacier National Park in 1910, then figuring

95. Nash, *Wilderness and the American Mind.*

prominently in the establishment of Denali National Park in Alaska, Everglades National Park, and Olympic National Park.[96] In the 1930s the head of the US Biological Service (now the Fish and Wildlife Service) declared that Madison Grant had been "the godfather to . . . wildlife conservation measures for the last 25 years."[97]

Since human beings were now to be seen as yet another part of the natural world, as Darwin had shown, Grant did not limit his biological perspective to the ecological protection and management of wild plants and animals. He was also a leading proponent at the time of human biological management—of "scientific racism," as explained by Grant in his 1916 book *The Passing of the Great Race*. The book proposes, as Grant writes in the opening sentence, "to elucidate the meaning of history in terms of race," as understood by the principles of survival of the fittest drawn from Darwin.[98] As his biographer Jonathan Spiro writes, Grant focused his entire theory of human history on the fundamental role of genes and evolution, thereby producing a "history of mankind [that] is actually a tale of the evolution, migration, and confrontation of races" that are the subspecies of the whole human species. Grant sees the history of Europe as shaped by three such subspecies, the "Nordics" of northern Europe, the "Alpines" of eastern and central Europe, and the "Mediterraneans" of southern and southwestern Europe. The Nordics, according to Grant, are the "Master Race."[99] The colder climate and harsher living conditions in the north in general, as he theorizes, have imposed a more ruthless evolutionary process of survival of the fittest, resulting in an evolutionarily superior Nordic race.

As a Darwinist true believer, who sought to apply Darwin's world view to the human species, Grant was an active proponent of the eugenics movement that became widely influential throughout the United States and in northern Europe. Grant warned that Darwinist biological science had shown the dangers that lay in humanitarian moralities that would perpetuate the less fit members to the detriment of the whole human species. The application of Newtonian science to establish human control over nature had produced extraordinary material benefits for the overall human condition on earth from the nineteenth century onward. Why should not a similar application of the most advanced evolutionary science, as Darwinism had more recently revealed it, not have similarly great long-run human benefits? Among those who closely studied Grant's writings and sought to apply them

96. Spiro, *Defending the Master Race*, 67.

97. Quoted in ibid., 28.

98. Grant, quoted in ibid., 145.

99. Ibid., 145, 148, 149.

in Germany was Adolf Hitler. In *Hitler's Millennial Reich*, American historian David Redles examines how the Darwinist messages of evolutionary salvation through racial competition penetrated all aspects of German life in the Nazi years. National Socialism was a new blend of old historic Christian ideas (the 1,000-year reich was the Nazi millennium) combined with a claim to apply newly modern methods derived from recent great advances in scientific knowledge provided by developments in evolutionary biology.[100] As Redles reports, this mixture of old and new religion was intoxicating for "many Germans and non-Germans [who] . . . accepted Hitler's messianic self-perception, his role as both prophet and messiah, interpreting him as a Christ or Godlike figure, sent from heaven to save Germany from utter annihilation"—all this based on using newly scientific methods. [101]

Michael Hoeltz writes with respect to the National Socialist belief system that it is "right to call it theology rather than to use the more neutral term ideology . . . because to talk about Hitler's ideology would miss the crucial point that the fascination with Hitler is based to a great extent on the symbolic power of theological language and the theological reference to a higher, greater transcendent reality," all this presented as the truth of the world as newly revealed by evolutionary biology in the wake of Darwin's great discoveries, now to be applied to the world of practical affairs in Germany.[102]

Looking back on their early involvement with National Socialism, many Germans later described the process as involving a "conversion experience." Redles writes that "in keeping with the religious nature of the Nazi conversion experience, the new faith was almost always referred to with a sense of righteousness; it was the 'correct' or 'right' path to salvation." It frequently invoked a profound sense "of moving from confusion to clarity, from darkness to light, . . . a [personal] perception of order collapsed into disorder and then having that sense of order reconstructed. The sense of order generated by Nazi apocalyptic cosmology was experienced as a revelation of simple but profound truths," explained in evolutionary biological terms.[103] Hitler himself explained that in encountering the reactions of his fellow Germans—and especially the young—to his Darwinist utopian message of earthly salvation in the early Nazi years,

> You will sense the inner conversion; then you will realize the new faith is awakening out of the lethargy of a corrupt epoch

100. Bucher, *Hitler's Theology.*

101. Redles, *Hitler's Millennial Reich*, 158.

102. Hoelzl, "Introduction," xvii.

103. Redles, *Hitler's Millennial Reich*, 85, 89.

and taking to the march—the faith in divine justice, in heavenly truth; the faith in an unworldly, paradisiacal future, where
the lust for power, force and enmity gives way to equality and
fraternity, the spirit of sacrifice, love and loyalty, and the will to
stand before the throne of the Almighty with the open heart of
one ready to believe in God. And they will have sufficient greatness to stammer out the prayer for their [German] brothers and
fathers, "Forgive them, Lord, for they knew not what they did."
It is on this basis alone that the new world will be built. To lay
this groundwork is our task.[104]

Historian Richard Steigmann-Gall similarly writes that "among wide circles,
Nazism was infused with key elements of Christian belief," and received
surprisingly large amounts of support from German Christian leadership—
especially among Protestant churches. Given that Nazism since then has become "the world-historical metaphor for human evil and wickedness, [that
it] . . . should have been related to Christianity can therefore be regarded
by many only as unthinkable."[105] True believing Darwinists today similarly
find it unthinkable that Darwinism played a large role in the events in Germany from 1919 to 1945. They have managed to suppress this lamentable
consequence of Darwinism from in their thinking. A whole industry of fictional accounts of Nazi Germany, therefore, has arisen, portraying National
Socialism as some form of bizarre, tortured, altogether unprecedented ab-
erration in Western civilization, an outbreak of irrationality on a national
German scale that could scarcely have been imagined before, and for which
there is no possible rational explanation.

    As Redles comments, however, "the perceived clarity of Nazi ideas
and goals, contrary to the view of many historians, was of paramount importance to many of the converted. The belief, then, that Nazi propaganda,
whether written or spoken, was a meaningless mishmash of ideas that had
little effect on its audience, is simply untrue."[106] When blended with elements
of Christian millenarianism, National Socialism was a surprisingly logical
application to the human situation of evolutionary biological science. As
modern physics had provided the scientific knowledge to manipulate the
natural world for great human benefit, evolutionary biology in Germany was
now providing the scientific knowledge for human beings to manipulate the
processes of human evolution also for great human benefit. Darwinism, as

---

104. Hitler, quoted in ibid., 78–79.

105. Steigmann-Gall, *The Holy Reich*, 265, 266. For a study from a Christian perspective of Hitler's frequent use of historical borrowings from Christianity, see Comfort, *Hitler, God & the Bible*.

106. Redles, *Hitler's Millennial Reich*, 90.

Dennett so naively declares as a positive feature, had in fact worked to apply a "universal acid" to traditional German morals and humanitarian culture that would otherwise have stood in the way of Nazi barbarism, even as many Nazis believed that they were pursuing the biological salvation of the world.

In *From Darwin to Hitler*, Richard Weikart takes the question head on: What is the connection between Darwinist evolutionary biology and the rise of National Socialism? As he notes, early in the twentieth century "most prominent advocates of Darwinian theory—including biologists, physicians, social theorists, and popularizers—believed Darwinism had far reaching implications for ethics and morality." Indeed, the proponents of most "visions of moral or social reform" often disagreed on the details but all of them "tried to give his or her particular agenda scientific imprimatur by claiming harmony with the laws of evolution." It reflected a basic shift in Western thought in "the 1890s and early 1900s, [when] race moved from the periphery to center stage with a veritable deluge of books and articles devoted to the topic." This included a growing number "of Aryan racists and anti-Semites—which included many scientists and physicians—[who] appropriated the mantle of Darwinian science to enhance their legitimacy," drawing connections that seemingly found strong support in Darwinism itself, especially given its implication that traditional morality was merely an evolutionary adaptation, thus never absolutely binding.[107] As Weikart sums up the impact of such thinking in Germany in the 1930s and 1940s:

> Nazi barbarism was motivated by an ethic that prided itself on being scientific. [For National Socialists] the evolutionary process became the arbiter of all morality. Whoever promoted the evolutionary progress of humanity was deemed good, and whatever hindered the biological improvement was considered morally bad. [As in the universal evolutionary struggle for survival of the fittest], multitudes must perish in this [natural] Malthusian struggle anyway, they reasoned, so why not improve humanity by [taking human actions] speeding up the destruction of the disabled and the inferior races? According to this logic, the extermination of individuals and races deemed inferior and "unfit" was not only morally justified but, indeed, morally praiseworthy.[108]

In 1946, drawing on a large body of Nazi documents that had recently become available with the end of World War II, the Yiddish Scientific Institute in New York published a comprehensive study, *Hitler's Professors*,

107. Weikart, *From Darwin to Hitler*, 229, 69, 117.
108. Ibid., 227.

describing the surprisingly large "part of German scholarship in Germany's crimes against the Jewish people." Max Weinrich writes—perhaps with some exaggeration—that "the whole ruling class of Germany was committed to the execution of this crime . . . [including] German scholarship [that] provided the ideas and techniques which led to and justified this unparalleled slaughter" of the Jews. This included almost every field of scholarship such as "physical anthropology and biology, all branches of the social sciences and the humanities." One might like to believe, Weinrich observes, that the Nazis had driven out the legitimate scholars, leaving only "sham scholars, nobodies elevated in rank by their Nazi friends and protectors."[109] But the clear documentary evidence shows that this view "is baseless." As Weinrich reports, in reality Darwinism was then regarded as the height of scientific knowledge, and many of the leading scholars of Germany had come to understand the world in Darwinist terms. The manipulation of scientific knowledge, following after Newton, and now after equally great Darwinist scientific advances, seemingly offered, moreover, a path to heaven on earth, the central goal of so much of modern thought since the Enlightenment.

Thus, as Weinrich wrote, in actual fact "the scholars whom we shall quote in such impressive numbers [in *Hitler's Professors*], like those others who were instrumental in any other part of the German pre-war and war efforts, were to a large extent people of long and high standing, university professors and academy members, some of them world famous, authors with familiar names and guest lecturers abroad, the kind of people Allied scholars used to meet and fraternize with at international congresses."[110] This German intellectual elite had such sure confidence in the National Socialist message because the message was in fact a surprisingly logical application of the principles of evolutionary biology—once all conventional morals had been dismissed, and as especially the scholarly elite knew, these morals had largely been grounded in fictitious biblical stories and other old mythology.

Rudolf Hess thus famously declared in 1934 that "National Socialism is nothing but applied biology." Weinrich writes that "the whole structure of anti-Jewish thought and action was erected upon the so-called 'racial science'" that supposedly originated in evolutionary biology and genetics. Among the key figures in its development were "some world-famous German scholars like Erwin Baur, Ernest Rudin, and, perhaps most of all, Eugen Fischer."[111] Illustrating the central role of Darwinist ideas, Rudin (with two coauthors) wrote in 1933:

109. Weinrich, *Hitler's Professors*, 5, 6, 7
110. Ibid., 7.
111. Ibid., 17.

Our whole cultural life for decades has been more or less under the influence of biological thinking, as it was begun around the middle of the last century, by the teachings of Darwin, Mendel, and Galton and afterwards has been advanced by the studies of [leading scholars such as] Ploetz, Schallmeyer, Correns, de Vries, Tschermak, Baur, Rudin, Fischer, Lenz, and others. Although it took decades before the courage was found, on the basis of the initial findings of the natural sciences, to carry on a systematic study of heredity, the progress of the teaching and its application to man could not be delayed any more. It was recognized that the natural laws discovered for plants and animals ought also to be for man, and this could be confirmed during the last three decades [through the further biological and genetic research that was in fact carried out].[112]

Should we in any way today hold Darwin himself—and later nineteenth- and early twentieth-century evolutionary biologists who spread his views with such religious enthusiasm—accountable for the terrible later consequences of their efforts? Obviously, it would have been impossible for them to anticipate the specific later uses to which their writings would be put in Germany, and therefore perhaps to have abandoned their evolutionary biological research in horror at any such prospect. Many evolutionary biologists, moreover, might well argue that their obligation is to do the best scientific research possible, and that it is the responsibility of others in society to decide what to do with the results. That is not their responsibility. From this perspective, the horrors in the name of Darwin of the first half of the twentieth century are simply a story of European civilization going off the rails, something for which it would be altogether unreasonable to assign any responsibility to evolutionary biologists themselves who had simply reported the scientific truth as they saw it.

This does not of course excuse the behavior of those many evolutionary biologists who did enter actively into the political fray to promote the social application of their Darwinist biological science—of whom there were many. Perhaps even more to the point, when evolutionary biologists exaggerated the scientific status of their Darwinist findings, as was often the case, this lent further scientific authority to the various political, economic, genetic, and other crusades that would later be presented—however much they went beyond the actual boundaries of science—in the name of Darwinist science. Even when they did not enter into these crusades themselves, many evolutionary biologists stood on the sidelines, remaining publicly silent as to the distortions of Darwinist thought being so widely

112. Rudin et al., quoted in Weinrich, *Hitler's Professors*, 33.

advanced. If there is a lesson to be learned in all this, it is that any attempt to apply Darwinism to wider human issues of the whole society can be an extraordinarily toxic brew. It is not clear that Dawkins, Dennett, and other of their new atheist brethren have much sense of history in this regard. Indeed, one might say that, far more than Christian religion, the greatest horrors of the twentieth century were justified in the name of "atheist religion," even as these forms of atheism implicitly drew heavily on Christianity for their great public appeal. As one might say, it was not traditional Christianity but a new "atheistic Christianity" in evolutionary biological disguise that wreaked havoc on the world over the course of a new "thirty years' wars" of modern religion from 1914 to 1945.

Conclusion

Although he died in February 2013, the distinguished American legal philosopher Ronald Dworkin—never known as a strong advocate for traditional religion—had completed by then a new book, *Religion Without God*, excerpts from which were soon published in the *New York Review of Books*. Reflecting the growing doubts about Darwinism—both scientifically and morally—that have been appearing in surprising places in the early part of the twenty-first century, Dworkin now rejected the Darwinist logic that "we hold the moral convictions we do only because they are evolutionarily adaptive."[113] He also observes that, as discussed above, there is nothing in the evolutionary account of history that guarantees the competitive survival of what is objectively "true."

But Dworkin wants something more absolute, more like the traditional Christian sense of the revealed "truths" of the world and of God—even if Dworkin does not argue that a specifically Christian God is necessary for this outcome. In broader terms, nevertheless, he writes approvingly of "the religious attitude [that] accepts the full independent reality of value." This means for one thing that "human life has objective meaning or importance"—we are not simply complex assemblies of chemicals and other material elements shaped by evolutionary forces. Endorsing a main tenet of "environmental religion" today, Dworkin writes that "what we call 'nature'— the universe as a whole and in all its parts—is not just a matter of fact but is itself sublime: something of intrinsic value and wonder" that transcends any biological or other scientific understanding. All in all, "the religious attitude" that will be required in the future for human beings on earth "rejects all forms of [evolutionary biological] naturalism. It insists that values are

113. Dworkin, *Religion Without God*, 14.

real and fundamental, not just manifestations of something else; they are as real as trees or pain," they are "true" in an absolute sense, all this in large contrast to the messages of our Darwinist fundamentalists both in the past and still commonly heard today—including among some who celebrate the ability of the Darwinist "universal acid" to undermine the old truths of Western civilization.[114]

Dworkin does not say so himself but in rejecting a naturalist world view, as advanced by many contemporary evolutionary biologists, he is taking a large step towards the conclusion that a god exists. When more fully exposed to the contradictions and other large failings of evolutionary biology in its Darwinist, and more recent neo-Darwinist, forms, surprisingly many other people—some of them self-professed atheists at present—might well come to agree, even if they do not know it yet.

114. Ibid., 10, 13.

5

Scientifically Inexplicable

The Mystery of Human Consciousness

HUMAN EXISTENCE IS HUMAN consciousness. There is nothing before it and nothing after it (that we can say about for sure). It is all you and I have. The "material" realm is simply a coding classification within human consciousness for certain mental events that we place in that category. Indeed, to belief that "the material world" actually exists as something outside our individual consciousness requires a leap of faith. As discussed earlier in this book, I happen to make that leap, as you the reader very likely also do, along with the vast majority of other human beings. But it is not a step that the scientific method by itself can justify. Indeed, it is closer to believing in a god, virtually equivalent if the necessarily supernatural power that establishes an exact correspondence between the interior "material" events of consciousness and the assumed outside material world is given the label of "god" (this god can of course have many other features).

There is no possible prospect of any actual "scientific" study of human consciousness. The events in human consciousness have no measurable reality in time and space, they do not have measurable size or form, their rates of change cannot be precisely calculated and objectively verified by any independent outside observer. Indeed, consciousness is inherently subjective; the only possible observer of my consciousness is me—and the same goes for you, dear reader. The accuracy of my reports about the workings of my consciousness to any other "outside" observer is speculative at best. Even my choice of language to describe events in my consciousness may mean different things to different people. Indeed, the core elements required for a rigorous application of the scientific method, as in the study of the natural world by physicists, are altogether missing. Freud once claimed to have developed a science of human consciousness but, while he was a brilliant writer, developed some insightful classifications of mental events, and offered many provocative hypotheses in his time, his claims to have developed an exact science of the mind—he claimed it was literally analogous to physics—appear to us today as bordering on another form of religious fundamentalism.

For much of the twentieth century, most scientific materialists ignored the intractable scientific problems of human consciousness (or pretended that Freud and his psychologist successors had or would solve them). Since the 1970s, however, the study of the events of consciousness has become a major growth area involving leading philosophers, psychologists, neuroscientists, and other contributors to the intellectual life of our time. For scientific materialists—who profess the belief that everything in the world can be explained in scientific terms—the new attention to consciousness has created a crisis of faith. Human consciousness simply will not fit the scientific method; in science, one clear counterexample is sufficient to invalidate a whole theory. Since the existence of human consciousness provides such a counterexample, scientific materialism is therefore necessarily false. But scientific materialism is the religion of large numbers of contemporary true believers—it provides their fundamental framework for understanding the world—who typically regard their core views as "modern," or perhaps "postmodern." All this poses an existential challenge for such people.

Like other religious groups confronting such a fundamental challenge—the Catholic Church 500 years ago in responding to the theories of Copernicus, for example—scientific materialists today have sought desperately to find a way to reconcile their long-standing scientific faith with the realities of human consciousness. Some of the better known philosophers of the past forty years have been called on to try to resolve the problem. One strategy has been something like the following. Since by assumption everything "real" in the world must be material, then human consciousness—having no material reality—cannot be real. What can be real for a scientific materialist is the physical human brain, so the study of consciousness must be reduced to the study of certain aspects of brain functioning that are then assumed to be the true essence of conscious experience. It is these physical brain activities (and their exact workings are largely unknown at present) that are said to form the real world of the human conscious mind. For scientific materialists, conscious ideas, thoughts, emotions, sensations, etc.—even mathematical theorems—cannot exist as real existing things in and of themselves. The strong internal impressions in our own minds to the contrary—the pervasive sense of being conscious, the conviction that our nonmaterial thoughts are real things that have a true existence—thus in some basic sense must be illusory, however counterintuitive this might seem to ordinary common sense.

The average person at this point might instead suggest that true-believing scientific materialists should check with a psychiatrist or psychologist soon. Indeed, scientific materialism rapidly leads to logical absurdities, such as the fact that the very materialist philosophies described above, as themselves ideas in human minds, can then not exist as real things—they are mere mental emanations of chemical events in the brain. As the discussion of evolutionary "racial science" in Chapter 4 illustrated, great scholarly accomplishment and high academic prestige provide no necessary guarantees against intellectual folly. In their desperation to find some way to preserve the materialist world view—their naturalist fundamentalist religion—the recent intellectual contortions of some naturalists might be compared with those of Christian creationists seeking a way to reconcile their literal biblical beliefs with the directly contradictory evidence of hundreds of millions of years of the plainly observed fossil record.

An Apostate Philosopher

Fortunately, a few philosophers, despite the intense peer pressures in the academy and elsewhere to declare that two plus two equals five, have kept their wits about them. New York University's Thomas Nagel is among the leading American philosophers of the second half of the twentieth century, who published a classic article in 1974 on "What Is It Like To Be a Bat?"— concluding that, no matter how much neurological and other scientific research might be done on bats in the future, in concept potentially resulting in a complete understanding of the physical workings of bat brains (and other parts of their anatomy), it would always remain impossible to know what the subjective experience of being a bat might be (what it would actually feel like in a mind, for example, to navigate the world by sonar methods). "Bat consciousness," in other words, would necessarily remain forever outside human understanding. Nagel has since written many more articles and books about the scientifically mysterious character of consciousness, focusing on the human case.[1]

In 2012 he published a major statement of his latest thinking in which he more explicitly took his past philosophical writings about consciousness to their logical conclusion. In *Mind and Cosmos: Why the Materialist Neo-Darwinian Conception of Nature is Almost Certainly False,* Nagel writes that "the aim of this book is to argue that the mind-body problem is not just

1. Nagel, "What is it Like to Be a Bat?"

a local problem, having to do with the relation between mind, brain and behavior in living animal organisms, but that it invades our understanding of the entire cosmos and its history"—in other words, it is ultimately about religion. There have been many efforts by philosophers and psychologists to explain human consciousness within the scientific materialist framework that sees the physical sciences as the foundational explanation of all of human existence. Nagel, however, considers all those efforts to be failures. As he states, "The starting point for the argument [of the book] is the failure of psychophysical reductionism, a position in the philosophy of mind that is largely motivated by the hope of showing how the physical sciences could in principle provide a theory of everything."[2]

It is not only that past efforts have failed but they will always fail because the hope for a physical explanation of human consciousness is in principle "unrealizable." It is inherently impossible for the physical sciences to explain an event occurring outside measurable time and space (such as human consciousness) by a physical cause itself occurring within measurable time and space. This is why no one as yet has been able to offer even a plausible hypothesis that might have any hope of explaining human consciousness in the terms of the physical sciences. To believe that such an explanation will necessarily be achieved at some time in the future is a statement of religious faith, not itself a scientific conclusion. Hence, as Nagel states, "I believe a true appreciation of the difficulty of the [consciousness] problem must eventually change our conception of the place of the physical sciences in describing the natural order."[3] In addressing the larger questions of human existence, it will seemingly require returning to methods of thought such as theology that were central elements of Western civilization long before the scientific revolution of the seventeenth century.

Nagel fully acknowledges the many large recent advances in the field of neuroscience that have successfully correlated the presence of particular events in human consciousness with corresponding physical activity in particular areas of the human brain. When a person feels deep anxiety, neurologists can tell us that certain parts of the brain show increased neural activity. Nagel concludes, however, that, like the consciousness of bats, such efforts do not—nor will they ever—resolve the scientific mystery of human consciousness. All attempts, he believes, will be "unsatisfactory for the same old reason: even with the [physical] brain added to the picture, they clearly leave out something essential, without which there would be no mind. And what they leave out is just what was deliberately left out of the

2. Nagel, *Mind and Cosmos*, 1, 2.
3. Ibid., 2, 1.

physical world by Descartes and Galileo in order to form the modern concept of the exclusively physical, namely subjective appearances," as they are experienced in human consciousness. These are mental events altogether lacking in any physical substance even as we mysteriously experience them during our lives on earth—if only within the context of the existence of a corresponding physical human brain.[4]

Descartes of course famously postulated a dualism of mind and body that exist separately and independently. By treating all the physical world as working according to discoverable physical laws, rather than being influenced by the arbitrary will of any human (or divine) mind, physical scientists from the seventeenth century onward could focus their efforts on discovering the strictly physical explanations for the workings of the solar system, the reactions of chemical substances, the workings of the human body and other biological entities, indeed all the parts of the physical universe. Even in Descartes's time, admittedly, some critics pointed out that there was a large problem with his postulated separation of mind and body—the ability of mental events in human minds to affect the bodily actions of the same people. (Right now, as I am thinking, my fingers are typing out my thoughts, demonstrating beyond any doubt to me that my conscious world is capable—however mysteriously—of causally moving the physical world, so they can never be said to be entirely separate.) The workings of gravity, as postulated by Newton, lacking any mechanical basis, were equally mysterious for him and others of his time. But such large philosophical problems could be conveniently neglected in the eighteenth century, given the extraordinary fruitfulness of the Cartesian dualist assumptions in supporting the development of modern science.

Nagel, however, now proposes to revisit the issue. Given what he sees as the scientifically "intractable" nature of human consciousness, he now states that "I believe we will have to leave materialism behind" as the one all-encompassing explanation of every aspect of human existence. What will be necessary, Nagel writes, is to develop "a post-materialist theory" (a "supernatural" theory, as I would today call it, although Nagel himself might not be comfortable with that term) that will "offer a unified explanation of how the physical and mental characteristics of organisms developed together."[5] He is hesitant—not surprisingly, given the intellectual (and religious) magnitude of the issues raised—to propose a simple clear "post-materialist" answer.

Among its many radical implications, Nagel's proposal would further undermine Darwinism as a complete explanation of the world. If

---

4. Ibid., 40.
5. Ibid., 41, 46–47.

consciousness itself has no material essence, how could it have evolved by biological evolutionary (material) means alone? Human brains with their atoms and molecules could in concept have evolved to enhance survival prospects (although it is challenging to understand exactly how such an extraordinarily complex instrument as the human brain could be the product of physical evolutionary processes in such a short time as the past two million years). It is impossible, however, to conceive how evolutionarily evolved workings of atoms and molecules, no matter how intricate their resulting interactions in my brain, would have developed to be able to create the ideas that occur in my consciousness and have no physical existence.

What would be the evolutionary point of such consciousness if all the actions of my human body are actually determined by physical events occurring in my human brain? In other words, how would I benefit in evolutionary terms from the add-on of consciousness if the real driving force for my bodily actions were the atoms and molecules in my brain alone? There would in fact be no evolutionary benefit. The deep sense of being conscious that I experience would thus seem to be biologically—and evolutionarily—superfluous, if consciousness itself is a mere reflection of physical processes in my brain.

Some people thus think that artificial intelligence, necessarily grounded in physical realities alone, will someday be able to replicate the full workings of every aspect of the human brain. But any computers that created such advanced forms of artificial intelligence will have no need for consciousness. Indeed, it is impossible to conceive how a machine might possess consciousness, even as this absence of consciousness poses no problem from an evolutionary standpoint—the computer would be able to simply direct our bodies to do the same things in the physical world that we now perceive our consciousness as directing us to do, in evolutionary terms both possibilities working equally well to advance our survival prospects.

As Nagel emphasizes, the interactions of mind and body remain to this day a total scientific mystery. It is not only impossible to understand how our consciousness directs our bodily actions but it is also impossible to understand how physical events in nature can produce the subjective experiences—themselves lacking any physical reality—that make up human consciousness. Various philosophers have pointed out, for example, that the color red in strictly physical terms is actually a particular wave length of light, something altogether different from my own conscious perception of red (and I have no way, moreover, of knowing even in concept whether your perception of red is the same as mine, even while it is not difficult to verify scientifically that the same wave lengths of light are reaching your eyes as are reaching mine, and that we are responding similarly, whatever is actually happening in our separate consciousnesses—you may be seeing green, where I see red, and there would be no way to know, or practical significance).

John Eccles is a distinguished neuroscientist who won the 1963 Nobel Prize for his research into the physical workings of the brain. Like Nagel, he also believes that human consciousness has a separate mental existence that has no scientifically explicable way even in concept of interacting with the chemical workings of the brain. In a 1989 book, he wrote that "when one adheres to the strict materialist theory of Darwinism, the existence of animal consciousness," including that of human beings, is "an inexplicable anomaly." Indeed, it is yet another large strike against Darwinism as a full scientific account of the workings of the universe. Deeply committed himself to maintaining the integrity of science, Eccles finds it "disturbing that evolutionists have largely ignored the tremendous enigma that is presented to their materialistic theory by the emergence of mentality in the [human and other] animal evolution."[6]

One obvious possibility is that the guiding intelligence of a supernatural god must be involved in all this. Nagel acknowledges this in *Mind and Cosmos* as one of the two main possibilities for a necessary "post-materialist" explanation of the world. As a lifelong and still self-declared atheist, however, Nagel rejects this conclusion for himself. As he writes, "I am not just unreceptive but strongly averse to the idea" of any "transcendent being"—such as the Jewish and Christian God—controlling the universe. Nagel is more comfortable with a second possibility he raises for moving past naturalism, a "teleological" explanation of the evolutionary history of the world. [7]

The physical universe would be seen as containing within itself non-material features that have resulted inevitably in the evolutionary emergence of living creatures possessing consciousness. The specifics of such a "teleological" theory would be new but in its spirit, as Nagel acknowledges, this direction of thought would be "a throwback to the Aristotelian conception of nature," in which motion in the world is conceived as a process of movement toward final causes (and which as a basic way of thinking was overthrown in the seventeenth century by Descartes and other pioneers of modern mathematics and physics). Nagel prefers the teleological explanation because, however mysterious it might be by conventional scientific standards, in his view it would remain secular, hypothesizing that there can be "natural teleological laws governing the development of organization [of the physical universe] over time, in addition to laws of the familiar [physical]

6. Eccles, *Evolution of the Brain*, 218, 176.

7. Nagel, *Mind and Cosmos*, 46, 95, 59.

kind governing the behavior of the elements."[8] These laws must, moreover, have somehow established in nature a direction of movement towards the current world, including the presence of human beings with consciousness and related intelligence. Nagel does not mention it but there is an interesting affinity here to the recent discovery by evolutionary biologists that cells may be able to engineer their evolutionary development in purposeful ways, that cells seemingly lacking altogether in consciousness nevertheless seem in laboratory experiments to demonstrate forms of "sentience," as discussed in the previous chapter.

Nagel has some other surprising company. From a much different starting point, the Princeton physicist John Wheeler—among the leading theoretical physicists of the second half of the twentieth century—offered a related idea, "the anthropic principle," for serious consideration. As Wheeler noted, and as discussed in Chapter 2 above, a variety of "constants in physics" have the ability to determine the future course of the universe.[9] The random probability that these constants—as the universe has turned out—would be suitable to create a world to sustain current life on earth is infinitesimally small, essentially zero. As a possible solution, as also noted previously, some physicists propose the idea of an extraordinarily large number of universes, the vast majority incapable of sustaining life, but that we just happen to live among one of the few exceptions. Wheeler quickly dismisses this hypothesis, however, as outside the bounds of science—as really a matter of theology—because he suggests that there is no way, even in concept, that we could measure or test anything about these essentially imaginary universes. As he puts it, "we can forgo the notion of an ensemble of universes as outside the legitimate bounds of logical discourse." Assuming there is only the one universe we inhabit, therefore, as Wheeler observed in 1994, "more and more physicists and astrophysicists [now] propose a perspective-shattering answer, not only is man adapted to the universe, the universe is adapted to man."[10] The universe, seemingly miraculously, came into existence for this ultimate purpose, the emergence of intelligence and consciousness, reaching new heights among human beings.

To the shock of mainstream evolutionary biologists, leading figures in the field such as Lynn Margulis and James Shapiro, as examined above, have recently been saying similar things. Since the discovery of quantum phenomena in the 1920s, it would seem that science itself has been increasingly finding that the supernatural—or at least outside any concept of nature with

8. Ibid., 59, 66.
9. Wheeler, *At Home in the Universe*, 185.
10. Ibid., 186, 185.

which we are familiar—is a routine part of the workings of our world. Now, as a leading philosopher, Nagel has been reaching much the same conclusion by a nonscientific route.

Placebos: A Natural Experiment

It is usually difficult or impossible in the social sciences to create new experiments involving human subjects that meet standards for empirical confirmation with full scientific rigor. In recent years, some social scientists have therefore sought to address this problem by identifying "natural experiments." These are situations that have arisen for non-experimental reasons that just happen to meet the requirements for a valid scientific experiment. For example, let us assume an interest in finding an answer to the question of whether Charter School A achieves a superior educational result, compared with public school alternatives. Some charter schools have much larger numbers of applicants than they are able to accept and are then required by law to decide which students they will accept by a random lottery. This creates two groups of students randomly selected from an initial overall population of all applying students, those accepted to the charter school and those rejected and going to public school, thus meeting the gold standard for a valid statistical comparison of the impact of different types of schools in achieving educational outcomes.

Although also never directly intended as a scientific experiment, there are also natural experiments available for studying the interactions of human consciousness and human brains. These involve drug tests in which some members of a group receive an actual drug under study and other members—without their knowledge—receive a "placebo," a non-drug specifically chosen because it has no significant chemical impact on the brain or other parts of the body. If a drug is to be deemed clinically effective, the success rate in treating a disease should be significantly higher (as can be accurately established by various statistical tests) for the people receiving the actual drug than for either those receiving the placebo or those who are outside the study altogether and thus not receiving anything medically.

Widely used in drug testing, such studies have served to reveal a remarkable human characteristic. In such tests it is common to observe that both those people receiving the actual drug and those people receiving the placebo often achieve significantly better results than the group of people not receiving anything, all this statistically significant at a high level of confidence. The placebo somehow—very mysteriously—also has a beneficial result for the participants in the test. Indeed, this has become a major problem in drug testing because it often leads to inconclusive results—everyone in the test population shows greater improvements than people not involved in the drug testing at all.

Paul Enck, Fabrizio Benedetti, and Manfred Schedlowski thus report in the journal *Neuron* that "in modern medicine, the placebo response or placebo effect has often been regarded as a nuisance in basic research and particularly in clinical research" because of the confusion it creates in interpreting the results of the research. Nevertheless, "the latest scientific evidence has demonstrated . . . that the placebo effect and the nocebo effect, the negative effects of placebo, stem from highly active processes in the brain that are mediated by psychological mechanisms such as expectation and conditioning. These processes have been described in some detail for many diseases and treatments."[11] Indeed, strong placebo effects can be found for all kinds of treatments for diseases but, not surprisingly, they are often particularly strong in tests of drugs seeking to relieve psychological disorders. One study of anti-depressants found that, overall, placebos were 82 percent as effective in relieving symptoms as the actual drugs themselves.[12]

As one might suggest, only half in jest, perhaps doctors should give their patients placebos while telling them that they are receiving the actual drug (which may be costly to manufacture and may also have adverse side effects). The placebo in some cases might do almost as much good as the actual drug at a lower cost to society and to the patient. Admittedly, aside from the ethical issues this would raise, medical professionals would be newly acting in a role that might be described as the modern equivalent of a "witch doctor." But the large beneficial results of placebos in modern drug testing suggest that many witch doctors of the past probably did a great deal of good for the physical health of their tribal "patients."

Indeed, current medical procedure produces a paradoxical result. If the actual drug and the placebo show no statistically significant difference, the current medical conclusion is to not use either the drug or the placebo (and the Food and Drug Administration probably will not approve the drug in the first place). But that will often do harm to the patient population. Prescribing either the placebo or the (perhaps chemically ineffective) drug itself—in the latter case sometimes working as an alternative form of placebo—will significantly benefit the physical health of many patients, and literally so. Because they regard medicine from a scientific materialist perspective that rejects medical use of any drug effectiveness outside physical

11. Enck, Benedetti, and Schedlowski, "New Insights into Placebo and Nocebo Responses," 195.

12. Angell, "The Epidemic of Mental Illness: Why?"

causation, doctors for reasons of their own ideological (or religious) antipathy to placebos thus seemingly end up violating a central ethical command of their own profession—do no harm. One might describe this as a "medical fundamentalism," a variation on the naturalist and Darwinist fundamentalisms discussed earlier, yet another indication of the pervasiveness of scientific materialist ways of thinking in society.

Given this awkward situation, the medical profession often finds it most convenient to ignore the whole puzzling issue. It was recently raised in *The Economist* magazine, however, with respect to the use of alternative medicines. For many of these alternative medicines, there is no known scientific mechanism by which the chemicals in the medicines could be doing any good—and yet they often do. As *The Economist* explained, alternative medicines "are very popular. Clearly, they have something that mainstream medicine does not. The question is, what?"[13]

As the natural experiment of placebos unmistakably shows, the simple mental act of having a conscious belief in the effectiveness of a drug in and of itself can produce strong curative effects. This illustrates the great confusion science experiences in dealing with mental phenomena such as human consciousness. From one scientific point of view, the placebo plainly works—the physical and psychological benefits to patients are well documented empirically according to strict scientific evidentiary standards. From another scientific viewpoint (the dominant viewpoint in the medical profession), however, the placebo effect is not "real." It does not have an immediate material cause, there can be no chemical physical explanation (the placebo is specifically chosen for the lack of any chemical effect); scientists are essentially clueless as to the scientific mechanism by which the placebo and the resulting positive thoughts in the mind of a person might actually improve that person's physical health (they cannot go beyond the statement that the positive thoughts in some altogether scientifically unknown way do in fact induce positive neurological changes in the brain that then can in fact be physically measured by neurologists, and correlated with resulting beneficial physical bodily changes). In lying outside any ordinary physical and natural explanation, placebo effects are thus yet another in the growing number of scientifically documented "supernatural" events.

Again, this might be taken as further evidence for the existence of a god—who else would be the actual source of the otherwise mysterious causation? Richard Dawkins of course would deny this—or at least the part about it implying the existence of an actually existing god. He might admittedly be willing to concede that the very idea of a god may itself be the

---

13. "There is No Alternative," 16

largest placebo effect ever. Dawkins probably would not deny that simply believing in a god can have wide-ranging physical impacts on actual human behavior and activity (in fact, he documents a whole range of them, mostly rather negative from his point of view).

He thus would seemingly be willing to agree specifically that newly accepting the idea of the Christian God in a human consciousness (those born again, for example) can by itself produce direct chemical changes in human brains and human behavior. But if he concedes the existence of such a placebo effect, an event of mind exerting control over matter, he would have to concede the existence of something lying outside natural scientific explanation, something supernatural in the world as ordinary human beings commonly experience and know it. Indeed, the very existence of any true placebo is in itself a contradiction of the basic tenets of physicalism and scientific materialism. By the method of contradiction, we can therefore logically conclude that scientific materialism is not true. QED.

Further evidence for the mysterious power—bordering on religious—of placebo effects was reported in 2015 in the *Washington Post*. While rejecting traditional "religion," many people today describe themselves as "spiritual," holding beliefs often associated with environmental values. A research team at a Swedish university conducted the following experiment. All students were asked to perform a mechanical and visual task that required some attention and effort, each student performing the task under light from the same incandescent lamp. For one group of students, the lamp was labeled in an eco-friendly manner; for the other students, there was no such label. Remarkably, the students working in physically identical light that was in their case generated by a lamp source that they perceived to be environmentally friendly performed much better. As the Swedish researchers revealed in a study published in the *Journal of Environmental Psychology*, as reported by the *Post*, "the mean number of errors made by those using the lamp bearing the conventional label was much greater than the number committed by those using the purportedly environmentally friendly lamp."[14] For the students in the latter group, using a seemingly environmentally friendly lamp meant that in their conscious awareness their efforts were apparently blessed by an environmental god, significantly improving their actual task performance without any contributing actual material causal mechanism, a recent graphic example of the scientifically inexplicable workings of placebo effects.[15]

14. Mooney, "Study Finds Placebo Effect in Eco-Labeling."

15. Nelson, "Environmental Religion"; Nelson, "Economic and Environmental Religion."

Scientifically Baffling

If it is not because of the existence of placebo effects, those who have
doubted that accepted scientific methods can ever be applied to understand
human consciousness include some illustrious figures. As noted earlier, the
great Danish physicist Niels Bohr considered that the study of the "soul"—
his way of characterizing human consciousness—might simply lie outside
the scope of the scientific method.[16] Ludwig Wittgenstein characterized this
situation as "the feeling of an unbridgeable gulf between consciousness and
brain-process" that seemingly defies any commonsense way of understanding how it works—again pointing towards the existence of a supernatural
power, of the existence of a god, although Wittgenstein did not propose to
go in this direction.[17] One of the outstanding scientific figures of the twentieth century, the physicist Freeman Dyson, who is also a leading contemporary student of theology, having given the Gifford lectures in Scotland
in 1984–1985, states that "the origin of life is a total mystery, and so is the
existence of human consciousness. We have no clear idea how the electrical
discharges occurring in nerve cells in our brains are connected with our
feelings and desires and actions," and vice versa.[18]

In 1992, Rutgers University philosopher Jerry Fodor affirmed that
"nobody has the slightest idea how anything material could be conscious.
Nobody even knows what it would be like to have the slightest idea how
anything material could be conscious."[19] Around the same time, Neil Ruden-
stine, then president of Harvard University, established five major themes
around which he assembled interdisciplinary working groups of Harvard
faculty, each theme chosen to be an area of especially large social significance and intellectual promise. One such group was the "Mind, Brain, and
Behavior Interfaculty Initiative" or "MBB." In 1994, a reporter for *Harvard
Magazine* interviewed MBB members to report on their progress to date.
The human brain, as the members of MBB considered, is "the most complex
organ known" in the living world (and maybe the nonliving as well). Yet,
the Harvard team found that in recent decades the field of neuroscience had
been making remarkable strides in understanding the physical workings
of the brain. As an extraordinarily complex system, "the brain contains a
hundred billion neurons, each one connected to at least a thousand others."
Somehow they all work together to sustain "every movement we make and

16. Bohr, *The Philosophical Writings of Niels Bohr*, 91.

17. Wittgenstein, *Philosophical Investigations*, quoted in McGinn, *Consciousness
and its Objects*, 65.

18. Dyson, "How We Know," 10.

19. Fodor, "The Big Idea," 5.

every sensation, emotion, and thought we experience [which] corresponds to the activity of particular neurons."[20]

As neuroscientists were rapidly discovering, it was quite feasible to trace close correlations between events occurring in human consciousness and related neurological activity in specific parts of the physical brain. Yet, despite such impressive advances in neuroscience, and as the members of MBB acknowledged, almost nothing was known about how "chemical signals" in the brain "give rise to thoughts and feelings." Reflecting the prevailing faith of scientific materialism, neuroscientists were confident that mental phenomena such as "love and hate, ecstasy and despair, [are] really the result of nerve cells passing molecules back and forth." Nevertheless, how all this actually worked remained a total scientific mystery; there were even some Harvard researchers who "wonder if anyone ever will" understand it, given the intrinsic problem for science of explaining a nonphysical event by means of a physical causal mechanism.[21]

In her 2005 book, *Consciousness*, psychologist Susan Blackmore observes that there has been a rapidly growing interest in the question of human consciousness and what it actually represents. Nevertheless, little had changed in the years since the Harvard program of research commenced; as she writes, there remains a "yawning chasm, or 'fathomless abyss' between the physical and mental worlds." Indeed, despite all the neurological research and renewed philosophical interest, the reality is that so far "the mystery has [not] gone away. Indeed, it is as deep as ever."[22] Summing up the thus far intractable problems faced by any scientific attempt to explain human consciousness, she writes,

> What is consciousness? This may sound like a simple question but it is not. Consciousness is at once the most obvious and the most difficult thing we can investigate. We seem either to have to use consciousness to investigate itself, which is a slightly weird idea, or to have to extricate ourselves from the very thing we want to study. No wonder that philosophers and scientists have struggled for millennia with the concept, and that scientists rejected the whole idea for long periods and refused to study it [as something that seemingly fell outside any methods available to science].[23]

20. Cuevas, "Mind, Brain and Behavior," 39.

21. Ibid., 36.

22. Blackmore, *Consciousness*, 2, 1.

23. Ibid., 1.

Six years later, despite the much greater study of phenomena of the human mind and brain, nothing much had changed. University of North Carolina psychology professor Barclay Martin again bluntly stated in 2011 that no one has "the foggiest idea of how a bunch of firing neurons in any kind of network produce consciousness." In a response, the Berkeley philosopher of the human mind John Searle affirmed that, even though "we know that brain processes cause all our conscious experiences," he had to admit that "I entirely agree [with Martin] that, at present, the way neurons produce consciousness remains [scientifically] mysterious."[24]

The Case of Daniel Dennett

All of the above amounts to an existential crisis for scientific materialism, which has claimed that it offers the full explanation for the human experience and situation in the world. Essentially, as Nagel now argues, this cannot be sustained philosophically as a plausible view of the world—even if this message has yet to reach much of the American public, partly because the elite media has not explained it. (Many of its members, as scientific materialist true believers, might themselves experience their own existential crises in doing so.) One large exception for many years has been *The New York Review of Books* (and the *Weekly Standard* in 2013 did publish a cover story discussing Nagel's recent apostasy and the fierce naturalist counterreaction it had provoked).[25] It would seem that this media self-censorship (the most effective kind) has reflected the high religious stakes. As the philosopher Edward Feser observes, the idea that "the physical world constitutes a vast 'machine' with material objects—including the human body—being but smaller machines operating within it, has come to dominate the thinking of modern philosophers and scientists alike."[26] It would require an unusually brash journalist to go against the naturalist fundamentalism that prevails across such wide circles of elite American opinion today.

When the problem of consciousness first began assuming a new philosophical prominence in the 1970s, a host of American philosophers initially rushed to defend scientific materialism. The basic philosophical strategy was to argue—sometimes more, sometimes less explicitly—that consciousness is not real; the real thing in the world is whatever physical is happening in the brain that is causing a conscious event. (And that however incapable

24. Martin, "The Mystery of Consciousness, Con't."; with Searle reply, "The Mystery of Consciousness, Con't."

25. Ferguson, "The Heretic."

26. Feser, *Philosophy of Mind*, 49.

we may now be, and conceivably may forever be, of fully explaining this causal relationship in scientific terms of measurable time and space, or even describing scientifically what a conscious event actually is.) Then, if consciousness is not itself real, the embarrassing scientific mystery goes away, and scientific materialism has escaped the large danger posed. Or, so many American philosophers in one form or another in essence asserted.

In 1991, the American philosopher Daniel Dennett published an argument of this kind in *Consciousness Explained*, concluding that human consciousness not only should be seen as lacking a distinct reality—and thus is of no large scientific interest in itself—but that consciousness literally does not exist at all. Dennett is to this day a leading contemporary philosopher and defender of scientific materialism (he is the author of *Breaking the Spell: Religion as a Natural Phenomenon* and many other books advancing a naturalist viewpoint). Whatever one thinks in the end of his line of argument in *Consciousness Explained*, Dennett was capable of putting on a brilliant literary performance. Dennett may also be admired because, unlike the intellectual confusions of many of his naturalist allies, he had the insight and courage to take their arguments to their full logical conclusion. In this respect, he made an important contribution to the overall contemporary philosophy of the mind, putting the issue of consciousness in its starkest terms.

In his 1991 book, Dennett begins by acknowledging that "with consciousness . . . we are in a terrible muddle. Consciousness stands alone today as a topic that often leaves even the most sophisticated thinkers tongue-tied and confused." But then Dennett boldly announces that he will finally resolve the philosophical conundrums in the pages to come. He warns his readers, however, that this could be problematic for some because his arguments may threaten their own commonsense beliefs about their own consciousness, indeed their very self-understanding of their own existence. If he succeeds in disabusing them or their simplistic ideas, they might be forced to "trade mystery," and its emotionally comforting illusions, for the potentially corrosive "rudiments of scientific knowledge of consciousness." Indeed, as Dennett writes, including as well those in secular circles, "some people [will] view [his] demystification [of consciousness] as desecration," causing them "to view this book at the outset as an act of intellectual vandalism, an assault on the last sanctuary of mankind," the human soul.[27]

But the readers should not worry too much, Dennett then offers reassurance, because "the losses, if any, are overridden by the gains in understanding—both scientific and social, both theoretical and moral—that

---

27. Dennett, *Consciousness Explained*, 22.

a good theory of consciousness can provide."[28] His readers, however confused and misled they may be at present, can deepen their understanding
of scientific materialism by now incorporating a new and genuinely correct
understanding of human consciousness.

Consciousness Explained is 468 pages long. As part of Dennett's grand
performance, much of it is filled with genuinely fascinating details about the
actual workings of the human mind. There is, for example, the remarkable
phenomenon of "blindsight." Some people have perfectly good eyes but the
part of the brain that processes the incoming sensory data has been dam-
aged, leaving them believing that they are unable to see at all. It turns out,
however, that such people can often actually locate objects placed in their
vicinity with surprising accuracy. Their eyes apparently transmit the data to
some part of the brain where, even though it never becomes a visual image
in their consciousness, the brain apparently still processes this information
in some fashion, allowing them to "see" without any conscious experience
of seeing.

After about 350 pages, including a number of chapters impressing
readers with his (genuinely) encyclopedic knowledge of the philosophy
of mind and the workings of the brain, Dennett finally gets to the heart
of the matter—in strictly naturalist terms, what is human consciousness?
Philosophers often use the technical term "qualia" to refer to the subjective
events occurring in human consciousness, the ordinary ideas and thoughts
we perceive that we are experiencing as mental events and seem to have
no physical substance. As Dennett explains, following many others, there is
no way that anyone can verify either the existence or the character of such
qualia in another person's consciousness. When someone reports to us a
sensory perception or an abstract idea, we have no measuring instrument or
other direct access to confirm, modify, or reject the individual report given
by the other person. All we can do is compare the reports of others with our
own conscious experiences and, then, when the two match up reasonably
well, draw the conclusion that we are two separate conscious beings whose
minds work similarly.

Yet, it could be that the other person is experiencing something altogether different from what we experience in our own consciousness, and
still might use much the same language to describe their subjective experiences. As Dennett explains, following many others, what you see as "yellow"
I might actually be seeing as "purple." Our color perceptions might thus be
inverted but this would have no practical significance whatsoever because
my behavior in response to "yellow" would be precisely the same as yours

28. Ibid.

with respect to what you saw instead as "purple." As a result, there would be no practical way to know whether our color perceptions—our experiences of color qualia—are in fact "inverted."[29] Indeed, the whole question of the truthfulness of our conscious perceptions would border on meaningless, since we can never know for sure what is actually happening in another person's consciousness, and can only in practice observe their physical actions, including their verbal speech, with our own sensory organs.

Dennett therefore draws the conclusion that "the very idea of inverted qualia is nonsense—and hence . . . the very idea of qualia is nonsense." So there is no point to any writing and talking about the events occurring in human consciousness because we have nothing to write or talk about. Given the scientific materialist premises from which Dennett begins, this is a surprisingly logical conclusion. For true believers in scientific materialism, everything that is "real" must exist in the physical world and must be at least in concept scientifically observable and thus measurable in time and space. As Dennett explains, however, since "no instrument can detect the presence of x [of any qualia] directly or indirectly; the way the world goes is not modulated in the slightest by the presence or absence of x." Rather, as scientific materialism assumes as a matter of faith, the physical world as we experience it is entirely determined by physical events. As Dennett asks, "How then, could there ever be any empirical reason to assert the presence of x [as a mental—a qualia—event]?"[30] The events of our consciousness, our qualia, fall altogether outside the realm of science and—in the terms of Dennett's strict scientific materialism—it is therefore logical to say that they simply do not exist.

If they are outside the realm of science and the physical world, what other kind of reason might be offered for believing in the existence of qualia? As Dennett writes, "Could there be another reason for asserting their existence? What sort of reason? An a priori reason, presumably. But what? No one has ever offered one—good, bad, or indifferent—that I have seen" and that is at all believable. Dennett acknowledges that people do have individual thoughts (quale) but "that quale of yours is [nothing but] a character in good standing in the fictional world of your heterophenomenology"— the fantasy world that you have heretofore called your own consciousness (a puppet world of thoughts that is in fact necessarily and entirely controlled by the strings of your physical brain). In the "*real* world in your brain," Dennett writes, whatever you are experiencing in consciousness "is just a complex of dispositions." The conclusion for Dennett is therefore inescapable; if

---

29. Ibid., 389–90.
30. Ibid., 390, 402.

the concept of qualia adds nothing to our scientific ability to understand the physical world, including the physical workings of the brain, the best answer is simply to recognize that "there are no such things" as conscious thoughts (qualia) that can have any kind of real impact on the physical world.[31]

Dennett anticipates that some critics will complain that in denying consciousness he has eliminated a core element in being a human being. I, Robert H. Nelson, the author of this book, for example, believe that my consciousness exists partly because I can perceive on the page the results of my conscious writing efforts. (I wonder how Dennett feels about his own book writing, whether he thinks it has anything at all to do with any events occurring in his own consciousness, or was written by atoms and molecules in his brain.) For Dennett, however, my conscious book writing is just another comforting illusion of mine that stands in the way of my accepting the disconcerting scientific truth—my consciousness can never be anything but a personal fantasy land of my own, necessarily scientifically inaccessible to any other person, and subordinate to my physical brain that actually controls all my actions in the physical world. Hence, for Dennett it would seem that it must be the mechanical workings of my physical brain that are actually creating the entire contents of this book.

Generalizing this thought, an actual "person" for Dennett is simply a mechanical system that obeys certain scientific laws; in concept, it would be possible to replicate the exact physical workings of a real-world human being, including the events occurring in a human brain, without having to invoke the existence of any internal subjective—any magical—mental domain of consciousness. Indeed, this is not far from the writings of Ray Kurzweil and other technology futurologists who suggest that a perfect computer simulation of a human brain (including simulated "thoughts") is in fact possible—and may well actually be attained surprisingly soon. In philosophy, the technical term for a strictly physical entity that otherwise acts just like a human being is a "zombie"—an entity that has a complete material existence that faithfully replicates a human being, even though it has no actual mental side to its existence.

In case anyone has missed the direction of his argument, Dennett now makes it crystal clear. "Are zombies possible? They're not just possible, they're actual. We're all zombies. Nobody is conscious" in a way that makes any real difference.[32] If we think otherwise, we are simply in the grip of a mysterious or magical self-deception. In actual reality, our brain atoms and molecules have simply been running a complex movie screen before us that

31. Ibid., 403, 389, 383.
32. Ibid., 406.

we somehow think we are actually responsible for creating as a mental act, and have thus mistaken for a real existing world of human consciousness.

Dennett, as noted, can be praised for his logical consistency. He has taken premises that underlie scientific materialism more generally, and strictly carried their logic to a final conclusion in the matter of human consciousness. If this conclusion is absurd, so be it. An absurd conclusion is preferable for Dennett to giving up his abiding scientific materialist fundamentalism, the set of organizing principles for his basic understanding of himself and his existence. Perhaps having to accept the truth of consciousness would be too painful to bear. Many other philosophers and neurologists agree on these premises but do not have Dennett's ruthless determination to follow the logic to its final conclusion. They solve the problem of consciousness with confused thinking, a solution Dennett refuses to adopt. Dennett, unlike many scholars, also seems to enjoy provocation; he not only takes controversial positions among philosophers but takes pains to make his writings, including their radical conclusions, accessible to a wider public than reached by most other professional philosophers (among whom professional obscurity of expression is instead a common form of self-protection against wider criticism).

There is another possibility, however, that Dennett simply excludes by assumption, along with other scientific materialists. This is, as Nagel concludes in his 2012 book, that the basic premises of scientific materialism are wrong; if that is so, the full development of their logic has no special truth warrant. Indeed, in the end, if inadvertently, Dennett has seemingly provided a strong argument for supernaturalism. Again employing the method of contradiction, it goes as follows. First, begin with the assumption that "scientific materialism is true"; then, following the logically developed argument made by Dennett, this implies that consciousness does not exist. But for anyone who is certain that consciousness does exist (I suspect the great majority of the readers of this book), the original assumption leads to a contradiction. By the method of contradiction, we are required to conclude that "scientific materialism is false." QED. This line of argument, of course, only holds for those people who are entirely sure that their consciousness does in fact exist. Dennett, for example, does not have to deal with such a contradiction—unless of course he is fooling himself in saying that his own consciousness does not exist (one wonders what for him is supposedly doing the saying).

Rejecting Dennett, Keeping Consciousness

A logical contradiction, moreover, also only arises, if I am correct, if Dennett's development of the logic of scientific materialism is valid, requiring us to reject from the scientific materialist framework the existence of any non-material human consciousness (for fear perhaps that we might otherwise end up in the same camp as Nagel). Some scientific materialists, however, seek to save both consciousness and scientific materialism by rejecting the logic of Dennett's argument that consciousness does not exist. In a 1995 exchange with Dennett, the Berkeley philosopher John Searle writes that, "to put it as clearly as I can: in his book, *Consciousness Explained*, Dennett denies the existence of consciousness." Most people, as Searle comments, "when first told this, would assume that I must be misunderstanding him. Surely no sane person could deny the existence of [conscious] feelings." But in Dennett's 1995 reply to Searle, he "makes it clear that I have understood him exactly. He says, 'How could anyone deny that!? Just watch.'" Speaking as a leading contemporary philosopher of the mind, Searle declares that "I regard his view as self-refuting because it denies the existence of the data which a theory of consciousness is supposed to explain"—the actual data of experienced conscious sensations, thoughts, and ideas, including at a minimum those personally found in the conscious mind of each individual.[33]

Dennett, as Searle regards him, is following a well-established pattern. Surveying the body of mainly 1980s writings by philosophers and neuroscientists in a 1992 book, Searle wrote there of the frequent "absurdity of" the results whenever the subject of human consciousness was under philosophical examination. Most such writers, Searle observed, tried "to study the mind as if it consisted of neutral phenomena, independent of consciousness and subjectivity." Some analysts excluded beliefs altogether as important factors in human existence (behaviorism) while others redefined them in other and more measurable terms "of cause and effect relationships (functionalism), or [said] that they [beliefs] do not really exist at all (reductive materialism), or that talk of beliefs and desires is just to be construed as a certain manner of speaking (the intentional stance)." For Searle, "the ultimate absurdity is to try to treat consciousness itself independently of consciousness, that is, to treat it solely from a third-person point of view, and that leads to the view that consciousness as such, as 'inner,' 'private' phenomenal events, does not really exist" at all—just the approach Dennett arrives at.[34]

---

33. Searle, "'The Mystery of Consciousness': An Exchange."

34. Searle, *The Rediscovery of the Mind*, 20, 19–20, 20.

As a prominent American philosopher himself, Searle regarded the tortured quality of philosophical argument—much of it coming from well-respected members of the philosophy profession—as perplexing. It presents "a very curious spectacle," as he observed. Indeed, "the most striking feature is how much of mainstream philosophy of mind of the past fifty years seems obviously false. I believe there is no other area of contemporary analytic philosophy where so much is said that is so implausible." How could it conceivably be, Searle asked, that "in the philosophy of mind, obvious facts about the mental, such as that we all really do have subjective conscious mental states and that these are not eliminable in favor of anything else, are routinely denied by many, perhaps most, of the advanced thinkers in the subject." A key factor, Searle speculated, must be the literal "terror" (Searle's word) felt by many philosophers at the prospect of having to deal with a real phenomenon of consciousness that nevertheless lacks any physical qualities.[35] As such, consciousness would be scientifically impossible to explain, threatening to undermine the entire edifice of scientific materialism (which assumes that all real things are scientifically explainable), thus creating an opening for new interpretations of reality that include a role for the supernatural and thus in at least some form a god. As noted previously, naturalist fundamentalists seemingly often react much as some Christian fundamentalists; when something threatens to undermine the true religion, it is the threatening element that will have to go, leading in both cases to contrived arguments that seek to paper over the problems.

Indeed, as Searle wrote, the greatest fear of many misguided philosophers of consciousness was that their efforts might somehow offer encouragement to the "antiscientism that went with traditional dualism, the belief in the immortality of the soul, spiritualism, and so on." As Searle explained, there had once been a widely held "Cartesian view that in addition to physical particles there are 'immaterial' souls or mental substances." Such views were often associated with a belief in God as the source of the soul. Whatever large problems he had with his fellow philosophers, Searle did agree with them that "nowadays, as far as I can tell, no one" of any high professional reputation in the philosophical study of the mind "believes in the existence of immortal spiritual substances except on religious grounds. To my knowledge, there are no purely philosophical or scientific motivations for accepting the existence of immortal mental substances" such as souls.[36]

But Searle's argument here becomes confusing as well. If consciousness exists, and yet is not explainable in physical terms, it must exist outside

35. Ibid., 3, 4.
36. Ibid., 3, 27.

physical nature. That is to say, it is by definition a supernatural phenomenon. The only escape would be to assume that, even if none is available now, some future natural explanation for consciousness will one day be discovered. But this in itself, as noted above, would be an act of faith, not empirically confirmable by any application of the scientific method. It would, moreover, be difficult to reconcile with the spirit of Searle's other main arguments that are critical of the mainstream philosophy of the mind. Still, Searle seems to be held back by much the same concern of other philosophers, that he will be labeled a modern heretic by the scientific materialist mainstream, himself accused of being a dualist, even of lending support to supernaturalism and of abetting an outright theism. In 2005, he would write that, whatever the many difficulties along the way, and the false paths taken by many others, he had not abandoned the true naturalist faith. One could still hope for some future great advance in scientific understanding of the brain, however remote it might be today, in which:

> Suppose we knew in exact detail all of the neurobiological mechanisms and their mode of operation, so that we knew exactly which neuronal events were causally necessary, or sufficient, or both, for which subjective feelings. Suppose all this knowledge was stated as a set of precise laws. Suppose such knowledge were in daily medical use to overcome human pain, misery, and mental illness. We are a long way from this ideal and we may never reach it. . . . [But this would be] a complete science of the sort I am imagining [of the biological workings of the brain as the precise determinants of consciousness].[37]

But even if all this were accomplished, it would fall well short of upholding naturalism, rather amounting to a perfection of the existing methods of neuroscience (where so many large successes in establishing correlations between conscious thoughts and the physical brain are already being achieved). That might even allow for the discovery of physical drugs that would affect particular identifiable areas of the brain in precise ways that would then predictably change conscious experiences—such as perhaps human memory improvements. If not at present a perfected science, current drugs such as Prozac already work in this manner, and further research might reveal yet more precisely how Prozac affects the neuronal workings of the brain, and as a consequence the specific events occurring in consciousness. With potentially even many more successful efforts with other drugs, it might even become possible to manage human conscious experiences—if admittedly not an attractive possibility in all respects—by chemical means.

37. Searle, "What is Consciousness?"

Even if such efforts should one day be perfectly successful, however, we would still be well short of a full scientific explanation for the events of human consciousness—events such as my writing this book whose contents I cannot conceive will ever be explainable by physical science alone.

It is similarly inconceivable, for example, that any such scientific strategy would ever be able to explain how strictly physical events in human brains have produced the analytical efforts within human consciousness that have now yielded the field of neuroscience itself, and the level of scientific knowledge that neuroscientists have thus far achieved. It is extremely unlikely that doing neuroscience at its highest levels will ever be reduced to a process of understanding the complex chemical interactions occurring within the brains of working neuroscientists. (If any such outcome is ever achieved, the managed "neural" interactions—or simulations of such—are most likely to be occurring in the electrical circuits, the "brain," of a physical computer, not of a biological human being. But who knows, perhaps the best neuroscience of the future will be done by physical computers, even as they have no consciousness themselves of what they are doing.)

The Dualist Possibility

In 1993 his fellow philosopher Thomas Nagel reviewed Searle's 1992 book in an article "The Mind Wins!" Overall, Nagel was quite favorable in his assessment, describing Searle as a valuable "dragonslayer by temperament" who had succeeded in showing that the dominant "materialist tradition" of recent years in the philosophy of the mind "is nonsense, for reasons some of which are obvious and some more subtle." Nagel agreed with Searle with respect to the confused reasoning introduced by many other philosophers of the mind that it is "the fear of dualism, with its spiritualist and otherwise unscientific associations, [that] drives them to embrace reductionist materialism at any intellectual cost." Invoking the language of psychology, Nagel (like Searle) agrees that among contemporary philosophers of the mind there has been a pattern of "constant repetition . . . [much like] a compulsive neurotic of the same destructive pattern of behavior. . . . It is evident . . . that [the many philosophical] reductionists are convinced in advance that some materialist theory must be correct: they just have to find it"—the consequences of failure would be unacceptable, potentially undermining their long-standing naturalist fundamentalism.[38]

For the philosophical reductionists of the mind, rather than a faith in a Christian God, as Nagel explains, their own religion is thus characterized by

38. Nagel, "The Mind Wins!"

an assumed "scientific worldview to which they can see no alternative" competing world view. Reinforcing Searle's conclusions about Dennett and his ilk,
Nagel says of such thinking that the unquestioning commitment to materialism has yielded "its most bizarre manifestation [that] is yet another theory,
called 'eliminative' materialism. This is the view that, because mental states
can't be accommodated within the world described by physics, they don't exist—just as witches and ghosts don't exist."[39] In Dennett's defense, however, it
might be pointed out that at least such thinking avoids the worst logical contradictions of some philosophers who concede the existence of consciousness
but then seek to explain it in scientific materialist terms. Indeed, if we start
from a certain faith that scientific materialism must be true, and the existence
of consciousness does in fact refute scientific materialism, then it does follow
logically, as Dennett argues, that consciousness cannot exist.

However, while Nagel much admired Searle's skillful dissections of
the confused arguments of many philosophers of the mind, he found, as
suggested above, that Searle seemingly also suffered from a deep fear of
his own—of being accused of dualism. While rejecting Dennett and other
scientific materialist reductionists, Searle still maintained that any future
correct argument about consciousness must be scientifically grounded in
material fact and theory. As Nagel concludes, however, this is not viable,
leading Searle to disguise what is really "an essentially dualistic claim [as
developed in his 1992 book] in language that expresses a strong aversion to
dualism"—and thus even Searle himself also falls prey to the philosophical
contortions that have plagued the philosophy of mind in desperately seeking to uphold the naturalist orthodoxy.[40]

As opposed to Searle's caution, Nagel was already showing signs in
1993 of the thinking that would lead in 2012 to his newly heretical book,
Mind and Cosmos, proposing there a "post-materialist" future. Nagel wrote
in 1993 that it was looking increasingly likely that there would be no choice
but to accept the fact that the "mental" cannot be reduced to the "nonmen-
tal" (i.e., the physical)—that "consciousness is an intrinsic subjective property of the brain [somehow mysteriously] caused by its [physical] neural
activity," outside any normal physical scientific framework of analysis and
understanding. If there is to be any hope at all to explain consciousness,
as Nagel was already writing more than twenty years ago, it will be necessary to depart from "the path which physical science has followed since
the seventeenth century, since that depended on excluding the mind of the

39. Ibid.
40. Ibid.

observer from the world being observed and described."[41] It was not only leading philosophers but also quantum physicists of the twentieth century and the more recent evolutionary biological discoverers of "sentience" in cells and the evolution of other microorganisms who have been concluding that mind and matter are inextricably intertwined in nature, however impossible, indeed completely heretical, this must be in normal scientific materialist terms

Nagel, as an avowed atheist himself, was averse to drawing any theistic conclusions, and was thus not inclined to follow the logic of his own argument to this logically consistent ending point. Indeed, it was beginning to look as though the word "god" might have to be brought back to respectability in philosophical discussions—which would now also become theological discussions as well. For devout scientific materialists, some of their worst fears were seemingly being realized. Along with other events in physical science itself, the new philosophical and neurological attention being given to the complete scientific mystery of human consciousness was working to undermine the true materialist faith. A future of existential confusion was looking ever more likely.

Colin McGinn's World of Mystery

The prolific and insightful American philosopher Colin McGinn is among the most outspoken members of the "pessimistic" camp about ever explaining consciousness in ordinary physical science terms. As he writes, "brain states cause conscious states—that is what observation suggests: but the question is how such a thing is so much as *possible*." In the workings of consciousness "something 'remarkable' seems to result from something unremarkable, and in a way that is unprecedented in nature." Indeed, the physical brain's ability to generate human consciousness seems virtually supernatural, like a "miracle," as McGinn himself characterizes it. How might it be possible that a set of mental events can be created by a set of physical events: "It seems no more intelligible that neurons should produce conscious states than that kidney cells should, or sawdust for that matter. We seem to be confronted with a kind of spontaneous generation in which a deep ontological gap is miraculously bridged."[42]

In the end, as McGinn concludes, using any of the known methods of physical science, "I do regard the mind-body problem as an insoluble

---

41. Ibid.
42. McGinn, "Solving the Philosophical Mind-Body Problem," 57, 56, 57.

(epistemic) mystery."[43] Moreover, he is well aware of the intellectual, scientific, and religious stakes, writing in 1999 that "I believe myself that the new interest in consciousness represents the next big phase in human thought about the natural world," representing as large an intellectual and philosophical development today as "the determination to understand the physical world that gathered force in the seventeenth century."[44]

But now the trend of events is in a new direction, posing a basic challenge to the materialism that began to take shape in the seventeenth century, and that underlay the modern development of the scientific method itself. As McGinn writes, "consciousness is threatening. It looks like an anomaly in our conception of the universe, a place where our usual [scientific] methods of understanding run out of steam. We are [only] now beginning to face up to the aspect of nature we do not understand," how a mental state even in concept could be created by a physical event. The current state of affairs, as McGinn sees it, is one of wide intellectual confusion—"discussion of consciousness is marked by divergences of opinion as wide as can be found anywhere" in the contemporary philosophical world. These differences, moreover, involve fundamental questions of the workings and character of the natural order. As suggested above, McGinn agrees that the conflicts are "as great as that which separates flat-earthers from round-earthers or Darwinists from Creationists." At the highest levels of thought, discussions of human consciousness leave us "in the uncomfortable position of having admitted a topic . . . about which we cannot agree, even about the basics."[45]

But McGinn, having said all this, and in this respect like the great majority of philosophers and neurologists of our day, distains any appeals to supernatural arguments. Indeed, he presents himself as yet another true believer in naturalism. Somehow, some way, he believes a naturalist explanation must exist for the emergence of mind from matter—this conviction amounting to an article of faith for McGinn as well. At the same time, he is also a strong critic of all existing efforts to understand or "explain" the existence of consciousness in naturalist terms. He agrees with Nagel and Searle that they are all in essence failures. Answers to the mystery of human consciousness will not be obtained from the likes of Daniel Dennett, Francis Crick, Steven Pinker, and the many others who have sought to understand consciousness—in principle at least, it may take a very long time in practice to work out the details—with the methods of physics, chemistry, and

43. Ibid., 60n2.

44. McGinn, "Can We Ever Understand Consciousness?"

45. Ibid.

biology, as applied to the study of the human mind by evolutionary biology and neuroscience.

In 1989, McGinn sought to help to fill the gap himself with an article in the philosophy journal *Mind*, and he then reworked his original argument into a 2004 essay, "Solving the Philosophical Mind-Body Problem."[46] McGinn is a philosopher and not a neuroscientist; he makes no claims to having discovered a neuroscientific answer now to explain the workings of human consciousness. Rather, he takes the discussion in a radically new direction. McGinn thinks that there is not likely to be any future natural explanation in the traditional sense; there will be no good physical scientific theory no matter how long we wait. But we can still be confident, he argues, that a natural explanation of some kind necessarily must exist. It must exist because we can take as self-evidently true that all existent phenomena must have natural explanations. It is just that any natural explanation in the case of consciousness will have to be outside our previous experience of the study of the workings of the natural world, and thus will not be discoverable by the use of the current scientific methods of physics and chemistry with which we have become familiar. Indeed, it may require a breakthrough as immense as Newton's discovery of the force of gravity, a force that seemed to work at a distance without any apparent intervening mechanical cause, leading some of Newton's contemporaries to regard it as a supernatural form of magic—and Newton himself to consider that the action of a god was the only explanation for gravity that he could conceive.

As McGinn thus writes, his goal is "to remove the suspicion that the world is behaving very strangely—almost paradoxically—when conscious states are generated by the [physical] brain, without having to produce the theory that explains how [such] things are actually working." As matters stand now, by demanding that an actual neuroscientific explanation of consciousness be established in physical terms, and given the actual impossibility of accomplishing this with our current scientific methods, we are forced into a circumstance of "intractable philosophical perplexity."[47] Given the present state of the discussion, any philosopher who is entirely honest in his arguments will have little choice but to accept the validity of some form of dualism—that there somehow exist separate mental and physical worlds. For McGinn, true believer in naturalism that he remains, this is an unacceptable outcome; some other answer, therefore, must exist, even if the only way is to postulate a brand-new natural force in the universe, hidden

---

46. McGinn, "Can We Solve the Mind-Body Problem?"; McGinn, "Solving the Philosophical Mind-Body Problem."

47. McGinn, "Solving the Philosophical Mind-Body Problem," 61, 60.

to this day from discovery by the conventional methods of physical science. This brand new element of nature will be defined by the fact that it is capable of explaining the existence and workings of human consciousness.

McGinn thus writes that in seeking a naturalist explanation for consciousness, "we do not have a plethora of theoretically adequate options from among which we cannot empirically choose." Rather, the much greater problem is that "nothing we can think of has a chance of explaining what needs to be explained" about consciousness in standard scientific terms. We are faced with a situation where "we don't know what a possible explanation of consciousness would even *look like*—hence the feeling of deep conceptual intractability" that for some true-believing naturalists can evoke feelings of an almost existential dread. We can overcame such inner anxieties, as McGinn suggests, by simply accepting that a naturalist answer must necessarily exist. As he explains this, "we solve the philosophical problem by diagnosing how it arises and asserting [as a foundational assumption] that consciousness is not non-natural despite all appearances to the contrary."[48]

McGinn acknowledges that this may seem a "mysterian" position to take. Yet, the choices are stark; if his solution is not accepted, intellectually honest philosophers will be pushed into proposing "supernatural dualisms of various forms," or alternatively at the other extreme of denying that any "such thing as consciousness" exists at all. Such outcomes, however, are themselves no less mysterious than his own proposed solution; indeed, for McGinn they are even less acceptable. Hence, as he explains, the "mysterian element" of his own theory "is invoked to an [ultimately] anti-mysterian agenda," that of dispelling the otherwise disturbing prospect that no natural explanation whatsoever for consciousness might exist, and the seeming inevitability at that point of having to appeal to some kind of supernatural explanation of human consciousness and indeed of human existence.[49] The real choice therefore is between one more limited form of mystery (McGinn's) and a greater mystery in which naturalism as a core world view will have to be abandoned (as Nagel, showing that McGinn's concerns were well founded, has recently concluded is in fact unavoidable). What this all really comes down to, however, is simply a pronouncement on McGinn's part that his naturalist faith is deeper than any faith he can conceive of accepting in the existence of a god. McGinn at this point is no longer speaking as a philosopher but as a theologian.

48. Ibid., 62, 64.
49. Ibid., 60, 63, 60.

McGinn the Theologian

McGinn thus recognizes that, once a supernatural dualism is conceded, it is only a short step to explaining consciousness in terms of the existence of some kind of supernatural being—a god, if not necessarily the Christian God. If naturalism is rejected, and given the long history of religion, some theorists of consciousness thus are bound to suggest, as McGinn fears, that "maybe God performs this miracle every time they close their eyes. This may make them take an attitude of unusual reverence toward unperceived objects, even arguing to the existence of God on the strength of what needs to be assumed in order to explain such a remarkable thing" as human consciousness. For McGinn, as for most philosophers and neuroscientists today, this turn to theism is a disturbing prospect that surely demands radical countermeasures. As McGinn sums up the situation, "I say it is like this with us and the mind-body problem." We must realize that "consciousness and the brain do have a nature that renders their union . . . natural, but we are blocked from grasping this nature" by the existing large limitations of our own mental capacities. We are therefore compelled to recognize that ultimately "consciousness exists, it is not non-natural, it is not something else in disguise, and it has a [natural] explanation: it is just that its nature is deeply hidden to us" at present and perhaps for the foreseeable future (although we can hope for a Newton or Einstein of consciousness who will finally solve the problem with some radically new insight).[50]

It is hard not to notice the surprising parallels between McGinn's argument and the arguments made by theologians over the centuries for the existence of a god. In Christian theology, a great mystery exists in the world; it cannot in principle be comprehended with the available powers of human reason; it is therefore necessary to look outside the range of normal human experience and rational understanding. The details differ but in many religions such thinking is a key part of the argument for the existence of a god. We have some glimpses of god's workings in the world (including conscious experiences), giving us some openings to knowing god's ways, but much will always remain a mystery, given the large limitations of human beings. For most religions, invoking the existence of a god is then a rational answer. Now in McGinn's case, as one might put it, he seemingly has unintentionally coined a new word for such "a god," his unknown form of "nature" that somehow mysteriously produces consciousness—but of which we otherwise know very little. In both the traditional religious case and now

50. Ibid., 66–67, 67–68, 68.

McGinn's case, we have to infer a conclusion from what little we do actually know as frail human beings.

In a common Christian understanding of dualism, the existence of God is invoked to explain the mystery of how nonmaterial events can cause material events, and vice versa. When a conscious thought to take some action occurs in a human brain (a nonmaterial event), God instantaneously exerts his powers to cause the necessary neural changes in the brain to make it happen. Or, if I accidentally touch a hot plate, God translates the neuronal reactions in my brain to the sharp pain experienced in my consciousness. In other words, among the many things a Christian God might do in the world, God may be the necessary link between the material and the nonmaterial sides of life—the otherwise separate realms of body and soul.

This is of course the same function performed by McGinn's new mysterious force of nature that he posits as necessary to understand human consciousness. One might suggest that the largest difference between the Christian explanation and McGinn's explanation is terminological—whether one calls this unknown presence in nature the mysterious workings of a "god" or calls it the unknown workings of something else that is equally invisible and mysterious to our present understanding of nature. It seems that we may have here yet another example of a widespread phenomenon of the modern age, the recasting of traditional religious messages to become secular religious messages even as they claim to say nothing about a god—indeed, may often even vigorously deny outwardly the existence of any god, while implicitly describing the workings of a god.[51] For Karl Marx, he thus substituted the all-powerful laws of economic history in place of the all-powerful Christian God, both equally omnipotent and equally capable of bringing heaven to earth, a future result that the Marxist economic god and the Christian God had already predetermined.

In a 1999 book, *The Mysterious Flame*, McGinn develops his theological thinking further, at one point explicitly bringing the possibility of a god into the discussion. McGinn recognizes, as discussed above, that there is a large—potentially fatal—problem for any forms of Darwinism if consciousness is recognized as a real but nonmaterial part of the world. As mentioned previously, how could the material workings of natural selection yield a nonmaterial outcome? Or, as McGinn puts it, the problem for Darwinism posed by "the conscious mind is that it is hard to see how any process—natural or divine—could possibly shape matter into mind.... [Indeed,] this seems impossible as a matter of principle." McGinn thus agrees

51. Bailey, *Implicit Religion in Contemporary Society;* Bailey, "Implicit Religion" (2009); and Bailey, "Implicit Religion" (2010).

that "sentience cannot be explained by means of Darwinian principles plus physics, because it needs to be *possible* to make mind from matter if natural selection is to explain how sentience arises by means of natural selection operating on material things." Stated another way, "a Darwinian explanation of consciousness works only if materialism about consciousness is true. But we have already seen that it is not true"—at least as materialism has long been understood by most philosophers and other true believers.[52] Given this clear counterexample, shockingly enough, the scientifically inexplicable character of consciousness is enough in itself to demonstrate that Darwinism is necessarily false—unable to account for a large part of human existence, the immaterial realm of our personal conscious experiences.

McCinn has no sympathy for traditional forms of Christian creationism—such beliefs are decisively refuted by an immense body of scientific inquiry and past discoveries in the fossil record. However, he thinks it may be possible to develop a new and more plausible form of "mental creationism," as McGinn calls it, based on the inability of scientific materialism—and thus necessarily also Darwinism—to explain or even comprehend the actual character of human consciousness. It would be reasonable then to argue that "only another form of consciousness could be sufficient to explain consciousness. Hence, the cause of sentience must be another sentience." Indeed, it must "be a conscious agent of some suitably impressive sort." As a result, as McGinn now writes, "It looks as if a new creative principle must be admitted into the universe."[53]

One possibility is that this new creative principle is to be found in the old idea of a human "soul." As McGinn writes, "It has been supposed since antiquity that consciousness and divinity go together. God is the author of the soul, and the soul is as supernatural as its [divine] creator." This is part of what it means to say that "human beings are made in the image of God." A typical understanding—found frequently in Christian theology—is "that God created your soul and adjoined it to your body for the duration of your mortal life." At the end of a person's life, "the soul can continue its existence, because it never depended upon the existence of the body to begin with. Each soul is itself a local miracle, a sign . . . of supernatural power in the empirical world." As McGinn writes, the physical human brain itself is then to be understood as "merely the organ or instrument of consciousness, not its cause or origin." As McGinn further suggests, an appropriate term for such a belief might be "theistic dualism."[54]

52. McGinn, *The Mysterious Flame*, 82.

53. Ibid., 83, 82.

54. Ibid., 83, 84.

McGinn acknowledges that such an argument for theistic dualism (there could be a number of possibilities in developing the details) is a strong one. It cannot be refuted simply as a matter of a flawed logical underpinning or a large body of factual errors upon which it relies—such as say literal biblical creationism. In the end, some element of religious faith might be necessary to believe in a theistic dualism but that is true of essentially all fundamental world views, even typically those that assert a secular character (whether their adherents recognize it or not). McGinn (like Nagel as discussed above) is personally averse, however, to theism in any form. Despite all his many sharp criticisms of its standard forms of expression, he is not willing to abandon his true-believing naturalist faith. To have to invoke a god would be for him a confession of personal failure.

A Christian Perspective on the Soul

True believing Christians (or other theists) obviously have no such reason to defend the implicit forms of secular fundamentalism that underlie contemporary naturalism. Hence, they are more open to thinking and writing about the soul as a real possibility. Indeed, questions of the soul are similar to issues of human consciousness, with to some extent a new word *consciousness* having today replaced a much older word *soul*, the latter seemingly having too many strong religious connotations. A recent scholarly exploration of such matters in 2011, however, reflected a more traditional Christian perspective, *The Soul Hypothesis*, an edited collection organized by Mark Baker, a professor of linguistics and cognitive science, and Stewart Goetz, a professor of philosophy, both of whom describe themselves as "theists."[55]

As they write, belief in a soul entails a form of dualism, a conviction that there exists a large realm of human existence that differs in some fundamental way from raw "matter." The monotheistic religions of Judaism, Christianity, and Islam "have all agreed that humans have a soul that survives the death of the body, will be judged by God, and will experience either punishment or reward in an eternal afterlife." For Descartes as well, the mental domain and the physical domain are separate worlds. Baker and Goetz comment that in the twentieth century, a more common form of dualism was "property dualism," the idea noted above that the one fundamental reality is the material world which somehow gives rise to—if quite

---

55. Baker and Goetz, "Introduction" to *The Soul Hypothesis*. See also Goetz and Taliaferro, *A Brief History of the Soul*; and Swinburne, *The Evolution of the Soul*.

mysteriously—the subjective experiences of human consciousness that are not themselves material in character even as they have a real existence.[56]

Baker and Goetz observe that ordinary people take for granted that they "inhabit a rich world of beliefs and desires, goals and purposes, pleasures and pains, sights and sounds, joys and sorrows whose nature has little or nothing to do with ordinary physical objects and the forces that act on them." It is equally obvious to most people that this mental realm is nevertheless closely tied to the physical world, including their brains, as when they experience a sensation in their consciousness caused by a physical impact on their body or when they cause their physical body to move as a matter of conscious intent. Yet, for most people, as Baker and Goetz write, the world of consciousness clearly "does seem different" from the material world of rocks and even of most plants and animals and other forms of life on earth. Over the course of human history, it is a fact that "most people have believed that a human being is a composite thing, made up of two distinct natures, a body and a soul. To use a technical term of Western philosophy, most people have been *dualists*," even if in recent times they might not describe their thinking in such terms.[57]

Historically, it is not only ordinary people who have typically seen the world in dualist terms. Plato was a dualist as were most early Christian writers. Indeed, the dualists of history include many of the greatest thinkers in the Western tradition, such as Augustine, Aquinas, Galileo, Descartes, Newton, Leibniz, Locke, and Kant. As Baker and Goetz write, "most western thinkers have thought in [dualist] terms from the beginning until (at least) the very recent past." Outside Western civilization, studies in the field of cultural anthropology have found that "such a belief [in dualism] is attested in almost all known human cultures."[58] The large majority of human beings thus have believed that both an "outside" material world of physical objects and events and an "inner" nonmaterial world of human consciousness coexist. Since the events of consciousness themselves have no physical existence (at least that can be examined and measured independently in time and space by any other observers), the conclusion long seemed inescapable—the material world and the world of human consciousness are dual realities in which human beings somehow live out their existence.

For scientific materialists, as noted above, the most distressing element of dualism is the large opening it provides for the supernatural. The very essence of a human soul, or of a human consciousness, for which there is no

---

56. Baker and Goetz, *The Soul Hypothesis*, 249, 164.

57. Ibid., 1.

58. Ibid., 2.

scientific explanation in principle, is almost by definition supernatural. If the supernatural is real, then a god may well be real. Indeed, one might attempt to speculate about the character of god based on observations of the workings of the supernatural, as they are available to each individual in observing introspectively the workings of their own human "soul," now more typically called their "consciousness." Baker and Goetz argue, however, that there is no "contradiction between believing that human beings have an immaterial soul and believing that there is no God," even as some philosophers have in fact argued this.[59] The soul (individual self-consciousness and the capacity for rational thought) can be hypothesized to exist without necessarily assuming the existence of a god, as illustrated by McGinn above, with his idea that there is an unknown physical force at work. Indeed, Baker and Goetz find that there are forms of dualism that are fully compatible with atheism.

Nevertheless, they acknowledge that the form of dualism that they favor in *The Soul Hypothesis* has "the additional fortune or misfortune of being strongly associated with traditional religious beliefs." They also acknowledge that it "is presumably not a coincidence" that all the other chapter contributors to their edited book collection about the soul are believing Christians of one sort or another.[60] At the very end of *The Soul Hypothesis* in a concluding section, the two editors address in greater detail the potential religious implications of dualism. Until this point, they and their other chapter authors have been examining the hypothesis that the soul exists without seeking to ground their arguments in explicitly religious terms. They also acknowledge differences among the two coeditors themselves in their own religious understandings of the relationship between Christianity and dualism. For one coeditor, as he characterizes his understanding of the relationship of Christianity and dualism:

> Theism is the more certain truth, and the one that . . . . pragmatic reasoning about these matters starts from. As a theist, [this coeditor] believes in a God that is distinct from the material universe, a God that is "a Spirit." Given this, he believes that there is a class of entities ("spirits"), which contains at least one member, such that those entities are not made up of matter or subject to physical laws but can interact causally with ordinary physical objects. But if there is one member of this class, [one] cannot automatically rule out the possibility that there are other members of this [spiritual] class—that human beings (created in the image of God) might also be things of this sort. He does

59. Ibid., 250.
60. Ibid., 249, 250.

not believe that this is entailed by his core Christian beliefs, but the possibility is raised by them. With this in mind, he looks at the evidence he can find from psychology and linguistics to see if there are observable phenomena that are better explained in this way, and concludes that there are. So for him, theism plus a consideration of relevant facts [about human consciousness and the human condition in the world more generally] leads toward dualism.[61]

The other coeditor (they do not identify which is which) has his reasoning working the other way around; it is his dualism that leads to theism.

The more certain truth is dualism. It seems obvious to [this co-editor] that he cannot be simply a physical object, subject to all and only the laws of physics, given his first-person experience, his ability to reason, and his ability to make free choices guided by his purposes. It is also evident that, as a soul, he is able to cause events in his body, such as voluntary movements; agency [from mind to matter] clearly is [somehow mysteriously] possible. This then raises the possibility that there is some other, greater soul, who can in a free and purposeful manner cause events not only in one particular animal body, but anywhere in the material universe. Such a being would be God. With this possibility arising out of his dualism, he looks at the experiential evidence that points to the existence of such a [supreme] being and concludes on the basis of this evidence that this being does exist. For him, dualism plus a consideration of relevant facts leads to theism.[62]

Neither Baker nor Goetz argues that such reasoning "proves" the existence of a god. One can merely offer arguments grounded in certain faith assumptions, plus observations of the world, as examined and developed by rational processes of thought. The naturalist, to be sure, stands on no higher ground. When someone demands that the existence of a god must be "proved" (implicitly assuming that the use of scientific methods is necessary in considering the question of a god), we can safely conclude that no god will ever be found. No further discussion is necessary. The naturalist, however, has to begin with some assumptions as well; he simply prefers his own assumptions. It is a large initial assumption, for example, to require that a god must be explained and understood in scientific terms—an assumption

61. Ibid., 251–52.
62. Ibid., 252.

that amounts to little more than declaring in advance as a matter of faith
that a god does not exist.

Freud: Psychiatrist of the Soul

It would be hard to dispute that Sigmund Freud had more influence on
thinking about human consciousness than any other person of the twentieth century. A core element of Freud's writings was the claim that, as a
medical doctor, he was engaged in a practice of scientific inquiry that was
yielding revolutionary consequences for the understanding of human consciousness. Indeed, Freud commonly compared his methods to those of
physics, once writing that we are now "in a position to establish psychology
on foundations similar to those of any other science such, for instance, as
physics." He insisted that "we have discovered technical methods of filling
up the gaps in the phenomena of our consciousness, and we make use of
those methods just as a physicist makes use of experiment."[63] With Freud's
new science of psychology, as he claimed, many of the great historic mysteries of the human mind could now finally be resolved.

Freud also saw himself as a follower of Darwin, Freud's theory of the
changes in individual mental processes from early childhood to adulthood
representing a transfer of evolutionary thinking to the study of the psychological development of the human mind. As such, the essence of this internal
mental evolution was competitive struggle among the various conscious and
unconscious forces in the mind from an early age. Indeed, as Karl Popper
once commented, Freud in this respect followed Karl Marx—another Darwinist disciple—in portraying the events of human consciousness as a mental form of "class struggle between the lower and higher parts of the soul."[64]

Whatever his many useful individual insights, Freud offers a caution-
ary tale for us today with respect to making large claims about the existence of a science of the mind and in particular the assertion that mental
phenomena are determined and can be understood in a manner analogous
to the workings of the natural world. It is notable that, in reviewing the
philosophic and neurological literature of consciousness of the past thirty
years, the name of Freud seldom comes up. If anything, he is seen today
as yet another embarrassment of what was in general an unduly credulous
twentieth century—Marx and Freud leading the evangelical parade. Examining the twentieth-century legacy of Freud in a 1998 review, Thomas Nagel
observes that Freud asserted a "causally complete physical system [in the

63. Freud, quoted in Nagel, *Other Minds*, 14–15, 15.
64. Popper, "Part I," 166.

brain], some of whose processes, however, have the property of consciousness in addition, or have conscious concomitants. The mental then appears as the effect of a certain kind of physical process" that Freud will now explore through a comprehensive examination of the mental and behavioral events that correspond to this process.[65]

Like many others at the end of the twentieth century, Nagel is deeply skeptical of Freud's whole project, at least in the terms in which he presented it. He writes that for Freud "to assume that an objective psychology, whose concepts refer to physical phenomena, will roughly preserve the distinctions and categories embodied in common sense mental concepts is to assume a great deal," and without much justification at all. Nagel criticizes Freud on the grounds that his "theory is essentially mentalistic in that its explanatory value cannot be recaptured by a nonanthropomorphic version." The phenomena studied by physicists can in principle be observed and measured equally well in time and space by any outside party (any "third person"), while the phenomena of human consciousness are directly observed only by the one individual (the "first person") experiencing the events in his own mind.[66]

Thus, the basic data of Freudian psychology are expressed by human beings in subjective human speech and in other communication of internal mental events (through poetry, for example), as the individual consciousness interprets its own internal experiences in order to try to convey them to other consciousnesses. Nagel comments that "until these subjective features are left behind, the hypotheses of a mentalist psychology will not be accepted as physical explanations." Indeed, "psychoanalytic theory will have to change a great deal before it comes to be regarded as part of the physical description of reality. And perhaps it, and other mentalistic theories, will never achieve the kind of objectivity necessary" to put it in the category of physics, Freud to the contrary.[67]

Nagel suggests that Freudianism is actually a disguised form of dualism. Freud's outward claims that his theories are grounded in physical processes occurring in the brain are merely window dressing. The postulated physical processes actually play little role in the psychological content of his theories. All the real action is occurring within the mental domains of the conscious (and the unconscious). Thus, despite Freud's strong assertions that he is following in the naturalist tradition, the Freudian world of the mind for all practical purposes exists independently of the physical world of the brain. As Freud speculates creatively and boldly about the workings of

65. Nagel, *Other Minds*, 15–16.

66. Ibid., 19, 24.

67. Ibid., 24, 25.

a distinct mental side of human existence, he would seem to be a latter-day follower in the Cartesian tradition.

Why, then, if his thinking had such large scientific failings, did Freud have such an immense influence on the intellectual life of the twentieth century? I would suggest that Nagel has given us the answer: Freud was a great modern explorer of the human soul. As Karl Popper writes, "in Greek philosophy, the soul played a role very similar to that of the mind in post-Cartesian philosophy. It was an [immaterial] entity, a substance, which sums up the conscious experience of the self."[68] Freud's great innovation was to develop a way for the twentieth century to continue to talk and think about the soul, all the while never having to use this old-fashioned word with it powerful theistic connotations. This was a necessary strategy for an age when so much elite—"sophisticated"—discussion had to be carried on in the language of scientific materialism, a language that did not admit of any interesting and illuminating way of discussing and analyzing matters of human consciousness (of the "soul"). Freud proved remarkably adept in showing how to create the necessary linguistic disguises in order to allow a far-ranging, modern discussion of a topic that was actually still of immense interest to most people, even if they no longer had the vocabulary to address it explicitly.

But times are slowly changing; the soul may be coming back. In a 2012 collection of essays by several well-known contemporary philosophers and theologians, the editor, Oxford University research fellow Benedikt Gocke, states in the Introduction that "since the middle of the last century, the default answer to the questions of what and who we are has been the physicalist's objectivist answer: because everything is physical—so it went—we, too, have to be physical." However, "for reasons well known"—including some discussed above in this book—"reductive physicalism failed" as an attempt to address the full dimensions of the human condition; moreover, "nonreductive physicalism . . . also failed." In retrospect, it has become clear that both forms of physicalism necessarily require assumptions that represent "an article of faith held by the physicalist"—that they thus belong at least as much to the domain of religion as to science.[69]

This is unusually blunt talk for a contemporary philosopher in now rejecting scientific materialism. But the more surprising part of the book is the direction in which many of the specific chapters turn, towards dualism and even towards a newly explicit discussion of the soul. Indeed, Gocke writes that there has been a "recent revival of dualism," as is illustrated by

---

68. Popper, "Part I," 159.

69. Gocke, "Introduction," 1, 2.

the five chapters in the book that "are concerned with ways to establish the truth of dualism"—this a book coming from a well-respected American university press. Two other chapters find that "there is a strong connection between [philosophical] metaphysics and spirituality." In one chapter, as Gocke summarizes it, Oxford philosopher Stephen Priest "argues that materialist and physicalist solutions to the problems in the philosophy of mind are guaranteed to fail because they do not do justice to the reality of one's own existence." Priest himself argues that a much better perspective is to recognize the existence of "an unbounded and unchanging inner space in which the time is always now," and this inner space is to be "identified with the immaterial soul."[70]

The "Hard Problem" of Consciousness

A key figure in the recent shift of scholarly opinion away from scientific materialism in the understanding of human consciousness is the Australian philosopher David Chalmers. Chalmers first came to wider professional notice with a 1995 article on "Facing Up to the Problem of Consciousness" in the *Journal of Consciousness Studies*. Chalmers expanded the article in 1996 to an influential book, *The Conscious Mind: In Search of a Fundamental Theory*.[71] Chalmers would later acknowledge in a 2010 book that his mid-1990s efforts were less successful in advancing a new theory of consciousness than he had hoped; rather, his greatest impact was in critiquing previous philosophical writings about consciousness, thus further helping to undermine the old materialist understandings. As Chalmers wrote in 1995, many naturalist philosophers of consciousness still use "reductive methods to address consciousness." Chalmers concluded, however, that "these methods inevitably fail to come to grips with the hardest part of the problem" of consciousness.[72]

Chalmers thus famously distinguished between "the easy problems" and the "hard problems" of consciousness. As he wrote, "the easy problems of consciousness are those that seem directly susceptible to the standard methods of cognitive science, whereby a phenomenon is explained in terms of computational or neural mechanisms" operating within the physical brain. For example, if I "see" an object, a scientist can in concept measure the light waves entering my eyes, the neural messages that are then transmitted from the eyes to the brain, the receipt of these messages in the brain, and

70. Ibid., 12, 17.
71. Chalmers, *The Conscious Mind*.
72. Chalmers, "Facing Up to the Problem of Consciousness," 200.

the further neural manipulation—potentially quite complex—occurring within the brain, finally resulting at some point in my conscious perception of the object. At present it is typically impossible to say exactly how the physical brain performs all these functions in full neural detail, even though we know that it somehow does so successfully. But we can be reasonably confident that in principle with further neurological study and research it will eventually all be fully understood in physical terms (at least up to the final moment when the conscious perception arises). As Chalmers writes, in terms of a full understanding of what is happening in the physical brain in such situations, "getting the details right will probably take a century or two of difficult empirical work. Still, there is every reason to believe that the methods of cognitive science and neuroscience will succeed."[73]

With respect to the "hard problems" of consciousness, however, Chalmers concludes that there can be no such confidence. These problems involve the subjective experiences in consciousness themselves such as "the felt quality of redness, the experience of dark and light, the quality of depth in a visual field, . . . the sound of a clarinet, the smell of mothballs"—all examples of "qualia" in the language of philosophy. Chalmers agrees that these features of the human mind are intrinsically "perplexing" in terms of our ability to explain them in any physical scientific way. As Chalmers observes, "how can we explain why there is something it is like to entertain a mental image, or to experience an emotion? It is widely agreed that experience arises from a physical basis, but we have no good explanation of why and how it so arises." Indeed, as others have said, it remains a complete scientific mystery, leaving us, Chalmers laments, in a circumstance in which "it seems objectively unreasonable that it should [arise], and yet it does."[74] And the examples of events in consciousness mentioned by Chalmers are elementary compared with say the development of higher mathematics by the community of mathematicians of the world.

Following in the path of Searle, and affirming his basic view, Chalmers delves into the details of a number of specific earlier theories of consciousness that he finds exhibit a common pattern of claiming more than they deliver. He finds that the "Neural Darwinism" model of Edelman (1989), for example, "addresses questions about perceptual awareness and the self-concept, but says nothing about why there should also be [conscious] experience." The "multiple drafts" model of Dennett (1991), despite his grand claims, actually diverts our attention by examining one of the easy problems, the "reportability of certain mental contents." In another case,

73. Ibid., 200, 201.
74. Ibid., 201.

"the 'intermediate level' theory of Jackendoff (1987) provides an account of some computational processes that underlie consciousness" but he candidly acknowledges that the hard problem "of how these 'project' into consciousness remains mysterious." The co-discoverer of DNA in 1953, Francis Crick turned to the study of the workings of the brain as the focus for much of his later research career. Working with Christof Koch, the two made extensive studies of the physical brain processes that give rise to consciousness, as identifiable with the methods of neurology. As Chalmers comments, however, their "strategy is clearly incomplete" in terms of understanding the hard problem. For that, "we need to know more than *which* processes [in the brain] give rise to experience; we need an account of why and how"—something that no neuroscientist or other student of the brain has yet succeeded in providing. In general, "the emergence of [conscious] experience goes beyond what can by derived from physical theory" as lies at the metaphysical heart of scientific materialism.[75]

Chalmers does not advocate giving up on the hard problem simply because it seems altogether intractable in terms of any standard "reductive explanation" of the physical sciences. Instead, philosophers and neuroscientists will have to turn to a method of "nonreductive explanation [which] is [now] the natural choice" in studying the hard problem. It will be, he acknowledges, "a variety of dualism, as it postulates basic properties [as part of human existence] over and above the properties invoked by physics." While they would not be the laws of the physical universe, the goal would still be a theory containing "fundamental laws" that connect the events occurring in consciousness itself—what Freud claimed to be discovering, if ultimately to be judged a failure. But perhaps a future follower in the path of Freud will be more successful; Chalmers thus suggests that such a theory might be described as a form of "naturalistic dualism."[76] It is perhaps better described, however, as a form of "theistic dualism," as labeled by McGinn, since the most direct interpretation of these nonphysical "fundamental laws" may be that they are actually the laws of a god who shares consciousness with human beings, if in god's case on a vastly grander scale.

The Matrix as Metaphysics

Even in the 1990s, Chalmers, like McGinn, is thus being drawn—perhaps unhappily but seemingly with no other choice—into the realm of religion and theology. He moves further in a 2010 book, *The Character of*

75. Ibid., 205, 207, 208.
76. Ibid., 209, 210.

Consciousness, in which he includes a chapter on "*The Matrix* as Metaphysics." As he writes there,

> Let's say that a matrix . . . is an artificially designed computer simulation of a world. . . . Let's also say that someone is *envatted*, or is *in a matrix*, if he or she has a cognitive system that receives its inputs from and sends its outputs to a matrix. Then, the brain at the beginning is envatted.
>
> We can imagine that a matrix simulates the entire physics of a world, keeping track of every last particle throughout space and time. . . . An envatted being will be associated with a computer simulation of a particular simulated body. A connection is arranged so that whenever this body receives sensory inputs inside the simulation, the envatted cognitive system will receive sensory inputs of the same sort. When the envatted [being's] cognitive system produces motor outputs, corresponding motor outputs will be fed to the motor organs of the simulated body.
>
> When the possibility of a matrix is raised, a question immediately follows. How do I know that I am not in a matrix? After all, there could be a brain in a vat structured exactly like my brain, hooked up to a matrix, with experiences indistinguishable from those I am having now. From the inside [first person perspective of my own consciousness], there is no way to tell for sure that I am not in the situation of the brain in a vat. So it seems that there is no way to know for sure that I am not in a matrix.[77]

The 1999 movie *The Matrix* offers a particular development of this theme. That we exist in a matrix, Chalmers suggests, is not a mere hypothetical thought experiment; rather it is a philosophical possibility that we must at least "take seriously." Indeed, extending the projections of technological futurists such as Ray Kurzweil into the indefinite future (see the discussion in Chapter 2), it may be an actual possibility that "technology will evolve that will allow beings to create computer simulations of entire worlds." If there are already many existing worlds outside our own earth, some existing beings may already be creating such simulations. You and I could be one of their creations. Hence, the chance that you or I would be existing as an envatted "brain" within such a computer simulation is at least in concept an actual possibility. Indeed, Chalmers suggests at one point that conceivably it is even "more likely . . . than . . . not" that you or I exist as part of a computer simulation. All our "perceptions" of the world could be nothing but accounts created by digital signals sent by a computer to our simulated

---

77. Chalmers, *The Character of Consciousness*, 456–57.

minds. As Chalmers writes, whether correct or not, "it certainly seems that we cannot be *certain* that we are not in a matrix."[78]

Given the mysteries of human existence posed by twentieth-century physics as reviewed earlier in Chapter 3, and the mysteries of human consciousness as reviewed in this chapter, Chalmers is open to exploring some radical reconceptions of the basic workings of the world. He proposes "the Metaphysical Hypothesis" in which "physical processes" are not to be understood as the movements and actions of material objects subject to various forces but instead as "fundamentally computational." He understands this as occurring in a dualist world in which "our cognitive systems are separate from physical processes but interact with them." Finally, a third foundational element of the Metaphysical Hypothesis is that "physical reality was created by beings outside physical space-time."[79]

In Chalmer's proposed new metaphysics, it follows that "physics as we know it is not the fundamental level of reality." Atoms and molecules do exist but they are—as are subatomic particles such as quarks, electrons, or photons—the creations of "a computational algorithm, which at a higher level produces the processes that we [have come to] think of as fundamental particles, forces, and so on." All of our daily perceptions that guide us in going about the process of living in the world will be unaffected. There are still objects in human consciousness such as "tables and chairs" as we routinely perceive them, but if we want to penetrate more deeply, it "just turns out that their fundamental reality is a little different from what we thought"— something that twentieth-century physics has told us as well.[80]

The hypothesis that the universe was created by "beings outside physical space-time" is of course long-standing in religion. As Chalmers comments, "If one believes that God created the world, and if one believes that God is outside physical space-time, then one believes in [one version of] the Creation Hypothesis."[81] The Cambridge University mathematician John Barrow similarly writes that we are now confronted with "an alarming thought . . . that we might be living in someone else's simulation right now." But Barrow then observes that this possibility is not as new as is commonly believed. Indeed, "Is it not very similar to many religious beliefs in which God is the Great Programmer who can choose to intervene in the world

---

78. Ibid., 457.
79. Ibid., 459.
80. Ibid., 460, 461.
81. Ibid., 462.

occasionally (as in orthodox Christian doctrine) or chose not to intervene after the start (as in Deism)?"[82]

As Chalmers explains, however, "one need not believe in God to believe the Creation Hypothesis." Contrary to the widespread naturalism of our time, the Creation Hypothesis "is clearly coherent, and I cannot conclusively rule it out." Chalmers accepts that the Matrix Hypothesis is a dualistic form of "Mind-Body Hypothesis"—that "my mind is (and has always been) constituted by physical processes outside physical space time and receives its perceptual inputs from and sends its outputs to processes in [this] physical space-time." As Chalmers acknowledges, "Descartes believed something like this." Summing up his new grand cosmogony, Chalmers explains that "the computational processes underlying physical space-time were designed by the creators as a computer simulation of a world."[83] In this framework, the intractable problem of the scientific inexplicability of human consciousness, approached in the terms of ordinary scientific materialism, simply becomes a non-problem.

Chalmers might not use the term but it is apparent that he is proposing a new religion. It is not any old religion but mirrors in key aspects Judeo-Christian religion. Indeed, "the matrix" is perhaps best regarded as a new word for a god, one that would not be so different in many ways from the Christian God, who is often also described in Christian theology as a nonphysical mind who created the universe and oversees everything that occurs in it. The inhabitants of the matrix have a nonphysical conscious experience of their existence, indeed rather similar to the workings of a Christian soul. So why not just say that "the Metaphysical Hypothesis" is a reworked Christianity to a new contemporary dress, even though Chalmers himself may not even be aware of this? As also noted above with respect to McGinn and Freud, the strong prejudices of the twentieth century and the early twenty-first century against discussing religion in explicit terms have made it necessary for many people to create whole new "secular" vocabularies to examine and discuss traditionally religious questions. As one might say, there are surprisingly many modern instances in which one might say of "secular" belief systems that they are in reality "Christianity in disguise."[84]

Chalmers may also prefer to talk about a god in the language of "the matrix" because it now adds an element of science fiction appeal. It is playfully offered in a postmodernist spirit. One might say that these features are part of Chalmers's packaging to make his new (or old) "religion" more

---

82. Barrow, *The Infinite Book*, 204.

83. Chalmers, *The Character of Consciousness*, 462, 463.

84. Nelson, "The Secularization Myth Revisited."

acceptable for the many people today who have a negative view of traditional "religion." Indeed, one might argue that over the past fifty years the most influential writers in advancing a Christian ethics and world view broadly— seeing the world as a battlefield of good and evil, for example—have been J. R. R. Tolkien, C. S. Lewis, and J. K. Rowling. Tolkien openly acknowledged that *The Lord of the Rings* and other fantasies of his were meant as Christian parables. Lewis was a leading Christian apologists of the twentieth century when not writing children's stories, and Rowling herself states that her own Christian beliefs were major influences on the Harry Potter series. The 1977 movie *Star Wars* and its sequels may have done more to advance historic elements of Christian thinking among the young than all the Sunday school classes of the 1970s and 1980s combined.

For adults, what is labeled "secular religion" often plays a similar role, including in its messages significant borrowings from traditional Jewish and Christian sources. Indeed, for many people, skeptical of anything officially labeled as "religion," it may be the only way that traditional religious ideas can reach them—they require an outwardly disguised "secular" form of Christianity (or a Christian heresy, as some might put it). Even if Chalmers may not himself be a devout apologist for a disguised Christianity in the manner of a Tolkien or Lewis, he would seem to be making an implicit case for a Christian world view to a considerably greater extent than he himself seemingly recognizes.

Mental Monism

It is conventionally assumed today that if dualism is rejected, the alternative is one or another form of material monism—as this belief is found today under various labels such as naturalism, physicalism, and scientific materialism. But material monism may have reversed things. If dualism is false, the most logical form of monism is instead mental monism. As Chalmers is exploring, there can be no sure belief in the existence of an outside physical world without introducing some element of conscious faith in the existence of my own physical brain. Consciousness thus has to come first, before "matter" can exist. Indeed, some historic religions have seen the world in terms of mind as the sole reality. One Buddhist writer, for example, as University of Helsinki theologian Ilkka Pyysiainen relates, "adopts an idealist position and thinks that the 'impressions' (*vasana*) of deeds enter into the series of consciousness (*vijnanasantana*) and fruition takes place there. In other words, everything happens in the 'mind only.'"[85]

85. Pyysiainen, *Supernatural Agents*, 157.

Let us as a thought experiment imagine a world without any faith in a material dimension of existence. In such a world, following Descartes (but without his dualism), we would have to begin with the workings of our own consciousness. In the end, without some faith assumptions, that is all we have. In other words, we would have a form of solipsism. The possibility of solipsism is a subject that comes up frequently in philosophical discussions but it is then typically dismissed with little or no further explanation as simply being "impossible." It is easy to escape the world of solipsism with a few "supernatural" assumptions such as the existence of a god (or a "matrix"). Without such assumptions, however, it is surprisingly difficult—I would say in fact it is logically impossible.

The existing attempts to refute solipsism from a perspective grounded in scientific materialism alone are not persuasive. For example, it is not a strong argument to argue for the actual existence of other minds (and then also other bodies) to say that I can develop close analogies between my own perceptions of the workings of other minds (necessarily occurring in my own mind) and the workings of my own mind. But this would not tell me much because all the action is still happening in my own mind alone. As with the matrix, I may be as a god myself, creating my own universe—how would I know?

Quantum mechanics seems to raise that possibility. Former Oxford theologian Keith Ward, for example, writes that some leading quantum physicists "are impressed by the fact that electrons are probability waves that only collapse into locatable particles when a measurement is taken or when an observation is made." This leads them to think—scientific materialism to the contrary—that "perhaps consciousness cannot be considered just a by-product of the physical activity of the brain." Indeed, the scientific materialists may have things just backwards: quantum mechanics may be taken to suggest, as Ward writes, and Chalmers is in effect getting close to, that "perhaps consciousness has to be present for there to be an actual physical world containing brains at all." If this is true (not all physicists would agree), it implies that "some sort of consciousness is needed to make the universe actual." It would have to be a "cosmic consciousness, a consciousness without a body."[86] It sounds a lot like a creator god.

Modern physics, Ward writes, harking back to Plato, thus raises the very real possibility that "the real basis for the universe is conceptual or mathematical"—in 2008 anticipating the 2014 book on *Our Mathematical Universe: My Quest for the Ultimate Nature of Reality*, by the MIT physicist Max Tegmark. There is a world, Ward suggests, of "mathematical possibilities

---

86. Ward, *The Big Questions in Science and Religion*, 24, 25.

[that first] exist in a cosmic consciousness, and it is this consciousness which, being necessary [in the beginning], can give actuality to some of these possible [mathematical] states and laws." Ward quotes approvingly the view of British physicist Roger Penrose (noted above in Chapter 3) that there is a "need for mentality to be 'ontologically fundamental' in the universe." If we conceive of God as mind, this is coming close to the classic Christian view that the universe was created according to a design that first existed in the mind of God. Ward is impressed by the parallels; as he writes, quantum mechanics leads to the search for "a principle of the actualization of some possible states" of some form of "cosmic consciousness," which easily recalls "the biblical principle enunciated in the book of Genesis" in describing the first six days.[87]

Conclusion

It is not only Nagel, Chalmers, Ward, and a few others, but in recent years a growing number of philosophers, neurologists, and other scholars of the mind have been challenging a strictly materialist world view. In a 2010 edited collection of essays by analytical philosophers, *The Waning of Materialism*, the editors Robert Koons, professor of philosophy at the University of Texas, and George Bealer, professor of philosophy at Yale, write that "materialism is a readily intelligible monistic worldview, appealing in its apparent simplicity, and a natural complement to the impressive ongoing successes in the natural sciences." They find, however, that today "materialism is waning in a number of significant respects—one of which is the ever-growing number of major philosophers who reject materialism or at least have strong sympathies with anti-materialist views." Indeed, there have always been a surprising number of leading thinkers—perhaps it helped to have a high intellectual status to be able to adopt more controversial views falling outside the mainstream—who were skeptical, including in the twentieth century Bertrand Russell, Rudolf Carnap, Alonzo Church, Kurt Godel, Stuart Hampshire, Peter Strawson, and Hilary Putnam.[88]

But now anti-materialist heresies are spreading more widely in the philosophical community. As Koons and Bealer write, among contemporary philosophers "a growing number—among them prominent philosophers who once had strong materialist sympathies—have come to the conclusion that some of the arguments against materialism cannot be overcome." While materialist philosophers such as Daniel Dennett have fought to overcome

87. Ibid., 25, 26.
88. Koons and Bealer, "Introduction" to *The Waning of Materialism*, ix.

the objections, even many current philosophers who subscribe to material-ist views "would acknowledge that the current extant responses [of such philosophers] are at best inconclusive." Among those who still profess to believe in materialism, they admit that at present they are simply taking it as an "article of faith that at some point in the future they, or someone else, will find ways" to more successfully defend materialism. As Koons and Bealer observe, however, "such a [faith] conviction does not rise to the standard of epistemic justification needed for theoretical knowledge" to be accepted as philosophical truth—certainly when such truth claims can influence dis-cussions in society concerning fundamental matters of individual religious world view and of the wider actions of a whole society.

Perhaps the greatest tensions working against full acceptance of a phi-losophy of scientific materialism have related to the mysterious character of human consciousness. Nothing is more central to human existence than consciousness. Any overarching world view that cannot accommodate hu-man consciousness in its framework of understanding is radically incom-plete—and thus must be rejected as a full account of the human condition. Redefining the workings of consciousness entirely in materialist terms—the desperation reductionist strategy of scientific materialism—is untenable. Put in the simplest terms, the events of consciousness are not observable other than to each individual with respect to his own consciousness; the events of my own consciousness are not measurable in time and space even by myself; therefore, much that happens in consciousness cannot be studied or understood with the methods of the physical sciences; therefore, natural-ism necessarily fails as an explanation of everything; therefore, some things in the world must lie outside any physical explanation grounded in a scien-tific understanding of the workings of nature—as one might say, they are in this respect "supernatural"; therefore, if the existence of the supernatural means the existence of a god (perhaps not a necessary conclusion in and of itself, but it is hard to imagine the alternative), we can conclude that a god in at least this limited sense exists. If the existence of some god is conceded, a main task becomes to discover additional features of this god by whatever methods may turn out to be possible and rationally defensible.

6

Divine Agency in Recorded Human History

Are There "Miracles"?

ALTHOUGH OUR AWARENESS IS dulled by familiarity, we are daily surrounded by miracles. An iPhone is a miracle, able to receive telephone calls and emails without any physical connection anywhere—through the air, as it seems (or in reality it could as well be through a "vacuum"). An airplane carrying 300 people from New York to London is a miracle. Modern medicine can restore the sight of some people, a miracle with biblical overtones. Google is a miracle, able to access vast troves of information worldwide seemingly instantaneously, at times seeming to take a large step towards omniscience. If any of these things and dozens of other products of modern technology had been suggested to a person as recently as 1800, they would have had no doubt that it is impossible, it would require a miracle, only a god can have such powers, and who could possible believe, other than a madman, that human beings would soon become as a god.

It also does not seem to be a miracle today because we have what seems to be an explanation—it is not God but science that makes it possible. Yet, our actual personal understanding of the daily miracles that surround us is no greater than if God were the actual source of the events. I have no clue how any of these miracles actually work. As Princeton physicist Eugene Wigner acknowledged, even the scientists who produce the knowledge to create the miracles have no real idea. They have no rational explanation, for example, of how electromagnetic waves exist or behave the way they do. They simply know that these waves (whatever they are, and they share with human consciousness the fact that they certainly have no material existence) follow exact mathematical rules (unlike consciousness) that can then be manipulated by human beings to create radio, television, electric lighting, and many other technological marvels. In this respect, one might say that science itself creates powers that are godlike. By some miracle, human beings have in the modern age come into possession of the powers of a god. Not surprisingly, then, the specific miracles produced by the new god of "science" are more impressive than the miracles Jesus performed in the Bible, not only in their reliable predictability but in the fact that we can personally verify their existence from our own experience. (Unfortunately, when human beings have sought to extend the godlike powers of science beyond the boundaries of the natural world, the results in politics, economics, and many other areas of life have been anything but godlike or miraculous.)

Our daily lives are also full of other miracles, as when I "decide" in my conscious mind to walk across the street. The ability of a nonmaterial mind to control a material event is indeed a miracle, as a growing number of philosophers have been observing in recent years (although typically not using the term *miracle*, even as they acknowledge that there is no known basis for such events in the workings of the natural world, for the time being at least we must consider them supernatural). Our lives, in short, are filled with direct experiences of the supernatural; they are so commonplace, however, that we no longer recognize them for their supernatural and miraculous qualities. For the many worshipers of science, moreover, to acknowledge explicitly the presence of supernatural, miraculous events in the world would be to concede that their god of science is less than the all-powerful being they conceive of—a concession that many of them will resist making at all costs, intellectual and otherwise. The god that exists is more than simply the laws of nature.

The existence of a few routinely supernatural features of the world of our daily lives is still a long way, however, from offering evidence for the existence of a traditional Jewish and Christian God. Our daily miracles tell us some things about god—his fondness for mathematics, for example—but large gaps remain. In the Bible, only one book, Genesis, focuses on the geological and biological early history of the earth, and this account is no longer credible. The remainder of the Bible is about—at least it is so presented—recorded human history up through the time of Jesus, all this history constituting the primary source of knowledge about God for Jews and Christians. As a source of information about human history for people living today, however, the Bible has three significant problems. First, its history deals with a small part of the total population of the earth—there is little or nothing about China or India, and the record of the entire Americas is missing. Second, this history stops about 2,000 years ago, and many important events—potentially revelatory of a god—have happened in the world since then. Third, the biblical historical account itself is of uncertain reliability, seldom supported by strong historical documentation or other independently verifiable evidence in its details.

Chapter 6 will therefore take the following approach. Filling in large areas missing from the biblical account, and limiting ourselves to historical events for which some definite historical evidence can be provided, is it possible to say anything further about the question of a god? While not relying on the specific details included in the Christian Bible, this approach nevertheless remains broadly biblical in two respects. First, it looks to recorded human history as a main potential source of religious knowledge. Second, it asks whether the record of human history offers any significant evidence of a supernatural force at work—the actions of a god—playing a large direct role in its outcomes. As noted above, we already know that there exist some supernatural events in direct human experience indicating the existence of some kind of a god. So there is nothing in principle that would exclude the possibility that such a god might also act directly in recorded human history to reveal further aspects of his thinking to the world.

A common response at this point will be to say that it is simply impossible that there could have been any such "miracles" in recorded human history. To assert absolutely that there are no such supernatural events, however, is simply another way of declaring that "I am a scientific materialist"—and therefore no such thing could even in concept be possible. But this is about like declaring in advance that I win the argument—further discussion is pointless—because I could not possibly be wrong.

Christianity makes a much different faith statement; a leading contemporary Protestant theologian at Duke University, Stanley Hauerwas, states that "Christ is written everywhere," not only in the Bible, "but also in the [full] pages of history."[1] How might one shed any rational light on the relative merits of the competing faith claims of scientific materialism and Christianity? If we are limited in addressing this question to the application of the scientific method alone, the answer is clearly no—nothing of rational interest can be said. If the scope of legitimate human inquiry is expanded to include other forms of historical analysis besides the scientific method, however, the answer is potentially yes. As has been discussed, the scientific method is in general of limited usefulness in studying matters of history; no great historian has ever relied on it as his or her central method of scholarship.

---

1. Hauerwas, "Go With God," 50.

The Problem of Identifying Miracles

The Oxford and then Cambridge University professor of medieval and renaissance literature, and also great Christian apologist, C. S. Lewis, explores
such questions in his book, *Miracles*. Lewis points to the problem for the
scientific materialist that if all of reality is grounded in the physical workings of the natural world, this excludes not only the possibility of supernatural miracles but of any fundamental historical explanatory power for
ideas (which have no physical reality). But if this is true, why do Dawkins,
Dennett, and other absolute naturalists make such heroic efforts to change
our minds? If they are hoping thereby to make a difference in the world,
this would seemingly be pointless; it would require a "miracle" within the
scientific materialist framework of their own thought. For a true-believing
naturalist, even the naturalist idea itself (as an idea, that is, which is something intrinsically non-measurable) must itself be irrelevant to anything real
and thus material that happens in the world.

As we have seen, the miracle of the mental altering the physical is a
daily occurrence in human affairs. Obviously, my thoughts can affect the
actions of my body. It is also a supernatural event when I can communicate
with other conscious minds—no plausible physical explanation exists for
the full process of something moving from my conscious existence, to my
physical brain, to another person's physical brain, and then to this person's
corresponding nonmaterial consciousness. How can it possibly happen?
What about this possibility: Does a god intervene to make it happen? We
might then also ask: Does a god intervene to alter the events of recorded human history by other "supernatural" means (by means other than through
the mysterious workings of mathematics and human consciousness discussed in previous chapters)?

One response is that if my mind can control my body, why should a
god—if he exists—be inferior in his capabilities with respect to the whole
wider world? Indeed, Lewis believes that such things can happen in human
history as well, including events in nature. Lewis suggests, however, that
"miraculous" (supernatural) events do not happen frequently; indeed, he
thinks they are exceedingly rare. After they do happen, moreover, there is
no continuing suspension of the physical laws of nature. Rather, it is a one-
time supernatural intervention that simply "resets" the starting point for the
course of natural history to follow; the normal workings of natural history
then continue according to the same familiar natural laws of physics (until
there is another reset).[2]

---

2. Lewis, *Miracles*, 100–107. See also Lennox, *Miracles*.

Thus, for Lewis "the divine art of miracle is not an art of suspending the [natural] pattern to which events conform but of feeding new events into that pattern. It does not violate the law's proviso, 'If A, then B': it says, 'But this time instead of A, A2,' and we will now evolve naturally from A2 instead of A."[3] Some scientific materialists might accept such an outside intervention of a god at least with respect to the case of the moment of the big bang. But they would argue, Lewis to the contrary, that the divine resetting of history has never happened again. Yet, that is a faith assumption on their part, not an empirically confirmed conclusion. Indeed, one well-respected contemporary physicist, Leo Smolin, has recently offered a scientific hypothesis that the laws of nature have varied routinely since the big bang, although he does not rely on the assumed existence of a god to make the changes in the workings of the natural order.[4] If the term *god* is interpreted broadly enough, however, we might say that Smolin is making the case for divine miracles.

What about miracles in human as opposed to natural history? For Lewis, the possible existence of miracles in human history is all about probabilities. Given a specific event in history, how difficult is it to explain that event in conventional historical terms—what is the probability that we can develop a persuasive historical account without invoking anything miraculous? Alternatively, what is the probability that God may have intervened—a very low likelihood for Lewis most of the time—to bring about the recorded historical result? For example, assuming the Red Sea actually parted to allow Moses and the Jews to escape the Egyptians, what is the probability that this was due to some extraordinary set of physical circumstances such as an immense earthquake or a hurricane, by chance occurring at just the right moment to allow the Jews to pass? Alternatively, what is the probability that the parting of the Red Sea instead must have been God's doing—assuming it happened?

A central possible miracle of human history is the resurrection of Christ, also from this perspective becoming a matter of probabilities. If the event occurred at all, it was clearly a miracle. So the probabilistic question here takes the following form: What is the probability that the biblical account of the resurrection is an exact historical account, versus the probability that it was later created by the followers of Jesus, and then incorporated into the canon of the Bible (which did not occur until a considerable number of years—there are scholarly debates about the exact number—after Jesus is said to have been resurrected)? In the past century, a large body of scholarly

3. Ibid., 60.
4. Smolin, *Time Reborn*.

analysis has in fact been devoted to this question, in effect developing competing estimates of resurrection probabilities (if not usually specified in such
numerically precise terms). The leading Oxford University scholar of early
Christianity, Geza Vermes, thus finds that "resurrection as a spiritual entity
is appropriately expressed by a vision. Anything more is suspect of hallucina-
tion," and thus it is appropriate to conclude that "the Resurrection becomes
a purely spiritual concept without requiring any accompanying physical
reality."[5] By contrast, the distinguished contemporary English theologian N.
T. Wright finds that, all things considered, "the best historical explanation . . .
is that Jesus was indeed bodily raised from the dead."[6]

Lewis recognizes full well the deep modern resistance to any idea even
in concept of a possible presence of divine miracles in recorded human history. This is because in the twentieth century "naturalistic assumptions . . .
will meet you on every side—even from the pens of clergymen." For those
living in the twentieth-century intellectual milieu, even including Lewis
himself, "we all have naturalism in our bones." Indeed, it requires a heroic
act of rational intellect and will—a willingness to defy a solidly entrenched
mainstream opinion in one's surrounding environment—"to work the infec-
tion [of naturalism] out of our system." If that can be done, however, Lewis
thinks that "the existing evidence will be sufficient to convince us that quite a
number of miracles have occurred" in the long record of human history. The
great majority of claims for miracles, however, are questionable. The matter, moreover, is not to be decided *a priori*. Indeed, Lewis thinks that "most
stories about miraculous events are probably false. . . . Lies, exaggerations,
misunderstandings and hearsay make up perhaps more than half of all that is
said and written in the world" about most subjects. The test of a true miracle,
Lewis argues, must therefore be decided by the "criterion of probability"—as
noted, following as rigorously rational an analysis as is possible.[7]

Three Candidate Miracles

Three things most fundamentally distinguish human beings from other
members of the plant and animal kingdoms, even those members such as
elephants and dolphins that, as we have been learning more and more in
recent decades, possess high levels of intelligence. These might have been
moments when a god chose to miraculously "reset" the circumstances of
human existence. The first such event was the human discovery of the ability

5. Vermes, *The Resurrection*, 148, 147.
6. Wright, *The Resurrection of the Son of God*, 8.
7. Lewis, *Miracles*, 164, 4, 100.

to make and use fire, likely within the past 500,000 years (although conceivably as long ago as 1,000,000 years)—the first practice of "chemistry," as one might say, by any creature of the earth (going well beyond the mere physical use of "tools," which long preceded the first direct human ancestors among, for example, chimpanzees). One might propose speech as another such unique feature of the human species but there is growing evidence that elephants, dolphins, whales, and some other species do have their own forms of communicating that might qualify as "speech." The more elaborate and complex human forms of speech, as we now know them, however, appear to have emerged around 100,000 years ago, a second transformative event in human history.

What is clearly unique to human beings is the capacity to translate speech, and related mental events in consciousness, into physical forms that can be preserved and exchanged among the members of the species—sometimes described as the development of "external memory." The earliest such developments were forms of artwork, much later followed by the capacity for writing, the latter emerging only about 5,000 years ago in the Middle East. If one considers the radical transformation of human existence since that time, writing has played a central role in much of it. The ability to control fire, the capacity for speech, and writing are all dependent on happenings originating in human consciousness. Other than brain size (presumably associated with intellectual capacity), changes in human physical anatomy alone do not seem to have been major evolutionary factors in the emergence of modern human forms of existence—although perhaps human thumbs and fingers reinforced significantly the evolutionary advantages of high intelligence.

Fire, speech, and writing all would thus seem to qualify as "candidate miracles," moments when a god might have reset the basic terms of human existence—for reasons known only to god, although one might simply speculate it was out of curiosity to see what would happen next. The information to make any kind of rational estimate of the probability that human control over fire emerged spontaneously, lacking any divine component, is simply not available in the historical record. The same can be said for human speech. The situation is somewhat more promising for writing, an event within recorded human history (not a coincidence obviously), but there is not enough information at present to make estimates of rational probabilities with any real level of confidence. Hence, in choosing between natural evolutionary processes and divine intervention in these three cases, archeological investigation and rational analysis are not much help. (Although we can know in general that the development

of human consciousness, as discussed previously, seems to defy material
evolutionary explanation.)

The Axial Age

A few animals do show evidence of self-consciousness, for example, the ability to recognize themselves in a mirror. So self-consciousness itself does not
appear to be limited to humans. What is clearly unique to human beings,
however, is the ability to engage in higher powers of abstract reasoning—
reaching remarkable levels in the workings of modern mathematics and
philosophy. Human beings are also probably unique in their self-conscious
desire to find an "explanation" for their own existence and to know its real
"meaning." These human features emerged gradually but there is a growing
scholarly agreement that a decisive "breakthrough" occurred in the "Axial
age," commonly dated from around 800 BCE to 200 BCE. As Harvard professor Benjamin Schwartz writes, during this period there were a series of "momentous developments" for the human condition on earth: "In the Middle
East we see the rise of classical Judaism through the prophets and the beginnings of rabbinical Judaism; in Persia the rise of Zoroastrianism; in India the
transition from the Vedas to the Upanishads, Buddhism, Jainism, and other
heterodox sects; in China Confucianism, Taoism, and the 'hundred schools';
and in Greece the evolution from Homer and Hesiod to pre-Socratic and
classical philosophy" including the writings of Plato and Aristotle.[8]

Even more remarkably, a large part of these momentous developments
for human history occurred in a narrow 300-year window from about 600
to 300 BCE. Confucius is said to have lived from 551 to 479 BCE, Plato
from 428 to 348 BCE, and Aristotle from 384 to 322 BCE. The exact dates
for the Buddha in India are not known but he is now generally thought to
have lived between about 600 and 400 BCE. In China, the years of the birth
and death of Lao-Tse (said to be the founder of Taoism) are also subject to
debate but he is generally thought to have lived somewhere between about
500 and 300 BCE. In other words, except for some of the Jewish prophets
who may have come in the preceding century, the pivotal events in three of
the four great Axial breakthroughs, despite being separated by great physical distances, and involving little cultural interchange, all occurred within
200 to 300 years of one another. Could this be due to a god?

Coming around 150,000 years after the emergence of modern man
in Africa, 10,000 years after the initial spread of agriculture, and 3,000
years after the beginnings of urban civilization, the compression of Axial

8. Schwartz, "The Age of Transcendence," 1.

developments into such a comparatively small time frame seemingly qualifies as a "candidate miracle." Indeed, while few professional historians believe
literally in any kind of "miracle" having occurred, they commonly employ
terms such as "remarkable," "astonishing," and "amazing" to describe this
strange confluence of Axial age events. As long ago as the mid-nineteenth
century, the German scholar Ernst von Lasaulx wrote that "it cannot possibly be an accident that, six hundred years before Christ, Zarathustra in
Persia, Gautama Buddha in Indian, Confucius in China, prophets in Israel
. . . all made their appearance pretty well simultaneously."[9]

Following after C. S. Lewis, a probability analysis in this case would
take the following form. What are the available historical explanations that
might explain this unprecedented set of near-simultaneous Axial events
and how plausible—how probable—do they seem without having to resort
to any supernatural explanation? Partly influenced by Max Weber and his
younger brother Alfred Weber (both of whom he had met), the German
philosopher Karl Jaspers in 1949 was the first to focus on developments
in the Axial age as such a critical moment in human history. It was a time,
Jaspers wrote, of "spiritual tension . . . questioning all human activity and
conferring upon it a new meaning," the precise moment when "man, as we
know him today, came into being."[10] Indeed, Jaspers himself was skeptical
that any adequate conventional historical account would ever be satisfactory. As Bjorn Thomassen in 2010 describes his thinking, "Jaspers saw
direct parallels between Buddhism, Confucianism, Hebrew prophecy and
Greek philosophy, but also claimed that their contemporaneity and their
commonalities remained a 'mystery' that could never be fully explained."[11]

Another interpreter finds that "by insisting that the world religions
arose simultaneously and independently from one another, he [Jaspers]
suggests an *immaterial* cause—that is, a movement of the human spirit that
is not accounted for by sociological factors such as social actors, organizations, or institutions."[12] Although Jaspers does not speak directly of a divine
intervention, his views might well be understood as an implicit suggestion
of a higher probability of a supernatural explanation, as compared with any
standard form of historical explanation. Later historians have stayed within
more conventional forms of analysis but few if any have seemed to have

9. Lasaulx, quoted in Stark, *Discovering God*, 384.

10. Jaspers, *The Origin and Goal of History*, 6, 1.

11. Thomassen, "Anthropology, Multiple Modernities, and the Axial Age Debate,"
327.

12. Boy and Torpey, "Inventing the Axial Age," 243–44.

much conviction that they had found a rational explanation for the extraordinary Axial developments.

Any form of economic determinism—a standard form of historical analysis throughout the twentieth century—fits the Axial circumstances poorly. The near-contemporaneous Axial developments all occurred in widely varying social and economic conditions. If social and economic events were the actual driving factors, one would have expected a much greater temporal distribution of the various Axial breakthroughs. Another possible explanation, that the Axial developments might have mutually influenced each other by a common exchange of ideas around the world at that time, also does not hold up. Given the great distances and the primitive state of travel and other communications around 500 BCE, some commercial trading of goods was occurring but there was little cultural interaction among China, India, ancient Greece, and the Jews. As far as a possible influence of China on Axial events elsewhere, for example, China expert Benjamin Schwartz finds that it was "probably non-existent."[13]

Rather than resulting from any economic advances (and geography faces similar problems as an explanation), another much different possible explanation sometimes given is that the Axial breakthroughs were instead the result of near-simultaneous, serious "breakdowns" in the various societies. It may be a severe crisis, not the successes of a society, that is required to explain such an astonishing departure as an Axial age. As Robert Bellah notes, however, breakdowns in history are very common, and Axial-type breakthroughs very rare. One might thus plausibly argue that "serious breakdowns may be the necessary predecessors of cultural breakthroughs" but at best this will be a "necessary" condition, certainly not a "sufficient" condition. Indeed, in his monumental 2011 book focusing on human religious history, Bellah raises the question with respect to the Axial age of "How did this happen?" In the end, however, like almost everyone else, Bellah seems essentially baffled by Axial events.

Events in even a single Axial civilization, ancient Greece, have seemed almost as inexplicable to many people. As Bellah comments, there was a time when some historians wrote in amazement of a "Greek miracle," although such language has increasingly been at odds with the professional self-image of historians. Bellah, however, cannot entirely contain his sense of amazement at the intellectual developments in Greece from about 500 to 300 BCE. Indeed, the very existence of Plato alone—for whom Bellah reserves his highest praise—is virtually a supernatural event in itself. As he writes, "Plato's work is a shoreless sea, touching on almost every subject

13. Schwartz, "The Age of Transcendence," 1.

(even on natural philosophy in the later dialogues), and the touchstone for Aristotle and all later ancient (and modern) philosophy." Indeed, it is virtually biblical in its scope and impact on human history, presenting a radical challenge to the existing order. Much of Christian theology—most prominently in the writings of Augustine—might well be described as a Christianized Platonism. In the end, as Bellah finally has to concede, perhaps it is unavoidable that we should simply concede that there was (in his words) a "Greek miracle."[14]

I would agree, both with respect to ancient Greece and the entire Axial age. No accepted form of historical analysis comes close to "explaining" the existence of Plato, Aristotle and other leading thinkers of ancient Greece in such a short time and in a geographic area containing such a tiny fraction of the total human population of the earth. The almost-simultaneous occurrence of three similarly remarkable events in other Axial civilizations in much different parts of the earth is even more difficult to "explain" rationally, compounding our amazement. So a supernatural "miracle" may simply be the best we can do; probabilistically, the best "explanation" might be a divine intervention in some form.

Of course, most of the educated elite today would find any such idea of a divine intervention and of actual miracles having occurred in recorded history to be impossible (if not absurd). Of my five rational ways of thinking about the question of a god explored in this book, this is the one that encounters the greatest resistance. The general elite assumption today is that, however mysterious some historical events appear to us at present, some rational explanation must exist (much as the philosopher Colin McGinn could only assume that, as discussed in Chapter 5, some "natural" explanation for human consciousness necessarily exists, however also unknown to us at present).

This assumption that a rational natural explanation must exist, even when none can be offered, is not, however, in itself a "rational" conclusion. It is instead yet another way of affirming a devout scientific materialist faith. Indeed, it would be more genuinely "agnostic"—and thus more "rational"— to simply accept that miracles in recorded human history might in fact occur and all the rational evidence must therefore be weighed in each case according to the specific candidate miracle under study. The great majority of such claims, as C. S. Lewis argued, will likely be false but this cannot be known *a priori* for all such claims, except as a statement of an individual religious faith of its own kind.

14. Bellah, *Religion in Human Evolution*, 387, 397.

A Mayan Axial Miracle?

Assuming at least for the purposes of discussion that the Axial age events were in fact a miracle, what would that tell us about the thinking of a god who might have produced this miracle? As stated above, this chapter is based on the assumption that god reveals himself through human history, as well as in the other ways discussed in earlier chapters. It would seem that a god who created the Axial age had decided to lay the foundations for a basic transformation of human consciousness to a higher order of self-awareness and of "transcendence"—that human beings might now be made in a more meaningful way "in the image of God." Whether god knew or controlled exactly how this would all play out, or simply wanted to "reset" the human condition in the Axial age, as Lewis's understanding of miracles would suggest, and then to leave it to normal social and natural events to determine the remaining details, there can be no doubt about the ultimate outcome. Human beings have begun to think and write widely and introspectively about human existence in the world and its meaning in a whole new way since Axial times.

This leaves, however, some difficult questions. The spread of the radically new powers of human thought largely occurred within the civilizations where the Axial developments occurred. These human capabilities in the past 200 years have now been spreading rapidly to the rest of the world but one might ask: Why did the Americas, Africa, and some other large parts of the world have to wait so long; why did they have such a small role over 2,500 years or so in the creation and then the working out of the Axial developments themselves? Also, why did women have such a small direct role in all this, leaving a true sexual revolution in human affairs again to occur only in the past 200 years? This is all the more surprising in light of the fact that the foundations for a changing status of women in the world were already being laid in the developments of the Axial age itself.

These are important questions for future theological examination, including the question of whether the ways of god ultimately will always be inscrutable—that may be why a god is a god. One potentially important addition to the discussion, however, is that a further possible Axial miracle may have occurred in the Americas, the development of Mayan civilization, mainly in the current Guatemala, Mexico, Honduras, and Belize. Knowledge of the Maya has greatly increased in the past thirty years, partly due to a new ability to decipher Mayan documents. Much of the literature of the Axial age since Karl Jaspers in 1949 thus was written with little awareness of the Mayan developments.

One reason the Mayan events are so remarkable is that they were occurring in complete geographic isolation and yet they closely coincide in historical time with pre-Axial and then Axial events elsewhere in the world. Mayan history is now divided into the Preclassic period from 1,500 BCE to 200 CE, and then the Classic period from 200 CE to 900 CE (after which Mayan society fell into what might be called a form of feudalism, a weakened condition of the Maya that still existed when the Spanish arrived in the early sixteenth century). The first Preclassic period is divided into three eras, the first known as the Early Preclassic from 1,500 to 900 BCE (similar in time to Bellah's "archaic" age that preceded the Axial age), the Middle Preclassic from 900 to 300 BCE (roughly corresponding to the Axial age), and then the Late Preclassic from 300 BCE to 100 CE.[15]

Unfortunately, we do not know as much about Mayan religious and philosophical thought as in the other Axial age cases. As the only pre-Columbian society in the Americas to have a full-fledged writing system (a writing system corresponding to the spoken language), the Maya produced thousands of "books" that were written on "beaten bark paper."[16] The Spanish, however, systematically burned all such books that they could find—why preserve communications inspired by the devil? Combined with natural deterioration, only four Mayan books are available to historians at present, and they have a limited scope. Most surviving Mayan documents thus had to have been written in stone or other materials more likely to survive.

Moreover, as compared with the other Axial developments, scholars have thus far devoted a much smaller amount of attention to Mayan developments. Many of the known Mayan ruins themselves are only partially excavated at present. Large numbers of other sites today sit below the forest canopy, altogether unexplored, and in some cases not even mapped for their precise locations. Who knows what might be found one day—conceivably a Plato or Aristotle of the Americas (although Mayan civilization, from what we know at present, is probably most directly comparable to the ancient Egyptian civilization that preceded the Axial age). It is seemingly possible to spend many hundreds of billions of dollars on space exploration to the moon, Mars, and elsewhere, seeking to learn more about the origins of life, while a few hundred million dollars spent on Mayan studies might teach us more of interest about the place of the human species in the universe.

Linda Schele and David Freidel are among the small group of 1970s and 1980s scholars who were engaged in studying Mayan life and history, and thus they might be excused for being enthusiasts for potentially important

15. Schele and Freidel, *A Forest of Kings*, 56–57.
16. Ibid., 50.

future revelations. In *A Forest of Kings: The Untold Story of the Ancient Maya*, they summarized the state of knowledge as of 1990. They write there that "with the [recent] decipherment of their writing system, the Maya joined the world's great pristine civilizations—Egypt, Mesopotamia, the Indus Valley, and China—on the stage of world history." As they explain further,

> [The Maya] developed a high religion and extraordinary state-craft that produced a stable society for over a thousand years. More than a collection of quaint mythology and exotic rituals, their religion was an effective definition of the nature of the world, answering questions about the origin of humanity, the purpose of human life on earth, and the relationship of the individual to his family, his society, and his gods. It is a religion which speaks to central and enduring problems of the civilized human condition: power, justice, equality, individual purpose, and social destiny.[17]

The low existing level of detailed knowledge of Mayan writing and thinking, however, may not be sufficient to conclude that, probabilistically, it qualifies as another likely "Axial miracle." It does seem, though, altogether remarkable that a sophisticated civilization, certainly comparable in many respects to that of ancient Egypt, and perhaps considerably more advanced in its thought, arose in the Americas. The fact that this occurred almost simultaneously with other pre-Axial and Axial age developments in ancient Greece, the Middle East, India, and China, and yet there was no contact at all with these developments, does seem in some way "miraculous." Perhaps further study will provide a stronger basis for judgment.

A Christian Miracle?

It was in the Middle East that a small Jewish group emerged 2,000 years ago made up of the followers of a local prophet, Jesus Christ. Beyond the fact of his existence, virtually nothing is known as a matter of recorded history. Christians rely on the New Testament for their knowledge of the life of Christ but, as Geza Vermes, the Oxford University historian of Judaism and early Christianity (considered by some to have been the leading such scholar of his generation) explains, "scholars all agree that the Gospels are not strictly speaking historical documents."[18] Their truthfulness may well be accepted as a matter of faith, as most Christians do. Since I have committed

---

17. Ibid., 19.
18. Vermes, *Christian Beginnings*, 32.

myself in this book to rationally developing arguments that do not depend mainly on faith, I do not propose to address here the question of whether the life of Christ was in fact a true "miracle," outside the workings of any natural processes.

That does not, however, preclude consideration of another candidate miracle, the rise and spread of the Christian church and religion itself. Unlike the life of Christ, there is in this case a vast amount of well-recorded history. A few moments of this recorded history, moreover, stand out as having special significance. As Rodney Stark reports, "by far the most important event in the entire rise of Christianity was the meeting around the year 50 [CE], when Paul was granted the authority to convert Gentiles without them also becoming observant Jews."[19] James, the brother of Jesus and the leader of the church, surprisingly supported Paul in this unusual (for a Jew) position.

Paul was closely involved in a second critical early development. As Vermes writes, "within decades from the crucifixion [the early Christian church] became very largely Greek in speech and thought."[20] Besides Paul, a second major Hellenizing influence was the Gospel of John, the last of the four Gospels to be written. Vermes explains that Judaism, and thus also the earliest Christianity, immediately after the death of Jesus, "was a religion of deeds." At the center of Jesus' preaching, moreover, was an eschatological expectation of the imminent coming to earth of the kingdom of God, and the need to prepare for this event. This of course failed to happen, requiring a rethinking of the Christian message. Even before that, as Vermes writes, Christianity was being reworked by Paul and then John "into a religion of believing." From the end of the first century of the common era the issues "dominating Christianity were belief concerning the nature of the Deity, the definition of Jesus Christ's person and his work of salvation, and the redemptive function of the one true church."[21]

A number of important early theologians such as Tertullian, Clement of Alexandria, and Origen emerged to explore the logic and full details of such beliefs. Vermes writes that as such questions were discussed and debated among the Christian faithful, "by the early fourth century the practical, charismatic Judaism preached by Jesus was transformed into an intellectual religion defined and regulated by [theological] dogma."[22] Two further developments within Christianity were then central. By the fourth century, Christianity had spread widely in the Roman Empire, including among its

---

19. Stark, *The Triumph of Christianity*, 413.

20. Vermes, *Christian Beginnings*, xiii.

21. Ibid., xvi.

22. Ibid., xvi.

adherents the mother of the future Emperor Constantine, who had a large religious influence on her son. In 312, having risen to high levels of power himself, Constantine appealed to the Christian God for help in a key battle for control over the western half of the Roman Empire. Constantine's triumph in this battle is sometimes said to be the moment of Constantine's conversion. (In fact, Constantine was not actually baptized as a Christian until much later, near his death.) In 313, Constantine issued the Edict of Milan, ending the persecution of Christians, and then also began to commit large resources to the widespread building of Christian churches and other structures. Contrary to a common impression, Constantine never required Romans to become Christians (the Emperor Theodosius made Christianity the official religion of the empire for the first time in 380).

After winning control of the empire in the East as well, Constantine took tight control of Christian affairs. Indeed, Constantine might be regarded in some sense as the first great "pope" (Sylvester, the bishop of Rome at the time, having little power). Unhappy with the theological feuding, Constantine in 325 convened the Council of Nicaea to address a longstanding fundamental question for Christian theology, the real nature of Jesus. Following the spreading Hellenization, Jesus had increasingly been transformed into a full-fledged divinity himself. As Vermes writes, however, Christians were then accused of abandoning monotheism and thus its theologians pressed to find an "escape route away from the trap of suspected formal polytheism." Indeed, partly reflecting such concerns, all the early church fathers had been "unwilling to place Father and Son on an equal footing in the divine hierarchy."[23] But any such concerns were swept away at Nicaea, establishing a Christian orthodoxy that has persisted to this day. As the Nicene Creed declared, Christians believe "in one Lord Jesus Christ the Son of God, . . . consubstantial with the Father."[24]

As Vermes comments, the meaning of "consubstantial" was to "underplay the image of Jesus of Nazareth, the itinerant preacher who in days long gone by was crisscrossing the rocky paths of Galilee, preaching the imminent arrival of the day of the Lord." Henceforth, Jesus would have a "new identity as the . . . co-eternal and co-equal only-begotten Son of God the Father"—a fully equal partner in heaven above (and there was also a third coequal partner, the Holy Ghost, thus forming the "Trinity").[25] In 325 years, the historical foundations of Christianity were established. As Paul Tillich writes, as a result of the events at Nicaea, "a new development in

23. Ibid., 226, 224.
24. Nicene Creed, quoted in ibid., 232.
25. Ibid., 234.

church history, indeed, of world history, had begun."[26] Christianity would subsequently spread across the earth to the extent that today it includes about one third of the total world population and has had immense impacts on the course of world history since Nicaea.

Would these first 325 years of establishing the Christian foundations qualify as a "miracle"? None of the usual modern explanatory variables— economics, geography, warfare, drive for power, and so on and so forth— would seem to have much traction. Modern historians look to such "real" events in the world in their search for explanations. The role of thoughts in human consciousness is always suspect, frequently seen as a by-product of other more fundamental developments. But what if the actual direction of causation normally runs the other way—that since the Axial age at least, it is the evolution of the workings of human consciousness, and above all the way of thinking about the world, that is the real driving force in history? Describing the rise of the "theoretic culture" that characterizes modernity, for example, the psychologist Merlin Donald explains that this "radical step in human cognitive evolution" that can be traced to Axial developments "emerged largely from a series of cumulative cultural innovations on the part of creative individuals. However, these innovations changed the nature of the cognitive games people played, and eventually altered how we perceive, think, remember, and conceive of reality; they even changed our sense of selfhood." This all happened without "any serious evolution of basic mental capacity, in the biological sense."[27] Christianity was the vehicle by which Axial developments reached the European world, as synthesized by Augustine in a Neoplatonic form that dominated Christian thought for 800 years until the writings of Aquinas in the thirteenth century brought together Christianity and Aristotle.

That is a large problem for modern historians. Among economic historians, for example, cultural explanations are always suspect, the last refuge of a failed economist. Max Weber played little role in twentieth-century economics, consigned to the field of "sociology" or "intellectual history." His sin was to explain the rise of capitalism in religious terms. The 325-year early rise of Christianity, eventually shaping the world as we know it today, appears, however, as a largely self-contained development within the ancient world of religion itself, driven by powerful individual religious concerns, theological controversies, and a variety of other religious factors. Even scholarly historians of religion typically focus on recording the events as opposed to explaining why religious developments took their actual direction.

26. Tillich, *A History of Christian Thought*, 73.

27. Donald, "An Evolutionary Approach to Culture," 48.

In other words, by modern historical standards, the origins of our own current world in the first 325 years of Christianity are difficult to explain.

Our actual choice, therefore, might be between "no good explanation" and a "supernatural explanation"—that a god, presumptively the Christian God in this case, reset history at that time through a few key events. Many people, as a matter of their modern scientific faith, will automatically rule out the possibility of a divine role. For other more "agnostic" people, however, some explanation may be better than no explanation. As discussed in Chapters 3 and 5, we can already be confident that some supernatural events do occur within the actual world as we experience it. Probabilistically, whatever the exact part Jesus may have played in this, it looks promising that the recorded history of the first 325 years of Christianity is best understood as a "miracle" reflecting some greater meaning and direction in world history. It would be difficult to deny that the consequences of it all have been altogether unexpected and astonishing in forming our world today.

The First Reformation

This raises an interesting theological question: can there be "negative" miracles? Indeed, Rodney Stark sees the final outcome of this 325 years, including especially the impact of Constantine, in such negative terms—negative within the framework of the development of the Christian religion itself. As he writes, "Constantine's involvement in Christian doctrinal disputes established the basis for an intolerant monopoly church responsible for centuries of negligence, followed by centuries of brutal heresy hunting and conflict." Constantine's efforts had the unfortunate consequence of setting "a precedent for future emperors who did invest the church with official status, as well as for popes who freely called upon the state to defend their monopoly against all significant dissenters." It would have been much better for the history of Christianity and of Western Europe, Stark suggests, to have maintained "effective and sincere religious competition," rather than the monopoly of the Roman Catholic Church.[28] This is a difficult case to make, however, given the immense success of Christianity as a religion of the world. History does not necessarily proceed in a straight line; perhaps the Roman Catholic monopoly—eventually abolished by the Protestant Reformation—was one phase of some larger grand design.

There was also more competition than Stark suggests. The long history of conflict between Christians and Muslims has obscure the fact that Islam at its beginnings was an effort to reform Christianity (and Judaism),

28. Stark, *The Triumph of Christianity*, 414–15.

reversing the Hellenizing consequences of the early centuries of Christianity, including the Council of Nicaea and its official establishment of a doctrinal Christian polytheism (as Muslims saw the matter). As Reza Aslan explains, Muhammad identified "himself repeatedly with the Jewish and Christian prophets and messengers who had come before him, particularly with Abraham." Indeed, in his own eyes Islam was "the religion of Abraham, [and] Muhammad was the *new* Abraham." As Aslan elaborates, Muhammad believed that "the Jews, Christians, and Muslims [not only] shared a single divine scripture [of the Bible] but also that they constituted a single divine Ummah [religious community]." From the "beginning of his ministry Muhammad revered Jesus as the greatest of God's messengers. Much of the Gospel narrative is recounted in the Quran, though in a somewhat abridged version, including Jesus' virgin birth, his miracles, his identity as the Messiah, and the expectation of his judgment over humanity at the end of time." Indeed, the same angel Gabriel explains Daniel's visions to him in the Old Testament, announces to Mary the forthcoming birth of Jesus in the New Testament, and accompanies Muhammad as he ascends briefly to heaven from the site of the Temple Mount in Jerusalem in order to receive instructions from God. All in all, for Muhammad, if they could be reformed, Judaism and Christianity were "nearly identical to Islam."[29]

Owing to "ignorance and error," however, Muhammed believed that Christianity had lost its way in the centuries immediately after Christ. Indeed, among the distortions introduced, the "chief among these was the concept of the Trinity." Jesus himself had never said that he "was himself God." As the Quran states, "it is the unbeliever who says 'God is the third of three"; rather, the biblical truth is that "there is only God the One." As Aslan writes, "it was Muhammad's belief that Orthodox Christians had corrupted the original message of Jesus, who the Quran contends never claimed divinity and never asked to be worshipped, but rather commanded his disciples to 'worship God, who is my Lord and your Lord,'"[30] culminating in the falsehoods of Nicaea. Spreading his message of Christian reformation in the early seventh century, Muhammad hoped to restore the true monotheistic faith in a one God of the universe.

Just as Christianity after Christ departed from its founding religious principles under Greek influence, Islam after Muhammad suffered a similar fate. As Aslan writes, "the Muslim scriptural and legal scholars of the following centuries rejected the notion that Jews and Christians were part of the Ummah, and instead designated both groups as unbelievers." As later

29. Aslan, *No god but God,* 44, 101, 103.

30. Ibid., 102, 103.

Muslims were taught, the "Quran had superseded, rather than supplemented the Torah and the Gospels." This partly reflected the desire of these Muslims that Islam should "establish its own religious independence," motivated perhaps by theological arguments but also no doubt by more earthly considerations.[31] Indeed, in contrast to other Axial age impacts, the spread of Islam would occur to a much greater degree by the exercise of military power.

During the early Middle Ages, Islamic civilization eclipsed Christian civilization in many respects, making important contributions to mathematics and philosophy (including the study of Aristotle whose writings did not reach the Christian world of Western Europe until the twelfth and thirteenth centuries). On the whole, however, Islam played a much smaller role in the full set of events that created the modern world. Muslims nevertheless represent today almost 25 percent of the population of the world. Combined with Christians, around 60 percent of the world's population are followers in one of the three religions of Abraham. Such numbers, moreover, do not take account of the fact that modern secular religions such as Marxism typically derived much of their message from Judaism and Christianity. The distinguished American Protestant theologian Max Stackhouse, professor emeritus at Princeton Theological Seminary, writes in *Globalization and Grace* that "certain influences from the classic Christian traditions of theology and ethics are at least partly responsible for the patterns and deeper dynamics that are driving globalization [today]."[32]

If modern secular religions are regarded as implicit forms of "Abrahamic religion" (see Chapter 7 below for further analysis of this question), one might say that most of the world today—leaving aside some isolated tribes—subscribes to beliefs shaped in significant part by the followers of Abraham, Jesus, and Mohammed. This radical transformation of world religion—the globalization of a single religious tradition—has occurred in only 3,000 years, a minute amount of time compared with the biological history of the earth, and even a tiny part of the two million years of the presence of human beings and their direct ancestors on earth. It does seem miraculous.

Does the rise of Islam itself qualify as a miracle? Given the large role of conquest in spreading Islam, the closest Christian equivalent might be the Spanish imposition of Christianity on its new possessions in the Americas. This probably does not count as a miracle. Perhaps the question of a possible Islamic miracle should be considered in the wider question of whether the rise of the modern world—potentially a new Axial moment—should be

---

31. Ibid., 104.
32. Stackhouse, *God and Globalization*, 35.

considered a miracle. If so, then a good case might be made for including Islam in that category as well.

The Second Reformation

Rodney Stark writes that after Paul and the redirection of Christianity in the first century to become a religion of Gentiles, and after Constantine in the fourth century, "the third great shift in the trajectory of Christian history was in response to the Reformations of the sixteenth century"—a second period of reformation (after Muhammad and Islam), now led almost a thousand years later by Martin Luther and John Calvin. Of particular importance, according to Stark, was the role of "dissenting Protestants, whether as unpopular minorities," or in some countries as a Protestant "monopoly state church," thus serving to encourage "other dissenters" and, all in all, creating a new diversity of religious belief—eventually extending to secular religion—within Europe. The large gains, according to Stark, extended to the Catholic Church that was itself renewed in response to Protestant competition (in this respect, Stark probably minimizes the downside that much of this new Catholic energy also went into strengthening the church monopoly in those many areas where the Catholic Church still retained its exclusive authority). As Stark concludes, "the end result of the Reformations was to reenergize Christianity," paving the way for its subsequent worldwide spread.[33]

It is often said that Max Weber was mistaken in arguing that the Reformation laid the basis for capitalism. It is more accurate, however, to say that Weber may have given too much emphasis to Calvinist theology even as the Protestant Reformation did in fact prove to be the opening wedge to the modern world, including capitalism. The Protestant encouragement of literacy in order for everyone, men and women alike, to be able to read the Bible, for example, was likely a key development in and of itself. It is thus necessary to speak of the influence the whole Protestant Reformation, including changes in church practices and many other features of institutional religion, not only the role of Calvinist theological precepts relating to predestination.

Moreover, the very term *capitalism* is a throwback to Karl Marx and the debates of the late nineteenth and early twentieth century; it is more appropriate instead now to speak of the "modern world," which necessarily includes a large economic dimension (which in the cases of some economic systems can be described—if rather crudely—as "capitalism"). Most importantly, Protestantism introduced a radical new individualism. The

33. Stark, *The Triumph of Christianity*, 416.

Protestant faithful were to study together with other faithful, and reach their own individual conclusions in matters of religious truth. There should be no hierarchy of authoritative church "experts" in matters of religious truth. If necessary, a person could leave one church for another, or even join a whole new religious community, as an exercise of free religious choice. In dissenting Protestant churches, the minister of the church was in essence an administrator of church affairs and a discussion leader—a radical change from the "top-down" structure of the Roman Catholic Church. Freedom in religious affairs then gradually extended into other parts of life, most importantly the political and the economic domains. As the distinguished German Protestant theologian Ernst Troeltsch once explained:

> The great ideas of the separation of Church and State, toleration of different Church societies alongside one another, the principle of Voluntaryism in the formation of these Church bodies, the (at first no doubt, only relative) liberty of conviction and opinion in all matters of world-view and religion. Here are the roots of the old liberal theory of the inviolability of the inner personal life by the State, which was subsequently extended to more outward things; here is brought about the end of the medieval idea of civilization, and coercive Church-and-State civilization gives place to individual civilization free from Church direction. The idea is at first religious. Later, it becomes secularized. . . . But its real foundations were laid in the English Puritan Revolution. The momentum of its religious impulse opened the way for modern freedom.[34]

The Protestant Reformation also paved the way for modern science. Nancy Frankenberry writes that "the historical titans of the scientific revolution—Galileo, Kepler, Bacon, Pascal, and Newton, all devout believers to a man—could interrelate their Christian faith and their scientific discoveries." The Lutheran Kepler "found religious ecstasy in the act of scientific discovery itself, seeing the Trinity revealed in the very structure of the heavens"—not so different from the ecstasies of scientific discovery of the American physicist Richard Feynman described above in Chapter 3.[35] Of the three greatest physicists of history, two were from Protestant England (Newton and Maxwell) and one from Protestant Germany (although Einstein was of course Jewish). In terms of providing a scientific base of knowledge for achieving a human mastery over nature for human practical benefit, Maxwell easily ranks first as the discoverer of the workings of electromagnetism, while

---

34. Troeltsch, *Protestantism and Progress*, 125–26.

35. Frankenberry, "Introduction" to *The Faith of Scientists in their Own Words*, ix.

Newton's and Einstein's greatest impacts actually lay in the revolutionary significance of their discoveries for the understanding of the true workings of the universe (neither gravity nor relativity was remotely comparable to electricity in changing the material circumstances of human existence).

In *The Great Transformation: The Beginning of Our Religious Traditions*, Karen Armstrong explores in depth the events of the Axial age, finding that they were carried forward by the great religions of the world. As she writes, "all the traditions that were developed during the Axial age pushed forward the frontiers of human consciousness and discovered a transcendent dimension in the core of their being." They did not "necessarily regard this as supernatural" but they also did not rule out the possibility. Armstrong considers that nothing comparable happened within human history until the past 500 years when a second Axial moment, "the Great Western Transformation, . . . created our own scientific and technological modernity."[36] Where it will eventually lead can only be conjectured, but we can be sure that it will be a radically different world from that of 500 years ago, based on Axial-like events since then. University of Notre Dame historian Brad Gregory in his 2012 book, *The Unintended Reformation: How a Religious Revolution Secularized Society,* explores with a great depth of scholarship how the modern world—and the modern mind that made this world—came into being as a result significantly of developments internal to religion. Such an unconventional analysis is possible for Gregory because he explicitly disavows the scientistic assumptions that continue to underlie not only the social sciences but so much else in modern scholarship. As he writes, for example, "science neither observes any *persons* nor discovers any *rights*—for the simple reason that there are none to be found given the metaphysical postulates and empiricist assumptions of science."[37] Gregory writes that,

> [My] principal argument is that the Western world today is an extraordinarily complex, tangled product of rejections, retentions, and transformations of medieval Western Christianity, in which the Reformation era constitutes the critical watershed. . . . On the eve of the Reformation, Latin Christianity comprised for good or ill the far from homogeneous yet institutionalized worldview within which the overwhelming majority of Europeans made sense of their lives. . . . Early twenty-first century Westerners live in and think with and even feel through the historical results of its variegated rejections and appropriations.

36. Armstrong, *The Great Transformation*, xvii, xviii, xvi.
37. Gregory, *The Unintended Reformation*, 19.

... In getting from the early sixteenth to the early twenty-first century, this study develops the claim ... that "incompatible, deeply held, concretely expressed, religious convictions paved a path to a secular society." ... The Reformation's influence on the eventual secularization of society was complex, largely indirect, far from immediate, and profoundly unintended.[38]

Was the Reformation a second Axial miracle? Some would argue that it simply reflected the growing power of northern German princes and their increasing demands for independence from the Holy Roman Empire and the Roman church. Calvinism, similarly, might be seen as the result of new demands among the spreading commercial classes of Europe to escape the restrictions of Catholic economic ethics. But Gregory concludes otherwise; such explanations, for one thing, do not explain the actual contents of Luther's and Calvin's theology, and it was these contents in particular that played a large role in creating the modern world—which is not to say that either Luther or Calvin would have approved of modern developments.

Gregory does argue that the Protestant Reformation can be explained in terms of developments internal to Christian theology and religion itself, some of them commencing well before the Reformation. If such explanations hold up to the scrutiny of future scholars, then perhaps the Reformation did not require a miracle to have occurred. It might be explained in human—essentially human religious—terms alone. But then again, God may have been acting through the key religious figures and events. Following after C. S. Lewis, the probabilities here are difficult to estimate.

The Industrial Revolution

In her 2010 book *Bourgeois Dignity: Why Economics Can't Explain the Modern World*, Deirdre McCloskey estimates that income per capita in England increased by at least a factor of sixteen in the past 200 years, perhaps by as much as thirty times or even more if the arrival of brand-new superior forms of goods and services is taken into account.[39] In terms of health, transportation, communications, food variety, and many other physical items of consumption, ordinary people in the developed world today live much better than royalty 200 years ago. Even to have conceived of such a possibility in 1800, it would have seemed to most people to require a miracle. Indeed, McCloskey concludes that existing attempts by economists and others to explain "the Great Fact" of the recent human mastery over nature and the

38. Ibid., 2.
39. McCloskey, *Bourgeois Dignity*, 48.

resulting transformation of the material conditions of human existence of the past 200 years have all failed.

McCloskey thus writes that economics "can't explain the onset or the continuation, in the magnitude as against the details of the pattern, of the uniquely modern—the widespread coming of automobiles, elections, computers, tolerance, antibiotics, frozen pizza, central heating, and higher education for the masses." This reflects the fact that "material, economic forces . . . were not the original and sustaining causes of the modern rise, 1800 to the present." Indeed, using the resources available to economists to study such matters, one can only conclude that the outcome was "inexplicable." Other historians outside economics have done little better because they focus on what they believe to be the "real" explanatory factors in history, things like class struggle, colonialism, great power international politics, warfare, and so forth. The real cause of the modern economic transformation, however, as McCloskey argues, lay in the domain of "ideas."[40] Indeed, it was a fundamental change that began in the seventeenth century in Holland and England, accelerating in the eighteenth century, in the ways of thinking about the morality of markets that allowed for an unprecedented expansion of private freedom of entrepreneurial innovation, the one most important factor in the later extraordinary modern developments. It remains to be more fully understood, however, how this change in the ethics of the market—along with similar freedoms extending to other areas of society such as politics and the pursuit of science—came about (McCloskey assigns less weight to the Protestant Reformation than I do). Adam Smith was not as much originally responsible for this ethical revolution as he was an observer of such developments in his own time whose efforts then served powerfully to further encourage them.

In 1981, the economic historian Eric Jones published the first edition of *The European Miracle*, reflecting his lifelong commitment to studying the revolutionary economic events that occurred in Europe in just two or three centuries. Jones does not literally believe that these events were a "miracle" but then again he acknowledges—showing unusual honesty—that he does not really have a good explanation. Indeed, when it comes to grand theories of modern economic history, he is more effective in showing the failings of other efforts than in supplying his own theory. Instead of a grand theory, his writings trace in great detail the historical record of the most important specific economic—and, equally important, political—events that we now can say with factual certainty did indeed lead to a brand-new modern economic world.

40. Ibid., 6.

If modern economic history is seen as the cumulative consequence of many such individual events—none decisive in themselves—there would be only a remote probability of realizing the actual economic path that is now a matter of record. One is then led to ask, if this actual path had not been followed (a high probability, although events did happen to turn out otherwise in this case), would a similar extraordinary modern level of economic development nevertheless have been achieved along a different path? Jones, like most economists and historians, offers no confident answer to this question. To develop an answer would require a fuller understanding of the true origins of modern economic growth and development than anyone has yet succeeded in providing.

Recognizing that this is not an altogether satisfactory outcome for a lifetime of work as an economic historian, Jones in the very last paragraph of the third edition in 2003 playfully suggests that some larger forces less subject to rational explanation might conceivably have been at work. As he writes, perhaps only half in jest, "perhaps there was something supernatural about Europe's rise after all." One key factor, for example, might have been "the miraculous preservation of the balance of power" in Europe, thus avoiding the concentration of central authority that occurred elsewhere in the world and which might have killed off the prospects for the political and economic freedoms so critical to modern developments. Jones does of course in the end affirm that the goal should be to provide "social science arguments [that] remain helpful in dealing with complex matters like development and the rise of one [Europe] among a handful of major civilizations." But "the task is a large one" that still remains for others in the future to accomplish—if it is to be accomplished at all.[41]

In *The Riddle of the Modern World: Of Liberty, Wealth and Equality*, Cambridge University anthropologist Alan Macfarlane also explores such questions from yet another disciplinary perspective. Macfarlane candidly acknowledges early on that "the emergence of our modern world and its very nature is a mystery. We are very confused as to how it came about." Macfarlane sees a key feature of modernity, similar to arguments made by Max Weber, as "the growth of rationality or the disenchantment of the world. There is a 'radical discontinuity' which exists between primitive and modern mentality." Macfarlane is an admirer of the work of philosopher and fellow anthropologist Ernest Gellner, who (in Macfarlane's words) argued that "the most fundamental aspect of the great [modern] transformation . . . is the effort to separate and balance the deepest forces in human life—the pursuit of power (politics), wealth (economics), social warmth

---

41. Jones, *The European Miracle*, 257.

(kinship) and meaning (religion)."[42] This new separation was central to the rise of modern freedoms.

These events, as Macfarlane thinks, actually do amount to a "miracle" and great "puzzle" in their "extraordinary" and "astonishing" features.[43] As Gellner himself writes, the central concern of a sociologist (and anthropologist) should be to "explain the circuitous and near-miraculous routes by which agrarian mankind has, *only once*, hit on this path; the way in which a vision [of freedom] not normally favored, but on the contrary impeded by the prevailing ethos and organization of most human societies, has prevailed. . . . It is most untypical. It goes against the social grain."[44] In seeking to solve this "riddle," Macfarlane expresses his dislike for the reductionist approaches characteristic of the social sciences, so often infected by the way of thinking of "the vulgar Marxist trap of seeing everything determined in the last instance by the relations of production, by the economic 'infrastructure.'" Instead, it is necessary to see the problem in terms of exploring the full interrelated workings of a "balanced set of cultural, legal, social and political conditions," recognizing that both "law and religion shaped the world through time, as much as they were shaped" themselves by external events.[45]

In addition to his contemporary Gellner, Macfarlane devotes much of his book to studying the explanations offered by Baron de Montesquieu, Adam Smith, and Alexis de Tocqueville, all of whom had lived recently enough to see the modern age taking shape, and sought to make sense of what they were observing (and were writing at a time when the current tight constraints of disciplinary boundaries of scholarship did not exist). Drawing on these four writers, Macfarlane in the concluding chapter attempts to provide his own answer to the modern miracle. It turns out, according to his interpretation, that it was really a miracle mainly of two countries, Holland and England, and in the end England was the most important. It was in England that the decisive rise of modern freedom occurred—of thought, of economic enterprise, of religion, of political expression, and in other areas of life. In explaining this, according to Macfarlane, one key factor was religion, dating from Henry VIII's separation from Rome, combined later with the fierce assertion of their own religious freedoms by the Puritans. The second key factor was geography, namely the island status of England, close enough to be part of the economic system of Europe, but far enough away and with enough ocean in between to be well insulated from military

42. Macfarlane, *The Riddle of the Modern World*, 2, 253.

43. Ibid., 256, 257.

44. Gellner, quoted in ibid., 257.

45. Ibid., 288.

invasion, thus limiting the need for large military expenditures (with related taxes) and a powerful state apparatus that other nations in Europe saw as necessary for their security. The English model was copied earliest and most successfully in the United States, another Protestant nation separated by an ocean from large military challenges. Once the economic miracle had been demonstrated in England and the United States, it no longer required a miracle to spread it to the rest of Europe and then to the rest of the world.

In the end, however, Macfarlane, like Jones, does not think that he has really succeeded in explaining the modern material transformation of the world. As he writes, despite his best efforts, "there is still a large gap in the explanation of how the transition to the modern world has occurred." It is possible to see that modern developments required a significant "overcoming [of the] political, religious and social predation" that has generally characterized the human condition (at least over the past 8,000 years). But how did this critical overcoming itself occur? While some plausible contributing factors can be identified, Macfarlane concludes that we still lack a persuasive full explanation of why "technological and scientific growth [did] occur so spectacularly and rapidly in western Europe . . . and why did it slow down, cease and even partially regress in other civilizations which had previously been far more 'advanced' than Europe."[46]

Given the lack of a better explanation, a preliminary verdict (at least until some better explanation comes along), is that, yes, the modern age may well be a miracle, inexplicable in conventional social and natural terms. To deny this possibility, even in concept, is not a scientific position but a statement of another form of religious faith, in this case a modern faith simply asserting that miracles are in principle impossible. But we already know that scientific materialism does not encompass the entire human condition, that the supernatural plays a role too.

Conclusion

The analysis of this chapter suggests that, since the Axial age, there have been a few critical events that are difficult to explain in conventional historical terms. When that is the case, one can then ask, is the existence of a miracle a higher probability, comparatively speaking? If these individual potentially miraculous events are cumulated as the recorded history of human beings of the past 3,000 or 4,000 years, the random probability of them all occurring becomes even lower, making the argument for a miracle in order to produce our current world yet stronger. Of course, some other and

46. Ibid., 293, 294.

much different world might have arisen that, considered as a single out-come, would itself be equally miraculous. But do we really believe that our lives and our world today are the product of such mere random chance? Many people say so but few actually follow through in their actions. Rich-ard Dawkins, for example, is obviously driven by a powerful proselytizing impulse that reveals his real hope to influence history—working with oth-ers of a similar cast of mind—in a certain religious direction that would fulfill its destiny.

Thus, while most people today doubt the existence of miracles in hu-man history, somewhat inconsistently, at the same time they often think that there is a purpose to their own lives and to the course of history (and history is of course the accumulation of the lives of all people on earth). If there is genuine purpose in human history—if the attainment of our current modern existence is not merely a random accident realizing an event of extremely low initial probability—it raises the question of what that pur-pose to history might be and how it is asserted. Christianity once supplied that purpose but in the modern age many people looked instead to secular "progress" as the path to a new heaven on earth. For them, it was not just an accident, moreover, but there were forces at work in history that were inevitably bringing such progress about—these forces now amounting to a secularization of the past role of "God" in history. To the extent that there was an inevitability to progress, one might say that there was in fact a belief in the existence of miracles (the required nonrandom supernatural events to bring about the progressive advance of history that would culminate in earthly perfection in the future), even as the particular term of *miracle*—owing to its strong biblical associations—would normally not be used. Human progress was instead said to be guaranteed by "science," exercising the miraculous powers of this new (and at the same time old) God of the modern age.

7

Secular Religion, Christianity, and Modernity

IN THE EIGHTEENTH CENTURY many of the leading thinkers of the Enlightenment saw it as a decisive turning point in all of human history—in the same way the incarnation of Jesus had long been regarded in the Christian world.[1] As many of them saw matters, since at least the collapse of ancient Greece and Rome, human beings had lived in ignorance, deceived among many others by the falsehoods of the Christian religion— above all by the Roman Catholic Church. But the development of the scientific method in the seventeenth century, and its ever-widening application in the eighteenth and further centuries to come, was changing all this. Newton and other physical scientists who followed after him had already made astonishing discoveries with respect to the true workings of the natural world. The eighteenth century was confident that there would be future similarly remarkable successes in all areas of human understanding, including the workings of human societies. It was as though in their own time the light had finally shone in Plato's cave (the En"light"enment), revealing a previously unknown world of scientific truth. If God had long been regarded as the ultimate authoritative source of knowledge for Christianity, Science would now assume that role in the world to come.

The nineteenth century, however, had to confront the disturbing events of the French Revolution at the end of the eighteenth century and other real-world disappointments. Pure reason was apparently not as powerful a force in human affairs as Enlightenment thinkers had assumed; the

---

1. This chapter draws on my writings about economic, environmental, and other secular religion over the past twenty years. The most important of these are the three books *Reaching for Heaven on Earth*, *Economics as Religion*, *The New Holy Wars*. See also my "Economics as Religion," "Economics as Religion: A Reply to the Commenters," and "Environmental Religion."

perfection of the world based on the rational applications of the scientific method apparently might be longer in coming than had been expected. Indeed, the nineteenth century returned to a more traditional way of understanding human existence, the biblical way of the study of the record of history. From Hegel to Marx, the most important intellectual developments of the nineteenth century were new understandings of history—mostly at odds, however, with the biblical account. The most influential of all, covering the entire biological history of life on earth, was that of Charles Darwin, as discussed in Chapter 4.

The twentieth century was then yet another period of basic reappraisal. It was forced to reexamine the fundamental assumptions of the nineteenth century—in physics and almost everywhere else. It was apparent in retrospect that leading nineteenth century histories such as Marxism and social Darwinism were less statements of scientific truth than new forms of religious dogma. The Russian revolution and its aftermath proved greatly disillusioning for progressive faith in the looming perfection of the human condition, the rise of Hitler and a new form of social Darwinism in Nazi Germany even more so. In retrospect, although Marxism and National Socialism seemingly rejected God, they had actually installed new "scientific gods" of history, no less all controlling than the biblical version, and also promising a future human heaven on earth as the culmination of history.[2] But of course, as the twentieth century advanced, this was all turning out to be yet another predictive folly, a newly secularized version of the many failed Christian predictions of the imminent arrival of the final days, an expectation which Jesus was originally convinced of himself.

In the last few decades of the twentieth century, reflecting such developments, a new type of secular religion, environmentalism, arose, the first widely influential secular gospel in at least 200 years (perhaps since Jean Jacques Rousseau) to challenge explicitly the basic idea of human "progress." Many others who turned away from the worship of progress, however, and contrary to the long-standing general expectation among secular thinkers, turned back to traditional religions such as fundamentalist Christianity—as illustrated by the recent "comeback" of religion noted in the Introduction. In one sense it was in fact a comeback but in another sense it was not. Religion had never actually gone away; it had merely changed its leading forms. The secular belief systems of the modern age, as was increasingly being recognized over the course of twentieth century scholarship, were genuine forms of religion themselves whose faithful showed no less

2. Nelson, "All in the Name of Progress"; Nelson, "The Theological Meaning of Economics."

devotional zeal—while saying little or nothing explicitly about a god—than the Christian true believers of old.

William Grassie is the founder of the Metanexus Institute on Religion and Science. As Grassie noted in 2008, appropriately understood, the term *religion* encompasses not only the familiar Christian kind but also any "bounded belief system and set of practices, as in the religions of the Greeks, Romans, Jews, Muslims, Hindus, Chinese and others." Recognizing the fact that some actual religions go so far as to deny their religious character—this may in fact be an important part of their modern appeal—Grassie describes the common worship in modern times of a "God-by-whatever-name." Ironically, it is even possible to have a "religion of no religion." There is, nevertheless, one common element: "every religion is . . . making universal truth claims . . . about the fundamental character of the universe as a whole."[3] Paul Tillich famously defined religion in a similar way, as addressing matters of "ultimate concern."[4]

Partly reflecting their frequently dismissive past attitudes with respect to (traditional) religion, our leading public intellectuals today typically have not committed much time and effort to theological reflection. This is partly because they have believed, in some cases perhaps unconsciously reflecting their own original Protestant roots, that religion is a matter of "faith alone," and thus that rational argument does not have much if any role to play in the whole matter of religion. Another important factor, however, as Grassie comments, is that "the social sciences—psychology, sociology, economics, and anthropology—were largely founded by thinkers who took for granted that there was no truth content or value to religions, that religions were irrational, superstitious, regressive, and dysfunctional." Indeed, "the social sciences were founded with a lot of *anima* toward religion, so it is little wonder that the faith factor is the forgotten variable in the social sciences in the decades that followed."[5] In retrospect, it now appears that the neglect of religion in the social sciences was actually the distain of one faith as expressed towards a religious competitor.[6]

As this book has emphasized, however, much is changing today. In 2007, Walter Russell Mead, formerly a Senior Fellow at the Council on Foreign Relations in New York, described a new version of modern religious history. He characterized "secular modernism" as constituting in reality a new "fourth faith" within the West. The first faith was Judaism, which 2,000

---

3. Grassie, "The New Sciences of Religion," 128, 130, 132, 130.

4. Brown, *Ultimate Concern.*

5. Grassie, "The New Sciences of Religion," 134.

6. Nelson, "Economic Religion versus Christian Values."

years ago gave rise to the second faith, Christianity, which was followed 650 years later by the third faith, Islam, all three tracing their origins to the biblical Abraham. In the modern age, as Mead argues, yet another Abrahamic faith emerged as a fundamental new religious movement, even as no one has yet given it a suitable name ("secular religion"—or perhaps "implicit religion"—seems to be about the best we have at present). Mead acknowledges that "believers in the fourth faith don't always like to be called believers" in any form of religion (they are often more comfortable with being described as "spiritual"). Indeed, many followers in the new secular religions "argue that unlike the superstitious and emotionally driven convictions of religious believers, the fourth faith is based in the clear light of science and reason."[7]

This sense of secular uniqueness has been largely an act of self-deception, however. As Mead comments, "the fourth faith, like the first three, fits the definition of faith given in the Epistle to the Hebrews in the New Testament." All four faiths are part of an "ongoing Abrahamic revolution in human affairs" that continues to shape the world; all "provide explanations of things that are seen and known, as well as predictions concerning things that are not yet seen."[8] Like Christianity, there are many "denominations" of the fourth faith—many different forms of secular religion.[9] The believers in fourth-faith forms of religion are often as righteously convinced of their own special access to the fundamental truths of the world as other religious believers of the past. Mead thus observes that "most devotees of the new [fourth faith] believe that their own particular version of it is the one sure way, and that history will culminate in the triumph of the true faith" across the whole earth.[10] While Marxism, social Darwinism, Freudianism, and many other twentieth-century "denominations" of the "fourth faith" have been fading into history, a more generic "scientific materialism," however, still retains much of its historic influence, often still dominating the intellectual life of the leading American universities as well as the thinking of the national media. As this book has suggested, however, the trends seem today to be going the other way.

My purpose in this book, as previously stated, is not here to "prove" the existence of a god—any such effort would already put the question of god's existence in the wrong category of human understanding, as something requiring scientific proof. God, if he exists, can never be known in the manner of a physical law of nature. While some people claim to be in direct

7. Mead, *God and Gold*, 283.

8. Ibid., 283, 282, 283.

9. Nelson, "Scholasticism versus Pietism."

10. Mead, *God and Gold*, 283.

communication with a god, this means of knowing about a god is not available to the majority. True believing Christians believe that God has directly communicated with the world through Jesus and the Bible, but this is an account that is impossible to verify in a manner that will convince those who begin with basic skepticism—and who demand actual recorded historical evidence of biblical events (in some other form than the Bible itself). The discoveries of physical science about the workings of the natural world do provide (almost) sure knowledge of the mind of god as mirrored in the workings of the natural world. However large and important it is, however, the natural world is still much less than the totality of human existence.

So thinking about a god today must necessarily be piecemeal and cumulative—as John Henry Newman had already emphasized in the nineteenth century must be the case. In pursuing this objective, the full history of religion in the modern age offers some additional valuable rational evidence. In particular, it is striking how Jewish, Christian, and Islamic understandings of the world have persisted with so little fundamental alteration, despite the radically different "secular" forms they have taken. The emergence of a "fourth faith," as Mead calls it, thus seems to me a remarkable, if perhaps not a fully miraculous, fact of modern religious history. Like the enduring power of the idea of natural law, now including many secular forms of its expression, the surprising modern persistence of the three Abrahamic faiths suggests that there may be habits of thought somehow embedded in the human mind and character that are unaltered even by large changes in external circumstances and the manner of their expression, yet cannot in any way be attributed to the material workings of Darwinist evolutionary forces. This is a fifth rational argument that illuminates the question of a god.

Christianity in Disguise

Although the religious character of secular religions such as Marxism and National Socialism is now in the twenty-first century widely accepted, the original source of these two religions is still surprising for many people. Indeed, such secular religions drew heavily on the Christian tradition; it might even be appropriate to describe them as secularizations of the Christian message, or as some others might prefer the label, as "Christian heresies."[11] The British political philosopher John Gray thus wrote in 2004 that the many modern political and economic "projects of universal emancipation are earthly renditions of the Christian promise of salvation." Indeed, "the

---

11. Nelson, "Ecological Science as a Creation Story"; Nelson, "The Secularization Myth Revisited."

idea of progress," central to so much of secular religion, "is a secular version of Christian eschatology. In Christianity, history cannot be senseless: it is a moral drama, beginning with a rebellion against God and ending with the Last Judgment. Christians therefore think of salvation as a historical event." This is in contrast, for example, to "Hindus and Buddhists, [for whom] it [history] means liberation from time."[12]

Igal Halfin is a contemporary Israeli historian who concluded in 2000, based on extensive archival research, that the "eschatological" elements of early Russian communism, borrowed from Christianity, were decisive influences in determining the very categories of thought that shaped the former Soviet Union's politics and economics in its first decades. It was not economics that determined religion, as so many committed Marxists and other economic determinists have firmly believed, but actually more the opposite. During the 1920s and 1930s, Halfin writes, Soviet universities functioned as "a grand laboratory, designing techniques for the perfection of humanity." Life in revolutionary Russia was everywhere a reflection of "messianic aspirations," as the teachings of Marxist religion "shaped the identity of the Soviet citizen; it did not just coerce pre-existing, fully formed citizens to adjust to a Soviet reality that was somehow external to them."[13] Rather, for the communist faithful Marxism formed the basis for their very way of comprehending their own existence in the world.

It was, moreover, the presentation of a Christian message in a disguised "scientific" form that was the key to the enormous impact historically of Marxism and communism—the Bolshevik Revolution, like the French Revolution, was yet another of the religious revolutions of history. As Halfin reports, "Marxists would doubtless have renounced notions such as good, evil, messiah, and salvation as baseless religious superstitions that had nothing to do with the revolutionary experience. Yet, these concepts, translated into a secular key, continued to animate Communist discourse" in Russia for many years. Most Russian communists were nevertheless altogether blind to the reality of the close "affinity" of Russian communism "with Christian messianism."[14] As described by Halfin, however, the parallels are obvious to us today:

> The Marxist concept of universal History was essentially inspired by the Judeo-Christian bracketing of historical time between the Fall of Adam and the Apocalypse. The Original Expropriation, at the beginning of time, represented a rupture in

12. Gray, "An Illusion with a Future," 12, 11. See also Gray, *Heresies*.
13. Halfin, *From Darkness to Light*, 2, 28, 37.
14. Ibid., 39.

the timeless primitive Communism, which inaugurated History and set humanity on a course of self-alienation. The universal Revolution, an abrupt and absolute event, was to return humanity to itself in a fiery cataclysm. . . . Imbuing time with a historical teleology that gave meaning to events, Marxist eschatology described [human] history as moral progression from the darkness of class society to the light of Communism.[15]

Also in 2000, another contemporary historian reached similar conclusions with respect to the messages on which the Nazi regime rode to power in Germany. As Michael Burleigh comments, "interest in political religions is currently undergoing a renaissance," partly reflecting the waning faith in standard economic and other materialist understandings of history and a new recognition of the power of religion in its various forms in shaping society. The conflicts between the Soviet Union and Germany were a revival of religious warfare in Europe—part of another Thirty Years' War centered again on Germany—now inspired by secular gospels. The leaders of both Nazi Germany and the Soviet Union "utilised sacred language and rites, even when they aggressively rejected religion" in any traditional form. As Burleigh finds, similar to writers already mentioned in Chapter 4, the popularity of Nazism partly reflected its wide use of "pseudo-liturgical rites and deliberate evocations of the Bible," all part of a wider European pattern in which "totalitarian ideologies themselves shadowed the belief patterns of conventional religion," promising in new secular credos that "salvation would not be long in coming."[16]

Amidst the social and economic chaos of Germany in the 1920s and 1930s, the "Nazi ideology offered redemption from a national ontological crisis." For German followers, "Nazism was not simply applied biology, but the expression of eternal scientific laws, revealed by God and in turn invested with sacred properties."[17] The swastika was the Nazi cross (also used historically as a religious symbol in Hinduism and Buddhism), the 1,000-year Reich the Nazi millennium. Burleigh explains that "Nazism was neither science run riot, . . . nor bastardized Christianity. . . . It was a creative synthesis of both. Armed with his religious science, Hitler was . . . God's partner in ordering and perfecting that part of mankind which concerned him."[18] Amazingly enough, a large part of the German population believed

15. Ibid., 40.

16. Burleigh, The Third Reich, 11, 12. See also Burleigh, Earthly Powers, and Burleigh, Sacred Causes.

17. Burleigh, The Third Reich, 12, 13.

18. Ibid., 14.

him; indeed, his mass popularity did not really fade until the early 1940s when World War II turned sharply against Germany and the population no longer believed the words of its latest messiah.

The Church of the American Nation-State

America has also been a fertile ground for secular religion, although fortunately much more lasting, putting a much greater emphasis on human freedom, and with long-lasting beneficial results sufficient to attract tens of millions of immigrants. A leading historian of the American Revolution, Gordon Wood, thus observes that "although some of the Founders . . . were fairly devout Christians, most leading Founders were not deeply religious men and few of them had much of a spiritual life." Indeed, "many of them shared the [common eighteenth-century] views of an enlightened speaker before the American Philosophical Society in 1793 who abhorred 'that gloomy superstition disseminated by ignorant [Calvinist] illiberal preachers.'"[19]

As long ago as 1932, however, the American intellectual historian Carl Becker was pointing out that the Founders may have rejected old-fashioned Calvinism but not Christianity altogether. Indeed, leading American and other thinkers of the second half of the eighteenth century took a vision of "life eternal in the Heavenly City of God," which they then "projected into the life of man on earth and identified with the desired and hoped-for regeneration of society." It was "to the future [that Enlightenment] Philosophers therefore look, as to a promised land, a new millennium." If faith in traditional Christianity was fading, they somehow understood that "the best hope . . . lay in recasting it, and in bringing it up to date" to fit the scientific expectations of the eighteenth century. In short, as Becker declared, "the task of the Philosophers was to present another interpretation of the past, the present, and the future state of mankind"—a seemingly new "religion of humanity" that in reality borrowed heavily from much older religious sources.[20]

One hears frequently of "anti-Americanism" in the world but seldom of "anti-Englishism," "anti-Germanism," or "anti-Chineseism." Harvard political scientist Samuel Huntington wrote in 2004 that "becoming an American" is a process "comparable to conversion to a new religion and with similar consequences."[21] Because America is the product of waves

19. Wood, "Praying with the Founders."

20. Becker, *The Heavenly City of the Eighteenth-Century Philosophers*, 139, 118, 123, 122.

21. Huntington, *Who Are We?*, 191, 127, 106.

of immigration over several centuries, the national bonding agent of the United States had to be a unifying secular faith. No one Jewish, Christian, or any other older faith could hold Americans of so many races, ethnicities, and other backgrounds together. This integrating force, Huntington explains, was thus "a nondenominational, national religion and, in its articulated form, not expressly a Christian religion." Its civil religion "converts Americans from religious people of many denominations into a [single] nation with the soul of a church."[22]

The unifying faith of America, however, is secular only in outward appearance. The reality, Huntington writes, is that the American nation-state in essence is "a church that is profoundly Christian in its origins, symbolism, spirit, accoutrements, and, most importantly, its basic assumptions about the nature of man, history, right and wrong. The Christian Bible, Christian references, biblical allusions and metaphors, permeate expressions of the [American] civil religion." The American religion is not, to be sure, identical to Christianity. As Huntington notes, America's civil religion allows for the frequent use of the word *God*, as on the nation's coins. However, "two words . . . do not appear in civil religion statements and ceremonies. They are 'Jesus Christ.'" This omission is of course of great religious significance. Many religions believe in a god, but only Christianity believes in the divinity of Christ. Again, though, the reality can be deceptive; as Huntington finds, even with little explicit mention "the American civil religion is Christianity without Christ."[23] Admittedly, this may raise basic theological questions for those who think of themselves as being both great American patriots and devout Christian believers as well. It may be a bit like declaring "I am a Catholic" and "I am a Protestant" in the same breath.[24] But it seems to work well for many millions of American faithful.

The American sociologist of religion Robert Bellah earlier developed similar themes in his much-discussed 1967 essay, "Civil Religion in America," one of the most influential articles of American social science of the past fifty years.[25] Bellah wrote there of a "civil religion" that for the United States had provided its "national religious self-understanding" and in this capacity had played a central role in shaping American history. The national religion was "a collection of beliefs, symbols, and rituals with respect to sacred things and institutionalized in a collectivity"—the American nation.

---

22. Ibid., 106.

23. Ibid.

24. Nelson, "Rethinking Church and State"; Nelson, "Wilderness, Church and State."

25 Bellah, "Civil Religion in America," 1.

For Bellah all this represented a "religion—there seems no other word for it" in a literal, not merely a metaphorical, sense.[26]

As with most secular religions, there were significant borrowings from Christianity, even though the American civil religion, in Bellah's view, "is clearly not itself Christianity." In terms of its content, as Bellah wrote, the "God of the American civil religion is not only rather 'unitarian,' he is also on the austere side, much more related to order, law and right than to salvation and love"—perhaps somewhat of a Calvinist God to reflect the American Puritan origins. But the deity of American civil religion was "actively interested and involved in history, with a special concern for America." In such respects, the American civil religion had more of an Old Testament than a New Testament character. Indeed, in the American civil religion, "Europe is Egypt; America, the promised land," as the Atlantic Ocean would be seen as the Red Sea across which a perilous journey had been undertaken to build a model kingdom of God in the Massachusetts wilderness.[27]

Bellah's article was important because, while he was far from the first to make the argument, it introduced more widely the idea of secular religion as having a literally religious character. It also showed clearly how the boundaries between secular religion and traditional religion were more blurred than many Americans realized. Bellah explained that "behind the civil religion at every point lie Biblical archetypes; Exodus, Chosen People, Promised Land, New Jerusalem, and Sacrificial Death and Rebirth. But it is also genuinely American and genuinely new. It has its own prophets and its own martyrs, its own sacred events and sacred places, its own solemn rituals and symbols. It is concerned that America be as perfectly in accord with the will of God as men can make it, and a light to all nations"—carrying on the old Puritan idea of a "city upon a hill," now translated to secular terms. George Washington was the Moses and Abraham Lincoln (he gave his life to save the Union) the Christ figure. Bellah also considered that it was not a fixed religion, that "it is not evident that it is incapable of growth and new insight."[28]

In 1988 Sanford Levinson published *Constitutional Faith*, a product, as he described it, of his own efforts to be a "legal theologian," supplementing his daily job as a law professor at the University of Texas.[29] Levinson explained that for most Americans the US Constitution is seen as in effect an American successor to the Christian Bible. The Constitution is America's "sacred text" that represents the foundational document for the American "civil religion."

26. Ibid., 8.

27. Ibid, 7, 8.

28. Ibid., 18, 19.

29. Levinson, *Constitutional Faith*, 27.

Quoting approvingly from a *Stanford Law Review* article on "The Constitution as Scripture," Levinson agrees that "America would have no national church . . . yet the worship of the Constitution would serve the unifying function of a national civil religion" for the people of the United States.[30]

As the ultimate adjudicators, the members of the Supreme Court not only dress and act like priests, but the American nation has in fact substituted a "priesthood of lawyers for a pontifical Court" in Rome. For Levinson, the contemporary legal debates about constitutional original intent versus a "living constitution" reenact much older theological disagreements between Roman Catholicism and Protestantism. The Catholic Church historically saw Christianity as refined through the prism of centuries of church interpretation, papal encyclicals, the writings of Catholic scholars, church councils, and other historic events. For Protestants, such Catholic thinking was heresy, effectively substituting the efforts of fallen human beings in place of God's directly revealed truths in the Bible. The real meaning of Christianity must be found by study of the Bible—in combination with study of the Book of Nature, the only other form of direct communication from God. Today, in the American legal system, according to Levinson, there is a similar clash among "protestant" and "catholic" legal experts in constitutional interpretation; the new "protestant position is that it is the [US] constitutional text alone [that is relevant], while the [new] catholic position is that the source of doctrine is the text of the Constitution plus unwritten tradition."[31]

Reenacting Christian Divisions

Levinson provides a specific American example of a much wider trend within modern religion, the reenactment of traditional divisions within Christian religion in newly secular—and thus partially disguised —forms. Despite its frequent outward antagonism to the Roman Catholic Church, the Enlightenment ironically owed a large debt to the Catholic tradition within Christianity. Instead of a Catholic priesthood of religious experts, a new modern priesthood of scientific experts would take its place. Science did not work in the Protestant manner of "faith alone"—from the bottom up—but instead sought with the use of the scientific method to establish authoritative expert truths by rigorously rational methods—a historically more Catholic approach. Few people, for example, could ever hope to repeat by their own personal efforts the technical thought processes of scientific discovery and no one would suggest that each individual person—in the

30. Ibid., 121, 55.
31. Ibid., 47, 29.

Protestant manner of individually discovering and verifying religious truth through biblical study and other means—should bear responsibility for making their own individual determinations of actual scientific knowledge. In Catholicism, the path to a final heaven on earth was a gradual "progressive" one in which the authoritative pronouncements of a church priesthood of religious experts would play a key guiding role. The Enlightenment faith in the continuing redeeming benefits of human "progress" now saw scientific experts playing a newly secularized version of such an originally Catholic priestly role.[32]

There was, however, one great challenger to the Enlightenment faith in the progress of the world, Jean Jacques Rousseau. Rousseau's perspective, however, was less novel than many people believed at the time. In opposition to the main directions of the Enlightenment, it was a reassertion of a Calvinist understanding, a biblical story of a terrible fall, of human beings now living in a fundamentally—and even increasingly—corrupted condition, all this now reworked to a secular vocabulary. Not coincidentally, Rousseau was born in Geneva, where John Calvin had ministered to the faithful for many years, and Rousseau's family had been followers in the Calvinist faith. As a leading biographer Jean Starobinski comments, Rousseau sees historical "change as corruption. As time goes by, man becomes disfigured and unrecognizable. This drastic (and, if you will, Calvinist) version of the myth of origin" shaped the very essence of his thought.[33]

The fall from the garden of Eden thus reappears in Rousseau's rendition as a terrible decline from a much happier "natural state" that once existed in the world. A first sign of this fall, many thousands of years ago, was the rise of organized agriculture, which was then followed by the spread of ancient cities and the rise of urban civilization. For Rousseau, the presence of sin in the world had now recently reached its most advanced stage with the scientific and material "progress" of the eighteenth century. For Rousseau, as Starobinski explains, "the cost of intellectual and technical progress has been moral degradation." The era of Enlightenment "progress" is for Rousseau a time in which "the human mind triumphs but man has lost his way"—humanity has succumbed to a new form of excess of pride and ambition. As Starobinski puts it, Rousseau "takes the religious myth and sets it in historical time." In order "to explain the fall of man [there is] no demon tempter or tempted Eve—no supernatural intervention is required; human causes [alone] will suffice." For Rousseau, "appearance and reality [once]

---

32. Nelson, *Reaching for Heaven on Earth*, 85–122; Nelson, "What is 'Economic Theology'?"

33. Starobinski, *Jean-Jacques Rousseau*, 16.

were in perfect [natural] equilibrium. Men [then] showed themselves and were seen by others as they really were. External appearances were not obstacles but faithful mirrors, wherein mind met mind in perfect harmony," but all this had been lost owing to the headlong human pursuit of scientific and economic "progress."[34] As Rousseau so well illustrated, and as Starobinski comments, the intellectual historians of the twentieth century increasingly recognized that in the Enlightenment the leading ideas were typically secular restatements of much older Christian messages.

Environmental Calvinism

For the next 200 years after Rousseau, as noted above, there would be many competing secular explanations of the correct route of human progress—social democracy, the American progressive "gospel of efficiency," European socialism, capitalism, social Darwinism, Marxism, the "market mechanism" of the welfare state, globalism, etc., etc. Owing to intellectual misunderstandings and confusions and other limitations among their proponents, some of these supposed paths of scientific and economic progress turned out to have consequences much different than expected by their proponents—in some cases actually impeding economic advance. No major secular religion over that 200-year period, however, followed Rousseau closely in rejecting the very goal of scientific and economic progress itself, and the expectation that its successful pursuit would radically change the human condition for the better. With the rise of environmentalism in the last few decades of the twentieth century, however, this could no longer be said.[35]

Perhaps the most influential book in spreading the new environmental gospel was Rachel Carson's *Silent Spring*, appearing in 1962.[36] Carson wrote that human beings had lived for many thousands of years in an Eden-like "natural environment" that, given the very limited tools available at the time, could not be altered in any essential way by human actions. Although there were cancer-causing elements in this environment such as the radiation of the sun, "over the eons of unhurried time that is nature's, life reached an adjustment with destructive forces" through the workings of biological evolution. Cancer-causing agents were thus few in number and they belong

---

34. Ibid., 29, 3, 12.

35. Nelson, *The New Holy Wars*. See also Nelson, "Unoriginal Sin"; Nelson, "Sustainability, Efficiency and God"; Nelson, "Does 'Existence Value' Exist?"; Nelson, "The Gospel According to Conservation Biology"; Nelson, "Economic and Environmental Religion."

36. Nelson, "*Silent Spring* as Secular Religion."

to that ancient array of forces to which life has been accustomed from the beginning." In almost an echo of Rousseau, however, there had been a recent moment of the fall: the modern spread of scientific and economic progress over the world. As Carson explains, "with the dawn of the industrial era the world became a place of continuous, ever-accelerating change. Instead of the natural environment there was rapidly substituted an artificial one composed of new chemical and physical agents, many of them possessing powerful capacities for inducing biologic change." Having turned away from the possibility of living in a natural and thus ecologically balanced world, modern human beings now experienced large exposures to "carcinogens which his own activities had created" and against which "man had no protection." The very gene structure of human beings, for example, had been "shaped through long eons of evolution." Our natural "genetic heritage" is for the human species "infinitely more valuable than individual life."[37] Here again, however, owing to their own misplaced human pride and greed, ending up in the pervasive human assaults on nature of the modern industrial system, human beings now faced a future of alienation and despair.

The terrible impacts of modern scientific capabilities had been seen in the nuclear radiation falling on human beings at Hiroshima and Nagasaki— the creation of nuclear weapons perhaps the ultimate danger resulting from a misplaced worship of science. Moreover, in their capacity to produce genetic damage, Carson wrote, "the parallel between chemicals and radiation is exact and inescapable." Indeed, *Silent Spring* warns that "genetic deterioration through manmade [chemical] agents is the menace of our time, 'the last and greatest danger to our civilization.'"[38] For environmentalists such as Carson, the modern age had made scientific and economic progress its god, only now to realize the disastrous consequences of the worship once again of a false idol.

A remarkable number of American environmental leaders, including not only Carson herself but also John Muir, David Brower, Edward Abbey, Dave Foreman, and still others were brought up in the Presbyterian church (the Scottish branch of Calvinism), or one or another of its American offshoots. Environmental historian Mark Stoll thus comments that today's "environmentalists rally in defense of virtuous nature against the amoral forces who let themselves be overcome by greed." This reflects the "Calvinistic moral and activist roots" of the contemporary environmental movement. Indeed, recasting in new language "the doctrines laid down by John Calvin," one finds today in the environmental movement a "moral outrage, activism,

37 Carson, *Silent Spring*, 219, 219–20, 220, 208.
38. Ibid., 208.

and appeal to government intervention [that] draw on the same account. [In this vision] the world has been transformed with new answers that are often only old ones rephrased" from past American religious history.[39]

In Europe, environmentalism has exerted a particularly large influence in northern nations with a Protestant heritage. Finding that all these Protestant connections are more than a mere coincidence, the distinguished environmental historian Donald Worster notes that the intense desire to purge the world of its spreading evils was combined in early Protestantism with a strong sense of "ascetic discipline." There was, as Worster explains, "a deep suspicion in the Protestant mind of unrestrained play, extravagant consumption, and self-indulgence, a suspicion that tended to be very skeptical of human nature, to fear that humans were born depraved and were in need of strict management." Worster now finds that the very echoes of this more pessimistic way of thinking are often prominently featured among current environmentalists for whom "too often for the public they sound like gloomy echoes of Gilbert Burnet's ringing jeremiad of 1679: 'The whole Nation is corrupted . . . and we may justly look for unheard of Calamities.'" Worster suggests that in our own time of wide devotion to personal pleasures and consumption "the Protestant ascetic tradition may someday survive only among the nation's environmentalists, who . . . compulsively turn off the lights."[40]

Worster's observation was amusingly illustrated by a Washington, DC, resident who recently wrote a book (endorsed by Bill McKibben and other leading environmentalists) about her heroic pursuit of environmental purity. As reported in the environmental news service Greenwire,

> A bitter billing dispute with her electric company changed environmentalist Keya Chatterjee's life.
>
> Battling Pepco over charges for electricity at her Washington, D.C., row house in the dead of winter six years ago, Chatterjee eventually just ordered the utility to shut off the power. She and her husband lived in the dark and cold for a few months, an experience that convinced them that even when they turned the lights back on, they could use less power.
>
> They went on a strict energy diet, one that has only increased since having a baby two-and-a-half years ago.
>
> "Getting mad at Pepco was like a gateway drug to sustainability," Chatterjee said. "Then we started getting rid of everything."[41]

39. Stoll, *Protestantism, Capitalism, and Nature in America*, 52.

40. Worster, *The Wealth of Nature*, 196, 197, 198, 197–98.

41. Winter, "How This Environmental Activist Learned to 'Walk the Walk.'"

Why, then, have we seen this revival of Calvinism, if in a disguised secular form? I would suggest that the required rethinking process, looking back on the disturbing history of the twentieth century, was particularly difficult for persons of a committed secular, Darwinist, and scientific materialist cast of mind. There was no possibility for them of finding adequate answers in an old-fashioned Calvinism—a belief system that in its essential pessimism about the human condition was actually consistent with the many terrible events of twentieth-century history. So a suitable secular disguise would have to be found—in other words, environmentalism.[42] It offered a Calvinist world view without all the old historical Calvinist baggage. As a secular belief system, environmentalism nevertheless proclaimed that the products of modern science were a large new threat to human (and plant and animal) existence. The rate of economic progress had been altogether unprecedented in Europe since the beginning of the nineteenth century, resulting in an astonishing material increase in living standards throughout the developed part of the world. Yet, other than in specifically material terms, it was not obvious that the full history of the twentieth century was a large improvement on the history of the nineteenth century—indeed, a good case perhaps could be made for the opposite, as environmentalism now raised the question.[43]

Conclusion

As I have explored in other writings, many more examples could be given of secular belief systems that are forms of religion, typically borrowing heavily in Western civilization from Jewish and Christian sources. Indeed, there may in fact be no such thing as an entirely secular belief system—at least having any significant following—that lacks an underlying traditional religious message. The most widely influential forms of scientific materialism of the modern era, Marxism and Freudianism, rather obviously had an essentially religious character, as is today widely accepted. It seems that human beings require meaning in their lives. If their self-professed beliefs do not explicitly provide that religious meaning, they will somehow still introduce it in some other surreptitious way. It is not surprising that, when they do so, they (often unconsciously) look back to the Jewish and Christian heritage of the West that shaped their civilization and its core beliefs and values. All the many "revolutions" in thought of the modern age were

---

42. Nelson, "Environmental Calvinism"; Nelson, "Calvinism Minus God"; Nelson, "Calvinism Without God."

43. Nelson, "Is 'Libertarian Environmentalist' an Oxymoron?"

thus radical changes in outward appearance to a much greater degree than in their inward content. It is yet another example of the frailties of human reason that so many people were so absolutely convinced of the contrary, that they were so certain that the Enlightenment meant a brand-new beginning for the human condition on earth. The remarkable persistence of old-fashioned Western religion in new post-Enlightenment forms must be regarded as one form of strong testimony to the enduring truthfulness of the old-fashioned beliefs—another rational argument to increase the probabilities that there is a god.

"Science" cannot provide the required meaning. Science has had extraordinary success in discovering the workings of the natural order and in giving human beings vastly greater abilities to put nature to use for human benefit. But there is nothing in the workings of the laws of physics—or of biological evolution—that gives meaning and purpose to human existence. Many people admittedly assert the contrary, that they experience awe and beauty and a strong sense of a shared community of all human beings in scientifically contemplating the physical universe. This is mainly an indication, however, of their lack of introspective awareness of the original religious sources of such thoughts and feelings, which have not been radically altered in their modern conversion to "secular" forms of expression. They are once again learning about a god from The Book of Nature, as it was long called in Christian theology. As Richard Feynman was honest enough to say, the laws of physics, the greatest success of modern science, say nothing at all about good and evil, the ultimate destination of history, or other core matters of human concern. Darwinism is barely a science, if at all, but in any case the actual morality of Darwinism consists of a belief in natural selection by means of the survival of the fittest. It is admittedly possible to interpret Darwinism in a manner that the selection of the fittest occurs among groups— and thus the evolutionary successful will have strong feelings of communal identity and a genetic willingness to sacrifice for the collective benefit. But in the end this does not bring human beings much above the moral status in the world of the members of an ant colony. These communal commitments will be justified, not in terms of their intrinsic merits, but in terms of their Darwinist survival advantages.

Whatever they say publicly, few people actually believe that—they are not indifferent to the fate of human beings in the world, to say nothing of their own and their children's fate. The real test is not survival but whether the destinations reached are worthy ones. Thus, when Darwinism is blended into a secular religion, the religion will in fact cease to be literally Darwinist. It will instead look outside natural evolution (and outside physics) to find some deeper sense of meaning and purpose that is then must be surreptitiously introduced because a contrary belief in Darwinism is part of their religion. In other words, the Darwinism is for outward show, intended to provide scientific legitimacy, and thus to give the actual secular religion that is implicitly present—and its normative beliefs and values—a greater legitimacy and authority in society. As the world learned in the first half of the twentieth century, however, this can be very dangerous—blending elements of Darwinism with elements of Christianity can create an extraordinarily toxic stew.

8

Conclusion

THE WORLD AS WE think we know it personally as a matter of our own common sense is an illusion, as least as the leading physicists, philosophers, and other authoritative experts of the twentieth century, and now the early twenty-first century, have been telling us. The existence of a physical world of matter, for example, is an illusion. Indeed, philosophers had long explained to us that we have access only to sense perceptions in our mind of an exterior reality. As the British theologian Keith Ward points out, "We see sights, hear sounds, feel touches and out of them construct a picture of a world of solid enduring objects. But the only world we immediately know is the world of our perceptions." Although we think we interact with and can understand a real world of our commonsense experiences, the deeper reality is that "what lies beneath our perceptions is unseen and unsensed, except in the intimations of transcendence that come to us in music and art, or in the demands of morality, in speculations about the new and strange reality of the quantum world, and in feelings that in our commerce with other persons [where] we occasionally reach out into depths beyond appearance and social conventions." The contrast with commonsense perceptions is clearest when it comes to the truths of the physical sciences, where "the world you experience looks very different from world physics tells you about."[1]

Twentieth-century physicists thus tell us that the seeming external reality of our routine existence actually consists of "wave functions" and other mathematical and statistical constructs that have been empirically verified to correspond to our internal perceptions of that external reality. Remarkably, in quantum mechanics the actual perceptions of external reality can depend on the observer and the manner of observation. The world of mathematics that is central to such scientific investigations has no "physical" existence itself but exists as an independent realm of mathematical truths

1. Ward, *The Evidence for God*, 59, 59–60, 35.

that seemingly has existed for eternity. By a process that is altogether mysterious, a key set of these mathematical truths (so far as we know not all of them) correlate exactly with our perceived workings of the external natural reality, thus establishing what we know as the "laws of physics." Our familiar mechanical world of physical cause and effect, the way you and I normally perceive the world, is seemingly a convenient figment of our imaginations, however much it may be practically useful for daily living.

Indeed, scientifically, it is not at all clear even who "I" am. For one thing, it seems that "I" am actually an ecological system that I share with a vast number of other living microorganisms in mutual symbiosis. Scientifically, perhaps it would be more accurate if I considered that the microorganisms actually use "me" as a convenient host. According to the evolutionary biological findings of the last few decades, microorganisms routinely exhibit purposeful behavior—the behavior of a simple cell might even be characterized as demonstrating a kind of "sentience." Again, it is far removed from the Darwinist stories of random mutations and natural selection taught to me in school. Indeed, leading philosophers and evolutionary biologists now explain that much of Darwinism, and its successor neo-Darwinism, is in its detailed explanations little more than a series of evolutionary tales—the new biblical parables of our times, as they might be described.

The introduction of the phenomenon of human consciousness is another element adding additional mystery to the question of who "I" am. I have the very strong sensation that I have a physical body that includes a brain. Is that the "real me"? But I also have an equally strong sensation that I have an immaterial consciousness that is filled with my own thoughts and emotions, that I am capable of making up my own mind outside the workings of my brain and other bodily chemistry. Is this immaterial reality the "real me"? Perhaps there are two separate forms of "real me"—as a photon can be either a particle or a wave. Yet, of course, they interact, as when my body creates a feeling of pleasure in my consciousness, or when my consciousness sends an instruction to my body to take some action. The manner of this interaction, however, is altogether mysterious, outside the explanation of the physical sciences—even in concept—which can deal only with relationships among objects and events both occurring in observable and measurable time and space. It is again far from the simple mechanistic world of a single scientific material reality of my childhood school lessons that were then so reassuring to me.

Since the Enlightenment, science has been the source of the scientific stories that have informed our understanding of a predictable and understandable world that corresponded to our commonsense perceptions. Indeed, it would be difficult not to have a deep faith in science when the knowledge it produces has so radically increased the human ability to transform the natural world to great human material benefit over the past 200 years, achieving levels of material abundance far beyond anything that might have been imagined a mere few hundred years ago. Yet, science is apparently a more mysterious god; physicists have now undermined—along with their philosophical and other expert compatriots today—the simple material stories of our childhood. The contemplation of such mysteries of human existence is admittedly not altogether new, having occupied the attention of many earlier philosophers and theologians over the centuries. But in its hubris the modern age dismissed most such past efforts, partly because most people were lacking—except for some specialists—in any detailed knowledge of the thinking (or even existence) of these earlier philosophers and theologians.

It may be time to go back to traditional philosophy and theology because we now have no better alternative, other than to stick to our current pleasant illusions. Do we want truth or pleasant illusion? It might stretch the traditional meaning of "a god," but perhaps we might begin now begin to say that the world as it actually exists in all its great mystery is the playground of a god with whom we are perhaps partial playmates. This is not a "god of the gaps" of the past that science often then rapidly succeeded in closing. This is a god of the mysteries of mathematics and of our human conscious existence that will not so easily yield to the scientific method—indeed, it seems that they lie in principle outside the scope of the scientific method altogether. At present, no one has any idea in concept how it might be possible that the immaterial world of mathematics came into existence. The only remotely plausible hypothesis would seem to be "a god" who favors mathematical truths in controlling the workings of the natural world. One might hope that, if theology is to be revived, we might learn more about what can be discovered about such a god through the various other indirect methods of learning that are available to us at present.

A Brief Historical Recapitulation

Modern science was a product of the Christian search to know God better, as could be achieved by studying the design of his creation, a religious motive finding especially fertile ground among English Calvinists and German Lutherans in the seventeenth century. Although not a Calvinist himself, the most important figure in the creation of modern science, Isaac Newton, was surrounded by Calvinists and was himself obsessed with religion, seeing himself as blessed with mathematical and other scientific skills that had made him

God's most important messenger, a thought that sometimes terrified him. For Newton, Galileo, and other leading figures in the scientific revolution of the seventeenth century, mathematics was the language of the divine.[2]

Newton would have been greatly disturbed by many of the later modern results of his own scientific efforts. Rather than bringing humanity closer to God, as was his intention, the modern science that followed after him ended up distancing the world from the Christian God. The monotheism of Jewish and Christian religion meant that it presented itself as offering the one "truth" of the world. For medieval society, the Bible was not only a collection of ethical principles but an actual true account of the most important events in human history. This proved to be a large weakness, however, when science established itself as a more accurate source of knowledge about many matters on which Christianity had long made authoritative pronouncements.

One possibility, then, was that science would be newly incorporated into Christian theology—as Newton hoped. In matters of the workings of nature (known then as the subject matter of "natural theology"), the scientific method was increasingly demonstrating that it was a much more authoritative source of theological knowledge, as compared with any previous resources (including the Bible) traditionally available to Christian theology. Institutional Christianity proved, however, unable to make such a radical transition in its thinking and methods. Science instead made its extraordinary advances outside Christian theology and the institutional settings of Christian religion. Forfeiting the field, few modern theologians ever mastered the methods of mathematics and physics.

By the mid-nineteenth century, there was another pivotal development. Up to then, science had been mostly a theological subject—it answered some of the most fundamental questions about the workings of the universe (about God's plan for the natural order, and the human ability to comprehend his plan). The great physicist James Clerk Maxwell and his 1860s theoretical discoveries in electromagnetism, however, soon had immense practical significance. The generation and use of electricity depended on a scientific understanding of its underlying mathematics. Until the second half of the nineteenth century, electricity had been a strange and obscure phenomenon in the natural world. After Maxwell, as we all now know from daily experience, the scientific understanding of electricity changed the physical realities of our own human existence.

Other areas of physics and of chemistry as well began in the second half of the nineteenth century to make similarly remarkable scientific

2. Koetsier and Bergmans, eds., *Mathematics and the Divine.*

discoveries also with immense practical consequences. Theoretical scientific knowledge from then on provided the basis for asserting an altogether unprecedented human control over nature. In the developed nations of the world, as noted previously, material outputs per capita soared by more than fifteen times from 1800 to 2000. In the late nineteenth and early twentieth centuries, the university was transformed from its religious origins to become a main source of scientific knowledge, as provided by new expert professional groups—organized on disciplinary lines—who would make possible the "scientific management" of society.

Such modern developments raised a profound theological question: God having strictly arranged the workings of the physical world according to scientifically discoverable mathematical laws, what about the other remaining large parts of human existence? What about the workings of society and of human minds? The initial modern response in the Enlightenment was to assume that God would necessarily be consistent. The physical sciences had made the great pioneering discoveries but it would seem that all of human existence—as many modern thinkers concluded from the eighteenth century onward—must be understandable by the application of the same scientific methods.

For thinkers such as Pierre Laplace in the late eighteenth and early nineteenth century, this would mean that all events in the world were ultimately reducible in principle to physical phenomena, the entire future of the earth including the lives of human beings at least in concept subject to exact scientific prediction. Applying his own version of such thinking to the workings of society, Karl Marx saw in the laws of economics the explanation for everything in human history. Richard Dawkins and his contemporary naturalist ilk today have the same faith but look to evolutionary biological science—along with physics—for their all-encompassing scientific explanation of the totality of human existence. For all three, a god, explicitly recognized as such, is unnecessary, an antiquated illusion.

A Waning of Scientific Faith

If he exists, a god, however, will have his own mind; he will not take instructions from human beings or necessarily conform to human assumptions of what a god must do. Once outside the physical workings of nature, the application of scientific methods to the workings of society and other parts of human affairs proved in the modern age to be a great disappointment. By the end of the twentieth century, the goal of the full scientific management of society appeared to have been yet another in a long list of utopian goals of history—originally religious in expecting God soon to establish his kingdom on earth, since the Enlightenment more often "secular" in now expecting the kingdom to arrive soon as the result of human scientifically guided actions.

Over the past century, the professionals of psychology, economics, sociology, and other social sciences have had to confront an embarrassing range of scientific failures. With each such failure—the Great Recession of 2008 and 2009 and its aftermath a very recent example for the members of the economics profession—the foundations of comprehensive modern scientific faith have been further eroded. We still believe in physics in its proper domain but most of the rest of life seems to fall outside the application of the scientific method strictly speaking—raising the interesting but difficult question of what methods we should be applying. Indeed, it is hard to make the case today that any large area of the "scientific" study of human affairs has made discoveries that can pass the essential test of the scientific method—prediction confirmed by empirical observation. There have been many confident predictions in the "human sciences" and many empirical failures.

This has admittedly not prevented many social scientists—economists in particular—from presenting the results of their scholarly efforts in the mathematical language of physics. Given the absence of any discoveries by economists even remotely analogous to those routinely made in physics, this is an indirect way, however, of making a religious claim. Economics has been more significant in the modern age for the religious blessings it has sought to confer on the economic culture and institutions of society than for its ability to discover the knowledge, for example, to plan and manage national and other large economic systems "scientifically."[3] Truth be told, it seems that random chance—or maybe a god's inscrutable will—plays a central historical role.

It is impossible to prove with certainty that the social sciences will never be able to succeed in their grand truth-telling aspirations. There is no time limit on demonstrating the success of the scientific method in new areas such as the workings of society. Perhaps a Newton of social science will be born a century from now. On the other hand, there is also no way to prove that such a great advance in scientific knowledge in the realm of human affairs will ever be forthcoming. Yes or no, it is a leap of faith, a religious conviction about the actual workings of the mind of a god in his design for the full universe, including the nonphysical—the social and cultural—elements of human existence.

---

3. Nelson, *Economics as Religion*.

As this book has made the case, however, there are at least two areas that will in principle remain forever inaccessible through the scientific method. One, as explored in Chapter 3, is the miracle of the very existence of a mathematical order to the physical world. Given that physical nature has seemingly obeyed mathematical laws for billions of years, this mathematical order had to have existed long before human beings or their ancestors ever conceived of anything about mathematics. How this mathematical order was imposed on physical nature as we perceive it is itself beyond any physical science explanation. Such a scientific explanation would have to be based in mathematics, and thus would already have to assume what is supposed to be explained—the initial mathematical ordering of the universe. It would be like seeking to demonstrate the existence of A by first assuming that A exists.

For Plato, the independent realm of mathematics was the realm of the gods. One might reason similarly today, a possibility that is frightening to true naturalist believers, which is why their resistance is so strong. This was well illustrated in a recent book review of an unabashedly Platonic way of thinking about mathematics, a book (discussed in Chapter 3 above) authored by a leading mathematician of our time, Edward Frenkel, now a professor of mathematics at the University of California at Berkeley. The book reviewer (not a mathematician) complains that "the problem with this Platonist view of mathematics—one that Frenkel . . . [dangerously] never quite recognizes as such—is that it makes mathematical knowledge a miracle." This is such a large problem because "if the objects of mathematics exist apart from us, living in a Platonic world that transcends the physical world of space and time, then how does the human mind 'get in touch' with them and learn about their properties and relations? Do mathematicians have ESP?"[4] There is another explanation, however, never mentioned by the reviewer. The old-fashioned explanation is that mathematics first exists in the mind of a god and human beings to some extent share in the capacity of this god's mind for mathematical thinking. For a true-believing naturalist, of course, this is a heresy whose spread should be aggressively contained as if it were a disease in society.

The prominent Harvard philosopher Hilary Putnam, a representative of the contemporary philosophical mainstream, is refreshingly candid about why mathematical Platonism must for people like him be ruled out from the outset. Mathematical Platonism, Putnam writes, "seems flatly incompatible with the simple fact that we think with our brains, and not with immaterial

---

4. Holt, "A Mathematical Romance," 29.

souls."[5] An "immaterial soul' is an old fashioned way of saying that we think with our "conscious minds." With mathematical Platonism we are entering the realm of a god and a religion, a threatening danger zone for any true believing naturalist. Despite conventional philosophical pieties today, the existence of mathematics and its ability to order what we call "the physical world" demonstrates that some fundamental realities of human existence lie outside the "material," an unacceptable idea to the large number of our current scientific materialist devout.

As explored in Chapter 5, the second and equally threatening area is human consciousness. Science can only explain that which can be observed and measured in time and space. Since this will never be true in the case of human consciousness, it follows that in principle physical science cannot explain consciousness—nor can evolutionary biology since it must work through a physical process. The power of naturalist religion is so great in our times, however, that many of its contemporary devout deny what is transparently obvious to most ordinary human beings, that consciousness exists outside what is conventionally labeled "the physical world." Remarkably for people who are often so critical of traditional religion, this naturalist behavior is surprisingly similar to fundamentalist Christian creationists who also make up implausible stories in a desperate attempt to defend their literal religion. Since the existence of consciousness directly contradicts the tenets of naturalism, they now do the same; some way must be found somehow to deny that consciousness exists at all (the Daniel Dennett solution)—or at least to assert that consciousness is some kind of mental illusion that mysteriously reduces to the chemical and electrical workings of neurons in the human brain.

In the end, the distinction between the world of physics and the world of consciousness may actually break down altogether. Most mathematicians are Platonists who believe that doing mathematics is an adventure in the discovery of a pre-existing mathematical universe—one that they often say has remarkable beauty along with its rational logical appeal. Like human consciousness, this pre-existing mathematical world does not belong to "the physical world," yet is laws exercise control over "the physical world." Yet, even "the physical world" exists only as a set of perceptions in human consciousness, aided by perceptions of "physical measuring instruments." It would seem that the final truest verdict is that all the world is consciousness, whether a generalized mathematical consciousness in principle shared by everyone who can think with sufficient rationality, or the specific experiences of individual consciousness that instead differ among individuals. It

5. Putnam, quoted in Holt, "A Mathematical Romance," 29.

comes close to the idea, as mentioned above, that god has no physical reality but is a cosmic mind. Human beings, miraculously, seem to share some parts of that cosmic mind of god—as more traditionally put in Christianity, they are made "in the image of God."

Unlike physics and chemistry after the mid-nineteenth century, the Darwinist theory of evolution has thus far had few practical consequences for human existence—confined to studying matters such as the evolution of viruses, the danger of pandemics, and the development of resistance to antibiotics. Darwinism thus still largely belongs to the realm of theology, as physics—once "natural theology" or "natural philosophy"—did until the mid-nineteenth century when knowledge of its laws became the basis for our present astonishing control over the "material" workings of the natural world. Now that the scientific miracles altogether transcended the biblical miracles, it was no contest for many ordinary people who observed all this—science had replaced the Bible as the most authoritative form of knowledge of the truths of the world.

The Christian Bible assumed such great religious—and thus also practical—significance because for more than a thousand years, it was regarded as the one authoritative account of the actual central events in human history. The Bible, however, is today no longer capable of sustaining this historical authority, partly because of the close scrutiny of biblical texts of the past few hundred years. Both the Old Testament and the New Testament have often been called into question with respect to their literal historical accuracy. One sees in the current efforts to create a new "big history," tracing the history of the world back to the big bang as the initial moment of "the creation," an attempt to write a new contemporary "Bible" of the billions of years of geological, biological, and most recently, human, life on earth that is said to be actually historically true—as science defines "truth."[6] But at least in their full specific details, many of the accounts of central events in the evolution of life on earth, as presented as "big history," cannot be considered as a part of recorded history. Indeed, some of them may be no less mythological than some of the specific stories of the biblical accounts.

The Unknown (to Him) Faith of Richard Dawkins

The large theological confusions of the modern age are well illustrated today in the thinking of Richard Dawkins, as developed in his many widely read books and articles over more than thirty years.[7] Dawkins, despite his many

6. Christian, Brown, and Benjamin, *Big History*.
7. McGrath, *Dawkins' God*.

protestations to the contrary, is a man of faith—a devout believer, as I will suggest here, in a god that in many respects resembles (if it is not identical to) the Christian God. In his failure to recognize this, Dawkins is, like many other modern men and women, exhibiting his own form of personal blindness and lack of historical religious knowledge.

For such religiously confused people, their actual faith is best revealed by their actions, not by their words. Rather than his professed "atheistic" beliefs, Dawkins by his actions shows a true believer most notable for his evangelical zeal and the disguised manner in which he seeks to promote his religious fundamentalism, a secular faith that is nevertheless surprisingly compatible with many aspects of Christianity.

1. **Dawkins has faith that a material world exists.**—As Bishop Berkeley long ago made clear, and David Hume more fully developed the idea later in the eighteenth century, a person can have no direct access to an external world of "matter." Twentieth-century physics then significantly further undermined any clear scientific basis for the existence of a "material world." To believe in its existence, as the great majority of human beings do (including me), is thus an act of deep religious faith. In his writings on evolutionary biology, Dawkins demonstrates that he is among these many true believers in the existence of a material world. This same belief has also been an important part of the Christian (and Jewish) message that emphasizes the bodily essence of human existence, in contrast to some Eastern religions for which a material existence may even be illusory. Our own material existence and material surroundings cannot be scientifically demonstrated, however: they have to be taken on faith.

2. **Dawkins has faith that other human minds exist.**—The same considerations apply to the existence of other human minds. In strictly scientific terms, we can never directly interact with either the mind or the body of another person. We can only experience a set of sensory impressions from which we must then indirectly impute the existence of other minds and bodies. To believe in their existence then again becomes ultimately a matter of faith. By the act of writing his many books that exhibit a deep desire to convert others to his own views, Dawkins demonstrates that he does believe deeply in the existence of other minds, again a faith fully shared with Christianity as well.

3. **Dawkins has a faith that actual "real truth" exists in the world.**—Again recalling the eighteenth-century arguments of Hume,

the scientific method is not an avenue to "real truth." Physical science is capable only of establishing that certain relationships among observed "natural" events in the world have thus far exhibited a 100 percent correlation. Science says nothing about why this correlation exists or whether it is guaranteed to continue indefinitely into the future. We can only believe that it will continue as a matter of faith. In arguing that the physical mechanisms of biological evolution explain all past history, and will explain all future history, Dawkins shows by this act that he has this faith. Belief in such a single intrinsic universal truth of the world, now and forever, is a distinguishing characteristic of Jewish and Christian monotheism as well.

4. **Dawkins has faith that "real truth" can be reached by processes of rational argument, both in his own mind, and in the minds of his readers whom he seeks to convert by such rational argument.**—In the physical world, the existence of a 100 percent correlation of repeatable events can be established by direct human observation and use of the scientific method. The truths of biological evolution, however, are not subject to such scientific methods. Rather, as discussed at various points in this book, evolution is a story of the history of the biological world with human beings part of this story for the past two million years. The truths of history must be reached by a process that combines observation of the biological facts of the world (some of them obtained using the outputs of physical science) and rational argument. In declaring that his books do advance knowledge of the actual true workings of nature, Dawkins demonstrates by this act that he believes that rational argument (outside the methods of physical science) can be an objective avenue to such "real truth." Thomas Aquinas would have fully agreed, indeed putting rational argument at the core of his theology (including five rational arguments for the existence of God). In Christian theology, the divine "logos," as contained originally in the person of Jesus Christ, is the rational order God imposed on the world, increasingly discoverable at least in part by human efforts.

5. **Dawkins has faith that there is more to human existence than a material reality.**—Rational argument is not a physical reality. The exercise of reason occurs in human minds. The actual existence of a "real truth," reached by rational argument, therefore cannot be established by processes occurring at the atomic and molecular levels of human brains. That is to say, human brain chemistry can never be "real truth." In effectively showing by his actions that he believes that real

truth exists, Dawkins demonstrates that he believes—and contrary to many of his assertions in other contexts—that there is a nonmaterial dimension to human existence in which rational thought processes operate and can prevail to establish the "real truth." For Christians as well, this is part of what it means to say that human beings are "made in the image of God."

6. For example, Dawkins has faith that he, Richard Dawkins, a live human being, wrote *The God Delusion*, as a free exercise of his own conscious powers of reasoning to reach the book's conclusions, as others can react freely to his arguments in his books by similar processes of their own individual conscious reasoning.—Dawkins's atheist compatriot Daniel Dennett is correct; if the workings of physical nature are all there is to human existence, then we are all, including Richard Dawkins, zombies. There is no Richard Dawkins, a real live person, who ever wrote *The God Delusion*. Rather, a functional robot (or a computer in a matrix), representing itself as "Richard Dawkins," wrote the book, as its contents were entirely determined by the scientific laws of nature operating in some physical system somewhere. By showing in his statements and other actions that he clearly holds a belief to the contrary, that he exists and as such did personally write *The God Delusion,* as the result of many individual human acts of free choice about its contents, Dawkins demonstrates that he has faith that he is not a zombie (or embedded in a matrix)—Dennett to the contrary. In other words, and in more old fashioned terms, Dawkins shows by his actions that he believes that human beings have free will to write their own books (and do many other things), according to independent thought processes in their minds, this also being a basic message of Christianity.

7. Dawkins does not believe in natural evolution as the final explanation of the world.—In a strictly evolutionary account, there is no such thing as "truth," only beliefs that advance evolutionary success. Dawkins thus demonstrates by his actions that he does not believe in natural evolution as determining what happens in his own mind and thus in the world as a whole—however confused his words may be about the supposed omnipotence of natural evolution.

I happen to share all these forms of faith with Dawkins, including that a real "me" wrote this book—that "you" are now reading—as an exercise of my own independent powers of free choice, operating outside any controlling laws of evolutionary biology or other physical laws of the natural universe. True-believing Christians would agree with all this as well. As matters of faith and reason, all conscious decision-making involves to some degree a transcendence of the purely physical existence of the human body. Broadly understood, free human actions thus involve the existence of something supernatural in the universe and this means almost by definition the existence of a god—certainly something mysterious that transcends scientific materialism. Dawkins, even if he does not know it, or even typically denies it explicitly, by his own actions actually shows that he believes in such a supernatural element to human existence. Like many other people in our own times, partly due to a lack of religious knowledge, he simply lacks the vocabulary (or the courage) to express explicitly his actual religious convictions that he has already demonstrated indirectly by his own actions.

Tests of Belief in a God

The act of believing, as I have been maintaining, in the existence of "real truth" in the world is to demonstrate in this manner one's actual belief in the existence of a supernatural element in the world—the existence of a god—if still leaving many questions to be answered about the full character of this god (beyond making "real truth" possible). That is to say, once again, since "real truth" that goes beyond physical brain workings and instinctual reactions cannot be the result of any mere physical forces in nature, belief in its existence requires something going beyond "the natural world" as we conventionally understand this term.

This is not the only good test for whether a person actually believes in a god, even when they might not know it. There are many things about the human situation that transcend conventional physical scientific explanation. If you believe in any of the following, whether or not you know it explicitly, your actions (of belief) demonstrate that you do believe in something supernatural working in the world that has traditionally been given the name of a "god." Nothing that is exclusively the product of the scientific method of Newton or the evolutionary biological method of Darwin will get you to a sure belief in the existence of these things below.

1. As noted, the existence of "real truth" as can be reached (or better and better approximated) by the exercise of human rational capabilities.

2. The existence of "real love" for other people in the world such as a spouse and/or child.

3. The existence of a belief in the "fundamental equality of all human beings."

4. The existence of "good and evil."

5. The existence of a "moral imperative to preserve the existence of other non-human species of the earth."

6. In the broadest terms, the existence of a "meaning and purpose to human existence."

These are all core principles of Christian religion. Is it necessary to believe in any one precise set of Christian doctrines in order to believe in their valid existence? The answer is clearly no. But it is necessary to believe in some supernatural elements of human existence that transcend the purely physical workings of the natural world. So if you answered yes to any of the six questions, as some readers of this book might be surprised to hear, you believe in the existence of a god.

This is not to say that religion—the belief in something fundamental and supernatural that is working in the world—is a universal force for good. Indeed, the term *religion* encompasses many forms of belief in the supernatural—in a god—some of which have contributed to terrible wars that have been fought in the name of religion and with many large evils committed. Some forms of religion can be the greatest force for the good in human existence, and other forms the greatest force for evil. It is even possible for the same religion in difference circumstances to function in these opposite roles. Religion is an ultimate feature that defines the human condition. The struggle to make religion a force for good is, at least so far, never-ending. The hope for "progress" in the world is ultimately a faith that the good influence of religion will in the long run prevail over the evil influence, due in part, as would seem necessary, to a supernatural partnership between a god and human beings made "in the image of god."

Writing This Book

I have long been like Richard Dawkins in that my most accurate statements about my own religious beliefs have typically taken the form of actions rather than words. I can see now that writing this book has been for me a religious act. I don't need the money and anyway none of my previous eight books has earned more than a few thousand dollars in royalties. I am not facing a publish or perish threat—I have been a tenured professor at the University of Maryland for more than twenty years and my next big academic move (hopefully not too soon) will be to retire. I do, I suppose, hope that the book will be a success and that I will win some recognition—and ideally even some plaudits—from friends and professional colleagues. But the biggest reason for writing the book is to make a statement of my participation in a community of those people deeply interested in discussing and debating the truth of a god's existence (or not). As a non-church attender most of my life, you might call this community my own form of church, even though it never gathers all its members in one place and time.

I also wanted to develop my own thinking about the question of a god. I think best by writing, so for me a book was a logical way to proceed. I also communicate best by writing ,so a book is also a good way to interact with others, if not to the exclusion of more direct personal interactions. As it now seems to me as this book is being completed, I already had assumed implicitly the existence of a god long ago, even as I did not then have the insight and vocabulary to say so out loud or perhaps even to acknowledge this belief explicitly in my own thinking. But I would have said "yes" to the following, all of which I now have come to think, similar to my observations above, would demonstrate a faith of mine in the existence of a god, broadly similar to the faith I see in Richard Dawkins, while we might disagree on many details.

1. I believe there is such a thing as "real truth" in the world in an absolute sense.

2. I believe this absolute "real truth" is in concept capable of being discovered by rational human endeavors within the conscious reach of each person.

3. I believe, more specifically, in my own pursuit of "real truth." I do have an autonomy to form my own views freely by means of my own internal thought processes, independent of the physical workings of atoms and molecules in my brain (although bodily circumstances can make such freedom of thought more or less difficult to maintain at any given moment).

4. I believe, similarly, that when I seek to persuade other people of my own understanding of "real truth" (as with this book, for example), they do have an autonomous capacity to think freely about my arguments and to form their own rational responses by means of their own independent thought processes—that their views about the book are not fully determined by electrical, chemical, or other bodily natural factors of their own.

This faith in "real truth," moreover, puts me in the broad historic category of a true believer in a central tenet of the Abrahamic religions—Judaism, Christianity, and Islam. As three contemporary students of international cultural differences write, "what distinguishes Western from the Eastern religions is their concern with Truth with a capital T. The Western revelatory religions share the assumption that there is an absolute Truth that excludes all other truth that human beings can possess."[8] While all of Christian religion seeks to reveal the one "Truth" of the world, there are large differences among Christian religions in how they go about this pursuit. Another student of international culture observes that Germans "believe that there is such a thing as scientific truth" that is to be sought with their usual ruthless efficiency. In their interactions with others, the Finns think that "stating the truth, whether pleasant or not, is the best way to achieve a successful outcome. They are astonished to find that only Germans, Canadians and U.S. Americans, Norwegians and Australians have the same attitude" to this degree (with Swedes close behind). The differences in practical commitment to Truth in everyday life are largest with the Catholic world; "in Italy truth is negotiable, in France it is dressed up, the Spanish play with 'double truth.'"[9] It seems that I am more a product of my Scandinavian heritage than I recognized until recently; I am descended from immigrants to the United States more than 100 years ago from Finland and Sweden.

Before writing the book, I may have occasionally had the thought that by my actions (including acts of belief), if not my words, I commonly show a belief in the existence of a god—as it now further seems, perhaps in some respects even a Protestant kind of a god. But, as I said, I was quite unlikely to make that statement explicitly in public. Unlike Dawkins, however, I have always had a favorable view of religion and its critical social importance for the world, even as I had my own large uncertainties about the specific details of religion. But with the advance in my own thinking that I hope this book represents, I can now say explicitly that I do believe that a god (very probably) exists. I also am more confident about various divine features—that god has a "mind" with no material essence and this god has a great fondness for mathematics, for example.

I recognize that many devout Christians will probably think that this is a pretty thin understanding of god that is well removed from their own more powerfully felt and personal Christian God. As I stated at the beginning, however, the purpose of this book has been to see how far rational analysis can take me (and possibly others) in thinking about the existence

---

8. Hofstede, Van Hofstede, and Minkov, *Cultures and Organizations*, 227.

9. Lewis, *Finland*, 57.

of a god. To get to the full Christian God would require going beyond such exercises in reasoning to make a larger leap of faith—certainly to get to the Protestant God of Martin Luther or John Calvin who said that religious belief is a matter of "faith alone." Maybe in the next book.

Bibliography

Angell, Marcia. "The Epidemic of Mental Illness: Why?" *The New York Review of Books*, June 23, 2011. http://www.nybooks.com/articles/archives/2011/jun/23/epidemic-mental-illness-why/.

Armstrong, Karen. *The Great Transformation: The Beginnings of Our Religious Traditions*. New York: Anchor, 2006.

Aslan, Reza. *No god but God: The Origins, Evolution, and Future of Islam*. New York: Random House, 2011.

Austin, Victor Lee. "How to Be a Sick Christian." *First Things* 249 (January 2015) 17–19.

Bailey, Edward. "Implicit Religion." In *The Oxford Handbook of the Sociology of Religion*, edited by Peter B. Clarke, 801–16. New York: Oxford University Press, 2009.

———. "Implicit Religion." *Religion* 40:4 (2010) 271–78.

———. "Implicit Religion: A Bibliographical Introduction." *Social Compass* 37 (1990) 483–98.

———. *Implicit Religion in Contemporary Society*. Kampen, Netherlands: Kok Pharos, 1997.

———. *Implicit Religion: An Introduction*. London: Middlesex University Press, 1998.

———. "'Implicit Religion': What Might That Be?" *Implicit Religion* 15:2 (2012) 195–207.

Baker, Mark C., and Stewart Goetz. "Introduction." In *The Soul Hypothesis: Investigations into the Existence of the Soul*, edited by Marc C. Baker and Stewart Goetz, 1–20. New York: Continuum, 2011.

———. "Afterword." In *The Soul Hypothesis: Investigations into the Existence of the Soul*, edited by Marc C. Baker and Stewart Goetz, 247–53. New York: Continuum, 2011.

Barbour, Ian G. *Religion and Science: Historical and Contemporary Issues*. New York: Harper Collins, 1997.

Barrow, John D. *The Constants of Nature*. London: Jonathan Cape, 2002.

———. *The Infinite Book: Where Things Happen That Don't*. London: Jonathan Cape, 2005.

Becker, Carl L. *The Heavenly City of the Eighteenth-Century Philosophers*. New Haven, CT: Yale University Press, 1968.

Bellah, Robert N. "Civil Religion in America." *Daedalus: Journal of the American Academy of Arts and Sciences* 96:1 (Winter 1967) 1–21.

———. *Religion in Human Evolution: From the Paleolithic to the Axial Age*. Cambridge, MA: Harvard University Press, 2011.

Bilbro, Jeffrey. *Loving God's Wildness: The Christian Roots of Ecological Ethics in American Literature*. Tuscaloosa, AL: University of Alabama Press, 2015.

Blackburn, Simon. "Taliban and Plato." *Times Literary Supplement*, July 2013. https://login.the-tls.co.uk/?gotoUrl=http%3A%2F%2Fwww.the-tls.co.uk%2Ftls%2Freviews%2Fphilosophy_and_religion%2Farticle1288833.ece.

Blackmore, Susan. *Consciousness: An Introduction*. New York: Routledge, 2010.

Bohr, Niels. "Atoms and Human Knowledge." In *Atomic Physics and Human Knowledge*, 83–93. Mineola, NY: Dover, 2010.

———. "Natural Philosophy and Human Cultures." In *Atomic Physics and Human Knowledge*, 23–31. Mineola, NY: Dover, 2010.

———. *The Philosophical Writings of Niels Bohr, Volume II: Essays 1933–1957 on Atomic Physics and Human Knowledge*. Woodbridge, CT: Ox Bow, 1987.

Boy, John D., and John Torpey. "Inventing the Axial Age: The Origins and Uses of a Historical Concept." *Theory and Society* 42:3 (May 2013) 241–59.

Brasier, Martin. "The Battle of Balliol." In *Lynn Margulis: The Life and Legacy of a Scientific Rebel*, edited by Dorion Sagan, 74–79. White River Junction, VT: Chelsea Green, 2012.

Breger, Herbert. "God and Mathematics in Leibniz's Thought." In *Mathematics and the Divine: A Historical Study*, edited by T. Koetsier and L. Bergmans, 485–98. Amsterdam: Elsevier, 2005.

Brown, D. MacKenzie. *Ultimate Concern: Tillich in Dialogue*. New York: Harper and Row, 1965.

Bucher, Rainer, *Hitler's Theology: A Study in Political Religion*. Translated by Rebecca Pohl. London: Continuum, 2011.

Burleigh, Michael. *Earthly Powers: The Clash of Religion and Politics in Europe, from the French Revolution to the Great War*. New York: Harper Collins, 2006.

———. *Sacred Causes: The Clash of Religion and Politics from the Great War to the War on Terror*. New York: Harper Collins, 2007.

———. *The Third Reich: A New History*. New York: Hill and Wang, 2000.

Carson, Rachel. *Silent Spring*. Boston: Houghton Mifflin, 1962.

Cavanaugh, William T. *The Myth of Religious Violence*. New York: Oxford University Press, 2009.

Chalmers, David J. *The Character of Consciousness*. New York: Oxford University Press, 2010.

———. *The Conscious Mind: In Search of a Fundamental Theory*. New York: Oxford University Press, 1996.

———. "Facing Up to the Problem of Consciousness." *Journal of Consciousness Studies* 2:3 (March 1995) 200–219.

Cherry, Kendra. "Freud and Religion." *About Education*. http://psychology.about.com/od/sigmundfreud/p/freud_religion.htm.

Christian, David, Cynthia Stokes Brown, and Craig Benjamin. *Big History: Between Nothing and Everything*. New York: McGraw-Hill, 2013.

Cohen, Daniel J. *Equations from God: Pure Mathematics and Victorian Faith*. Baltimore: Johns Hopkins University Press, 2007.

Comfort, Ray. *Hitler, God & the Bible*. Washington, DC: WND, 2012.

Cornwell, John. *Darwin's Angel: An Angelic Riposte to* The God Delusion. London: Profile, 2007.

———. *Newman's Unquiet Grave: The Reluctant Saint*. New York: Continuum, 2010.

Coyne, Jerry A. *Why Evolution is True*. New York: Viking, 2009.

Craig, William Lane. *On Guard: Defending Your Faith with Reason and Precision.* Colorado Springs, CO: David C. Cook, 2010.

———. *What is God Like?* N.p.: Create Space, 2013.

Cuevas, John De. "Mind, Brain and Behavior." *Harvard Magazine,* November/December 1994, 36–43.

Darwin, Charles. "Letter to William Graham." July 3, 1881. *Darwin Correspondence Project.* http://www.darwinproject.ac.uk/letter/entry-13230.

Davies, Paul. *God & the New Physics.* New York: Simon & Schuster, 1983.

———. *The Goldilocks Enigma: Why is the Universe Just Right for Life?* New York: Mariner, 2008.

Davies, Paul, and John Gribbin. *The Matter Myth: Dramatic Discoveries that Challenge Our Understanding of Physical Reality.* New York: Simon & Schuster, 2007 [1992].

Davis, Philip J., and Reuben Hirsch. *The Mathematical Experience.* Boston: Mariner, 1998.

Dawkins, Richard. *The Blind Watchmaker: Why the Evidence of Evolution Reveals a Universe Without Design.* New York: Norton, 1987.

———. *The God Delusion.* Boston: Houghton Mifflin, 2006.

———. *The Selfish Gene.* New York: Oxford University Press, 1976.

DeMartino, George, and Deirdre McCloskey, eds. *Oxford Handbook of Professional Economic Ethics.* New York: Oxford University Press, 2014.

Dennett, Daniel C. *Consciousness Explained.* Boston: Little, Brown, 1991.

———. *Darwin's Dangerous Idea: Evolution and the Meanings of Life.* New York: Simon and Schuster, 1996.

———. "Darwin's Strange Inversion of Reasoning." In *In the Light of Evolution: Volume III, Two Centuries of Darwin,* edited by John C. Avise and Francisco J. Ayala, 343–54. Washington, DC: National Academies, 2009.

———. *Evolution and the Meanings of Life.* New York: Simon and Schuster, 1996.

de Pater, Cornelis. "An Ocean of Truth." In *Mathematics and the Divine: A Historical Study,* edited by L. Koetsier and L. Bergmans, 459–84. Amsterdam: Elsevier, 2005

Donald, Merlin. "An Evolutionary Approach to Culture: Implications for Study of the Axial Age." In *The Axial Age and its Consequences,* edited by Robert N. Bellah and Hans Joas, 47–76. Cambridge, MA: Harvard University Press, 2012.

———. *Origins of the Modern Mind: Three Stages in the Evolution of Culture and Cognition.* Cambridge, MA: Harvard University Press, 1991.

Donlan, Thomas G. "A Slippery Course of Study." *Barron's,* April 6, 2015. http://www.barrons.com/articles/a-slippery-course-of-study-1428114145.

Dudley, Underwood. "Introduction to Chapter 2." In *Is Mathematics Inevitable?: A Miscellany,* edited by Underwood Dudley, 15–16. Washington, DC: Mathematical Association of America, 2008.

Dworkin, Ronald. "Religion Without God." *New York Review of Books,* April 4, 2013. http://www.nybooks.com/articles/archives/2013/apr/04/religion-without-god/.

———. *Religion Without God.* Cambridge, MA: Harvard University Press, 2013.

Dyson, Freeman. "How We Know." *New York Review of Books,* March 10, 2011. http://www.nybooks.com/articles/archieves/2011/mar/10/how-we-know/.

Eccles, John C. *Evolution of the Brain: Creation of the Self.* New York: Routledge, 1989.

Eddington, Arthur Stanley. *Science and the Unseen World.* New York: Macmillan, 1929.

Einstein, Albert. "Maxwell's Influence on the Evolution of the Idea of Physical Reality." In *Ideas and Opinions,* 266–70. New York: Three Rivers, 1982.

————. "On the Generalized Theory of Gravitation." In *Ideas and Opinions*, 341–56. New York: Three Rivers, 1982.

————. *Relativity: The Special and General Theory*. Translated by Robert W. Lawson. New York: Random House, 1961 [1920].

————. "Religion and Science." In *Ideas and Opinions*, 40. New York: Three Rivers, 1982.

————. "The Religious Spirit of Science." In *Ideas and Opinions*, 40. New York: Three Rivers, 1982.

Eldredge, Niles. "Foreword: Undreamt Philosophies." In *What is Life?*, by Lynn Margulis and Dorion Sagan, xi–xv. Berkeley, CA: University of California Press, 1995.

Enck, Paul., Fabrizio Benedetti, and Manfred Schedlowski. "New Insights into Placebo and Nocebo Responses." *Neuron* 59:2 (July 2008) 195–206.

Epstein, William M. *Psychotherapy as Religion: The Civil Divine in America*. Reno, NV: University of Nevada Press, 2006.

Ferguson, Andrew. "The Heretic." *The Weekly Standard*, March 25, 2013. http://www.weeklystandard.com/articles/heretic_707692.html.

Feser, Edward. *Philosophy of Mind*. Oxford: One World, 2006.

Feynman, Richard P. *The Meaning of It All: Thoughts of a Citizen-Scientist*. New York: Basic, 1998.

————. *QED: The Strange Theory of Light and Matter*. Princeton, NJ: Princeton University Press, 1985.

————. *Six Easy Pieces: Essentials of Physics Explained by it Most Brilliant Teacher*. New York: Basic, 1989.

Fish, Stanley. "God Talk." Opinionator Blog, *New York Times*, May 3, 2009. http://opinionator.blogs.nytimes.com/2009/05/03/god-talk.

Fleming, Thomas. *The Illusion of Victory: America in World War I*. New York: Basic, 2004.

Fodor, Jerry. "Against Darwinism." *Mind & Language* 23:1 (February 2008) 1–24.

————. "The Big Idea: Can There Be a Science of the Mind?" *Times Literary Supplement*, July 3, 1992, 5–7.

Fodor, Jerry, and Massimo Piattelli-Palmarini. *What Darwin Got Wrong*. New York: Farrar, Straus and Giroux, 2010.

Frankenberry, Nancy H. "Introduction." In *The Faith of Scientists in their Own Words*, edited by Nancy H. Frankenberry, vii–xv. Princeton, NJ: Princeton University Press, 2008.

Frenkel, Edward. *Love & Math: The Heart of Hidden Reality*. New York: Basic, 2013.

Gallup Poll, "Landing a Man on the Moon: The Public's View." July 20, 1999. http://www.gallup.com/poll/3712/landing-man-moon-publics-view.aspx.

Gleick, James. *Genius: The Life and Science of Richard Feynman*. New York: Vintage, 1992.

Gocke, Benedikt Paul. "Introduction." In *After Physicalism*, edited by Benedikt Paul Gocke, 1–29. Notre Dame, IN: University of Notre Dame Press, 2012.

Goetz, Stewart, and Charles Taliaferro. *A Brief History of the Soul*. Malden, MA: Wiley-Blackwell, 2011.

"Going Round in Circles." *The Economist*, December 4, 2010. http://www.economist.com/node/17626874.

Goodwin, Doris Kearns. "Foreword." In, *Baseball as a Road to God: Seeing Beyond the Game*, by John Sexton, xi–xiv. New York: Gotham, 2013.

Gould, Stephen Jay. "Darwinian Fundamentalism." *New York Review of Books*, June 12, 1997. http://www.nybooks.com/articles/archives/1997/jun/12/darwinian-fundamentalism.

———. "Evolution: The Pleasures of Pluralism," *New York Review of Books*, June 26, 1997. http://www.nybooks.com/articles/archives/1997/jun/26/evolution-the-pleasures-of-pluralism/.

———. *Punctuated Equilibrium*. Cambridge, MA: Harvard University Press, 2007.

Grassie, William. "The New Sciences of Religion." *Zygon* 43:1 (March 2008) 127–58.

Gray, John. "The Closed Mind of Richard Dawkins: His Atheism is its own Kind of Narrow Religion." *New Republic*, October 2, 2014. http://www.newrepublic.com/article/119596/appetite-wonder-review-closed-mind-richard-dawkins.

———. *Heresies: Against Progress and Other Illusions*. United Kingdom: Granta, 2004.

———. "An Illusion with a Future." *Daedalus* 133:3 (Summer 2004) 10–17.

Gregory, Brad S. *The Unintended Reformation: How a Religious Revolution Secularized Society*. Cambridge, MA: Harvard University Press, 2012.

Hahn, Scott, and Benjamin Wiker. *Answering the New Atheism: Dismantling Dawkins' Case Against God*. Steubenville, OH: Emmaus Road, 2008.

Halfin, Igal. *From Darkness to Light: Class, Consciousness, and Salvation in Revolutionary Russia*. Pittsburgh: University of Pittsburgh Press, 2000.

Hardy, G. H. *A Mathematician's Apology*. New York: Cambridge University Press, 1992 [1940].

Harris, Sam. *The End of Faith: Religion, Terror and the Future of Reason*. New York: Norton, 2005.

Hauerwas, Stanley. "Go With God." *First Things*. November 2010. http://www.firstthings.com/article/2010/10/go-with-god.

Heisenberg, Werner. *Philosophical Problems of Quantum Physics*. Woodbridge, CT: Ox Bow, 1979.

———. *Physics and Beyond: Encounters and Conversations*. New York: Harper, 1971.

———. "The Representation of Nature in Contemporary Physics." *Daedalus* 87:3 (Summer 1958) 95–108.

Himmelfarb, Gertrude. *Darwin and the Darwinian Revolution*. Chicago: Ivan R. Dee, 1996.

Hitchens, Christopher. *God is Not Great: How Religion Poisons Everything*. New York: Twelve, 2007.

Hoelzl, Michael. "Introduction: The Study of the Phenomenon of Adolf Hitler in Theology." In Rainer Bucher *Hitler's Theology: A Study in Political Religion*, translated by Rebecca Pohl, xiii–xx. London: Continuum, 2011.

Hofstede, Geert., Gert Van Hofstede, and Michael Minkov. *Cultures and Organizations: Software of the Mind: Intercultural Cooperation and Its Importance for Survival*. New York: McGraw Hill, 2010.

Holder, Rodney. *Big Bang, Big God: A Universe Designed for Life?* Oxford: Lion, 2013.

Holt, Jim. "A Mathematical Romance." *New York Review of Books*. December 5, 2013. http://www.nybooks.com/articles/archives/2013/dec/05/mathematical-romance.

Huntington, Samuel P. *Who Are We?: Challenges to America's National Identity*. New York: Simon and Schuster, 2004.

Jaspers, Karl. *The Origin and Goal of History*. New York: Routledge, 2010 [1953].

Johnson, Paul. *Darwin: Portrait of a Genius*. New York: Viking, 2012.

Jones, Eric. *The European Miracle: Environments, Economies and Geopolitics in the History of Europe and Asia.* 3rd ed. New York: Cambridge University Press, 2003.

Kanigel, Robert. *The Man Who Knew Infinity: A Life of the Genius Ramanujan.* New York: Washington Square, 1991.

Kenny, Anthony. *The Five Ways: St. Thomas Aquinas' Proofs of God's Existence.* Notre Dame, IN: University of Notre Dame Press, 1980 [1969].

Kerr, Hugh T., ed. *Calvin's Institutes: A New Compend.* Louisville: Westminster John Knox, 1989.

King, Gary, Robert O. Keohane, and Sidney Verba. *Designing Social Inquiry: Scientific Inference in Qualitative Research.* Princeton, NJ: Princeton University Press, 1994.

Kirschner, Marc W., and John C. Gerhart. *The Plausibility of Life: Resolving Darwin's Dilemma.* New Haven, CT: Yale University Press, 2005.

Koetsier, T., and L. Bergmans, eds. *Mathematics and the Divine: A Historical Study.* Amsterdam: Elsevier, 2005.

Koonin, Eugene V. *The Logic of Chance: The Nature and Origin of Biological Evolution.* Upper Saddle River, NJ: FT Press Science, 2011.

Koons, Robert C., and George Bealer. "Introduction." In *The Waning of Materialism,* edited by Robert C. Koons and George Bealer, ix–xxxi. Oxford: Oxford University Press, 2010.

Kurzweil, Ray. *The Singularity is Near: When Humans Transcend Biology.* New York: Viking, 2005.

Langevin, Paul. "Preface" to II:1. In *Quantum Theory and Measurement,* edited by Archibald Wheeler and Wojciech Hubert Zurek, 217–18. Princeton, NJ: Princeton University Press, 1983.

Lennox, John. *God and Stephen Hawking: Whose Design Is It Anyway?* Oxford: Lion, 2011.

———. *Miracles: Is Belief in the Supernatural Rational?* Cambridge, MA: The Veritas Forum, 2013.

Levinson, Sanford. *Constitutional Faith.* Princeton, NJ: Princeton University Press, 1988.

Lewis, C. S. *Mere Christianity.* New York: Macmillan, 1952.

———. *Miracles.* New York: Macmillan, 1947.

Lewis, Richard D. *Finland: Cultural Lone Wolf.* Boston: Intercultural, 2005.

Lindley, David. *Uncertainty: Einstein, Heisenberg, Bohr, and the Struggle for the Soul of Science.* New York: Anchor, 2008.

Livio, Mario. *Is God a Mathematician?* New York: Simon and Schuster, 2009.

London, Fritz, and Edmond Bauer. "The Theory of Observation in Quantum Mechanics." In *Quantum Theory and Measurement,* edited by John Archibald Wheeler and Wojciech Hubert Zurek, 217–59. Princeton, NJ: Princeton University Press, 1983.

Macfarlane, Alan. *The Riddle of the Modern World: Of Liberty, Wealth and Equality.* New York: Palgrave, 2000.

MacIntyre, Alasdair. *Marxism and Christianity.* Notre Dame, IN: University of Notre Dame Press, 1984.

Mann, Charles. "Lynn Margulis: Science's Unruly Mother." *Science* 5004 (April 19, 1991) 378–81.

Manski, Charles F. *Public Policy in an Uncertain World: Analysis and Decisions.* Cambridge, MA: Harvard University Press, 2013.

Manuel, Frank E. *The Religion of Isaac Newton.* Oxford: Clarendon, 1974.

Margulis, Lynn. *Symbiotic Planet: A New Look at Evolution*. New York: Basic Books, 1998.

Margulis, Lynn, and Dorion Sagan. *Acquiring Genomes: A Theory of the Origins of Species*. New York: Basic, 2002.

————. *Dazzle Gradually: Reflections on the Nature of Nature*. White River Junction, VT: Chelsea Green, 2007.

Martin, Barclay. "The Mystery of Consciousness, Con't." *New York Review of Books*, September 29, 2011. http://www.nybooks.com/articles/archives/2011/sep/29/mystery-consciousness-cont/.

Mayr, Ernst. *What Evolution Is*. New York: Basic, 2001.

McCloskey, Deirdre N. *Bourgeois Dignity: Why Economics Can't Explain the Modern World*. Chicago: University of Chicago Press, 2010.

McCloskey, Donald N. *The Rhetoric of Economics*. Madison, WI: University of Wisconsin Press, 1985.

McGinn, Colin. *Basic Structures of Reality: Essays in Meta-Physics*. New York: Oxford University Press, 2011.

————. "Can We Ever Understand Consciousness?" *New York Review of Books*, June 10, 1999. http://www.nybooks.com/articles/archives/1999/jun/10/can-we-ever-understand-consciousness/.

————. "Can We Solve the Mind-Body Problem?" *Mind* 98 (July 1989) 349–66.

————. *Consciousness and its Objects*. New York: Oxford University Press, 2004.

————. "Consciousness and Space." *Journal of Consciousness Studies* 2:3 (1995) 220–30.

————. *The Mysterious Flame: Conscious Minds in a Material World*. New York: Basic, 1999.

————. "Solving the Philosophical Mind-Body Problem." In *Consciousness and its Objects,* 56–76. New York: Oxford University Press, 2004.

McGrath, Alister E. *Dawkins' God: From the Selfish Gene to the God Delusion*. 2nd ed. Oxford: Wiley-Blackwell, 2015.

————. *A Fine-Tuned Universe: The Quest for God in Science and Theology*. Louisville: Westminster John Knox, 2009.

McGrath, Alister E., and Joanna Collicut McGrath. *The Dawkins Delusion? Atheist Fundamentalism and the Denial of the Divine*. Downers Grove, IL: InterVarsity, 2007.

Mead, Walter Russell. *God and Gold: Britain, America, and the Making of the Modern World*. New York: Knopf, 2007.

Merton, Robert K. *Science, Technology and Society in Seventeenth-Century England*. New York: Howard Fertig, 2001.

Micklethwait, John, and Adrian Wooldridge. *God is Back: How the Global Revival of Faith is Changing the World*. New York: Penguin, 2009.

Midgley, Mary. *Evolution as a Religion: Strange Hopes and Stranger Fears*. New York: Routledge, 2002 [1985].

Mooney, Christ. "Student Finds Placebo Effect in Eco-Labeling." *Washington Post*, April 24, 2015.

Mueller, Ian. "Mathematics and the Divine in Plato." In *Mathematics and the Divine: A Historical Study* edited by T. Koetsier and L. Bergmans, 99–121. Amsterdam: Elsevier, 2005.

Nagel, Thomas. *Mind and Cosmos: Why the Materialist Neo-Darwinian Conception of Nature is Almost Certainly False*. New York: Oxford University Press, 2012.

————. "The Mind Wins!" *New York Review of Books*, March 4, 1993. http://www.nybooks.com/articles/archives/1993/mar/04/the-mind-wins/.

————. *Other Minds: Critical Essays, 1969-1994*. New York: Oxford University Press, 1995

————. *Secular Philosophy and the Religious Temperament: Essays, 2002-2008*. New York: Oxford University Press, 2010.

————. "What is it Like to Be a Bat?" *Philosophical Review* 83:4 (October 1974) 435–50.

Nash, Roderick. *Wilderness and the American Mind*. New Haven, CT: Yale University Press, 1973.

Nelson, Robert H. "All in the Name of Progress: An Essay Review of Paul R. Josephson's *Industrialized Nature*." *Politics and the Life Sciences* 23:2 (October 2005) 46–54.

————. "Bringing Religion into Economic Policy Analysis." *Regulation* (Spring 2014) 52–57.

————. "Calvinism Minus God: Environmental Restoration as a Theological Concept." In *Saving the Seas: Values, Scientists and International Governance*, edited by L. Anathea Brooks and Stacy D. VanDeveer, 87–105. College Park, MD: Maryland Sea Grant College, 1997.

————. "Calvinism Without God: American Environmentalism as Implicit Calvinism." *Implicit Religion* 17:3 (2014) 249–73.

————. "Does 'Existence Value' Exist?: An Essay on Religions, Old and New." *The Independent Review* 1:4 (March 1997) 499–521.

————. "Ecological Science as a Creation Story." *The Independent Review* 14:4 (Spring 2010) 513–34.

————. "Economic and Environmental Religion." In *Oxford Handbook of Christianity and Economics*, edited by Paul Oslington, 337–58. New York: Oxford University Press, 2014.

————. "Economic Religion versus Christian Values." *Journal of Markets and Morality* 1:2 (October 1998) 142–57.

————. "Economics and Environmentalism: Belief Systems at Odds." *The Independent Review* 17:1 (Summer 2012) 5–17.

————. "The Economics Profession and the Making of Public Policy." *Journal of Economic Literature* 25:1 (March 1987) 49–91.

————. "Economics as Religion." In *Economics and Religion: Are They Distinct?*, edited by H. Geoffrey Brennan and A.M.C. Waterman, 227–48. Boston: Kluwer Academic, 1994.

————. "Economics as Religion: A Reply to the Commenters." *Case Western Reserve Law Review* 56:3 (Spring 2006) 663–83.

————. *Economics as Religion: From Samuelson to Chicago and Beyond*. University Park, PA: Pennsylvania State University Press, 2001.

————. "Environmental Calvinism: The Judeo-Christian Roots of Environmental Theology." In *Taking the Environment Seriously*, edited by Roger E. Meiners and Bruce Yandle, 233–55. Lanham, MD: Rowman & Littlefield, 1993.

————. "Environmental Colonialism: 'Saving' Africa from Africans." *The Independent Review* 8:1 (Summer 2003) 65–86.

————. "Environmental Religion: A Theological Critique." *Case Western Reserve Law Review* 55:1 (Fall 2004) 51–89.

————. "The Gospel According to Conservation Biology." *Philosophy and Public Policy Quarterly* 27:3–4 (Summer/Fall 2007) 10–16.

———. "Is 'Libertarian Environmentalist' an Oxymoron?: The Crisis of Progressive Faith and the Environmental and Libertarian Search for a New Guiding Vision." In *The Next West: Public Lands, Community and Economy in the American West*, edited by John A. Baden and Donald Snow, 205–32. Washington, DC: Island, 1997.

———. *The New Holy Wars: Economic Religion versus Environmental Religion in Contemporary America*. University Park, PA: Pennsylvania State University Press, 2010.

———. "The Office of Policy Analysis in the Department of the Interior." *Journal of Policy Analysis and Management* 8:3 (Summer 1989) 395–410.

———. *Reaching for Heaven on Earth: The Theological Meaning of Economics*. Lanham, MD: Rowman & Littlefield, 1991.

———. "Rethinking Church and State: The Case of Environmental Religion." *Pace Environmental Law Review* 29:1 (Fall 2011) 121–217.

———. "Scholasticism versus Pietism: The Battle for the Soul of Economics." *Econ Journal Watch* 1:3 (December 2004) 473–97.

———. "The Secular Religions of Progress." *The New Atlantis* 39 (Summer 2013) 38–50.

———. "The Secularization Myth Revisited: Secularism as Christianity in Disguise." *Journal of Markets and Morality* (forthcoming, Fall 2015).

———. "*Silent Spring* as Secular Religion." In *Silent Spring at 50*, edited by Roger Meiners, Pierre Desrochers, and Andrew Morriss, 61–96. Washington, DC: Cato Institute, 2012.

———. "Sustainability, Efficiency and God: Economic Values and the Sustainability Debate." *Annual Review of Ecology and Systematics* 26 (1995) 135–54.

———. "The Theological Meaning of Economics." In *Economics and Religion*, edited by Paul Oslington, 502–6. Northampton, MA: Edward Elgar, 2004.

———. "Unoriginal Sin: The Judeo-Christian Roots of Ecotheology." *Policy Review* 53 (Summer 1990) 52–59.

———. "What is 'Economic Theology'?" *Princeton Seminary Bulletin* 25:1 (2004) 58–79.

———. "Wilderness, Church, and State." *Liberty* (September 1992) 34–40.

Noble, Denis. "Science, Music, Philosophy: Margulis at Oxford." In *Lynn Margulis: The Life and Legacy of a Scientific Rebel*, edited by Dorion Sagan, 80–85. White River Junction, VT: Chelsea Green, 2012.

O'Meara, Dominic J. "Geometry and the Divine in Proclus." In *Mathematics and the Divine: A Historical Study*, edited by T. Koetsier and L. Bergmans, 133–45. Amsterdam: Elsevier, 2005.

Pais, Abraham. "*Subtle is the Lord . . .*": The Science and the Life of Albert Einstein*. New York: Oxford University Press, 2005.

Penrose, Roger. *The Emperor's New Mind: Concerning Computers, Minds, and the Laws of Physics*. New York: Oxford University Press, 1989.

———. *The Road to Reality: A Complete Guide to the Laws of the Universe*. New York: Vantage, 2007.

Plantinga, Alvin. *God and Other Minds: A Study of the Rational Justification of Belief in God*. Ithaca, NY: Cornell University Press, 1967.

———. *Knowledge and Christian Belief*. Grand Rapids: Eerdmans, 2015.

———. *Warranted Christian Belief*. New York: Oxford University Press, 2000.

————. *Where the Conflict Really Lies: Science, Religion, and Naturalism.* New York: Oxford University Press, 2011.

Polkinghorne, John. "Foreword" to Rodney Holder, *Big Bang, Big God: A Universe Designed for Life?,* 8–9. Oxford: Lion, 2013.

————. *Science and Religion in Quest of Truth.* New Haven, CT: Yale University Press, 2011.

Popper, Karl R. "Part I." In *The Self and its Brain: An Argument for Interactionism,* by Karl R. Popper and John C. Eccles, 3–234. New York: Routledge, 1977.

Pyysiainen, Ilkka. *Supernatural Agents: Why We Believe in Souls, Gods, and Buddhas.* New York: Oxford University Press, 2009.

Randall, John Herman. *Hellenistic Ways of Deliverance and the Making of the Christian Synthesis.* New York: Columbia University Press, 1970.

Redles, David. *Hitler's Millennial Reich: Apocalyptic Belief and the Search for Salvation.* New York: New York University Press, 2005.

Richards, Robert J. "Darwin's Place in the History of Thought: A Reevaluation." In *In the Light of Evolution: Volume III, Two Centuries of Darwin,* edited by John C. Avise and Francisco J. Ayala, 329–41. Washington, DC: National Academies, 2009.

Robinson, Daniel N. *Consciousness and Mental Life.* New York: Columbia University Press, 2008.

Ruse, Michael. "The Darwinian Revolution: Rethinking its Meaning and Significance." In *In the Light of Evolution: Volume III, Two Centuries of Darwin,* edited by John C. Avise and Francisco J. Ayala, 287–305. Washington, DC: National Academies, 2009.

Schacht, Richard. *Nietzsche.* Boston: Routledge and Kegan Paul, 1983.

Schele, Linda, and David Freidel. *A Forest of Kings: The Untold History of the Ancient Maya.* New York: William Morrow, 1990.

Schrodinger, Erwin. *Nature and the Greeks.* New York: Cambridge University Press, 1996.

————. *Science and Humanism.* New York: Cambridge University Press, 1996.

————. *What Is Life? With Mind and Matter and Autobiographical Sketches.* New York: Cambridge University Press, 1992.

Schwartz, Benjamin I. "The Age of Transcendence." *Daedalus* 104:2 (Spring 1975) 1–7.

Searle, John R., "The Mystery of Consciousness, Con't." *New York Review of Books,* September 29, 2011. http://www.nybooks.com/articles/archives/2011/sep/29/mystery-consciousness-cont/.

————. "'The Mystery of Consciousness': An Exchange." *New York Review of Books,* December 21, 1995. http://www.nybooks.com/articles/archives/1995/dec/21/the-mystery-of-consciousness-an-exchange/.

————. *The Rediscovery of the Mind.* Cambridge, MA: MIT Press, 1992.

————. "What is Consciousness?" *New York Review of Books,* June 23, 2005. http://www.nybooks.com/articles/archives/2005/jun/23/what-is-consciousness/.

Sexton, John. *Baseball as a Road to God: Seeing Beyond the Game.* New York: Gotham, 2013.

Shapiro, James A. *Evolution: A View from the 21st Century.* Upper Saddle River, NJ: FT Press Science, 2011.

Shermer, Michael. "Glorious Contingency." *Metanexus,* February 15, 2000. www.metanexus.net/print/4482.

Smolin, Lee. *Time Reborn: From the Crisis in Physics to the Future of the Universe.* New York: Houghton Mifflin Harcourt, 2013.

Soloveichick, Meir Y. "Torah and Incarnation." *First Things*, October 2010. http://www. firstthings.com/article/2010/10/torah-and-incarnation.

Spiro, Jonathan Peter. *Defending the Master Race: Conservation, Eugenics, and the Legacy of Madison Grant.* Lebanon, NH: University of Vermont Press, 2009.

Stackhouse, Max. *God and Globalization, Volume 4, Globalization and Grace.* New York: Continuum, 2007.

Stark, Rodney. *Discovering God: The Origins of the Great Religions and the Evolution of Belief.* New York: Harper One, 2007.

———. *The Triumph of Christianity: How the Jesus Movement Became the World's Largest Religion.* New York: Harper One, 2011.

Starobinski, Jean. *Jean-Jacques Rousseau: Transparency and Obstruction.* Chicago: University of Chicago Press, 1988.

Steigmann-Gall, Richard. *The Holy Reich: Nazi Conceptions of Christianity, 1919–1945.* New York: Cambridge University Press, 2003.

Stoll, Mark. *Protestantism, Capitalism, and Nature in America.* Albuquerque: University of New Mexico Press, 1997.

Swinburne, Richard. *The Evolution of the Soul.* Rev. ed. Oxford: Oxford University Press, 2007.

———. *Is There a God?* Rev. ed. New York: Oxford University Press, 2010.

Takacs, David. *The Idea of Biodiversity: Philosophies of Paradise.* Baltimore: Johns Hopkins University Press, 1996.

Tallinn, Jaan. "Weekend Confidential." *The Wall Street Journal,* interview by Alexandra Wolfe, June 2013.

Tegmark, Max. *Our Mathematical Universe: My Quest for the Ultimate Nature of Reality.* New York: Knopf, 2014.

"There is No Alternative: Virtually All Alternative Medicine is Bunk; But the Placebo Effect is Rather Interesting." *The Economist*, May 21, 2011.

Thomassen, Bjorn. "Anthropology, Multiple Modernities, and the Axial Age Debate." *Anthropological Theory* 10:4 (December 2010) 321–42. http://www.economist. com/node/18712290.

Tillich, Paul. *A History of Christian Thought: From Its Judaic and Hellenistic Origins to Existentialism.* New York: Simon and Schuster, 1967.

Tindol, Robert. "Physics World poll names Richard Feynman one of 10 greatest physicists of all time." Caltech, February 2, 1999. Online: http://www.caltech.edu/ article/12019.

Torrance, Thomas F. "Preface" to *The Dynamical Theory of the Electromagnetic Field* by James Clerk Maxwell, edited by Thomas F. Torrance, ix–xiii. Eugene, OR: Wipf and Stock, 1996.

Troeltsch, Ernst. *Protestantism and Progress: A Historical Study of the Relation of Protestantism to the Modern World.* Boston: Beacon, 1958 [1912].

Valiunas, Algis. "Einstein's Quest for Truth." *The New Atlantis,* 20 (Spring 2008) 121–41.

Vermes, Geza. *Christian Beginnings: From Nazareth to Nicaea.* New Haven, CT: Yale University Press, 2013.

———. *The Resurrection: History and Myth.* New York: Doubleday, 2008.

Vitz, Paul C. *Psychology as Religion: The Cult of Self-Worship.* Grand Rapids: Eerdmans, 1994.

Wallis, Faith. "'Number Mystique' in Early Medieval Computus Texts." In *Mathematics and the Divine: A Historical Study*, edited by T. Koetsier and L. Bergmans, 179–99. Amsterdam: Elsevier, 2005.

Ward, Keith. *The Big Questions in Science and Religion*. West Conshohocken, PA: Templeton Foundation, 2008.

———. *The Evidence for God: The Case for the Existence of the Spiritual Dimension*. London: Darton, Longman and Todd, 2014.

———. *Why There Almost Certainly Is a God: Doubting Dawkins*. Oxford: Lion, 2008.

Ward, Peter, and Joe Kirschvink. *A New History of Life: The Radical New Discoveries about the Origins and Evolution of Life on Earth*. New York: Bloomsbury, 2015.

Weikart, Richard. *From Darwin to Hitler: Evolutionary Ethics, Eugenics, and Racism in Germany*. New York: Palgrave Macmillan, 2004.

Weinrich, Max. *Hitler's Professors: The Part of Scholarship in Germany's Crimes Against the Jewish People*. New York: Yeshiva Scientific Institute, 1946.

Wheeler, John A. *At Home in the Universe*. Woodbury, NY: American Institute of Physics, 1994.

Wigner, Eugene P. "Remarks on the Mind-Body Question." In *Quantum Theory and Measurement*, edited by John Archibald Wheeler and Wojciech Hubert Zurek, 168–80. Princeton, NJ: Princeton University Press, 1983.

———. "The Unreasonable Effectiveness of Mathematics in the Natural Sciences," *Communications in Pure and Applied Mathematics* 13:1 (February 1960). http://www.dartmouth.edu/~matc/MathDrama/reading/Wigner.html.

Winter, Allison. "How This Environmental Activist Learned to 'Walk the Walk.'" *Greenwire*, July 31, 2013.

Wisnewski, Gerhard. *One Small Step: The Great Moon Hoax and the Race to Dominate Earth from Space*. East Sussex, UK: Clairview, 2007.

Witt, Annick Hedlund-de. "Worldviews and Their Significance for the Global Sustainable Development Debate." *Environmental Ethics*. 35:2 (Summer 2013) 133–62.

Wolfe, Alexandra. "Weekend Confidential." *The Wall Street Journal*, June 1-2, 2013.

Wood, Gordon S. "Praying with the Founders." *New York Review of Books*, May 1, 2008. http://www.nybooks.com/articles/archives/2008/may/01/praying-with-the-founders/.

Worster, John. *The Wealth of Nature: Environmental History and the Ecological Imagination*. New York: Oxford University Press, 1994.

Wright, N. T. *The Resurrection of the Son of God*. Minneapolis: Fortress, 2003.

Yao, Shing-Tung., and Steve Nadis. *The Shape of Inner Space: String Theory and the Geometry of the Universe's Hidden Dimensions*. New York: Basic, 2010.

Index

Comfort, Ray, 150n105
communitarian account of evolution,
        136
computer simulation
    of humans, 45–48
    of universes, 44
    of the world, 198–201
concentration camps of Germany, 15–16
the condemned, 9
Confucianism, 213–15
Confucius, 213–15
*The Conscious Mind: In Search
        of a Fundamental Theory*
        (Chalmers), 195
consciousness
    apprehension of Platonic
        mathematical world, 66
    blended with natural world in
        quantum mechanics, 82
    evolutionary theory and, 128
    human participation in God's, 51,
        114
    as internal reality, 94–95
    as part of universal cosmic mind,
        84–85
    as reality, 3–5
    role in physics, 54
    as separate world, 65, 91
    solipsists' view of, 4–5, 7, 20–21
    as supernatural miracle, 2–5
    Wigner on development of, 56–57
Consciousness (Blackmore), 169
Consciousness Explained (Dennett),
        171–75, 176
consensus reality, 95
conservation biology, 117
Constantine, 220, 222
Constitutional Faith (Levinson), 243–44
Constitution of the United States, 243
Convoluta roscoffensis, 133–34
Copernicus, 101, 157
Cornwell, John, 19n35, 28–29
cosmic optimism, 100
cosmic pessimism, 100–101
Council of Nicaea, 220, 223
Coyne, Jerry, 119, 127
Craig, William Lane, 19n36, 38n35

creation, 59–62, 199–200. *See also*
        physical world; universe
Creation Hypothesis, 199–200
creationism, 187, 199–200
Crick, Francis, 182, 197
crisis, 214
Cudworth, Ralph, 74
culture wars, 16–17
cumulative probabilities, 28–29

D

Darwin, Charles
    acceptance of his theory, 120
    bacteria vs., 132–38
    Descent of Man, 103
    discussion of new species, 136
    doubts of, 112
    faith of, 115
    on higher power guiding evolution,
        115–16
    Margulis' view of, 135
    method of research, 98
    on natural selection as teleological
        and moral construction, 115–16
    The Origin of Species, 98, 115, 133,
        136
    theory of evolution, 17, 119, 137,
        235
Darwin and the Darwinian Revolution
        (Himmelfarb), 115
"Darwinian Fundamentalism" (Gould),
        108
    Darwinism as religion, 100–103
    inquisitors versus evolutionary
        heresy, 103–107
    evolutionary theology, 114–17
    Darwinism as story telling, 129–31
    Margulis at Oxford, 138–41
    as universal acid, 145–54
Darwinism
    acceptance of, 120
    as alternative to Abrahamic
        religions, 101–2
    application of method of
        contradiction, 110–14

Z

Made in the USA
Columbia, SC
15 February 2020

88004563R00193